# Roman Urbanism in Italy

## Recent discoveries and new directions

*Edited by*
Alessandro Launaro

University of Cambridge Museum of Classical Archaeology
Monograph 5

**OXBOW** | books
Oxford & Philadelphia

Published in the United Kingdom in 2024 by
OXBOW BOOKS
The Old Music Hall, 106–108 Cowley Road, Oxford, OX4 1JE

and in the United States by
OXBOW BOOKS
1950 Lawrence Road, Havertown, PA 19083

Paperback Edition: ISBN 979-8-88857-036-4
Digital Edition: ISBN 979-8-88857-037-1

A CIP record for this book is available from the British Library

Library of Congress Control Number: 2023946676

Printed in the United Kingdom by CMP Digital Print Solutions

Typeset in India by Lapiz Digital Services, Chennai.

For a complete list of Oxbow titles, please contact:

| UNITED KINGDOM | UNITED STATES OF AMERICA |
|---|---|
| Oxbow Books | Oxbow Books |
| Telephone (0)1226 734350 | Telephone (610) 853-9131, Fax (610) 853-9146 |
| Email: oxbow@oxbowbooks.com | Email: queries@casemateacademic.com |
| www.oxbowbooks.com | www.casemateacademic.com/oxbow |

Oxbow Books is part of the Casemate Group

*Front cover:* Aerial view of the thatre of Interamna Lirenas (Alessandro Launaro)
*Back cover:* The Porta di Giove at Falerii Novi (Alessandro Launaro)

# Contents

# List of contributors

PATRIZIA BASSO is Full Professor of Classical Archaeology at the University of Verona and director of the excavation of the area of the Late Antique market and walls at Aquileia. From 2018 to 2023 she was Principal Investigator of the 'Food and Wine in ancient Verona' project (research of scientific excellence funded by Cariverona) and since 2023 she is the Principal Investigator of the 'Archaeology of Adriatic Wine' project (PRIN 2022).

GIUSEPPE CERAUDO is Full Professor of Ancient Topography at the University of Salento. His research is carried out as part of the activities of the Laboratory of Ancient Topography and Photogrammetry at the Department of Cultural Heritage. His scientific interests include archaeological cartography, field and architectural survey, aerotopography and photogrammetry applied to archaeology, with a specific attention to the development of new methodological approaches to archaeological prospection and to the innovative research field of finalized photogrammetry.

ANDREA U. DE GIORGI is Professor of Classics at the Florida State University. His interests are the archaeology and visual culture of Roman Italy and the East. He directs the Cosa Excavations, co-directs the Caesarea Coastal Archaeological Project, and studies the Antioch collections at Princeton University. His publication records include monographs, edited books and more than 30 essays among articles and book chapters.

GIROLAMO FERDINANDO DE SIMONE received his DPhil at the University of Oxford. He has led the Apolline Project, a multidisciplinary research project on the north slope of Mount Vesuvius and inland Campania, since 2004. For his innovative studies and the commitment to public archaeology he received the 2011 European Archaeological Heritage Prize. His research centres on the connections between the ancient landscape and the economy, especially in the Roman and Late Antique periods.

FRANCESCA DIOSONO studied at the University of Perugia and is Researcher at the Institute of Classical Archaeology of the Ludwig Maximilian University in Munich (DE). Her fields of interest include Roman archaeology, landscape archaeology and Roman material culture. She has worked since the 2000s on a range of projects in Italy, Spain, France and Jordan; among her main excavations are the colony of Fregellae (Frosinone), the Sanctuary of Diana at Nemi (Rome), the site of Villa San Silvestro in Cascia (Perugia) and the Sanctuary on Monte S. Angelo in Terracina (Latina).

CÉCILE EVERS is Keeper of Antiquities at the Royal Museum of Art and History in Brussels and curator of the Etruscan, Roman and Gallo-Roman collections. She teaches Roman Art History and Archaeology at the Université Libre de Bruxelles and is specialised in Roman sculpture (ideal and portraits) and the history of collections. She has been leading the Belgian excavations on the forum of Alba Fucens since 2007.

SOPHIE HAY works for the Archaeological Park of Pompeii in the Press and Communications Office. Between 2003 and 2017 she worked at the Department of Archaeology, University of Southampton undertaking archaeological geophysical surveys in Italy and the wider Mediterranean in collaboration with the British School at Rome.

IAN HAYNES is Professor of Archaeology at Newcastle University and Chair of Archaeology at the British School at Rome. With Paolo Liverani, Ian co-directed the Lateran Project, which focused on the archaeology of the Archbasilica of the St John Lateran, and SGL2, which examined sites in the grounds of the Hospital of San Giovanni - Addolorata. Ian is Principal Investigator of the *Rome Transformed* Project.

STEPHEN KAY is the Archaeology Manager at the British School at Rome, a Visiting Fellow at the University of Southampton and a Visiting Researcher at the Newcastle University. He has published widely on archaeological prospection with a principal focus on applications to Roman urbanism. He is a co-director of the *Falerii Novi Project*, a partner in the *Rome Transformed* project and has led excavations at Matrice (Molise), Segni (Lazio) and Pompeii (Campania).

ALESSANDRO LAUNARO is Associate Professor in Classics at the University of Cambridge and a Fellow of Gonville & Caius College. A Roman archaeologist with an expertise in landscape archaeology and ancient topography, he is specifically interested in the archaeology and history of ancient Italy, in both its urban and rural dimensions, cast against the long-term political, social, economic and cultural transformations of the broader Mediterranean world. He directs the Interamna Lirenas Project (Lazio, Central Italy).

PAOLO LIVERANI served as Curator of Classical Antiquities at the Vatican Museum (1986–2005) with responsibility for archaeological sites in the Lateran extraterritorial area. Later, as professor for Ancient Topography at the University of Florence, he maintained his interest in the Caelian Hill and co-directed with Ian Haynes the Lateran Project and the SGL2 research programme at the Hospital of San Giovanni - Addolorata in Rome. Paolo has worked at the heart of *Rome Transformed* from the project's inception.

ROCCO MARCHESCHI is a PhD student in Roman Archaeology and Ancient Topography at the University of Pisa. His research interests include the landscape evolution of the *ager Lunensis* and its settlements patterns in diachronic perspective.

SILVIA MARINI graduated in Archaeology at the University of Pisa, where she was awarded a Specialization Diploma in Archaeology and a PhD in Ancient History. Her research interests include pottery production and trade. She recently published the volume *Lucerne bollate in Italia centrale e settentrionale (I-II sec. d.C.). Aspetti tecnici, epigrafici e commerciali.*

SIMONETTA MENCHELLI is Professor of Ancient Topography and Underwater Archaeology at the University of Pisa. Her research interests include archaeological excavation and survey methodology; landscape and townscape archaeology; the archaeology of production, trade, and transport systems. She has conducted research in Italy (Tuscany, Liguria, Marche) and Europe (Corsica, Albania, Montenegro, Hungary).

MARTIN MILLETT is Emeritus Laurence Professor of Classical Archaeology at the University of Cambridge and a Life Fellow of Fitzwilliam College, Cambridge. He is currently President of the Society of Antiquaries of London, and he is also a Fellow of the British Academy and a Member of the Academia Europaea. During his career he has been involved in field projects across western Europe, working in the UK, Spain, Portugal and Italy.

ALESSIA MORIGI gained her BA/MA degrees and PhD in Archeology from the University of Bologna. She is currently Associate Professor of Archeology at the University of Parma and has qualified as Full Professor for the Italian University system. She is President of the *Società di Studi Romagnoli* and director of the archaeological excavations at Theoderic's Palace at Galeata. Her research focuses on the Roman city and its territory, including their development since Antiquity and their dialogue with the contemporary world.

JOHN R. PATTERSON is Associate Professor in the Faculty of Classics at the University of Cambridge, and Director of Studies in Classics at Magdalene and Lucy Cavendish Colleges. Among his publications on the history of Roman Italy is *Landscapes and Cities: Rural Settlement and Civic Transformation in Early Imperial Italy* (Oxford, 2006).

THEA RAVASI is the Archaeology Research Associate for *Rome Transformed*. She researches Roman residential and thermal architecture, but she has also extensively published on Roman trade and economy. Prior to joining *Rome Transformed*, Thea was a Post-Doctoral Researcher on the SGL2 project, and during that time began her work on both the imperial and Late Antique elite housing preserved beneath the Hospital of San Giovanni - Addolorata, and the Severan bath complex underneath the Lateran Baptistery.

BEN RUSSELL is Professor of the Archaeology of the Roman Empire at the University of Edinburgh. He is an expert in Roman urbanism and construction, and especially the supply and use of materials for artistic and architectural projects. He works on projects in Italy, Britain, Tunisia and Turkey. He has a DPhil from the University of Oxford and has previously worked at the University of Oxford and King's College London.

PAOLO SANGRISO graduated in Ancient History at the University of Pisa, where he was awarded a Specialization Diploma in Archaeology and a PhD in Ancient History. He is affiliated researcher at the University of Pisa and supervisor of the excavations at Vada Volaterrana and Lunae. He is author of many publications dealing with the landscapes of northern Etruria and the production of terra sigillata. His volume *Paesaggi romani nell' ager Lunensis, Il golfo di Spezia* was published in 2023.

CHRISTOPHER SMITH is Executive Chair of UKRI. He was previously Professor of Ancient History at the University of St Andrews and Director of the British School at Rome from 2009 to 2017. His research explores constitutionalism and state formation with particular emphasis on the development of Rome as a political and social community. He is the author or editor of over 20 books and in 2017 he was awarded the prestigious *Premio Cultori di Roma*.

FRANK VERMEULEN is a Full Professor of Roman Archaeology and Archaeological Methodology at Ghent University. He has a keen interest in Roman settlement archaeology and geo-archaeological approaches to ancient Mediterranean landscapes, including intensive aerial photography and geophysical prospection. During the past two decades he directed large field projects in Italy, Portugal and France and recently his research has focused on the study of Roman colonialism and urbanism, in particular concerning Central and Adriatic Italy.

# Chapter 1

## Introduction

### *Alessandro Launaro*

Towns and urban life have existed for a very long time, well before the Romans, and yet they came to represent a quintessential feature of the Roman world. Throughout Antiquity most of the population lived in the open countryside, but their settlements and lives almost invariably gravitated around – and indeed supported – a sprawling network of towns. Their relationship was very much symbiotic as urban sites 'were administrative centres, they were garrison towns, they were centres of exchange both as between towns and regions, and between townsmen and the surrounding countryside' (Hopkins 1978, 75; also Zuiderhoek 2017, 37–55). The specific conditions brought about by the Roman political unification of a vast empire could not but enhance the role towns played in connecting peoples and cultures, easing the (re)distribution of resources whilst extending the reach of political control and effective administration. Even more than this, the Roman empire could not have existed the way it did without towns and urban life: to understand Roman urbanism is to understand a fundamental dimension of Roman civilization.

Luckily for us, the sources at our disposal for the study of Roman urbanism are numerous, varied and – as this volume attests – ever-increasing. Towns not only occupied central stage in the lives of the literate elite whose accounts are preserved in ancient texts, but they left plenty of archaeological traces. The exploration of individual urban sites has undoubtedly added the most to our understanding of Roman urbanism, highlighting not only recurring features, but also the varied range of solutions adopted by different people in different places at different times. These individual studies, and the specific evidence they are based on, constitute the very foundation without which no synthesis of higher level could effectively exist (de Ligt & Bintliff 2019, 28).

The study of Roman urbanism – especially its early (Republican) phases – is indeed extensively rooted in the evidence provided by a series of key sites, several of them located in Italy. Some of these Italian towns have received a great deal of scholarly attention in the past and they are routinely referenced as 'textbook examples' in scholarly discussion, framing much of our understanding of the broad phenomenon of Roman urbanism (Gros & Torelli 2007, 5–270; Sewell 2010; Laurence *et al.* 2011, 37–63; Yegül & Favro 2019, 4–111). However, some discussions of these sites tend to fall back on well-established interpretations, with relatively little or no awareness of more recent developments. This is remarkable, since our understanding of these sites has evolved significantly thanks to new archaeological fieldwork, often characterised by the pursuit of new questions and the application of new approaches. Similarly, new evidence from other sites has prompted a reconsideration of time-honoured views about the nature, role and long-term trajectory of Roman towns in Italy.

This awareness lies behind the decision to devote the 2022 Laurence Seminar to a conversation about *Roman Urbanism in Italy: recent discoveries and new directions*. This event, which took place at the Faculty of Classics of the University of Cambridge on 27–28 May 2022, aimed at bringing together scholars whose recent work at key sites is helping to expand, change or challenge our current knowledge and understanding of Roman urbanism in Italy. The selection of case-studies was also guided by the desire to offer as representative a picture as possible of Roman urbanism in Italy, in terms of variety of urban types, chronological range (Mid Republic to Late Antiquity – and beyond), and geographic coverage (North, Central and Southern Italy; both Tyrrhenian and Adriatic side of the Peninsula). The individual contributions were grouped thematically, and this structure is reflected in the parts in which this volume is divided.

The body of available evidence for the study of Roman urbanism has been steadily increasing, thanks in no little part to the integrated application of new approaches (Part I). As several of the contributions in this volume make clear, remote sensing has played a crucial role in this. The case of Falerii Novi (Millett) is especially notable: one of the earliest Roman towns to be subjected to full-scale geophysical prospection, it provides concrete illustration not only of what these methods can reveal about the layout of ancient cities, but also the range of questions such evidence can be used to answer. The systematic application of non-intrusive methodologies within an overbuilt environment and the integration of different datasets is what allowed the 'Rome Transformed Project' (Haynes *et al.*) to reconstruct and visualise the development of a sector of Rome's periphery, the eastern Caelian, in the 1st–2nd centuries AD. It is indeed by combining and integrating a varied range of archaeological approaches, methods and techniques – and their resulting evidence – that best results can be obtained, as illustrated by ongoing fieldwork at Aquinum (Ceraudo).

The availability of new evidence is naturally bound to affect existing interpretations, even in the case of those 'textbook sites' whose understanding is often taken as more or less established (Part II). Nowhere this is more evident than at Cosa (De Giorgi), a site which has much contributed to framing the study of Roman urbanism generally, and (Latin) colonies specifically: once again its interpretation is being enriched by new data, prompting a further reappraisal of its early phases.

At Fregellae (Diosono), a unique site due to its being a 'closed context' from the Republican period, a review of the available evidence and associated documentation provides new insights about the development of key buildings and aspects of daily life in a period which is not particularly well known. New work around the *forum* of Alba Fucens (Evers) has expanded our understanding of this other important site, providing new evidence of the monumental transformation undergone by the town at the end of the Republic and during the Principate.

Recent work has further confirmed the varied range of urban solutions adopted across Roman Italy in response to local conditions (Part III). Not the only site known to have done so, Lucus Feroniae (Kay *et al.*) featured the bare essentials of a Roman town (i.e. a *forum* and a series of public buildings around it) even though it served a fundamentally rural population living dispersed in the countryside. As the case of Septempeda makes clear (Vermeulen), the process of town formation could vary significantly, and new towns could develop organically as a local initiative aimed at taking advantage of the territorial infrastructure promoted by the Romans.

As conditions changed, so did towns. The long-term development of Roman urbanism therefore reflects – and may thus be used to illuminate – broader transformations taking place both locally and across Italy more generally (Part IV). Recent excavations at Lunae (Menchelli *et al.*) have revealed a series of distinctive phases of occupation that are quite indicative of the general development of the town. A combination of full-coverage geophysical prospection, systematic analysis of the ploughsoil assemblage and excavation has made it possible to outline the long-term trajectory of Interamna Lirenas (Launaro), with potential implications for our understanding of Italy in the 2nd century AD. Comparable patterns have been identified at Aeclanum (Russell & De Simone), another relatively small town whose place in relation to the communication network guaranteed its success, particularly from the 2nd century AD onwards.

As several Roman towns continued to be occupied in the Late Antique and medieval periods, these changes became even more significant (Part V). However, patterns of both continuity and marked transformation are attested at Aquileia (Basso), whose strategic position guaranteed its continued relevance in relation to trade and supply in the 4th–5th centuries AD. The crucial importance of Parma (Morigi) in relation to the communication network can be clearly appreciated when considering the long and articulated history of its bridge – or rather bridges – along the route of the *via Aemilia*.

Notwithstanding the thematic organization adopted by this volume, the significance of each of these case studies is undoubtedly much broader. All these recent discoveries can indeed contribute to review and revise our understanding of the development of Italy in the Roman period (Patterson). In this sense, we hope that this volume will provide not only an accessible and up-to-date overview of current approaches to the study of Roman urbanism, but also a useful resource for those researching the archaeology and history of Roman Italy.

## Acknowledgements

The 2022 Laurence Seminar was organized by Alessandro Launaro and Martin Millett. Both the seminar and the publication of this volume were generously supported by the Faculty of Classics of the University of Cambridge. I am immensely grateful to Martin Millett for his invaluable advice, support and encouragement at every step of the editorial process.

## Bibliography

de Ligt, L. & Bintliff, J. (2019) Introduction. In L. de Ligt & J. Bintliff (eds) *Regional Urban Systems in the Roman World, 150 BCE - 250 CE*, 1–34. Leiden & Boston, Brill.

Gros, P. & Torelli, M. (2007) *Storia dell'urbanistica. Il mondo romano*, New Ed. Rome-Bari, Laterza.

Hopkins, K. (1978) Economic growth and towns in Classical Antiquity. In P. Abrams & E.A. Wrigley (eds) *Towns in Societies. Essays in Economic History and Historical Sociology*, 35–77. Cambridge, Cambridge University Press.

Laurence, R., Esmonde Cleary, S. & Sears, G. 2011. *The City in the Roman West, c. 250 BC – c. AD 250*. Cambridge, Cambridge University Press.

Sewell, J. (2010) *The Formation of Roman Urbanism, 338-200 B.C.* Portsmouth RI, Journal of Roman Archaeology.

Yegül, F. & Favro, D. (2019) *Roman Architecture and Urbanism: from the origins to Late Antiquity*. Cambridge, Cambridge University Press.

Zuiderhoek, A. (2017) *The Ancient City*. Cambridge, Cambridge University Press.

# Part I

## Methods and approaches

# Chapter 2

# Approaches to Roman urbanism in Italy: the example of Falerii Novi

## Martin Millett

## 2.1. Introduction

It is widely acknowledged that cities are fundamental to any understanding of the Roman empire. They were central to Rome's mode of administration, which had adapted to a world of slow and imperfect communications and which came to rely on distributed systems of political control that often integrated local social leaders. Furthermore, as nodes in the network of communications that thereby developed, they grew as centres of social systems and as key foci for economic activity. Hence, cities are central to the debates about the mechanisms behind the development and working of the Roman world. It is equally obvious that, whilst the amounts of textual and epigraphic evidence available are unlikely to increase, evidence produced by archaeological work is constantly growing, so one might hope that it has the potential to increase historical knowledge and enhance understanding. Whilst I remain optimistic that this is possible, I also believe that this will only happen if we are aware that any such progress relies not on simply producing more information from fieldwork, but in rethinking our questions and approaches. Recent trends in the analysis of archaeological data on an empire-wide scale (especially the Oxford Roman Economy Project: https://www.romaneconomy.ox.ac.uk) clearly illustrate some potential, although with our present imperfect data there is a danger that such studies may simply confirm the presuppositions of the analyst. This problem is perhaps illustrated in recent studies of Roman cities which support maximalist economic models whilst also tacitly assuming that all urban centres across the empire were essentially similar (Hanson 2016). For myself, I see the character of Roman urbanism as highly regionally variable, with the differences potentially providing key evidence for the nature of the changing social and economic structures within the Empire (Millett 2010). On this basis, I think that a more profitable approach is to map and analyse urban structures through space and time.

The challenge in doing this is that our evidential base is actually rather limited. Although there has long been an interest in the archaeology of Roman cities, such work has been heavily constrained. With the exception of the few places where there has been large-scale clearance of cities, mostly in locations that are not overlain by modern towns, we rely on interventions that have only sampled a small proportion of these ancient sites. Sampling theory shows that even very small sample(s) can be useful if they are truly representative of the 'population' under study, but only if we know, or can hypothesise, the relationship between the samples and the target 'population' and can assume that the target 'population' is homogeneous. This raises two issues for those using archaeological evidence of Roman urban centres. First, except in unusual circumstances, small excavation sites (our samples) are neither carefully selected to provide a *representative* sample, nor are they truly *random* samples. Instead, they are most often either situated as a result of modern development pressures – i.e. excavating in advance of building work – or located where an archaeologist thinks there is something interesting to investigate. Second, and important in cases where the archaeologist is deciding where to dig, our models of Roman urban centres have too often assumed that all Roman towns were basically similar in layout. This has led to excavations focusing on what are assumed to be key building types (most often the public monuments) or targeting areas at the centre of a town as these are assumed to be the most significant. This brings us back to the dominance in the literature of a limited number of extensively excavated towns – Pompeii and Ostia in Italy, and examples like Leptis in North Africa or Silchester in England – which have naturally dominated past thinking. In an era when scholars assumed that the Roman world was broadly homogenous, it was entirely reasonable to extrapolate from such widely explored examples and use them as models for the understanding of other sites, implicitly assuming that small, excavated examples could be interpreted in relation to them. Given our current knowledge of the heterogeneity of the Roman world, this approach is no longer tenable. On this basis, I would contend that we need both new approaches and different ways of thinking if we are to better understand both Roman towns and the dynamics of the Roman world itself.

Excavation – when well conducted – provides very high resolution and granular evidence about comparatively small areas (i.e. samples of cities). It has the potential to allow us to understand the development through time of such areas, and – with the analysis of finds – to make inferences about the lifeways of the inhabitants, their economy and society. It essentially provides detail that is very localised and context specific. There are exceptions, notably projects that have involved the large-scale clearance of extensive areas of ancient cities like Pompeii or Ostia. In the past, these campaigns, however, have generally resulted in a much poorer quality of evidence, with issues of lack of chronological detail which limits the research that can now be done on the finds assemblages (e.g. Berry 1997 and Allison 2004 on Pompeii). In both these cities, the benefits of the broad view of the urban landscape provided by large-scale clearance have allowed the creation of low resolution, big pictures (e.g. Lawrence 1994; Lawrence & Newsome 2011). The desire to enhance detail has also of course stimulated projects that are producing higher-resolution evidence of smaller sample areas within the cleared sites (e.g. Insula I.9.11–12, Pompeii: Fulford & Wallace-Hadrill 1999; Porta Stabia, Pompeii: https://classics.uc.edu/pompeii). Such complementary work is enhancing our understanding of these sites by treating previously cleared areas in new ways, often involving the stratigraphic recording of the standing structures as well as stratigraphic excavation within previously cleared areas. Such excellent work means that we have an increasingly sound understanding of these iconic sites. Alongside this, there is also a different trend, especially associated with studies of Pompeii, which has taken advantage of the large-scale of these cleared sites to look at overall patterns within the urban landscape, thereby characterising the townscape as a whole (Lawrence 1994).

## 2.2. Potential and limitations of remote sensing

Archaeological remote sensing has been increasingly widely used in archaeology in Italy and elsewhere over the last 25 years or so as several of the papers in this volume illustrate (also Johnson & Millett 2013; Vermeulen *et al.* 2012). Although aerial photography has a long history as a research tool in Italy, it has only recently been widely used, whilst at the same time access to both satellite imagery and cheap drones has widened the scope of aerial mapping very considerably. The use of various geophysical survey methods on a large scale is also a recent phenomenon (Campana 2018), although small-scale experimental geophysical survey has a longer history in Italy. Electrical resistance survey has not been used much on a large scale, largely because of the dry soil conditions and the fact that it is comparatively slow, although the development of mechanized systems of data collection, especially in France, suggests that it may become more common (Dabas 2009).

Fluxgate gradiometry, measuring variations in the earth's magnetic field (and commonly referred to as magnetometry) has been much more widely used as the equipment has become widely available and data can be collected rapidly and without much difficulty. After the spectacular success of the survey at Falerii Novi in the 1990s (Keay *et al.* 2000), a significant number of major urban sites in Italy have been surveyed using this method, with varying degrees of success (e.g. Kay *et al.*, this volume; Launaro, this volume; Vermeulen, this volume). In aggregate, they have provided a mass of new evidence, much of it of a very high quality. The resolution of data collection has gradually improved, as has the software for processing, so we are now familiar with the types of greyscale images that map buried structures.

More recently the ground-penetrating radar (GPR) has been used on an increasingly large scale. The technology has been under development for several years, but the cost of the equipment and the computing requirements for processing meant that it was generally only used on a small scale until the last decade. It can now be deployed on a large scale and this has produced some excellent results (Verdonck 2023).

All these methods have the potential to provide large-scale evidence at high resolution across past urban landscapes. All work well on agricultural land, unencumbered by buildings, so they have been most valuable in mapping now deserted Roman town sites. GPR does have the potential to map areas beneath hard surfaces, and so has the capacity to allow us to map features in towns that are still occupied, even if that potential is only now beginning to be fully realised (Piro *et al.* 2020; also Haynes *et al.,* this volume).

In general, the results from any method of remote sensing are constrained by a variety of factors, both inherent to the method and by the environment within which they are used. Hence, although in certain circumstances any particular method can produce visually spectacular results, in practice the evidence is invariably somewhat patchy, with the reasons for gaps in the data not always obvious. We therefore need to be careful about interpretation, and there is a general view amongst practitioners that we should ideally cover the same survey area with a variety of techniques to optimise the information obtained (Keay *et al.* 2013). Even in these circumstances and with the best of results, we should also bear in mind that evidence from remote sensing has basic limitations. First, all the methods are best at mapping solid structures, so more ephemeral evidence – e.g. timber buildings or secondary modifications to buildings – are not generally visible. Second, all are most effective in mapping relatively shallowly buried deposits. Whilst the depth penetration varies between different environments and with the scale of the buried structures, in most archaeological work mapping is limited to the upper 1–2 m, so understanding very deeply stratified sites is generally very difficult, if not impossible. Finally, although GPR differentiates features at different depths below the surface, thus making it possible to develop hypotheses about the chronology of buried structures, for the most part, remote sensing provides rather two-dimensional images which effectively show a palimpsest which requires careful analysis if different phases of activity are to be differentiated. Even where this is possible, the dating of the different phases is impossible from the remote sensing data alone – we rely either on sample excavation to provide stratigraphic dating or on drawing parallels with excavated structures to identify and thus infer a chronology. It is also notable that although many geophysical surveys have now been completed and images published, the number of sites where the results have been fully analysed and critically evaluated remains remarkably small.

These constraints do not mean that the results of such remote sensing surveys lack value, but they do mean that we need to think very carefully about how they can best be used. In doing this, I think it is important to appreciate also that excavation is not a universal panacea: the commonly held idea that digging a trench to examine a geophysical anomaly may be seen as 'ground-truthing' is false as it implies that excavation reveals an 'objective truth'. This is based on a positivist fallacy which will be obvious to anyone who has seriously wrestled with the analysis of the complex stratigraphy of an excavation. All archaeological interpretation is subjective and requires the careful weighing of different forms on evidence. Interpreting remote sensing data is no different, no more or less reliable that interpreting the stratigraphy in an excavated trench. Recognising this and understanding that we need to draw on the whole range of evidence available and weigh it very carefully are fundamental to good archaeological practice.

Returning to the points made above about the nature of excavated evidence from sites like Pompeii that have been the subject of large-scale clearance, we can see parallels with the nature of the data from remote sensing. Essentially, this also provides low-resolution, large-scale data in which relative chronology is difficult to assess, but where spatial patterns are laid bare. In that sense, these data sets are comparable and provide potentially valuable insights into characterising Roman urban landscapes.

## 2.3. The example of Falerii Novi

### 2.3.1. *The geophysical surveys*

Our work at Falerii Novi (Keay *et al.* 2000; Hay *et al.* 2010; Verdonck *et al.* 2020; Millett *et al.* forthcoming) provides an illustration both of the application of methods of remote sensing and of the ways in which that evidence can enable us to approach the subject of Roman urbanism in different ways. The site of Falerii Novi, which is now largely covered by farmland, offers a good opportunity to evaluate geophysical survey. The Roman town was established after Rome's destruction of its predecessor, now known as Falerii Veteres (Civita Castellana), following the Faliscan revolt in 241 BC. The new town was constructed some way to the West, astride the line of the *via Amerina* which was constructed to link Rome with Ameria (Amelia, Umbria) and ultimately Perusia (Perugia). According to the Byzantine writer Zonaras (8.18), the site of the new town was chosen to make it less defensible than its predecessor. In the absence of the relevant section of Livy's narrative, it is difficult to evaluate this statement, but it has generally assumed that the refoundation of Falerii was part of Rome's pacification strategy. Aside from its imposing circuit of walls that are generally assumed to date to the period of its foundation, there is little of the Roman period now visible on the site. Following a series of excavations in the 1820s (evaluated by Di Stefano Manzella 1979), the only major exploration of the site came with unpublished excavations in 1969–75.

In 1997–98 our team completed a survey of the available area within the walls, combining a fluxgate gradiometer survey with a topographic survey that enabled us to produce a close-interval contour map (Keay *et al.* 2000). The resolution of the magnetic survey was comparatively low by present-day standards, but the results were excellent and the publication stimulated considerable interest and encouraged others to undertake similar work elsewhere in Italy. On the basis of an interpretation

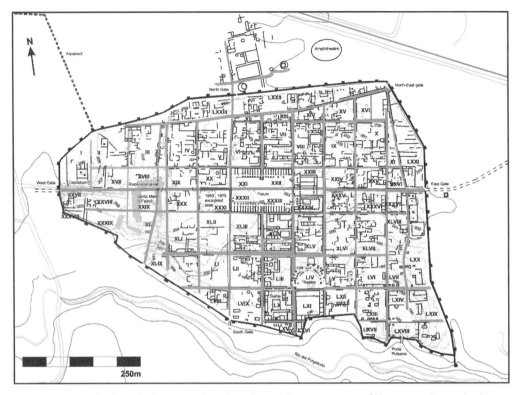

*Figure 2.1. Overall plan of Falerii Novi based on the gradiometry survey (illustration by Paul Johnson based on Keay* et al. *2000).*

of the geophysical anomalies, we published an interpretative plan that mapped the street layout and buildings (Fig. 2.1), alongside a commentary that discussed the different buildings identified. Further work in the area outside the walls to the north, completed in 2008, complemented the intramural study (Hay *et al.* 2010), and I published a discussion paper which developed ideas about the suggested phasing for the development of the town plan based on an analysis of its layout (Fig. 2.2) (Millett 2007). Whether or not the conclusions of that analysis were correct, the study did show how it was possible to use magnetic survey evidence as the basis for a broader historical discussion, and indeed this stimulated a response which proposed a slightly different sequence (Wallace-Hadrill 2013). Following on from the initial geophysical survey there was some further work surveying the town walls (McCall 2007), whilst the whole area was successfully mapped using LiDAR data (Opitz 2009).

This work was followed up in 2015–17 by a new project that collected high resolution GPR data across the walled area (Plate 2.1, Figs 2.3–5). This project, *Beneath the surface of Roman Republican cities* (funded by the AHRC), involved innovative geophysical work undertaken Dr Lieven Verdonck of Ghent University, with the survey of Falerii Novi completed in parallel with comparable work at Interamna Lirenas

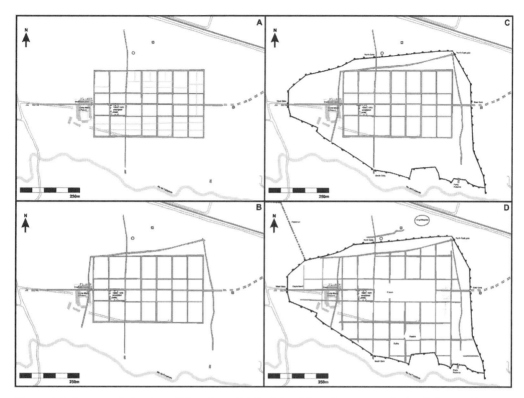

*Figure 2.2. Suggested phasing of the plan of Falerii Novi based on an analysis of the gradiometry survey: (A) the primary street grid, (B) the development of the peripheral road around the primary grid, (C) the construction of the walls and (D) the southern extension of the street grid up to the walls (illustration by Paul Johnson, based on Keay* et al. *2000).*

(Launaro & Millett 2023; also Launaro, this volume). It produced outstandingly good results which complement and extend knowledge of the town plan provided by the magnetic survey (Verdonck *et al.* 2020). A complete analysis of the results of this survey is soon to be published (Millett *et al.* forthcoming), so I do not want to discuss the detail or methodology here. Instead I would like to draw on the results to highlight how we can use remote sensing data to think about Roman town plans in new and comparative ways. In doing this, we should acknowledge that we are generally relying on the use of analogies with excavated data in the identification and classification of particular building forms. Hence, the interpretations offered should be seen as models or hypotheses that should be critically evaluated using other data sets and alternative ideas. Only by doing this will ideas be refined.

### 2.3.2. Phasing the town plan
Building on the idea first developed in discussion of the magnetic survey data, a sequence for the development of the street grid now seems to have been broadly

confirmed with the GPR survey (Fig. 2.2). This reveals that the first phase of the new town involved the laying out of a grid centred on an east–west axis along ridge parallel with the stream to the south. This was laid out three blocks wide (north–south) by seven blocks long (east–west), with the central set divided into pairs of smaller insulae by the east–west street (conventionally the *decumanus maximus*, although we should note that this terminology is a modern invention: Haverfield 1913, 73, 107). The east–west street intersected with the *via Amerina* (conventionally the *cardo maximus*), at the entrance to the *forum* with three rows of *insulae* to its West and five rows to its east. It now seems likely that the *insulae* occupied by the *forum* were reserved for this purpose from the outset as the street that runs through this area identified in the magnetic survey has been shown by the GPR survey to be post-Roman in date.

The axial east–west street passes through the East Gate and the so-called 'Porta di Giove' at the western limit of the town. On the highest point within the walls, just inside this gate, there is evidence for a major temple, interpreted as the *capitolium*. This location on the edge of the settlement and outside the street grid perhaps indicates that the temple was established at the foundation of the town and before the grid was laid out.

It seems clear that after the establishment of the primary grid a routeway was laid out around it. This connected to the valley of the Rio dell Purgatorio at the southeast via the so-called Porta Puteana, and a shallow side valley, then followed the eastern, northern and western sides of the grid before linking back to the valley floor at the southwest via a now lost side gate. This seems to have formed a processional way that linked Falerii Novi back to the sanctuaries at Falerii Veteres. It seems most likely that this routeway was conceived of as part of the original planning of the new town, with the town wall built after it had come in to use, although Andrew Wallace-Hadrill (2013) has argued that the Wall predates the grid and this routeway.

The final stage in the development of the grid involved the addition of a series of slightly less regular, but basically square *insulae* along the south side of the primary grid. These include various public buildings including baths and the theatre. The form of the theatre would perhaps imply that this expansion of the grid dates to the early imperial period.

### 2.3.3. *Land allotment – primary and secondary grid*

Within the grid plan, we can identify different patterns of house plots (Plate 2.1). These are broadly legible because of the scale and high resolution of the GPR survey despite there being substantial evidence for the long history of modification to many individual houses. It is notable that there are several types of building plot which broadly correlate with the proposed phasing of the plan. In the core area of primary grid we can identify a series of east–west properties laid out across the *insulae*. These are most clearly visible in the areas flanking the *forum* to the north and south. The widths of the plots, many of which are occupied by identifiable *atrium* houses, shows some variation in width. This may suggest that the allocation of plots was less regimented that in colonies (contrast with Interamna Lirenas: Launaro & Millett 2023, 83–92; Cosa: Fentress 2003). Elsewhere in the primary grid *insulae* were subdivided with a north–south division running through them. This is most clearly seen in the two rows of *insulae* at the eastern end of the grid where the east–west strips subdivided in this way were occupied by smaller houses. The regularity of this pattern suggests that it was part of the initial planning and implies social differentiation in the initial land allotment. Finally, the square *insulae* in the later grid to the south were divided into quarters, with some of the quarters further split in two. In contrast to the *insulae* in the primary grid, in these the house plots were not all aligned east–west but instead show a range of orientations although they are of standard sizes. This provides strong evidence for the systems of town planning and land allotment within the town, but this is less systematic than shown in colonies (as noted above). It seems likely that these irregularities indicate a more gradual pattern of development, perhaps with housing lots initially defined but only gradually being built upon. Nevertheless, the regularity of layout and allocation of space surely indicates the operation of a central authority, but one that may have been subtly different from that seen in contemporary colonies.

### 2.3.4. Population structure and density

The evidence of plot layouts and house types also provides a sound basis for the estimation of the urban population. In contrast to methods that rely on multiplying a proposed figure for average population density by the walled area (e.g. Hanson 2011, 250–259), we are able to count the actual number of houses of different sizes and provide estimates based on the size of the group occupying them (Millett 2013; Launaro & Millett 2023, 97–99). Although this still leaves some margin of error as not all houses will have had the same number of occupants it enables much more rigorous assessment of population to be made, especially given the high resolution of the GPR survey. Similarly, the number and distribution of houses of different sizes provides evidence for the analysis of the town's social structure, and also comparison with other extensively known towns.

### 2.3.5. Structure of routes

We have already noted the oddity of the peripheral street, interpreted as a processional route, that runs round the primary grid (par 2.3.2; also par. 2.3.7), but the GPR survey also provides other information about routes through the town. The main north–south route along the via Amerina seems to have been key and this is reflected in its unusual width (Fig. 2.3). There remains a question about the slightly offset position of the North Gate, the evidence for which has been made clearer by the GPR survey, although its interpretation remains difficult. By contrast the east–west route along the ridge is less strongly emphasized and, indeed it is interrupted by the *forum.* Nevertheless, its importance in the western part of the town is shown by the location of public buildings including the *forum* itself, a *macellum* and the *capitolium,* all of which open on to it. In the eastern part of the town, street widths suggest that a key east–west route that avoids the *forum* but follows the southern and eastern sides of primary grid. This wider street has properties set back from the frontage, but it is not clear why this east–west route has a kink in it towards its eastern end.

As well as the evidence for key thoroughfares, the GPR survey also shows streets that were constricted in some ways. Some features obstructing streets are probably street fountains, but there are also routes that seem to have been cut, with some structures built across streets. This is especially the case to the West of the *via Amerina* in the southern part of town. These encroachments provide key evidence

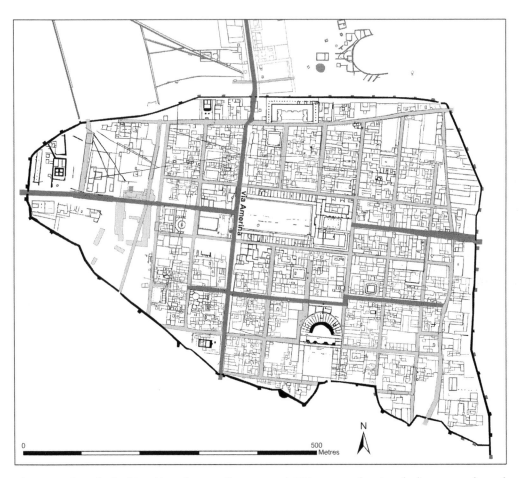

*Figure 2.3. Plan of Falerii Novi based on gradiometry and GPR surveys showing the key routes through the city (illustration by Alessandro Launaro, based on data from Keay et al. 2000 and collected by Lieven Verdonck for the AHRC-funded* Beneath the surface of Roman Republican cities *project).*

for understanding the changing use of space within the town and its transformations through to the later Empire.

### 2.3.6. *Disposition of public space*

Survey evidence is especially important for seeing overall patterns in the use of space across the whole townscape, and with the results of the GPR survey we have been able to identify a wide range of public buildings, even though the interpretation of some remains uncertain (Fig. 2.4). The principal public building and facilities identified (in addition to the temples discussed below) are the *forum* and *basilica*, two suites of baths, the theatre, the amphitheatre, two *macella*, a *nymphaeum* and the aqueduct.

*Figure 2.4. Plan of Falerii Novi based on gradiometry and GPR surveys showing the distribution of key public buildings in dark grey (illustration by Alessandro Launaro, based on data from Keay et al. 2000 and collected by Lieven Verdonck for the AHRC-funded* Beneath the surface of Roman Republican cities *project).*

The disposition of these is partly determined by chronological factors. In general, and with the exception of the *forum*, there are few public buildings in the area of the primary grid, perhaps because it was largely occupied by private buildings from an early stage. The exceptions are the two *macella*, both of which lie on key thoroughfares but are comparatively marginal in their location and may be relatively late in date. The theatre and associated *porticus* as well as the two suites of baths lie in the area of the later southern extension to the grid. This, together with aspects of their design, suggests that they are later in date. Other factors, including the physical topography, may also have influenced the location of these public monuments, with the theatre's *porticus* situated in a slight hollow. The location of the baths is also likely to be related to access to the water supply. The aqueduct enters the town at the northwest, with its pipe raised high on a series of piers that brought the water in at the level of the top of the wall. The surface here lies at about 208 m a.s.l., meaning that the pipe was at *c.* 212 m a.s.l. The present surface in the area where the baths are both located is at about *c.* 203 m a.s.l., providing a good head of water and a reasonable operating pressure. Only parts of the town lie at or below this level, where any baths perhaps would need to have been located to maintain water pressure. Furthermore, they were also situated not far from the South Gate, the main entrance to the town from Rome and therefore convenient for travellers arriving from Rome.

### 2.3.7. *Disposition of sacred buildings*

Perhaps the most surprising feature of Falerii Novi, as we now understand it through survey, is the extraordinary number of temples as well as their locational pattern (Fig. 2.5). We have identified ten likely temples in the town plan. Three of these are located in not unexpected positions – the probable *capitolium* lies at the highest point within the town facing south just inside the West Gate (the 'Porta di Giove'), whilst there is a temple axially situated in the middle of the eastern end of the *forum* square, with a third adjacent to this. The other temples are mostly peripheral within the town and show overlapping patterns of regularity. Several are in the northern half of the town with four of them adjacent to the irregular processional route that surround the primary grid, three of these (in addition to the *capitolium*) are known to face south. In addition to the *capitolium*, three temples are situated close to the principal gates while the final one is positioned to the southwest of the street intersection at the front of the *forum*. This, together with the two temples beside the South and West Gates, all face east. The liturgical and religious implications of these patterns of temple location and orientation are not presently understood but do seem clear and must surely be of significance for understanding the character of the town, which seems to have an unusually prominent religious topography. The peripheral situation of many of the temples is notable and raises the question of whether Falerii is unique or, alternatively, if a failure to explore marginal areas of other towns means that this is a common pattern that has previously escaped notice.

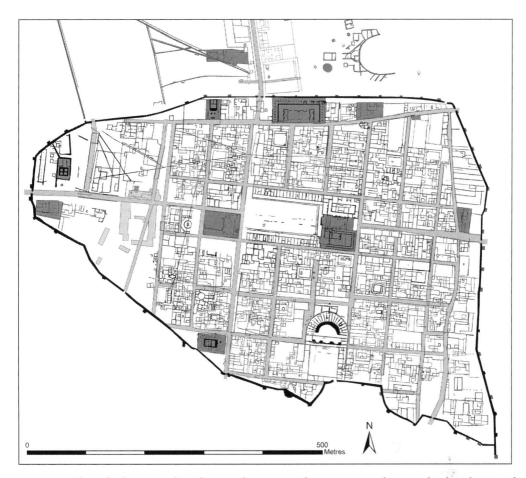

*Figure 2.5. Plan of Falerii Novi based on gradiometry and GPR surveys showing the distribution of temples in dark grey (illustration by Alessandro Launaro, based on data from Keay et al. 2000 and collected by Lieven Verdonck for the AHRC-funded* Beneath the surface of Roman Republican cities *project).*

## 2.4. Future prospects of comparative urban research

I trust that this brief account has illustrated both the benefits of large-scale and high-resolution survey and also the need to think about the kinds of question that such evidence now allows us to ask about whole town plans. It is my belief that such surveys do not provide the same types of evidence as comes from excavation, but they are of equal value. The information that comes from high resolution remote sensing is thus complementary, giving extensive views and across whole townscapes which can and should be used for comparative urban research, opening up new ways of seeing and assessing variation in Roman urbanism. As research of this type increases, it is my hope that we will be able to explore the dynamics that led to the heterogenous patterns of Roman urban forms much more effectively, moving away from the hegemony of sites like Pompeii and Ostia, and thus understanding society in the Roman world more fully.

## Acknowledgements

This paper could not have been written without the work of a large number of people who have been involved in the surveys at Falerii Novi over many years. The gradiometry surveys were undertaken in the *Roman Towns in the Lower and Middle Tiber Valley* project co-directed with the late Simon Keay and funded by the then AHRB. The GPR work is the outcome of work on the AHRC-funded *Beneath the surface of Roman Republican Towns* project (grant ref. AH/M006522/1) undertaken as a collaboration with Alessandro Launaro, Lieven Verdonck and Frank Vermeulen.

## Bibliography

Allison, P. M. (2004) *Pompeian Households: analysis of the material culture.* Los Angeles, Cotsen Institute of Archaeology, UCLA.

Berry, J. (1997) Household artefacts: towards a reinterpretation of Roman domestic space. In R. Lawrence & A. Wallace-Hadrill (eds) *Domestic Space in the Roman world: Pompeii and beyond*, 183–195. Portsmouth RI, Journal of Roman Archaeology.

Campana, S. (2018) *Mapping the Archaeological Continuum: filling 'empty' Mediterranean landscapes.* Cham, Springer.

Dabas, M. (2009) Theory and practice of the new fast electrical imaging system ARP. In S. Campana & S. Piro (eds) *Seeing the Unseen: geophysics and landscape archaeology*, 105–126. London, CRC Press.

Di Stefano Manzella, I. (1979) *Falerii Novi negli scavi degli anni 1821-30.* Rome, L'Erma di Bretschneider.

Fentress, E. (2003) *Cosa V: an intermittent town. Excavations 1991-97.* Ann Arbor MI, University of Michigan Press.

Fulford, M.G. & Wallace-Hadrill, A. (1999) Towards a history of pre-Roman Pompeii: excavations beneath the House of Amarantus (I.9.11–12), 1995–98. *Papers of the British School at Rome* 67, 37–144.

Hanson, J.W. (2011) The urban system of Roman Asia Minor and wider urban connectivity. In A. Bowman & A. Wilson (eds) *Settlement, Urbanization and Population*, 229–275. Oxford, Oxford University Press.

Hanson, J.W. (2016) *An Urban Geography of the Roman World, 100 BC to AD 300.* Oxford, Archaeopress.

Haverfield, F. (1913) *Ancient Town Planning.* Oxford, Clarendon Press.

Hay, S., Johnson, P., Keay, S. & Millett, M. (2010) Falerii Novi: further survey of the northern extramural area. *Papers of the British School at Rome* 78, 1–38.

Johnson, P. & Millett, M. (eds) (2013) *Archaeological Survey and the City.* Oxford, Oxbow Books.

Keay, S., Millett, M., Robinson, J., Taylor, J. & Terrenato, N. (2000) Falerii Novi: a new survey of the walled area. *Papers of the British School at Rome* 68, 1–94.

Keay, S., Earle, G., Beale, G., Davis, N., Ogden, J. & Strutt, K. (2013) Challenges of port landscapes: integrating geophysics, open area excavation and compute graphic visualization at Portus and Isola Sacra. In P. Johnson & M. Millett (eds) *Archaeological Survey and the City*, 303–357. Oxford, Oxbow Books.

Launaro, A. & Millett, M. (2023) *Interamna Lirenas: a Roman town in Central Italy revealed.* Cambridge, McDonald Institute for Archaeological Research.

Lawrence, R. (1994) *Roman Pompeii: space and society*. London, Routledge.

Lawrence, R. & Newsome, D.J. (eds) (2011) *Rome, Ostia, Pompeii: movement and space*. Oxford, Oxford University Press.

McCall, W.F. (2007) *Falerii Novi and the Romanisation of Italy During the Mid-Republic*. Unpublished PhD thesis, University of North Carolina at Chapel Hill.

Millett, M. (2007) Urban topography and social identity in the Tiber Valley. In R. Roth & J. Keller (eds) *Roman by Integration: dimensions of group identity in material culture and text*, 71–82. Portsmouth RI, Journal of Roman Archaeology.

Millett, M. (2010) Town and country in the early Roman west: a perspective. In C. Corsi & F. Vermeulen (eds) *Changing Landscapes. The Impact of Roman towns in the Western Mediterranean*, 17–25. Bologna, Antequem.

Millett, M. (2013) Understanding Roman towns in Italy: reflections on the role of geophysical survey. In P. Johnson & M. Millett (eds) *Archaeological Survey and the City*, 24–44. Oxford, Oxbow Books.

Millett, M., Launaro, A., Verdonck, L. & Vermeulen, F. (forthcoming) *Falerii Novi: the ground-penetrating radar survey of the Roman town*. Cambridge, McDonald Institute for Archaeological Research.

Opitz, R. (2009) Integrating lidar and geophysical survey at Falerii Novi and Falerii Veteres (Viterbo). *Papers of the British School at Rome* 77, 1–27, 335–43.

Piro, S., Haynes, I.P., Liverani, P. & Zamuner, D. (2020) Ground-Penetrating radar survey in the Saint John Lateran Basilica Complex. In L. Bosman, I.P. Haynes & P.Liverani (eds) *The Basilica of Saint John Lateran to AD 1600*, 52–70. Cambridge, Cambridge University Press.

Verdonck, L. (2023) The urban survey methodology. In A. Launaro & M. Millett *Interamna Lirenas: a Roman town in Central Italy revealed*, 19–38. Cambridge, McDonald Institute for Archaeological Research.

Verdonck, L., Launaro, A., Millett, M. & Vermeulen, F. (2020) Ground-penetrating radar survey at Falerii Novi: a new approach to the study of Roman cities. *Antiquity* 94, 705–723.

Vermeulen, F., Burgers, G.-J., Keay, S. & Corsi, C. (eds) (2012) *Urban Landscape Survey in Italy and the Mediterranean*. Oxford, Oxbow Books.

Wallace-Hadrill, A. (2013) Planning the Roman city: grids and divergences at Pompeii and Falerii Novi. In H. Eckhardt & S. Rippon (eds) *Living and Working in the Roman World*, 75–94. Portsmouth RI, Journal of Roman Archaeology.

## Website references

https://classics.uc.edu/pompeii
https://www.romaneconomy.ox.ac.uk

# Chapter 3

## The changing face of the eastern Caelian in the 1st–4th centuries AD: work by the Rome Transformed Project

*Ian Haynes, Paolo Liverani, Thea Ravasi & Stephen Kay*

### 3.1. Introduction: Rome Transformed

Situating Rome within wider debates on Classical Urbanism is notoriously challenging. It cannot be ignored; the city was the point of reference for a civilization built on urban centres. Rome's resilient power to absorb, adapt and re-present itself underpinned its longevity. Yet while this rightly ensures Rome has a profound significance in discussions of the Classical and Late Antique city, the pulse that sustained the *urbs Roma aeterna* was also very much its own. No urban centre in the Mediterranean world could match its sustained dynamism, and as Purcell (2007) observed in his discussion of the *horti* of peri-urban Rome, the drivers that underpinned its evolution were often particular to the circumstances of the city itself. The European Research Council-funded 'Rome Transformed' Project https://research.ncl.ac.uk/rometrans/ (grant agreement No. 835271, Haynes *et al.* 2020; 2021; 2022) seeks to understand better this dynamism and its implications, through detailed study of a neighbourhood on the periphery of the Late Republican city, outside Rome's *pomerium*, which went on to become the centre of western Christendom for a millennium. The project's focus is on the eastern Caelian, and most particularly, on the eight formative centuries that ran from the Principate of Augustus to the Pontificate of Leo III. This paper concentrates on the first four of those centuries.

Before proceeding, we would argue that the word 'transformation' needs to be reclaimed. In one of the biggest debates in the study of Classical Urbanism, discussion of the 'end' of ancient cities, the term has become baggage laden. For some, notably Ward-Perkins (2005, 4) it is too neutral to apply to what befell Rome and her empire. While for others, amongst them participants in the European Science Foundation's wide ranging 'Transformation of the Roman World Project' (https://brill.com/display/serial/TRW), it seems the best term to cover a raft of political, economic, religious, and military changes that reshaped society in between the 4th and 8th centuries AD. We see Rome's transformation differently; Rome was repeatedly transforming itself from its earliest days. The form of the city thus understood, while intimately bound up with shifts of power and ideology, is reshaped in terms not only of buildings added and removed, of expansion and of contraction, it is also a transformation in depth: of earth, debris, and subsurface infrastructure, built-up and, sometimes, excavated away. The dynamic remodelling of the city has produced a depth of archaeological deposits which present both remarkable opportunity and profound challenge. Accessing the evidence is one part of the challenge, synthesising and integrating it is another.

A key consideration is, therefore, the ongoing need to develop systems that facilitate analysis in three and four dimensions, visualising not only plans and structural elevations, but also subsurface infrastructure, and the interconnected nature of changes through time. As students of Rome, we are indeed fortunate to work with a rich body of topographical research (Coarelli 1997; 2012; 2014; Steinby 1993–2000), but such research is constrained by the imaging of spaces and structures in two dimensions.

What is true of the historiography of Rome's topography in general is no less true of our area. The research synthesised in Colini's magistral study of the Caelian (1944) and its updates (Pavolini 2006; Consalvi 2009), and further explored by Liverani (1999; 2020), has been augmented by excellent studies of individual monuments and locations (Krautheimer 1937; Colini 1955; Pavolini 1993; Englen 2003; Guidobaldi 2004; Brandt & Guidobaldi 2008; Pavolini & Palazzo 2013; Englen *et al.* 2015), which have also proven essential in our work.

The challenges confronting researchers in the Caelian, as throughout Rome, and indeed in many of the world's great cities, are all linked to the need to work in multiple dimensions simultaneously. Centuries of development mean that elements of earlier buildings have been destroyed or are so deeply buried that their recovery is largely impossible. The same forces have obscured the natural topography to a degree that even the very contours of the hills which shaped the antique city are only very partially known. Yet for those who drove those developments, the locations of pre-existing buildings, together with the underlying contours, will have been of fundamental concern. As with every great city, there are multiple instances in the history of Rome when dramatic programmes of demolition and earth moving changed both the built and natural landscapes out of recognition: building programmes did not emerge in a vacuum. What existed before could be co-opted for symbolism, convenience and often with regards to both. Roads and city walls framed evolving spaces, of course, but less obviously – particularly when viewed through the prism of so many two-dimensional plans – terracing and the installation of water supply and drainage networks played a central and ongoing role in determining what can be developed successfully where. Subsurface engineering lay at the heart of what made many Roman cities distinctive, but its implications are still often underappreciated in much discussion of Roman urbanism.

## 3.2. Non-intrusive methodologies

With these considerations in mind Rome Transformed has sought to develop a suite of integrated non-intrusive methodologies, many first trialled in the Lateran Project (Haynes *et al.* 2017; 2018; 2019; Piro *et al.* 2020), to allow the changing form of the research area to be modelled. These were developed to allow integration of work above ground with that undertaken in subterranean areas, surrounded by complex exposed archaeology. With some twelve areas of what we call Open Historic Excavations in the Rome Transformed area, most inaccessible to the public, and many requiring special safety measures to enter, this experience proved invaluable. It has also proved essential in advancing research in otherwise undocumented pozzolana quarries. In addition to being of more general archaeological interest, these quarries sometimes reveal further structural evidence.

Data capture consists of four strands: structural archaeology, geophysical survey, archival analysis and borehole survey. For ease of reference, the research area was divided into nine areas, on the basis of structural and functional coherence in property development. To aid readers these area codes are given in parentheses in this paper (Fig. 3.1).

In addition to the depth challenge, a major consideration when undertaking structural analysis of the surviving archaeology is its scale. Amongst other buildings

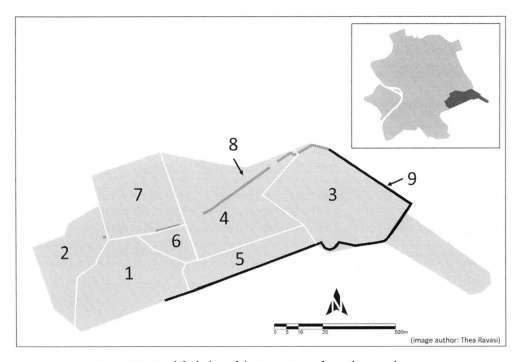

(image author: Thea Ravasi)

*Figure 3.1. Simplified plan of the Rome Transformed research area.*

under investigation, for example, are two basilicas (1, 3), an amphitheatre (3), the Varian Circus (3) – the largest circus ever built in Rome – a particularly complex stretch of the Aurelian Wall (9), and extended elements of the Claudio-Neronian aqueduct (8). This, and the commitment of the project to largely non-intrusive approaches, guided the selection of methods used. Mindful of the need to integrate all data within the same geospatial framework, the team generated digital clones through a comprehensive terrestrial laser scanning (TLS) and structure from motion (SfM) photogrammetry programme of all archaeology accessible above and below ground. Above ground, the surviving height of many of the structures necessitated the use of SfM based on UAVs, a complex task particularly in a busy urban area such as Rome. At ground-level and below, comprehensive TLS survey posed its own problems, requiring registration of chains of interlocking scans through often narrow passageways with limited lines of sight. On site before, during and after these surveys, and in the latter case also drawing further insights from the desk-based analysis of the resultant digital models, was the structural analysis itself. Employing the project's standardized recording method, and informed by existing research on these complexes, this took place wherever possible in an integrated fashion alongside colleagues with a research track record at the sites concerned. Thus, for example, work in the S. Croce archaeological area (3) took place alongside an established team, led by Anna De Santis, which had already studied the complex array of buildings found there for over a decade. The overall work programme is also augmented by minimally intrusive testing of key structures. These tests largely focus on the characterisation of mortar, to allow further insight into the comparative dating of major public works.

Thea Ravasi developed the Structural Analysis programme and coordinated the teams working across the project area. Results from the programme have allowed for the development of phased 3D models of each complex, and in the process have driven the reinterpretation of several sites, together with the generation of markedly more accurate plans and elevations than previously available. In some areas, most notably in the area (2) now occupied by the Azienda Ospedaliera San Giovanni - Addolorata, this work exposed fundamental errors in reports published by previous excavators. There it allows the formulation of new hypotheses on the incorporation of private properties in the imperial domain and on their transformations until the 4th century AD (Ravasi *et al.* 2020). Assisting the analytical process by generating digital clones of the archaeology repeatedly proved invaluable in understanding structural transformations, especially in underground spaces where a comprehensive viewing of coeval structures is often made impossible by later interventions. Furthermore, the resulting models will, we believe, open up all these areas to fresh approaches long after Rome Transformed has concluded.

A concurrent programme of geophysical survey was undertaken deploying electrical resistance tomography and ground-penetrating radar, the latter variously deploying 70, 80, 200 and 400 MHz antenna, and on modern road surfaces a multi-frequency, multi-channel towed system. This programme, the largest single geophysical survey to be undertaken for archaeological purposes in Rome, was conducted by three teams, provided by the British School at Rome, the Consiglio Nazionale delle Ricerche (CNR) and Geostudi Astier. Where appropriate a mixture of geophysical methods was deployed over the same areas.

Clearly the use of archaeological geophysics in urban areas presents multiple challenges. Of these, perhaps the most obvious is the depth of investigation. Radar signal attenuation is inevitably an issue, but the project attempts to mitigate this limitation by the comparative testing of innovative methods of data processing, with the use of multiple GPR antenna arrays, ERT, borehole survey, archival sources and observations from the structural analysis programme. Unmapped modern services and pipes (for example water, electricity, telecoms, sewerage, gas), access routes, and anomalies generated by traffic, bus routes and tramlines, the Metro, and urban furnishings, trees, and plant beds, must all be considered. Complicating matters include the implications of various weather conditions (though this of course applies to most geophysics surveys), gaining access to areas under diverse jurisdictions and owners, electromagnetic disturbance, and the passage of pedestrians and tourists.

In addition to cartographic sources, the histories of individual properties require investigation, together with details of both published and unpublished excavations. Accordingly the archival analysis programme, led by Francesca Carboni (Carboni & D'Ignazio 2023), has drawn on resources from the *Archivio Apostolico Vaticano/ Biblioteca Vaticana,* the *Biblioteca di Archeologia e Storia dell'Arte* at Palazzo Venezia, the *Archivio Storico Capitolino,* the *Archivio di Stato di Roma,* the *Archivio di Documentazione Archeologica* at Palazzo Altemps, the *Archivio Storico e Disegni* of the Sovrintendenza Capitolina and the *Archivio Centrale dello Stato.* An imperative is to source data from *ArcheoSITAR Project* (https://www.archeositarproject.it/) and *Forma Romae* databases (http://www.formaromae.it/), and to ensure that project data can in turn be uploaded into these systems.

The last main source of data is that derived from the project's borehole programme, targeted drilling at sixteen locations across the project area. Location is determined by the need to avoid unnecessary replication of work at areas where such data is already available (for example, that undertaken as part of the Metro C line works), but also by other factors. First, the need to avoid services of any sort, or to drill through highly sensitive areas. Second, selection of sites likely to have better organic preservation. The drilling campaign's main priority is to elucidate the natural topography of the project area, but reconstructing ground cover is of vital importance too. The final major consideration has been to see how data from the borehole campaigns can best enrich, and in turn be informed by, the results of the project's geophysical survey. Here the project draws on pioneering work undertaken at Portus, where the examination of cores alongside the reading of ERT profiles harvested at the same locations enhanced understanding of subsurface deposits (Kay *et al.* 2019). The cores are subjected to geological, micro-botanical and archaeological analysis, and samples submitted for radiocarbon dating.

## 3.3. Methods of data integration

Data capture is, of course, only the first part of the research process. Rome Transformed has developed a series of systems to enable the integration and synthesis of different data types. These systems consist of three main elements: RT 3D, RT SCIEDOC and the project's own 3D GIS.

Given the, often dramatic, shifts in ancient and Late Antique land surfaces during the period under study, the project team identified the requirement for an enhanced system to model successive landscapes. Early indications were that at least six different Digital Surface Models (DSMs) needed to be generated if the physical transformation of the eastern Caelian was to be understood, and accordingly, a system had to be developed to deliver those models. The result is RT 3D, produced by a project team led by Margherita Azzari and Vincenzo Bologna (Bologna & Azzari 2023). Working from a high-resolution DSM of the contemporary ground surface, the system draws upon an array of source material. Thus, existing geological maps, borehole data (both extracted by the project and from legacy sources), georeferenced historical cartographic data, geophysical data and the height point data recovered from the project's structural analysis programme can all be incorporated. In the latter case, there is a special emphasis on noting the level of ancient road surfaces, thresholds to exterior spaces and, in structures built into hill slopes, the height of windows. These data points then allow DSMs to be generated which can then be incorporated into the project's 3D GIS.

Integral to the project's interdisciplinary approach to the built landscape is RT SCIEDOC (https://rometrans.ncl.ac.uk/rtsciedoc/). The exercise of developing such 3D models has multiple advantages over the long-established practice of generating 2D images. Perhaps the most obvious strength of the approach lies in the fact that it is harder to conceal unresolved aspects of the structural interpretation. While a single angle, or the artistic addition of figures and shadows may obscure important detail in a 2D image, digital models can be viewed from multiple angles and their basic structural integrity tested. But the advantages of such models go beyond this, for their production readily facilitates interdisciplinary collaboration, as colleagues can connect and exchange information in visual form, something that allows greater precision than knowledge of one another's technical vocabularies may otherwise permit. Structural analysis of accessible fabric, archival images, and geophysics results can all feed into the model. In the latter instance the team seeks to progress what are variously termed three-tier visualisations, or full-data set models, based on an integration of geophysics anomaly interpretation with TLS/SFM-aided structural survey.

The risks of misrepresentation inherent in visualising cultural heritage, were set out by those who framed the original London Charter (Beacham *et al.* 2006; Denard 2012). Various responses have evolved, notably that developed by Marc Grellert and his colleagues at Darmstadt Technical University. Their system, SCIEDOC 'Scientific Documentation for Decisions' was conceived to make clear the source material that each stage of the generation of 'reconstruction' images (http://www.sciedoc.org/). With the generous collaboration of Dr Grellert, colleagues on the Rome Transformed team have developed their own variant, RT SCIEDOC (Haynes *et al.* 2023). RT SCIEDOC seeks to turn the risks of digital visualisation into assets, an approach that starts with the argument that such images should be regarded as arguments, or better still 'provocations'. Rather than suggesting that what is generated is in some sense a digital rebuilding of a past structure, the term provocation is used to solicit a constructive critical response from the viewer. Within the team, and it is hoped continually without, the generation of provocations is seen as essential to weighing evidence openly, justifying claims transparently, and equipping others to join in and develop the discussion more easily. Following a series of internal and open public sessions presenting provocations, the project team move on to completion of technical reports on individual structural reports and subsequently to the population of project's 3D GIS.

Critical to the development of the project's GIS, and with a view to maximising its capacity to address key questions about the transformation of the Caelian, is ensuring that the underpinning system adopted is both capable of managing 3D shape files and yet accessible to as large a range of users as possible. This question of accessibility is, we would argue, too often lost in complex projects where the interrogation of spatial data ends up the province of only a small number of team members. Rather than developing a new system from scratch, it is important to employ one which a wide range of professionals within and beyond the project can use. Accordingly, therefore, the project makes use of ESRI ArcGIS Pro. It has, however, sought to innovate in its use of this package. Alex Turner, geomatician on the project, has emphasised the importance of relating good GIS use to good practice in metadata management (Turner 2023). Metadata is recorded in an easily accessible format and linked to the visual spatial data generated by the project GIS. This ensures that it not only produces something with immediately tangible results, thus motivating team members to deliver on the otherwise unpopular task of detailed metadata management, but also makes a thorough ongoing exploration of data integrity much easier.

Fuller discussion of the efficacy and implications of the harmonised use of these systems of data integration will follow, but key themes when attempting to appreciate the transformation of the southeast Caelian are emerging. Rome Transformed has as a stated aim to consider the role of the area in developing, illuminating, and in many cases promoting and projecting powerfully influential ideas about politics, security, and religion. While these can, and should, be explored in terms of specific architectural forms, the approach of the project is to go beyond this and to integrate architecture, with topography, in a dynamic environment. Our systems therefore aim to situate all these spaces and places within models of movement. Crucially all these themes can also be studied in 3D through simulating movement, the movement of people and animals, of water and of sound. The first theme of these is linked to access, not just in the sense of doorways and roadways, of paths and barriers, but also in terms of walls, heights and hills. A particular aspect here, sometimes archaeologically visible even when key sections of path or road cannot be readily recovered or observed, is the use of terracing. Also, relevant here is the occupation of space in a way that transforms access, such as the appropriation of areas for burials. Second in the discussion is water. Here again there is a need to go beyond the, undoubtedly important, matter of the course of major water supply infrastructure – aqueducts and sewers – and to look at water holistically. An approach truly informed by hydraulic engineering brings these macro systems, and the micro systems at the level of homes, baths and backyards, not only into contact with one another, but with the wider landscape. Flow modelling systems have a role to play here and adapted to the incomplete nature of the archaeological record, have the further benefit of enabling more refined hypotheses about the use of space than would be otherwise possible. Sound carries too, carrying with it signals about activity and the identity of different parts of the urban fabric. Accordingly, it warrants careful attention. Thus far most of the work undertaken by the project has involved the modelling of sound within buildings, but the project also sees the application of ODEON software for the interrogation of exterior spaces and streetscapes in this landscape of hills and valleys.

## 3.4. Transforming the eastern Caelian

The eastern Caelian was not a single administrative entity in antiquity. The hill was divided in two separate administrative regions by Augustus (*regio II* to the north and west and *regio V*, the Sessorian, to the East). It became part of the ecclesiastical *regio II* in the 4th century AD (Spera 2013). As noted above, the project seeks to focus in particular on a succession of key episodes in the physical transformation of the eastern Caelian. In broad terms, each episode is selected on the basis of developments which have profound implications both for the general character of the neighbourhood at their time, and for its capacity to illuminate through detailed analysis big themes in the political, military and religious life of the Roman world. The project's point of culmination comes with the transformations that marked the area in the late 8th and early 9th centuries AD, a time when new architectures not only articulated Leo III's synthesis of religious and secular rulership, but also – in the form of his development of the Lateran Palace – inspired the most powerful king of the era, Charlemagne, to emulate his achievement in the building of his own royal residence at Aachen.

This paper will, however, focus on a narrower chronological range. It covers key transformations from the early imperial period through to the 5th century AD, focussing more specifically on the project's own archaeological and geographical contribution to our understanding of these changes. As mentioned, to assist the reader in navigating through the different parts of the eastern Caelian, each location in question will be referred to in relation to the project's area codes (as shown in Fig. 3.1).

From at least the 4th century BC, elements of the eastern Caelian had been given over to cemeteries (Scrinari 1968–69a; La Rocca 1973; Coates-Stephens 2004). By the end of the 1st century BC, areas of high ground were marked by a striking density of burials. Close study of the tombs on the via Statilia (4), for example, shows how successive funerary monuments were squeezed into the spaces left between their predecessors, all projecting onto the so-called *via Caelemontana*. This is an area where radical changes in ground surface in antiquity is particularly marked, for not only does it account for the standard of preservation of the via Statilia group, but it is also vividly conveyed in the remodelling of the 1st-century AD *columbarium* of Tiberius Claudius Vitalis (4), unearthed in the 1860s (Bergau 1866). The latter lies within the grounds of the Villa Wolkonsky, West of the via Statilia, but it clearly belongs to the same necropolis. Here successive phases of the tomb show how builders had to raise the entry of the building to keep pace with rising ground levels. Such indications are proving invaluable in developing RT3D-generated DSMs for the ancient landscape.

Here we see too the importance of height, not just for the area itself, but for the entire city of Rome. Traces of a Republican underground aqueduct are visible within the excavations at the via Statilia, and these appear, for the short stretch that can be followed, to take much the same line as that subsequently traced by the *Arcus Neroniani* (8). During the imperial period, the eastern Caelian was to emerge as a crucial point in the city's hydraulic system, ultimately seven out of Rome's eleven aqueducts passed through, converging at *ad Spem Veterem*, near the Porta Maggiore. For those with interests in the neighbourhood, this clearly had fundamental implications for the supply and development of an array of activity, but it is important to note that it was not the only way in which water shaped life here.

In the lower-lying land immediately the south of the research area, water represented both an opportunity and a liability. The scale of the opportunity has been made most clear through the archaeological research that has accompanied Metro C works for San Giovanni station. Here the assiduous and sophisticated channelling of water from the Marrana was integral to the development of the *horti*. The advanced horticulture practiced here in the early 1st century AD, evidenced by the discovery of peach pits in the excavations, was enabled by careful hydraulic management (Rea 2011; 2016). As noted below, however, later changes to the area, and in particular the construction of the Aurelian Wall, were to disrupt some of this management and, in time, to create their own problems. Certainly, the course of the waterlogged valley now concealed deep below the raised ground of the gardens on Via Carlo Felice (5), would have discouraged all but the most ambitious, and well-resourced building projects. The project team's own drilling in this area permits a still more nuanced picture of the range and evolution of this water course.

It is within this undulating landscape that we must place the buildings that completed the *horti*, providing facilities for rest, relaxation and hospitality. Surviving traces of these buildings indicate, unsurprisingly perhaps, that high ground was particularly desirable, but more than that, that there was great investment in terracing the slopes. Here then were rooms with views, mere minutes from the *forum* complexes to the northwest, but with a prospect that looked to the south and east. This configuration is particularly noteworthy in the luxurious series of properties that lie today underneath the Lateran Basilica (1). Here, and in sharp contrast to the later remodelling of this location for the *Castra Nova* (1), the buildings wrap around the slopes of the Caelian, permitting the occupants views out beyond the city to the delicately managed countryside beyond. That this was a significant and ongoing engineering effort is further evidenced by the addition of buttresses within one of the passages within the house here. The passage had been built up against the hillside, and this passage had been in use for some time before buttresses were added; sometime in the first half of the 2nd century AD the whole scheme was then overlain with painted wall plaster. When the passageways were first constructed is difficult to determine, but earlier excavations at the site yielded quantities of decontextualised wall plaster of a calibre and style that stands most direct comparison with imperial properties of Julio-Claudian date elsewhere (Moormann & Mols 1998). This observation, coupled with clear evidence that other walls within the complex were covered in marble up to a height of at least 5 m indicates very luxurious properties indeed, certainly consistent with the quality of imperial palace decoration. This need not indicate that the Lateran property was already part of the imperial *patrimonium*, as elite properties in Rome at this time could clearly be of the very highest quality, but the possibility should not be ruled out.

A short distance from the Lateran Basilica, in the grounds of what is today the *Azienda Ospedaliera San Giovanni – Addolorata* (2), lie the remains of the *Horti* of Domitia Lucilla, an identification affirmed by stamped fistulae (Liverani 2004). This was the childhood home of the future emperor Marcus Aurelius. A far-reaching reappraisal of the original excavations of Santa Maria Scrinari (1995) has enabled the project team to reassess the structural sequence here, which stretches back well before the 2nd century AD. Appropriately, the picture here is of sophisticated terracing and of production: the project research led by Thea Ravasi suggests that a *doliarium* discovered here, which may have been part of the imperial property, remained in use into the 3rd century AD.

The precise configuration of the building(s) that underlie what is today the *Scala Santa* complex (6) will likely never be known, but surviving evidence points strongly to the presence here of another lavish property. Here too terracing provided height and prospect to the house. Access to what would once have been south-facing rooms is possible in the crypt of the *Oratorio dell'Arciconfraternita del Ss.mo Sacramento* (6), where alongside stretches of intact wall plaster, again from the first half of the 2nd century AD, still earlier architectural elements can be observed. Indeed, the team recorded the presence here of a Corinthian capital, dated on stylistic grounds to between the late 1st century BC and early 1st century AD. Ground-penetrating radar survey south of this area (Fig. 3.2), and immediately East of the façade of the Lateran Basilica, may indicate the presence of a further contemporary structure, but these results are still being reviewed in the light of new dating evidence, and core data.

Turning now to the eastern extremities of the project area, it is difficult to characterise what is today the S. Croce archaeological area in the 1st and 2nd centuries AD (3), but new evidence from this area, from both geophysical survey and structural analysis, indicates that the massive building programmes of the

Figure 3.2. Visualisation of anomalies identified adjacent to the Lateran Basilica in Ground Penetrating Radar survey by Salvatore Piro and modelled by Alex Turner.

Severan period led to its wholesale redevelopment. The advantage of large, elevated surfaces, so obviously important in parts of the Caelian already, were to take on a new significance here at the turn of the 2nd–3rd century AD.

Archaeologically, the changes associated with the Severans are very striking indeed. These are most notable in the area beneath the Lateran Basilica (1) (Haynes & Liverani 2020). Thanks to epigraphic evidence (AE 1935, 156; 157) we now know the period in which the *Castra Nova*, the New Fort of the *equites singulares* (the emperor's guard cavalry) was constructed. As its name suggests, the *Castra Nova* was not the first military foundation in the area, and indeed, Lanciani documented the discovery of great hall at nearby Via Tasso (Lanciani 1897, 338), complete with multiple altars dedicated by *equites singulares* stationed at another base (CIL VI 31138–31187), the *Castra Priora* (7) (Buzzetti 1993). The current consensus dates the foundation of the *Castra Priora* to Trajan, but it remains uncertain exactly what area the fort itself occupied. Thus far, work by the project team has yet to identify compelling evidence for the precise location of the *Priora,* and a possibility remains that the fort itself lay further north than Lanciani's site. What we can reasonably say, though, is that the addition of the *Castra Nova* here substantially augmented a strong body of horseguards in the area. The implications of this for daily life in this part of the city, and for other imperial initiatives, warrant careful consideration.

Both the date of the foundation of the *Castra Nova,* in operation by AD 197, and the location also speak to broader themes in the city of Rome and beyond.

First, Septimius Severus presented himself in his coinage as *Restitutor Urbis* (RIC 167, 168): as is increasingly evident, this was more than just rhetoric. Though one particular feature of Rome's urban pulse and dynamism was that successive emperors boasted of their own programmes to 'restore' the city, the scale of Severan work remains remarkably extensive (Lusnia 2014). Reconstruction after substantial fire damage to Rome took place alongside the creation of an array of remarkable monuments. What gets lost in much of the discussion of this work, however, is the timeline. The *Castra Nova* was amongst the first construction projects and must accordingly reflect the emperor's priorities.

The selection of the location of the *Castra Nova* (1), which was to have multiple consequences, also attests to certain priorities. At one level, it lay outside the *pomerium*, respectful in theory of long precedent, but at another, it was extremely close, mere minutes by horseback, from the Senate House and *fora*. But there is surely more to the location than that, for as our modelling of the setting indicates, standing on a purpose-built platform elevated above the higher slopes of the Caelian, the fort dominated the high ground and the approach of anyone entering Rome from the southeast. This is a textbook location for a Roman fort, recalling the tactical strictures in *De Munitionibus Castrorum* (56, 57) on the positioning of campaign bases in hostile territory. When seen in the context of the ongoing use of the *Castra Priora* (7), the likelihood that detachments of guardsmen were present elsewhere within the city (Coulston 2000; Busch 2011), and imperial estates beyond, as at *Ad duos lauros* where many were buried in the *via Labicana* cemetery, the military aspect of this transformation is at once apparent. That the area repurposed at Albano to make way for the *Castra Albana* fortress of the *Legio II Parthica* at the same time was itself previously an imperial property makes this transition still more interesting.

There is a further consideration here, water. Interestingly the Severan enhancement of the Claudio-Neronian aqueduct post-dates by a few years the construction of the *Castra Nova*. This might seem surprising, but in fact it is likely that the hydraulic system could already deliver the volumes of water required without augmentation. The restoration of the aqueduct must therefore be seen in a wider setting, both in terms of Rome's needs, and secondarily perhaps, as something that could then sustain the bath complexes restored or added to the eastern Caelian in the Severan period. Amongst these we must include reference to the building of the bath complex now under the Lateran Baptistery (1), an enterprise team members believe was completed in the reign of Caracalla, but which was ideally suited to serving the *equites*, and the addition of another separate one, a few metres away, but most likely for an entirely separate clientele. Further to the East, other substantial baths were added, notably the so-called 'Baths of Helena', were in operation from this time. Water was also integral to the military/security dynamic of the city. As noted above, seven of the eleven major aqueducts ran through the eastern Caelian. The capacity to cut the supply of water to large parts of Rome will have been apparent to the city's occupants. Indeed, in AD 238 precisely this strategy was deployed by the Praetorians

(SHA *Max. et Balb.* 8.4; Hdn. 7.12.3–7). Though the camp itself lay north of the eastern Caelian, its water supply originated here, at the Porta Maggiore (Evans 1997, 126).

Security and plentiful water are both essential assets for Imperial palaces. The development of the large imperial complex known as *Horti Spei Veteris* (SHA *Heliogab.* 13.5), much of which is now contained within the S. Croce archaeological area (3), must be understood in these contexts (Colini 1955; Colli 1996; Borgia & Colli 1998; Borgia *et al.* 2008a; 2008b; Bottiglieri *et al.* 2016). Our knowledge of the S. Croce complex has benefitted greatly from ongoing collaboration with the established team of researchers working there, and a fuller analysis will be published in due course. It is nevertheless important to note the following themes, all of profound relevance to the study of Roman cities. First, here, on the very outskirts of the city, there is clear evidence for another colossal programme of monumental construction, a programme that once again, as with the Lateran hill, only on a still greater scale, requires a radical elevation and levelling of the ground. Second, this initiative, the creation of what later becomes known as the Sessorian Palace (3), foreshadows an important trajectory in Roman urbanism. Looking particularly at later developments under the Tetrarchy, Dey (2014, 33) has noted the phenomenon of the palatial quarters (for example at Antioch, Thessaloniki, Trier) that are 'veritable "new cities" annexed to the older urban nuclei'. Many of these features (*circus*, reception halls, baths, and porticoes) appear in the Sessorian in the Severan period.

The circus and main reception hall are quite connected, along with its associated and well-preserved amphitheatre, the *Amphitheatrum Castrense,* by a lavishly appointed *porticus.* This connectivity was assuredly part of the original design of early Severan date and represents, therefore, an interesting conceptual step to Dey's 'veritable new city' model, but it also clearly underwent significant change within a few decades. This is most evident in the Varian Circus, the largest monumental circus ever built in Rome. While the circus form was to endure for centuries at other sites around the Roman world, the Varian Circus had a life measured only in decades. Even before the Aurelian Wall cut across its circuit, other buildings had rendered the complex unsuited to chariot racing. A structural analysis team, led by Francesca Carboni from the Rome Transformed team with Laura Bottiglieri, has demonstrated that there was an intermediary structural phase, sandwiched between the construction of the circus and the building of the Wall.

Lest we imagine that this means the impact of the Aurelian Wall on this southeast corner of ancient Rome was therefore somehow less important than it might otherwise appear, it is important to acknowledge that the balance of evidence rather points the other way. The Wall now embraced an area that had previously lain beyond the city's traditional boundaries. Access to some buildings, notably the *Amphitheatrum Castrense* (3), was transformed. While previously its arcades were open on all sides, the construction of the Wall led to their blocking, though the overall form and function of the amphitheatre endured. The same appears to apply to many of the buildings within the S. Croce archaeological area, and if anything, the sense of a 'new city' now walled to the south and east, and indeed partially to the West, was only further enhanced. An intensification of occupation is suggested by the reuse of the passageways beneath the seating banks of the circus, now repurposed as part of a new structure within the palace complex.

Further West, the construction of what becomes known as the 'Porta Asinaria' (1) provides a new monumentalised and fortified entry point to the city, albeit one still overlooked by the *Castra Nova*. As elsewhere on the Aurelian Wall circuit, the original height is approximately half that of what it later becomes when Honorius reworks the city's defences. Excavation work underneath the Asinaria, conducted by Lucos Cozza (Gatti 1954, 97–104), and further contextualised by survey and borehole drilling by the Rome Transformed team in association with Marianna Franco, demonstrates that the original ground surface and entry portal lay much lower than envisioned by earlier researchers, a realisation that further enhances our appreciation of the monumentality of the entryway from its earliest phase. This observation is of particular interest in the light of Ian Richmond's own observations. Richmond (1930, 245), whose comment 'The world was not to know that its greatest City had become a fortified castle... The essential part of the plan was to build a wall which was strong, but inconspicuous', was perhaps partially influenced in this by his own study of the gate.

Contributing to the ground-level changes here, as elsewhere on the southern edge of the research area, were flood deposits from the Marrana (Capelli 2015; Rea 2016; Liverani & Haynes 2022, 153–154; Figs 3.3 and 3.4). Structural analysis led by Francesca Carboni with Marianna Franco further East along the Wall (5) has

*Figure 3.3. Project visualisation ('provocation') showing views into the city looking northwest at the time of the construction of the Aurelian Wall in the AD 270s (Francesca Carboni & Iwan Peverett).*

*Figure 3.4. Project visualisation ('provocation') showing views into the city looking northwest following the Honorian rebuilding (Francesca Carboni & Iwan Peverett).*

demonstrated that the waterlogged and thus unstable nature of the ground between the Porta Asinaria and the S. Croce archaeological area, meant that when Honorian works on the Wall took place, much of the curtain wall had to be replaced from the ground level up.

Returning to the early 4th century AD, however, the next substantive transformation of the eastern Caelian came with Constantine. While the building work associated with this will have been spread over several years, it is not unreasonable to conclude that within days of his victory at Milvian Bridge on October 28, AD 312, Constantine's impact on the area was palpable. The destruction and/or dissolution of the *equites singulares* on that day meant that large areas previously under military occupation, would have become vacant. There is no surviving archaeological evidence for what happened to the base of the *equites singulares* of the *Castra Priora* (7) at this time, but the *Castra Nova* (1) was demolished. As our modelling work makes evident, the Lateran Basilica, consecrated most probably in AD 318, was built over the central range of the fort, dwarfing what were once the largest and most magnificent buildings of the cavalry base. Builders were able to take advantage of the massive platform constructed for the fort, and by adding to it, ensured that the emperor's cathedral, seat of the Pope, towered over those entering the city from the south. A new religious foundation at the heart of Constantine's new model of rulership therefore obliterated, both literally and figuratively, a complex that formerly had exemplified the military strength and vulnerability of his predecessors (Fig. 3.5).

Imagining the world's first cathedral was a major step with far more implications than the standard discussions of repurposing the remarkably adaptable basilica plan would suggest (Bosman *et al.* 2020). Its internal architecture, with its ceremonial

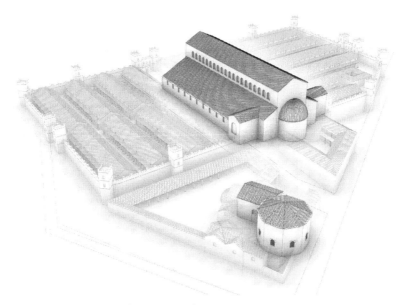

*Figure 3.5. Project visualisation ('provocation') showing the Constantinian Basilica's spatial relationship to the Castra Nova that previously occupied the same site (Iwan Peverett and Ian Haynes, incorporating a visualisation of the Constantinian Basilica developed by Lex Bosman, Paolo Liverani, Iwan Peverett & Ian Haynes, and work on the baths/Baptistery by Thea Ravasi).*

adaptations – a *solea* fencing the route from the entrance, through towards the apse, aligning most likely on the centre of the basilica's ornate *fastigium* and centre altar – marked a new synthesis of procession and audience with a new idea of the divine. Exciting new work by Gianluca Foschi is demonstrating the acoustic force of this architecture. As evolutions in liturgy informed architectural form, so the Lateran Basilica shaped and articulated new ideas about worship. Furthermore, it is also now possible to demonstrate conclusively, thanks to work by Elettra Santucci and Thea Ravasi, that the repurposing of other buildings previously associated with the *Castra* also served the new order. Thus, elements of the water supply system of the baths of the *Castra* were pressed into service for the new baptistery (1), itself an innovative architectural form which was to be widely emulated. In the direct context of the Lateran though, the location was assuredly partly selected to exploit purely local factors, namely the ready availability of good drainage close to the cathedral. Cathedral and baptistery forms were both to play an important role in Roman urbanism from the early 4th century AD onwards. Here in Rome, they served as the nexus of a growing array of religious buildings that were ultimately to manifest themselves in ideas of palatial architecture that would influence guest kings and inspire them in turn.

The Lateran area was not, however, the only site in the research area where the long-term impact of the Severan transformation was to shape 4th-century AD topography. The Sessorian complex (3) endured and was embellished under the

Constantinian dynasty, and the great hall at its centre retains its importance as the Basilica of S. Croce today. Existing features were similarly enhanced and transformed at this time, notably the elaborate bath complex, the Baths of Helena (3), that lay nearby. The presence of baths such as these pose their own questions about the peculiar nature of urbanism in the southeast of the city: who did such extensive baths serve – staff from the Sessorian or a wider public? Further work may hope to resolve this question.

In the following centuries, the Lateran Basilica and, to a lesser but still significant extent, the Basilica of S. Croce, were to remain key foci. Where there was ongoing monumental construction, it coalesced amongst the former. At the Lateran lay the home of the Bishop of Rome, but there were other high-status buildings too, the precise significance of which remains unclear. The remains of a substantial structure now located beneath the INPS building on Via dell'Amba Aradam (1) (Scrinari 1991), has attracted widespread interest on account of its megalographic frescoes, interpreted by McFadden (2013) as a Constantinian image programme, must be understood in its topographical context (Liverani 1993). Further work on the setting and architecture, now being undertaken by project team member Thea Ravasi in association with Simona Morretta (*Soprintendenza Speciale Archeologia Belle Arti e Paesaggio di Roma*), problematises previous interpretations, but also highlights the significance of the structure's setting. This needs to be seen, once more, within a context of hillside terracing on the extremities of the city. Here the elements of the building, notably the main corridor, are of Severan date; the celebrated frescoes added a century later.

Houses of antiquity, such as the *domus* complex excavated beneath the *Ospedale di S. Giovanni* (2) at Corsia Mazzoni (Scrinari 1968–69b) and now substantially reinterpreted by the project team in work led by Thea Ravasi, remained in use into Late Antiquity and beyond (Plate 3.1). Evidence from the Ospedale's Corsia Folchi site, shows how even as the ground floor was raised, spaces were retained; what had been a heated apsidal room at ground level, was retained as an underground chamber. Some buildings were adapted to accommodate the needs of the Christian religious communities now drawn to the area. An important example of an early oratory, with frescoes dating to the second half of the 4th century AD, was also uncovered in the hospital's grounds, a mere 80 m West of the Corsia Mazzoni *domus*. It remains the focus of a major Italian-Japanese research project (Cerrito & Yamada 2019).

This intensity of ecclesiastical activity coalescing around a cathedral building was, as is well known, to be repeated at many major urban centres in the Roman world. The Lateran operated as a point of reference for those other centres in Italy and across much of the empire, not of course in a simple aping of form, but undoubtedly as exemplars for new uses of architecture and rite. That is, however, another story, and rather than plot its ongoing evolution here, we direct readers to further publications by the Rome Transformed team.

## 3.5. Conclusions

In addition to arguing that advances in digital technologies can facilitate step changes in how we visualise and debate the dynamics of Roman urbanism, we would suggest that the experience of Rome Transformed offers some other general lessons. At a generalised level, the ebb and flow of development in the eastern Caelian accords with the well-attested phenomenon of the 'fringe belt', a dynamic area as integral to the story of large cites as any of other aspect of the panoply of urban infrastructure (Liverani & Haynes 2022). The applicability of the 'fringe belt' concept to Rome more generally has already been explored by Mandich (2015; 2019). More specifically, though, we can see in this area the playing out of what are clearly key themes in evolution of the Roman empire's cities, notably in the nuanced adaptation of sophisticated engineering strategies, here deployed on monumental scale, to landscape transformation. Without its hydraulic engineers, without its terraces, without its concrete substructures, the city could never have undergone the pattern of transformation it did. This has multiple implications of course, and opens areas for new experimentation such as, for example, the palatial complex of the Sessorian, the design of which arguably pioneers its own model of urbanistic enclave. By the late 3rd century AD, the eastern Caelian has acquired – within wider Rome – what has become an essential urban characteristic, an enclosing wall, and, in the course of time, this is adapted to situate the pomp and procession of Late Antique ceremonial. The capacity of ecclesiastical centres to generate new forms of growth is also a dominant theme emulated across much of the empire, fostering a new kind of urban life, as the pulse of Classical cities weakened.

There are also features that are more particular to Rome. As has been argued, the Severan transformation plays a key role in the longer-term evolution of the area, and while the fundamental role of the military in this may seem at a variance with general trends in Italian urbanism under the empire, it connected with currents elsewhere, notably urban development on the Danubian frontiers, and with the particularities of Rome itself. At one level, seen especially from the perspective of changes in land ownership, it can be seen as a successor to a process specific to the power play of the City of Rome's peripheries from the Principate onwards. The uniquely dynamic nature of Rome's *horti* is intimately linked to Roman power politics, as places where wealth might be displayed and influence pedalled. In such an environment, it is scarcely surprising that sometimes through inheritance, and sometimes through outright brutality, successive imperial proprietors and agents acquired steadily more land requiring, and facilitating, a new environment open to new forms of development.

## Acknowledgements

The authors thank their colleagues Francesca Carboni, Gianluca Foschi, Salvatore Piro and Alex Turner for comments on the contents of this paper, and indeed all members of the Rome Transformed team for their contributions to the project's research. Rome Transformed receives funding from the European Research Council (ERC) under the European Union's Horizon 2020 research and innovation programme (grant agreement No. 835271), the project team wishes to thank the following organisations and individuals without whom the work discussed here would have been impossible: *Soprintendenza Speciale Archeologia Belle Arti e Paesaggio di Roma* (especially Mirella Serlorenzi, Anna De Santis, and Simona Morretta), *Sovrintendenza Capitolina ai Beni Culturali* (especially Marianna Franco and Simonetta Serra), *Musei Vaticani* (especially Barbara Jatta, Giandomenico Spinola, Sabina Francini, and Leonardo Di Blasi), *Azienda Ospedaliera San Giovanni - Addolorata* (especially Maria Luisa Velardi, Francesco Pontoriero, Cinzia Martini), the British Ambassador to Italy and San Marino and the Embassy staff of Villa Wolkonsky (especially Allegra Serrao). Margherita Azzari, Vincenzo Bologna and colleagues (for RT3D), Gianfranco Morelli and colleagues from Geostudi Aster for further GPR survey, Stefano Campana and Matteo Sordini of the University of Siena oversaw UAV SFM survey of the Aurelian Wall and Claudio-Neronian Aqueduct. The specialists working at S. Croce have generously collaborated with the Rome Transformed Team throughout work in their area. *Roma Sotterranea* provided expertise and safety cover (co-ordinated by Elettra Santucci).

# Bibliography

Beacham, R., Denard, H & Niccolucci, F. (2006) An introduction to the London Charter. In M. Ioannides, D. Arnold, F. Niccolucci & K. Mania (eds) *The e-volution of Information Communication Technology in Cultural Heritage. Where Hi-Tech Touches the Past: Risks and Challenges for the 21st Century,* 263–269. Budapest, Archaeolingua.

Bergau, R. (1866) Sepolcro antico scoperto nella villa Wolkonsky. *Bullettino dell'Instituto di Corrispondenza Archeologica,* 112–117

Bologna, V. & Azzari, B. (2023) RT3D stratigraphies: analysis and software design to manage data. In Haynes, I.P, Ravasi, T., Kay, S., Piro, S. & Liverani, P. (eds) (2023) *Non-Intrusive Methodologies for Large Area Urban Research,* 1–3. Oxford, Archaeopress.

Borgia, E. & Colli, D. (1998) Roma, Santa Croce in Gerusalemme. Nuove acquisizioni topografiche. *Bullettino della Commissione archeologica comunale di Roma* 99, 243–250.

Borgia, E., Colli, D., Palladino, S. & Paterna, C. (2008a) Horti Spei Veteris e Palatium Sessorianum: nuove acquisizioni da interventi urbani 1996–2008. Parte I. *Fasti On Line Documents & Research* 125, 1–17.

Borgia, E., Colli, D., Palladino, S. & Paterna, C. (2008b) Horti Spei Veteris e Palatium Sessorianum: nuove acquisizioni da interventi urbani 1996–2008. Parte II. *Fasti On Line Documents & Research* 125, 18–41.

Bosman, L., Liverani, P., Peverett, I. & Haynes, I.P. (2020) Visualising the Constantinian Basilica. In L. Bosman, I. P. Haynes & P. Liverani (eds) *Saint John Lateran to 1600,* 134–167. Cambridge, Cambridge University Press.

Bottiglieri, L., Colli, D. & Palladino, S. (2016) Il comprensorio archeologico di Santa Croce in Gerusalemme a Roma: nuovi interventi di riqualificazione e recenti scoperte (2013–2014). *Bollettino di Archeologia Online* 7.1–2, 133–144.

Brandt, O. & Guidobaldi, F. (2008) Il battistero lateranense: nuove interpretazioni delle fasi strutturali. *Rivista di Archeologia Cristiana* 84, 189–282.

Busch, A.W. (2011) *Militär in Rom: Militärische und paramilitärische Einheiten im kaiserzeitlichen Stadtbild* (Palilia 20). Wiesbaden, Dr. Ludwig Reichert Verlag.

Buzzetti, C. (1993) *Castra Equitum Singularium, Singulariorum.* In E.M. Steinby (ed.) *Lexicon Topographicum Urbis Romae,* vol. 1, 246–248. Rome, Quasar.

Capelli, G. (2015) La Marrana dell'acqua Mariana. Un corso d'acqua al servizio dei Papi. *Acque Sotterranee – Italian Journal of Groundwater* 4.4, 79–82.

Carboni, F. & D'Ignazio, E. (2023) Conducting archival research in an interdisciplinary context for Rome Transformed. In I.P. Haynes, T. Ravasi, S. Kay, S. Piro & P. Liverani (eds) *Non-Intrusive Methodologies for Large Area Urban Research,* 21–27. Oxford, Archaeopress.

Cerrito, A. & Yamada, J. (2019) Scoperta di nuove pitture nell'oratorio paleocristiano sotto l'Ospedale dell'Angelo (complesso ospedaliero S. Giovanni-Addolorata, Roma). *Atti della Pontificia Accademia Romana di Archeologia. Rendiconti* 91, 275–321.

Coarelli, F. (1997) *Il Campo Marzio: dalle origini alla fine della Repubblica.* Rome, Quasar.

Coarelli, F. (2012) *Palatium: il Palatino dalle origini all'impero.* Rome, Quasar.

Coarelli, F. (2014) *Collis. Il Quirinale e il Viminale nell'antichità, Rome.* Rome, Quasar.

Coates-Stephens, R. (2004) *Porta Maggiore. Monument and landscape.* Rome, L'Erma di Bretschneider.

Colini, A.M. (1944) *Storia e topografia del Celio nell'antichità.* Vatican City, Tipografia Poliglotta Vaticana.

Colini, A.M. (1955) *Horti spei veteris. Palatium Sessorianum.* Vatican City, Tipografia Poliglotta Vaticana.

Colli, D. (1996) Il palazzo Sessoriano nell'area archeologica di S. Croce in Gerusalemme: ultima sede imperiale a Roma? *Mélanges de l'Ecole française de Rome. Antiquité* 108, 2, 771–815.

Consalvi, F. (2009) *Il Celio orientale: contributi alla carta archeologica di Roma, tavola VI settore H.* Rome, Quasar.

Coulston, J.C.N. (2000) 'Armed and Belted Men': The soldiery in imperial Rome. In J.C.N. Coulston & H. Dodge (eds) *Ancient Rome: The Archaeology of the Eternal City,* 76–118. Oxford, Oxbow Books.

Denard, H. (2012) A new introduction to the London Charter. In A. Bentkowska-Kafel, D. Baker & H. Denard (eds) *Paradata and Transparency in Virtual Heritage,* 57–71. Aldershot, Ashgate.

Dey, H.W. (2014) *The Afterlife of the Roman City.* Cambridge, Cambridge University Press.

Englen, A. (ed.) (2003) *Caelius I. Santa Maria in Domnica, San Tommaso in Formis e il Clivus Scauri.* Rome, L'Erma di Bretschneider.

Englen, A., Filetici, M.G., Palazzo, P., Pavolini, C. & Santolini, R. (eds) (2015) *Caelius II. Le case romane sotto la Basilica dei Santi Giovanni e Paolo.* Rome, L'Erma di Bretschneider.

Evans, H.B. (1997) *Water Distribution in Ancient Rome: the evidence of Frontinus.* Ann Arbor, University of Michigan Press.

Gatti, G. (1954) La riapertura della Porta Asinaria. *Capitolium* 29, 97–104.

Guidobaldi, F. (2004) Sessorium e Laterano. Il nuovo polo cristiano della Roma costantiniana. *Mélanges de l'École française de Rome. Antiquité* 116.1, 11–15.

Haynes, I.P. & Liverani, P. (2020) The Castra Nova and the Severan transformation of Rome. In L. Bosman, I.P. Haynes & P. Liverani (eds) *Saint John Lateran,* 91–113. Cambridge, Cambridge University Press.

Haynes, I.P., Liverani, P., Heslop, D., Peverett, I., Spinola, G. & Turner, A. (2017) The Lateran Project: interim report for the 2016–2017 Seasons (Rome). *Papers of the British School at Rome* 85, 317–320.

Haynes, I.P., Liverani, P., Ravasi, T., Kay, S. & Peverett, I. (2018) The Lateran Project: Interim Report for the 2017–2018 Season (Rome). *Papers of the British School at Rome* 86, 320–325.

Haynes, I.P., Liverani, P., Ravasi, T., Kay, S. & Peverett, I. (2019) The Lateran Project: Interim Report for the 2018–2019 Season (Rome). *Papers of the British School at Rome* 87, 318–322.

Haynes, I.P., Liverani, P., Kay, S., Piro, S., Ravasi, T. & Carboni, F. (2020) Rome Transformed: researching the eastern Caelian c1–c8 CE (Rome). *Papers of the British School at Rome* 88, 354–357.

Haynes, I. P., Liverani, P., Carboni, F., Ravasi, T., Kay, S., Piro, S. & Morelli, G. (2021) Rome Transformed: interdisciplinary analysis of the eastern Caelian. *Papers of the British School at Rome* 89, 342–346.

Haynes, I.P., Liverani, P., Carboni, F., Ravasi, T., Kay, S., Piro, S. & Morelli, G. (2022) Rome Transformed: fieldwork in South-East Rome. *Papers of the British School at Rome* 90, 337–341.

Haynes, I.P., Ravasi, T., Peverett, I., Grellert, M., Simpson, M. & Ravasi, T. (2023) From interpretation to 'provocation' and back again: Rome Transformed SCIEDOC and the Ospedale di San Giovanni in Laterano. In I.P. Haynes, T. Ravasi, S. Kay, S. Piro & P. Liverani (eds) *Non-Intrusive Methodologies for Large Area Urban Research,* 49–55. Oxford, Archaeopress.

Kay, S., Pomar, E., Keay, S., Strutt, K., Chapkanski, S. & Goiran, J-P. (2019) Integrating geophysical and geoarcheological surveys for the reconstruction of a Roman port infrastructure: the Claudian harbour at Portus. In J. Bonsall (ed.) *New Global Perspectives on Archaeological Prospection,* 99–103. Oxford, Archaeopress.

Krautheimer, R. (1937) *Corpus Basilicarum Christianarum Romae: the early Christian basilicas of Rome (IV–IX Centuries),* I. Rome, Pontificio Istituto di Archeologia Cristiana.

Lanciani, R. (1897) *The Ruins and Excavations of Ancient Rome: a companion book for students and travellers.* Boston and New York, Houghton, Miffin & co.

La Rocca, E. (1973) Tomba di San Giovanni. In F. Coarelli (ed.) *Roma Medio Repubblicana. Aspetti culturali di Roma e del Lazio nei secoli IV e III a.C.,* 244–256. Rome, L'Erma di Bretschneider.

Liverani, P. (1993) Note di topografia lateranense: le strutture di via Amba Aradam. A proposito di una recente pubblicazione. *Bullettino della Commissione Archeologica Comunale di Roma* 95, 143–152.

Liverani, P. (1999) Dalle Aedes Laterani al patriarchio lateranense. *Rivista di Archeologia Cristiana* 75.1–2, 521–549.

Liverani, P. (2004) L'area lateranense in età tardoantica e le origini del Patriarchio. *Mélanges de l'École française de Rome. Antiquité* 116.1, 17–49.

Liverani, P. (2020) The evolution of the Lateran: from the domus to the episcopal complex. In L. Bosman, I.P. Haynes and P. Liverani (eds) *The Basilica of Saint John Lateran to 1600,* 6–24. Cambridge, Cambridge University Press

Liverani, P. & Haynes, I.P. (2022) Cinture di margine: la Cerniera tra città e campagna a sud est di Roma. *Atlante Tematico di Topografia Antica* 33, 151–165.

Lusnia, S.S. (2014) *Creating Severan Rome: the architecture and self-image of L. Septimius Severus (AD 193–211).* Brussels, Latomus.

Mandich, M.J. (2015) Re-defining the Roman '*Suburbium*' from Republic to Empire: a theoretical approach. In T. Brindle, M. Allen, E. Durham & A. Smith, A. (eds) *TRAC 2014: Proceedings of the Twenty-Fourth Annual Theoretical Roman Archaeology Conference, Reading 2014,* 81–99. Oxford: Oxbow Books.

Mandich, M. J. (2019) Ancient city, universal growth? Exploring urban expansion and economic development on Rome's eastern periphery. *Frontiers in Digital Humanities* 6, Article 18.

McFadden, S. (2013) A Constantinian image program in Rome rediscovered: the Late Antique Megalographia from the so-called domus Faustae. *Memoirs of the American Academy in Rome* 58, 82–114.

Moormann, E. & Mols, S.T.A.M. (1998) Le pitture romane - Frammenti in situ. In P. Liverani, S.T.A.M. Mols, E.M. Moormann & G. Spinola (eds) *Laterano 1. Scavi sotto la Basilica di S. Giovanni - I materiali,* 115–131. Vatican City, Monumenti, Musei e Gallerie Pontificie.

Pavolini, C. (1993) *Caput Africae I. Indagini archeologiche a Piazza Celimontana, 1984-1988. La storia, lo scavo, l'ambiente.* Rome, Istituto Poligrafico e Zecca dello Stato.

Pavolini, C. (2006) *Archeologia e topografia della regione II (Celio). Un aggiornamento sessant'anni dopo Colini. Lexicon Topographicum Urbis Romae, Supplementum III.* Rome, Quasar.

Pavolini, C. & Palazzo, P. (eds) (2013) *Gli dei propizi: la Basilica Hilariana nel contesto dello scavo dell'Ospedale Militare del Celio (1987-2000)*. Rome, Quasar.

Piro, S., Haynes, I.P., Liverani, P. & Zamuner, D. (2020) Ground penetrating radar survey at St John Lateran. In L. Bosman, I. P. Haynes & P. Liverani (eds) *Saint John Lateran to 1600*, 52–70. Cambridge, Cambridge University Press.

Purcell, N. (2007) The horti of Rome and the landscape of property. In A. Leone, D. Palombi & S. Walker (eds) *Res Bene Gestae: ricerche di storia urbana su Roma antica in onore di Eva Margareta Steinby*. 361–377. Rome, Quasar.

Ravasi, T., Liverani, P., Haynes, I.P. & Kay, S. (2020) San Giovanni in Laterano 2 Project (SGL2). *Papers of the British School at Rome* 88, 350–354.

Rea, R. (2011) Metropolitana di Roma Linea C. Stazione San Giovanni. Dati sulla cintura ortiva intorno a Roma tra la fine del I sec. a.C. e il III secolo. *Bollettino di Archeologia Online* 2, 21–42.

Rea, R. (2016) Archeologia nel suburbio di Roma. La stazione S. Giovanni della Linea C della metropolitana. In A.F. Ferrandes & G. Pardini (eds) *Le regole del gioco: tracce, archeologi, racconti. Studi in onore di Clementina Panella*, 425–442. Rome, Quasar.

Richmond, I.A. (1930) *The City Wall of Imperial Rome. An account of its architectural development from Aurelian to Narses*. Oxford, Clarendon press.

Scrinari, S.M.V. (1968–69a) Tombe a camera sotto la via Santo Stefano Rotondo. *Bullettino della Commissione Archeologica Comunale in Roma* 81, 17–24.

Scrinari, S.M.V. (1968–69b) Scavi sotto sala Mazzoni all'Ospedale di S. Giovanni in Roma. *Rendiconti della Pontificia Accademia d'Archeologia* 41, 167–189.

Scrinari, S.M.V. (1991) *Il Laterano imperiale, 1. Dalle Aedes Laterani alla Domus Faustae*. Vatican City, Pontificio Istituto di archeologia cristiana.

Scrinari, S.M.V. (1995) *Il Laterano imperiale, 2. Dagli Horti Domitiae alla cappella cristiana*. Vatican City, Pontificio istituto di archeologia cristiana.

Spera, L. (2013) Il vescovo di Roma e la città: regioni ecclesiastiche, tituli e cimiteri. Ridefinizione di un problema amministrativo e territoriale. In *Atti del XV Congreso Internacional de Arqueologia Cristiana*, 163–198. Vatican City.

Steinby, E.M. (ed.) (1993–2000) *Lexicon Topographicum Urbis Romae*. Rome, Quasar.

Turner, A. (2023) Marvellous metadata: managing metadata for the Rome Transformed Project. In I.P. Haynes, T. Ravasi, S. Kay, S. Piro & P. Liverani (eds) *Non-Intrusive Methodologies for Large Area Urban Research*, 117–119. Oxford, Archaeopress.

Ward-Perkins, B. (2005) *The Fall of Rome and the End of Civilization*. Oxford, Oxford University Press.

## Website references

https://brill.com/display/serial/TRW
https://research.ncl.ac.uk/rometrans/
https://rometrans.ncl.ac.uk/rtsciedoc/
https://www.archeositarproject.it/
http://www.formaromae.it/
http://www.sciedoc.org/

# Chapter 4

# Luck is in the research method: Aquinum, the rediscovery of an 'invisible' town

*Giuseppe Ceraudo*

## 4.1. Introduction

Excavations conducted since 2009 have contributed to our understanding of the Roman triumviral colony of Aquinum (Castrocielo, Frosinone – Lazio), making it one of the most important sites in the Italian archaeological panorama. The urban streets, the *domus*, theatre and monumental bathhouse complex, brought to light over the last thirteen years, have provided crucial data for understanding the entire ancient Roman town. This intense period of fieldwork activities has aroused the interest and curiosity of a wide public, while the discoveries have placed the ancient site into the national and international spotlight, defined by the media and social networks as a 'lucky' archaeological excavation.

It must, however, be reiterated that behind these surprising and 'fortunate' discoveries lies careful and painstaking research work, carried out over the last 25 years, and developed as part of the '*Ager Aquinas* Project'. This preface introduces the 'history' of topographical research at Aquinum which has been characterized by a multidisciplinary study, a well-established approach that has achieved remarkable results that will be discussed in this paper. The research activity, in which non-invasive remote sensing and ground-based survey activities have been fundamental, is helping to expand, modify and challenge our knowledge of this important urban site situated along the *via Latina* between Rome and Capua.

The '*Ager Aquinas* Project' forms part of the activities of the Laboratory of Ancient Topography and Photogrammetry (LabTAF) at the Department of Cultural Heritage of the University of Salento, Lecce. Research first began in 1998 with the purpose of developing, through a wide-ranging application, an operational model aimed at the identification of archaeological evidence in the area, its understanding, cataloguing and interpretation, within a Geographical Information System designed for the management and dissemination of data (Ceraudo 2012).[1] The project encompassed the territory that once belonged to the triumviral colony of Aquinum, in the middle of the Liri Valley, at the centre of a vast plain dominated by the Monte Cairo massif to the north and the Aurunci mountain range to the south, on the western edge of three ancient lakes that have since disappeared.[2] The study was conducted using long experience accumulated in the field of Ancient Topography as well as making use of the latest methodologies and techniques.[3]

Field and laboratory activities were carried out along the lines of inquiry that have always characterized the Lecce research group's topographical work: archaeological exploration of the territory by means of direct and systematic surveys, archaeology-targeted photogrammetry, use of specific applications for vertical and oblique aerial photography, low-altitude aerial surveys, applications linked to the use of different UAV sensors (RGB, thermal, multispectral, Lidar, and others), survey and analysis of monuments, geophysical prospections and setting up of a database linked to cartography and a Geographical Information System developed by the LabTAF (Guaitoli 2009) (Fig. 4.1). Regular archaeological excavation campaigns have been underway since 2009, continuing the aforementioned research activities and aimed at verifying previous hypotheses. Trenches were opened in a central sector inside the urban area, within an area owned by the Municipality of Castrocielo. It is with this context that we would like to trace the history of research at Aquinum, a research characterized by a consolidated method, with field and laboratory activities featuring a multidisciplinary approach, focusing in particular on the integrated and systematic use of non-invasive remote-sensing and ground-based analyses.

## 4.2. Earlier work

Despite some important topographical work carried out at different times in the last century by Cagiano de Azevedo (1949) and Giuliani (1964), Aquinum lacked an adequate cartographic base for the drafting of a detailed archaeological map. All that existed of the Roman town were reconstructed plans of the settlement layout and the articulation of its internal street network, which made it possible to outline, albeit schematically, the main features of its urban topography.

## 4.3. Methodology

### 4.3.1. Topographical survey

With a view to developing this line of research, without losing sight of the fundamental objectives to be achieved through the topographical study of the territory, this type of activity necessarily requires the use of well-established techniques of direct ground-based survey, both integral and systematic. New methods of recording – also cartographically – the presence and distribution of archaeological evidence were applied to the results acquired from field survey, taking into account absences and geographical-environmental factors that may have influenced, conditioned, limited or prevented field recording, showing the degree of legibility in 'visibility' maps of the

Figure 4.1. This image visually summarises some of the research activities carried out in the field at Aquinum by the LabTAF. From top left to right: topographic reconnaissance; aimed photogrammetry; archaeological cartography; photo-interpretation; aerial reconnaissance; oblique aerial photography; survey, technical analysis and 3D modelling of monuments; geophysical prospecting.

surveyed terrain. In addition, to facilitate field recording operations, a new software capable of supporting topographical survey – Project Ulixes – designed to run on compact systems (handheld PCs and PC tablets), is currently being implemented and tested. The system includes an internal module for the acquisition of Topographic Unit sheets that automatically associates the position of the find with its description (Di Giacomo & Scardozzi 2008).

As for the internal structure of the settlement of Aquinum, this has been reconstructed, using aerial photography and the few still-visible features on the ground, by Giuliani (1964), who identified the regular but not orthogonal pattern of the triumviral colony, with axes that did not intersect at right angles but gave rise to parallelogram-shaped *insulae*.

### 4.3.2. *Aimed photogrammetry and archaeological photo-interpretation*

LabTAF is one of the few existing operational centres in Italy for archaeological cartography. It was established to respond to the need for methodological criteria and the acquisition of modern technologies, to be applied in turn to the collection of data and the cataloguing of existing evidence in an area. The aim was to produce a cartographic base (drawn-up by archaeological operators), developed according to the highest current technological standards and which would constitute an ideal base for the drafting of Archaeological Maps.

Since no adequate cartography existed for this type of activity, a specific numerical aerophotogrammetric restitution at a scale of 1:2000 of the urban and suburban area of the ancient town of Aquinum was produced at the LabTAF. The aerophotogrammetric restitution, supplemented by fieldwork, allowed questions to be posed and certain hypotheses to be formulated which, promptly verified on the ground, made it possible to trace the shape of the town, in particular the eastern sector, in greater detail. It was thus possible to reconstruct a much more extensive wall circuit, nearer the edge of the valley and better suited to meet the town's defensive needs. With this change, the settlement surface area now corresponds to approximately 100 ha, compared to the previously estimated 85 ha (Ceraudo 1999). In addition to fieldwork, therefore, a great deal of attention was dedicated to the specialized analysis of vertical aerial photography, a fundamental tool for knowledge and documentation in studies of 'archaeological topography', which with its multiple applications represents one of the sources that has provided the most useful results for studies in the field. All the evidence duly acquired offered new insights into the study and understanding of the urban layout, allowing the revision and modification, not so much in form as in substance, in what must have been Aquinum's urban plan.

As is now well known, the Roman town was characterized (1) by the route of the *via Latina* (which crossed it in an east–west direction, dividing it into two parts), (2) by its imposing defensive system (consisting of an enclosure wall and, on three sides, a large ditch), (3) by the regular but non-orthogonal arrangement of the axes of the road network (whose unusual layout – east–west the *decumanus*, northwest–southeast the *cardo* – gave rise to parallelogram-shaped *insula* blocks), and (4) by the presence, at various points within the settlement, of monumental remains of a number of ancient buildings.[4] The latter, once surveyed and reported in a specially developed numerical aerophotogrammetric map, made it possible to clarify and redraw certain aspects of the *forma urbis* of Aquinum (Ceraudo 1999).

With regard to this aspect in particular, which allowed for prediction of the presence of infrastructure and the typology of structures in the ancient urban area, work was based on the first reconstruction of the *insulae* proposed by Giuliani (1964), thanks to the photointerpretation of aerial images taken in 1944 by the Royal Air Force and published in a fundamental article, although the absence of photogrammetric requirements in the photos made it impossible to define the exact size of the blocks. Only more recently was it possible to ascertain, by means of a detailed survey, the exact size of the largest *insulae*, with a module of 212 × 140 metres (6 × 4 *actus*).[5] Furthermore, it was possible to note an additional internal division with the height of the blocks corresponding to 70 m (2 *actus*). This reconstruction is based on the presence, in addition to the *decumanus maximus* formed by the *via Latina*, of a total of 14 *decumani*: 7 to the north of this and 6 to the south (Fig. 4.2). The plan shows a change from the fourth *decumanus* to the north, up to the line of the walls, where the last two blocks appear longer. These *insulae*, probably constrained by the presence of a large temple, the so-called *Capitolium* (Ceraudo & Murro 2018, 30–33), measure 4.5 *actus*, and are in turn divided in half (270 feet, about 80 metres) (Ceraudo 2004a, 13–17).

More articulated, and therefore more complex, is the attempt to reconstruct the width of the *insulae*, given the dislocation (not always constant), discontinuity and fragmentary nature of the *cardines* identified so far. Only five, in fact, have been recognized with certainty, almost all based on the continuation of modern roads and field boundaries that roughly follow the ancient route: the *cardo maximus*, the so-called 'via Montana', which basically follows the via Civita Vetere in the northern part and via Saudoni (from San Pietro Vetere) in the southern; the eastern *cardo*, identified thanks to the preservation of via Campo Spinello, and the western *cardo*, reconstructed thanks to the features visible in aerial images and located in a field to the east of the so-called *Capitolium* (Ceraudo 2004a, 17, fig. 5).

All these elements seem to confirm a constant width of 6 *actus* for the *insulae* adjacent to the *cardo maximus*. There are, however, some irregularities in this reconstruction, which do not always seem to fit into this module even though they follow the *actus* as the basic unit of measurement. These are recognizable in the line of walls on the western side, on which via Santa Maria Maddalena runs, in some cadastral parcels oriented according to the *cardines* and in 'via della Palestra', the only ancient road with a northwest–southeast orientation excavated so far, brought to light beneath the Casale Pascale in correspondence with the main entrance on the southern side of the *palaestra* of the 'Veccian baths'. All these data seem to suggest a much more complex layout than the one hypothesised, which only the continuation of research activities will be able to clarify.

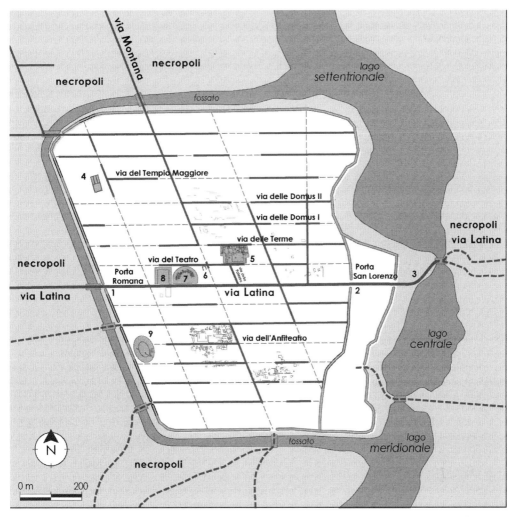

*Figure 4.2. Schematic representation of the urban layout and the main monuments of Aquinum: 1. Porta Romana; 2. Porta S. Lorenzo; 3. via Latina; 4. Major temple (the so-called Capitolium); 5. Central or 'Veccian baths'; 6. Apsidal building (the so-called Temple of Diana); 7. Theatre; 8. Porticus duplex; 9. Amphitheatre.*

### 4.3.3. Low-altitude aerial survey

Research activities tied in to remote sensing were not limited to the acquisition of vertical aerial photos and the production of specific cartography. Agreements with bodies or institutions qualified to fly, such as the *Nucleo Tutela del Patrimonio dei Carabinieri*, the *Corpo Forestale dello Stato* and the *Nucleo Elicotteristi dei Vigili del Fuoco di Roma*, made it possible to monitor and document the entire area under investigation via targeted flights. Starting in 2005, a specific aerial reconnaissance program of the

*Figure 4.3. Oblique aerial view (2005) with the traces of four decumani located north of the via Latina.*

area was initiated, with low-altitude photographic surveys and oblique aerial shots along the entire valley. Some of the numerous aerial images available have shed light on a central sector of the urban area just northeast of the theatre, which previously had not yielded any evidence useful for defining the layout of the urban structure (Fig. 4.3). The favourable combination of the agricultural work carried out in the fields and the choice of an optimal period for the identification of features allowed for the discovery of an extensive sector of the settlement. Prior to the flights, thanks to field survey, areas with considerably higher concentrations of ancient material had been identified. As a result of the aerial photographs, it was possible to see how these concentrations were related to the remains of isolated buildings aligned along the urban road axes and clearly visible the recently acquired aerial images. It is therefore possible to reconstruct, within a sector that seems to have been intended for residential structures, the presence of several large complexes, certainly *domus*, with large unbuilt spaces left within the *insulae*. This situation is distinct from that identified in the southern part of the settlement to the east of the amphitheatre, where it was possible to recognize, before the area was cleared by excavation work carried out inside an equestrian centre, several *insulae* with a greater concentration and articulation of buildings, including perhaps a bath complex (Chouquer 1987, 274) (Fig. 4.4).

*Figure 4.4. Oblique aerial view with the traces of three* decumani *south of the* via Latina *(photo: G. Chouquer 1982 – CNRS: collection de l'École française de Rome).*

### 4.3.4. The use of Unmanned Aerial Vehicle (UAV): drones

Research activities at Aquinum have undergone a continuous evolution over the years, in line with the tradition and methodology of the aforementioned aerial survey but renewed through the use of new and more up-to-date technologies. Recently, in fact, a considerable amount of data deriving from the study of traditional aerial photographs (historical and recent, vertical and oblique) has been integrated through aerial recording by way of remotely piloted aircraft, namely drones. The UAV sector is currently going through a period of considerable development with increasingly sophisticated vehicles and technologies which, thanks to their practicality and cost-effectiveness, guarantee a wide range of uses in the field of archaeology. From the first interventions, more oriented towards addressing simple documentation, their deployment has moved on to meet the demands of multiple fields of application such as, for example, the aerophotogrammetric survey and topography of archaeological areas, surveys of monuments and excavations as well as the mapping and monitoring of vast areas of the landscape. A flexible tool that lends itself to a wide range of uses for the documentation, conservation, prevention and management of archaeological and landscape heritage. The most interesting aspect, however, not yet fully grasped, is the enormous potential of these tools for acquiring a more in-depth knowledge of the territory. Beyond the understandable advantages in terms of cost-effectiveness, repeatability and autonomy of operations, the use of drone remote sensing has constituted a formidable research opportunity for Aquinum, with the possibility of constantly monitoring vast portions of the ancient settlement, strategic areas as well as areas of specific interest (Ferrari *et al.* 2015).[6] Our aim was to acquire data through the recording of new archaeological marks, taking advantage of the possibility of replicating flights at different times of the year, as the fields are worked seasonally, or even at different times of the day, as the terrain is better exposed according to the different inclination of the rays of the sun.[7]

### 4.3.5. Survey and analysis of the monuments

The remains of ruined monuments are still visible in various parts of the settlement (Nicosia 2006, 87–104), for which a specific program of survey and analysis was initiated, followed by a detailed study for an accurate reconstruction, implemented with the use of 3D models. This made it possible to highlight the structural and architectonic peculiarities of the buildings and their construction techniques, also in relation to the period to which they belonged. In the western sector these are: the remains of the amphitheatre, the Porta Romana, a tower just to the north, and the temple building known as *Capitolium*. In the eastern sector, we have the honorary arch known as 'Arco di Marcantonio', the Porta San Lorenzo, and the long wall to the south of the latter. Lastly, in the central sector, are the theatre and building with an apse. Crucial was the involvement of young researchers specialized in the field, who collaborated with great commitment in these phases of research.[8]

Significant results relate in particular to the two large buildings used for spectacles: the theatre and amphitheatre, which fit perfectly into the urban grid, even though they are not chronologically coeval.[9] All that is still visible of the theatre today are the remains of the load-bearing part of the *cavea*, parts of the 22 radial walls (1.05 m wide and preserved for a maximum length of 16.5 metres), the inner nucleus in *opus caementicium*, covered externally by slightly irregular *opus reticulatum* facing. The side of the quadrangular *cubilia*, made of local travertine, indeed vary between 10 and 14 cm. These curtain walls constituted the supports of the concrete barrel vaults, some of which are still partially preserved, providing in all probability the necessary support for the overlying tiers of seats in the *media cavea*, inclined at an angle of approximately 27° (Bellini 2001; Ferrari 2007, 145–146).[10] At present, no elements related to the *scaena*, which must have originally occupied an area about 15 m wide running between the still-preserved supports and the northern edge of the *via Latina* (Ferrari 2007, 145), are visible. In the absence of reliable excavation data, the chronology of the building – on the basis of the construction technique alone – can be set between the establishment of the *municipium* (Bellini 2001, 100; also 2004, 90–91, dating both spectacle buildings to the 'Municipal period'), the dedication of the triumviral colony (Coarelli 1964, 53), the 1st century BC (the most likely hypothesis), the Augustan period (De Rossi 1980, 246) or, more generally, the early Imperial period (Cagiano de Azevedo 1949, 42).

The amphitheatre was located in the southwestern sector of the town against the walls, *intra moenia* but in a decentralized position, as was usually preferred for buildings of this type. It stood on the site where Casale Bonanni, which, trapezoidal in shape, was built at the end of the 18th century (recently demolished along with large portions of the Roman building) incorporating four of the radial *septa* of the *cavea*. Although the monument was severely damaged by the construction of the *Autostrada del Sole* (the A1 motorway) which obliterated about a third of it, thanks to the survey of the surviving parts prior to their demolition it was possible to reconstruct the general plan and size (58 × 35 m) of the arena.[11] A number of the structure's radial supports, built in *opus reticulatum* with tufa block facings, were incorporated in the external structure of the farmstead and its cellars. On the other hand, short sections of wall in mixed technique (*opus reticulatum* and *opus latericium*) of the annular corridors of the arena are still visible along the northern shoulder of the motorway. Also in this case, due to the lack of excavation data and on the basis of the construction technique alone, the chronology of the building – surely established after the dedication of the triumviral colony – cannot be related to that of the theatre but must be attributed to the early Imperial period.[12]

Once documented in detail, the remains of the ancient features were positioned inside the developed numerical aerophotogrammetric map, allowing us to highlight and redraw, in combination with data garnered from archaeological photo-interpretation, hitherto unknown aspects of the form and urban layout of Aquinum, paying special attention to its positioning within the urban grid.

### 4.3.6. Geophysical surveys

The need to experiment with innovative tools and new survey methodologies stems from the long experience acquired with the previously illustrated methods, the awareness of their intrinsic limitations and the observation of a progressive erosion of surface evidence. For this reason, a series of geophysical prospection campaigns were launched with the aim of testing the potential of this type of investigation, integrating and cross-referencing it with the data already available. The prospection works carried out so far have covered a total surface area of 15 ha with magnetometry and *c.* 10 ha with georadar, conducted in areas rich in archaeological material and features, and where field surveys had already been carried out.[13] Once again, results have been exceptional, fully confirming the data obtained from the survey and archaeological photo-interpretation work, highlighting more clearly the location of the buried structures (Fig. 4.5).

### 4.3.7. Archaeological excavation

With the start of regular excavation campaigns in 2009, an attempt was made to provide an initial answer to aspects related to the road network. The first two test trenches were, in fact, opened in correspondence with the two *decumani* rebuilt north of the *via Latina* but not detected as features in the aerial photos, in order to understand the reasons why the traces, clearly visible in the neighbouring fields, were absent in the targeted area. At the end of the first campaign, the discovery of two finely paved streets with white limestone blocks in the locations already suggested has allowed us to show with certainty the validity of the hypothesised *insula* module and realize that all traces of the road axes identified so far in the aerial images referred with absolute certainty only to portions of *viae glareatae*. The paved streets, on the other hand, were not clearly visible in the traces and could only be detected in a few cases, especially thanks to the geophysical prospections conducted in various sectors of the town (Ceraudo *et al.* 2010; Piro *et al.* 2011).

In the *insula* brought to light between the two road axes, conventionally identified as 'Via del Teatro' and 'Via delle Terme', the excavations uncovered an enormous public bathhouse complex: the Central Baths or *Balneum* of M. *Veccius*, named after the magistrate who founded them (Ceraudo *et al.* 2019). Consistent with the urban road system of *Aquinum* (Ceraudo 1999), the structures are arranged according to a double east–west and northwest–southeast orientation. In addition to the bathhouse building, now almost entirely excavated (Ceraudo 2019), it was also possible to investigate around and near other monuments that are still visible but that have seen only limited study. Recent test trenches opened in the area of the theatre documented the presence of part of the stone elements of the annular corridor and the external pillars, already hypothesized in an earlier three-dimensional reconstruction of the monument (Ferrari 2007). On the other hand, work carried out near the so-called Temple of Diana, an imposing apsidal building oriented according to the urban *cardines*, confirmed the presence of two fundamental road axes already theorized in the reconstruction of the road

*Figure 4.5. Vertical aerial view (2017) and geo-magnetic prospections of the central section of the urban plan of* Aquinum *north of the* via Latina; *in the field in the centre of the frame, now owned by the Municipality of Castrocielo and where the annual excavation campaigns have been carried out since 2009, traces of two* decumani *and several* domus *are visible.*

Figure 4.6. *Vertical aerial view (2016) of the central sector of the town north of the* via Latina, *featuring the theatre, the so-called Apsidal building and the Central baths.*

network: one close to the eastern side, the *cardo maximus* ('via Montana'), and one in contact with the apse and corresponding to 'via del Teatro' (Fig. 4.6).

### 4.3.8. IT applications (databases and Geographical Information Systems)

The complexity of the strategy adopted and the substantial volume of data acquired made it essential to create a GIS system for the storage, management and processing of the data collected up to this point, a logical consequence of the territorial research, finalized cartography and photo-interpretation. The LabTAF Geographic Information System was created by bringing together the experiences and technologies developed over a decade of applications through successive refinements in a number of sample territories representative of the national panorama (Guaitoli 2001). The GIS is based on a general cartographic reference framework and various datasets specifically structured for the various areas of research (urban centres, territory, monuments, excavation finds, museum materials, and others). All the archaeological elements are included in a numerical cartography and associated to a database developed according to the knowledge of the individual territorial assets. This contains the information on all the various elements existing on the ground, indicating their condition, damage, risk, cadastral data and type of documentation (historical, geographical, photographic and cartographic).

Like all GIS systems, the structure allows spatial, geographic and alphanumeric queries integrated in several directions and with great operational power. As previously stated, most of the data was obtained through systematic survey and analytical filing, including information already known from historical-bibliographical research, perusal of archival sources, analysis of aerial photographs and various types of aerial images, including satellite images, with the primary purpose of knowledge, conservation and valorisation of the cultural heritage as a strategic resource for the growth of the territory. This line of research is not only aimed at the historical-archaeological reconstruction of the landscape, but also at the renewal of the protection system as part of an overall valorisation strategy.

## 4.4. Results and conclusions

The planned work program for Aquinum was tailored to the enormous archaeological potential and research perspectives offered by the site. A key aspect of the project was the primary need for knowledge and management of the area, subjected to a gradual but constant destruction caused by agricultural work and, in some areas, deep and extensive ploughing. The planning and exploratory work carried out over the last few years has also taken into account the results of data processing and documentation relating to systematic field surveys, aerial reconnaissance and geophysical prospections carried out in more than a decade of research activities by the University of Salento (Ceraudo 2007; Ceraudo *et al.* 2010). The current state of knowledge, the consistency of the archaeological deposits, the abundance of materials and the considerable traces revealed during the aerotopographical investigations, all constitute univocal indicators of favourable conditions for the planning of future survey projects aimed at ascertaining and verifying what has been identified through the aforementioned scientific research activities. Fundamental results have thus been achieved within the general framework for the reconstruction of the urban layout of the ancient town and, in particular, through the excavation of a central sector of the settlement, characterized by public buildings, some of which were already known (the theatre and apsidal building) and others newly acquired to the archaeological patrimony (the public baths). All this, it is hoped, will serve as a driving force for a better management of the site, also in view of a future strategic valorisation of the area.

### Notes

1. The project, aimed at the study of the Roman town and its territory, is part of the research programs of the LabTAF, launched in agreement with the Superintendence of Archaeology, Fine Arts and Landscape for the provinces of Frosinone and Latina, with the support of the Municipality of Castrocielo.
2. In anticipation of the final publication of the Archaeological Map of Aquinum, which is currently at an advanced stage, some of the most interesting results of the research work carried out at the site have been presented in Ceraudo 1999; 2001; 2003; 2004a; 2004b; 2012; 2017; 2019; 2020a; 2020b; 2023; Nicosia & Ceraudo 2007; Ceraudo *et al.* 2017; Ceraudo & Murro 2018.

3. Guaitoli 1999; Gianfrotta 2002; Quilici Gigli 2004; 2010; Ceraudo 2015.
4. On the *via Latina* in the territory of Aquinum: Ceraudo 2023. As for the wall enclosure, its eastern side was naturally defended by the presence of three lakes, as testified by Grossi (1907, 22), drained and reclaimed towards the end of the 16th c. by Giacomo Boncompagni (Duke of Sora from 1579 to 1612) following the purchase of the fiefs of Aquino from the d'Avalos family in 1583 (Coldagelli 1969). This would seem to be confirmed by a wall-painting in the *Salone dei 18 Paesi* ('Hall of 18 Countries') in the Boncompagni-Viscogliosi Castle on the Island of Liri, which depicts Aquino and its territory towards the end of the 16th c. with the lakes already drained.
5. Thus correcting the measurments proposed by Paolo Sommella (1988, 170–171, fig. 47). The module that has been reconstructed is that of the programmatic plan which, within the urban space, does not always coincide with the measurements of the actual plan. The alignments of the ideal mesh did not always fall in the same point, but could vary, coinciding with different elements such as the centreline of the roadway, one of its two sides or even with the front of the *insula*.
6. We employed multi-rotor and fixed-wing UAVs, cross-referencing data with geophysical surveys and experimenting with new aero-photo image processing techniques.
7. Scheduling the flight and acquiring aerial images requires very little time (compared, for example, to using an aircraft), making it possible to achieve adequate photogrammetric coverage of areas of several hectares in just a few minutes. Its simplicity allows to carry out numerous flights, verify data onsite and, if necessary, repeat shots in order to obtain the best results. The possibility of repeating flights is essential to ensure a more complete coverage of the archaeological context with numerous high-quality images in different conditions and with different exposures, in search of the best possible conditions.
8. e.g. Murro (2007) on the '*Capitolium*', the honorary arch and Porta San Lorenzo; Ferrari (2007) for the theatre and amphitheatre.
9. The specific building technique adopted for the theatre is completely different from that of the amphitheatre (an aspect never properly emphasised) and implies that the dating of the two monuments – set at different times during the 1st c. BC, or the early 1st c. AD – should, in my opinion, be revised (Ceraudo 2020b).
10. Parts of the barrel vaults are preserved between row 19, 20 and 21, counting from the first row to the east.
11. The arena measured 58 x 35 m; see Ferrari 2007, 148–150.
12. Golvin (1988, 168–169, 217) proposed a Julio-Claudian date on the basis of the available published evidence.
13. Magnetometric prospections (with a gradiometric magnetometer, an Overhouser GSM-19GW by Gemsystem) were conducted in collaboration with colleagues from the Laboratory of Landscape Archaeology of the University of Siena under the direction of Stefano Campana. The most recent ground-penetrating radar (GPR) prospections were instead carried out in collaboration with Frank Vermeulen and Lieven Verdonck from the Department of Archaeology of Ghent University (the GPR network, towed by an all-terrain vehicle, comprises 15 500MHz antennae, a frequency which has previously proved effective for the prospection of other Roman urban sites).

# Bibliography

Bellini, G.R. (2001) *Note sul teatro di Aquinum*. In *Il 'Latium' meridionale e Roma*, 95–125. Rome, Sintesi D'Informazione.
Bellini, G.R. (2004) *L'ager di Aquinum*. In G. Ghini (ed.) *Lazio e Sabina 2*, 77–92. Rome, De Luca.
Cagiano de Azevedo, M. (1949) *Aquinum*. Rome, Istituto di Studi Romani.

Ceraudo, G. (1999) Il contributo dell'aerofotogrammetria per la ricostruzione dell'impianto urbano di Aquinum. *Terra dei Volsci. Annali* 2, 161–168.

Ceraudo, G. (2001) Nuovi dati sulla topografia di Aquinum attraverso la fotointerpretazione archeologica e la ricognizione diretta. *Daidalos* 3, 161–175.

Ceraudo, G. (2003) *Aquinum.* In M. Guaitoli (ed.) *Lo sguardo di Icaro. Le collezioni dell'Aerofoteca Nazionale per la conoscenza del territorio,* 178–184. Rome, Campisano.

Ceraudo, G. (2004a) Aquinum: la città romana. In G. Ceraudo (ed.) *Ager Aquinas. Aerotopografia archeologica lungo la valle dell'antico Liris,* 13–23. Rome, Caramanica.

Ceraudo, G. (2004b) La via Latina tra Fabrateria Nova e Casinum: precisazioni topografiche e nuovi spunti metodologici. *Archeologia Aerea* 1, 155–181.

Ceraudo, G. (2007) Progetto Ager Aquinas. 10 anni di ricerche: risultati e prospettive. In A. Nicosia & G. Ceraudo (eds) *Spigolature Aquinati. Studi storico-archeologici su Aquino e il suo territorio,* 39–48. Aquino, Museo della Città.

Ceraudo, G. (2012) Progetto *'Ager Aquinas'.* Indagini aerotopografiche finalizzate allo studio della Città Romana di *Aquinum* (Lazio, Italia). In F. Vermeulen, G.J. Burgers, S. Keay & C. Corsi, C. (eds) *Urban Landscape Survey in Italy and the Mediterranean,* 94–103. Oxford, Oxbow Books.

Ceraudo, G. (2015) Carta Archeologica d'Italia ricerche in Puglia. In G. Cera (ed.) *Topografia e popolamento nell'Alto Salento. Il territorio di Mesagne dalla Preistoria alla Tarda Antichità,* 5–7. Foggia, Claudio Grenzi.

Ceraudo, G. (2017) Aquinum e il suo territorio. Un progetto multidisciplinare per la valorizzazione delle conoscenze. In G. Mastrocinque (ed.) *Paesaggi mediterranei di età romana. Archeologia, tutela, comunicazione,* 125–134. Bari, Edipuglia.

Ceraudo, G. (2019) Il balneum di Marcus Veccius ad Aquinum. Considerazioni sull'edificio termale e sulle sue potenzialità ricettive. *Atlante Tematico di Topografia Antica* 29, 89–112.

Ceraudo, G. (2020a) Considerazioni topografiche a margine della scoperta del cosiddetto Cesare di Aquinum: la fortuna è nel metodo. *Rendiconti della Pontificia Accademia di Archeologia* 91, 249–274.

Ceraudo, G. (2020b) Gli edifici da spettacolo di Aquinum tra distruzione, ricerca e valorizzazione. *Atlante Tematico di Topografia Antica* 30, 125–137.

Ceraudo, G. (2023) Entrando ad Aquinum dalla via Latina. 'a due tiri di schioppo a palla' da Porta Romana. *Atlante Tematico di Topografia Antica* 33, 301–310.

Ceraudo, G. & Murro, G. (2018) *Aquinum. Guida ai monumenti e all'area archeologica.* Foggia, Grenzi.

Ceraudo, G., Piro, S. & Zamuner, D. (2010) Integrated GPR and archaeological investigations to study the site of Aquinum (Frosinone, Italy). In *Proceedings of the XIII International Conference on GPR,* 96–100. https://doi.org/10.1109/GPR15825.2010 [accessed 4 May 2023]

Ceraudo, G., Guacci, P. & Merico A. (2017) The Use of UAV technology in topographical research: some case studies from Central and Southern Italy. *Scientific Research and Information Technology* 7.1, 29–38.

Ceraudo, G., Molle, C. & Nonnis, D. (2019) L'iscrizione musiva di M. Veccius M. f. nelle terme centrali di Aquinum. *Rendiconti della Pontificia Accademia di Archeologia* 90, 1–53.

Chouquer, G. (1987) *Le ville et le cadastre.* In Chouquer, G., Clavel-Lévêque, M., Favory, F. & J.P. Vallat (eds) *Structures agraires en Italie Centro-Méridionale. Cadastres et paysage ruraux,* 263–283. Rome, École française de Rome.

Coarelli, F. (1964) *Note sulla topografia extraurbana di Aquino. Quaderni dell'Istituto di Topografia Antica* 1, 51–54.

Coldagelli, G. (1969) s.v. Boncompagni, Giacomo. In *Dizionario Biografico degli Italiani* 11, 689–692. Rome, Istituto dell'Enciclopedia Italiana.

De Rossi, G.M. (1980) *Lazio meridionale.* Rome, Newton Compton.

Di Giacomo, G. & Scardozzi, G. (2008) Integration between high resolution satellite images, GPS and Tablet PC with a new software for archaeological survey: the Ulixes system. In R. Lasaponara & N. Masini (eds) *Proceedings of I International EARSeL Workshop 'Advances in Remote Sensing for Archaeology and Cultural Heritage Management',* 339–342. Rome, Aracne.

Ferrari, I. (2007) Archeologia e grafica 3D. Il teatro e l'anfiteatro di Aquinum. In A. Nicosia & G. Ceraudo (eds) *Spigolature Aquinati. Studi storico-archeologici su Aquino e il suo territorio*, 145–152. Aquino, Museo della Città.

Ferrari, V., Guacci, P. & Merico, A. (2015) Archeologia Aerea e Telerilevamento di prossimità con Sistemi Aeromobili a Pilotaggio Remoto. *Archeologia Aerea* 9, 66–68.

Gianfrotta, P.A. (2002) Prefazione. In A. Milioni, *Viterbo* I, *Carta Archeologica d'Italia. Contributi*, ix–x. Viterbo, Università degli studi della Tuscia.

Giuliani, C.F. (1964) Aquino. *Quaderni dell'Istituto di Topografia Antica* 1, 41–49.

Golvin, J.C. (1988) *L'amphithéâtre romain. Essai sur la théorisation de sa forme et de ses fonctions*. Paris, De Boccard.

Grossi, E. (1907) *Aquinum. Ricerche di topografia e di storia*. Rome, E. Loescher.

Guaitoli, M. (1999) Appendice III. Nota sulla metodologia della raccolta, dell'elaborazione e della presentazione dei dati. In P. Tartara, *Torrimpietra (IGM 149 INO) (Forma Italiae 39)* 357–365. Firenze, Leo S. Olschki Editore.

Guaitoli, M. (2001) I sistemi informativi territoriali in rapporto al patrimonio archeologico. In *Problemi della 'Chora' Coloniale dall'Occidente al Mar Nero*, 385–402. Taranto, Istituto per la Storia e l'Archeologia della Magna Grecia.

Guaitoli, M. (2009) Metodologie per la conoscenza e la gestione dei beni culturali e del territorio. Le attività del Consiglio Nazionale delle Ricerche per il Progetto 'Sistema Informativo Geografico Territoriale della regione Campania'. In *Sistema Informativo Geografico Territoriale della regione Campania. I risultati del progetto*, 39–62. Soveria Mannelli, Rubbettino Editore.

Murro, G. (2007) *Aquinum: cosiddetto Capitolium, Porta S. Lorenzo, arco onorario*. In A. Nicosia & G. Ceraudo (eds) *Spigolature Aquinati. Studi storico-archeologici su Aquino e il suo territorio*, 133–144. Aquino, Museo della Città.

Nicosia, A. (2006) *Museo della Città e del Territorio. Aquino*. Rome, Istituto poligrafico e Zecca dello Stato.

Piro, S., Ceraudo, G. & Zamuner, D. (2011) Integrated geophysical and archaeological investigations of Aquinum in Frosinone, Italy. *Archaeological Prospection* 18, 127–138.

Quilici Gigli, S. (2004) La ricerca per la Carta archeologica della Campania: continuità e innovazione in un antico progetto. In S. Quilici Gigli & L. Quilici (eds) *Carta archeologica e ricerche in Campania*, 9–18. Rome, L'Erma di Bretschneider.

Quilici Gigli, S. (2010) La Carta archeologica della Campania. L'impegno per la promozione di una conoscenza culturale e civile. In S. Quilici Gigli & L. Quilici (eds) *Carta archeologica e ricerche in Campania*, 11–24. Rome, L'Erma di Bretschneider.

Sommella, P. (1988) *Italia antica. L'urbanistica romana*. Rome, Jouvence.

# Part II

## Beyond the textbook

# Chapter 5

# Cosa, Orbetello, and the genesis of a colony

*Andrea U. De Giorgi*

## 5.1. Introduction

Cosa never ceases to amaze. Granted, the extraordinary scholarly output of the site hardly matches the modest remains on the Ansedonia promontory. To the visitor, Cosa may be a disappointment, if not a downright projection of the vision of Frank Brown, the first archaeologist to shed light on the colony and its material record. Today, the presentation of Cosa and its monuments is vastly obscured by the macchia, while the current archaeological itinerary reflects Brown's tenet that Cosa was a miniature copy of Rome, projecting, as it were, an idea of urbanism and monumentality that was expected to mirror the realities of the capital in the 3rd century BC (Fig. 5.1). Much research has debunked this myth and altogether positioned Cosa in the context of Roman expansion, and, more fundamentally, in the narrative of southern Tuscan cities whose settlement lingered for centuries. What is more, the discourse of Roman colonization has decisively parted company with frameworks taken up by Brown and Salmon, among others (Bispham 2006; Bradley 2006; Broadhead 2008; Erdkamp 2011; Stek & Pelgrom 2014; Termeer 2015; Coles 2017).

Extensive though Cosa's archaeological record may seem, it primarily illustrates the floruit of the colony during the 2nd century BC and the Augustan period. Accordingly, this same perspective permeates most of Cosa's scholarly output, with the discussion of the material record typically couched in narratives of foundation, floruit, and decline. The critique of Cosa's scholarly tradition, however, does not concern us here. Rather, it needs to be stressed that the early days of the colony and, in turn, the post classical phases of the town, still offer plenty of room for discussion. While the former is being taken up by new research (De Giorgi *et al.* 2023), questions about the incubation of the Roman settlement, and the political climate that brought to bear the establishment, remain paramount. In that vein, this essay formulates new questions about old problems, highlighting the colony of Cosa and its unique relationship with the territory, a dynamic connection that veers from the tropes of centuriation, *iugera* distribution, and civic allotments. In particular, this

*Figure 5.1. Cosa: general view of the Ansedonia promontory and Orbetello in the background (photo by the author).*

study takes up Cosa's genealogy and growth, vis à vis the cultural and environmental realities of Cosa's settlement in its formative years. How the colony nucleated and negotiated its layout and urban plan, perhaps falling short of meeting the long-term expectations of its stakeholders, yet showcasing a remarkable degree of resilience, is the main thrust of this research. To that end, this essay probes the Tyrrhenian seaboard of Cosa and brings into sharper focus discrete areas of the ancient town: the axes near the *forum*, the *horreum*, a sector of the town now tentatively defined as the *macellum* and the Portus Cosanus, that is Cosa's anchorage. What is more, the corollary of water management and delivery offers a lens to discuss the nucleation and growth of this community and, last but not not least, their sense of belonging and knowledge of the place.

## 5.2. The setting of Cosa

Perched on a karstic promontory overlooking the Tyrrhenian Sea and measuring approximately 13 ha, the town commanded a vast territory of 550 km$^2$, extending from the mouth of the Albegna River all the way to Vulci and plausibly, the Marta River (Fig. 5.2). Much of this very fertile land was to be occupied by the early colonists, at

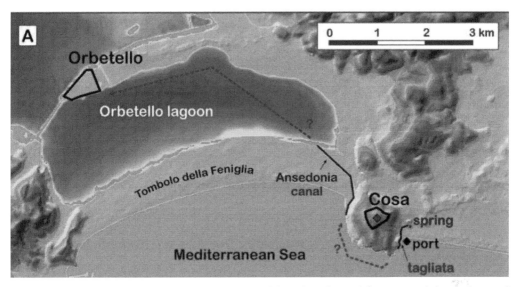

Figure 5.2. Cosa, Orbetello, the lagoon and a possible paleo-channel (courtesy of the author and Jean-Philippe Goiran).

least in the expectations of the agency behind the project, whatever that might be. The core of the district was the triangle today referred to as 'Valle d'Oro' which included the site of Settefinestre and where traces of centuriation also survive (Castagnoli 1956; Dyson 1978; Rathbone 1981; Carlsen 1984; Carandini & Cambi 2002; also Levi 1927). In geological terms, the site of Cosa is nested on top of a dolomitic rock promontory, 114 m a.s.l. The compact limestone has been susceptible to the formation of sink holes, with at least one such feature north of the *forum* and a series of fissures in the port area. As with the climate, rain here is scarce, 460 mm a year, some of the lowest figures in Tuscany. Earthquakes, too, may have taken a toll on the built environment of the town with episodes in AD 408 and 618 (Guidoboni 1989); the collapse of the vaulting of one of the baths, in particular, offers compelling evidence of the violent, instantaneous destruction of a sector of the building. More fundamentally though, Cosa does not have water resources. The promontory is bereft of any source of perennial water and not conducive to the construction of aqueducts. These limitations, however, never hindered or brought to a halt a long and complicated history of settlement. And it should be borne in mind that east of the promontory, where the Portus Cosanus grew in synchrony with the colony, is a strip of prehistoric marshes and lagoons that extended for several kilometers. Rodenwaldt and Lehmann (1961) were the first to address the role of this ecosystem as it impacted human settlement. They noted that the strip of marshes east of the Ansedonia promontory was a fundamental corollary to settlement in the region, as it offered key sources of sustenance, other than an ideal setting for the development of fisheries after the foundation of Cosa. Our programme of coring, undertaken with Jean Philippe Goiran at the University of Lyon near the area that was occupied by Cosa's small port, has aimed at producing a sedimentary history of the Ansedonia promontory and adjacent harbour. So far, this research has demonstrated that this paleoenvironment intersected with human agency as early as the early 1st millennium BC. This signature of early anthropic intervention in one of our cores does not, of course, offer a fixed benchmark, and firm material evidence is in short supply. Nevertheless, the data informs us about the early interaction between human agency and the environment at an early stage, long before the establishment of the Latin colony in 273 BC. Moreover, Iron Age settlements on the Feniglia sandbar as well as the floruit of the Orbetello settlement in the 7th–6th centuries BC (Calastri 2019), offer tantalizing evidence for the uptick of settlement in this district starting in the 1st millennium BCE.

## 5.3. Orbetello and vicinity

Located 6 km northwest of Cosa, Orbetello owes its renown to the lagoon and wetland adjacent to it. Two sandbars, the Tombolo della Giannella and Tombolo della Feniglia separate the lagoon from the Tyrrhenian Sea. In the centre of the lagoon is Orbetello, lying on a sandbar now connecting the mainland to Mt. Argentario by a causeway. Orbetello is notoriously girded by a system of polygonal fortifications that stylistically duplicated that of the Latin colony of Cosa. Previously though, it may have initially served as *epineion* of Cosa, that is a military port (Ciampoltrini 2019). Yet Orbetello and its obscure history of settlement, in particular, remain a cultural facet that has not been sufficiently explored, for all the implications that this harbour community may have had with the foundation and development of the colony of Cosa. As the Etruscan and Punic threats were looming in the region, the Roman presence near the Orbetello peninsula and the Tuscan archipelago, was driven by the necessity to secure northbound maritime traffic (McCann *et al.* 1987, 22–23). The position of colonial settlements in this districts would have thus cemented a sense of Roman presence over the corridor that included the islands of Giglio (Igilium) and Giannutri (Dianium), all the more as the role of the port of Talamone (Portus Telamonis) seemingly dwindled down in the early decades of the 3rd century.[1] The addition of a docking facility for military ships at Portus Herculis on the Argentario peninsula in the last decades of the 3rd century BC casts further light onto this flurry of building initiatives, while also illustrating a picture of increasing volume of navigation and related infrastructure.[2] Ad hoc adjustments and the appearance of new local interlocutors seem to have been the pattern as Roman presence was setting its foothold on a region, that of the Tuscan seaboard, that regulated traffic to the archipelago and, beyond, Sardinia as well as Liguria. We shall return to Orbetello and its role below; for now, it needs to be stressed that this local perspective helps shed further light on the occupation of the Ansedonia hill and the foundation of the colony of Cosa. Simply put, a local angle of opportunism and possibilities, wedded, however, with the political realities of the 3rd and 2nd centuries BCE, unpacks new scenarios above and beyond the realities of foundation and conquest.

For starters, one may consider the environmental corollary. Heavy-handed human intervention appears to be the signature for the region during the 3rd century BC. In particular, a host of proxies suggest trends of interest that began long before the *deductio* of colonies in the region. The last three millennia of the c. 15,000-year pollen record from Lago di Mezzano, some 50 km west of Cosa, illustrate the effects of human impact, and, not least, deforestation, with values steadily increasing between 700 BC and the 1st century AD, when there is also a significant presence of *avena/triticum*, along with herbs linked to human disturbance (Sadori 2018). This information also seems to dovetail with other paleobotanical datasets, not least from the Lago di Accesa, Poggio San Martino, and Poggio dell'Amore: they signal the gradual reconfiguration of the vegetation canopy in the greater Tuscan region, with trends of wholesale replacement of select taxa, and heavy exploitation of *quercus* (Rattighieri *et al.* 2013). It is safe to infer that said trends began in the Etruscan period and gained traction at the time of the Roman conquest. We should posit a similar environmental impact on the Ansedonia hilltop, when around 273 BC the Latin colony was established. While the deforestation of the promontory cannot be documented, ubiquitous scarping and levelling of limestone outcrops for quarrying purposes attests to the forethought and labour that accompanied the early days of the colony and the wholesale reconfiguration of the hilltop of Ansedonia. More to the point, the foundation of the colony was powerfully demarcated by its perimeter of polygonal walls, still in great condition. The circuit ran for about 1.5 km in length with 21 towers, and an interior line surrounding the *Arx* of slightly less than 200 m (Brown 1949; Barker *et al.* forthcoming). Towers were projecting rectangles, with the exception of one of circular form (possibly of the Augustan period), and concentrated on the sea sides of the fortification, designed as they were against threats from the sea, plausibly pirates or Carthaginians (Brown 1949; 1980; Brown *et al.* 1994). The scale of the project is the crux of the problem: was there a need for a so potent and conspicuous ring of walls? Was this a clear statement of conquest, or rather the by-product of current anxieties, with possible pockets of Etruscan resistance and a looming threat moving from Carthage? All the same, the planning and execution of the monument are nothing short of remarkable. Our ongoing study of the colony's energetics shows that expediency in the execution and local quarrying were key to this project (Barker *et al.* forthcoming). Calculating the project's labour time, we suggest that approximately 80 days of labour may have sufficed for the completion of the project, by the hands of 2,500 presumed families of settlers. Of course, the demographics of colonial enterprises in the 3rd century BC are a matter of dispute, and those of Cosa are no exception. For too long, studies have suggested tallies grounded in 258 alleged living structures (Hanson & Ortman 2017, rehashing Fentress 2003 and Fentress & Perkins 2016); this projection is no longer tenable, as shown by the recent GPR analysis of the site, which shows vast sectors of the town devoid of any building activity (Bandalat *et al.* 2019; Scott *et al.* 2021). Rather, the nature and scale of the early construction projects at Cosa help us assess the original investment and, not least, the size of the community. Based on contemporary similar enterprises at Cales and Luceria, one can argue that the initial number of colonists should not have exceeded those figures. All the same, going back to the construction of the walls and labour involved, it is apt to say that the homogeneity of the project and its solid character make it plain that forethought, design, and architectural know-how effectively coalesced in a project that was designed to attract new constituencies and investments, but still fundamentally tied to the territory. Lastly, it needs to be stressed that a synchronic project of defences was implemented at Orbetello (Calastri 2019): this perimeter of defences presumably superseded fortifications that girded the 7th-century BC settlement and encircled the promontory with their 1,926 m long circuit. While the masonry of the walls of Cosa was mimicked in the following years by projects like the Villa delle Torrette in the Valle d'Oro, Orbetello was no mere imitation (Dyson 1978). The masonry style (Lugli III/IV) and the execution make it plain that this project was germane to that of Cosa, probably executed by the same hands.

As a flurry of building initiatives were unfolding on the Ansedonia hilltop site, much was also happening in the vicinity of Cosa's anchorage, the site typically referred to as Portus Cosanus, an anchorage that has been brought into sharper focus by the study of Ann Marguerite McCann, and later Giulio Ciampoltrini (De Giorgi 2022). The configuration of the port is well known, from the breakwaters to the imposing silhouette of a temple dedicated to an unknown deity and destroyed by modern development.[3] Nevertheless, for too long its establishment synchronic with that of the colony has been sidelined, while its relevance has been pigeonholed into the commercial fortunes of the elites of the region, not least the Sestii family during the last decades of the 2nd and the 1st century BC (out of a vast bibliography, see Rathbone 1981; Carandini & Cambi 2002). Instead, the archaeological record of the site bespeaks a project that brought to bear the stamina and forethought of the Cosa planners. In particular, the polygonal masonry lining up the structure on its north side betrays a project that was in harmony with the 3rd-century BC fortifications on the hilltop (McCann *et al.* 1987).[4] Furthermore, its topography makes it plain that two axes of traffic from the northeast and southeast gates were designed to reach Cosa's *forum* and its adjacent commercial areas (Fig. 5.3). Wheel ruts along the 'Road of Porta Romana' document the flow of goods in and out of the town, while the archaeological collections of the port suggest that alleged recession that unfolded on the hilltop of Cosa needs to be reconsidered (Will & Slane 2019, 7–10; also McCann *et al.* 1987, 33). More importantly though, the Portus Cosanus was the locus where less visible, yet equally paramount, modifications took place. Behind the harbour and its infrastructure of backwaters and piers was an intricate system of southwest–northeast water canals, consisting of two natural clefts in the dolomitic rock of the promontory and one man-made. The latter and its role in serving the fisheries and the draining of the lagoon have been amply discussed by McCann and needs not to be taken up here (McCann *et al.* 1987).

*Figure 5.3. Portus Cosanus (courtesy of the American Academy in Rome).*

*Figure 5.4. Spacco della Regina, Portus Cosanus: scarping and cutting of the limestone rock (photo by the author).*

At 262 m in length, the 'Spacco della Regina' is the longest of these channels, and, with its shorter pendant 'Piccolo Spacco', it offers a glimpse into the formation of natural clefts in the rugged Ansedonia promontory. The greater of the two owes its evocative name to medieval myths: its eerie character amid occasional skylight, dark tunnel and a cave must have stoked its reputation of haven for brigands. What needs to be stressed, however, is that its entrance has been cut back at least 1.5 m thanks to heavy pounding and scarping of the rock wall. Further, amid 1–6 m wide twists and turns and occasional trickling of water from a no longer visible spring, the 'Spacco della Regina' canal vividly bears witness to substantial man-made manipulation. In particular, large-scale scarping of the walls of rock inside the cave may suggest the preparation of the surface for the accommodation of water-lifting devices of sorts (Fig. 5.4) (De Giorgi 2018).[5] By that rationale, said technology would have lifted the water of the spring to a location (some 30 m above) on the hilltop, seemingly outside Cosa's town walls. Only a handful of holes can be noted in the immediate vicinity of said apparatus, which suggests that the projects may have only supported some light, makeshift mechanisms, or, at worst, had never been brought to completion. While this evidence was noted by McCann and her team, it was, however, never discussed and integrated in the greater discourse of the colony and its maritime outlet. The potential hydraulic implication of this evidence is paramount on two counts: first, it enlarges the breadth of engineering applications that secured a steady supply of fresh water to the hilltop settlement – which had none. Second, and more fundamental, it sheds light on stringent water needs and cultural responses that only local folks could articulate. In short, the community that transformed this promontory in the early 3rd century had a strong command over the technology of the day, whether for construction or hydraulics. They also had an intimate knowledge of the ecology of this region, from the nature of its stone to the amount of rain the area would get each year, as well as the possibilities to capture the few water resources available nearby. That these people were local, and indeed very steeped in this territory, is a cogent possibility.

This hypothesis thus advances the well-known historical narrative of Cosa's foundation in the context of the Roman conquest of the 3rd century BC. It also invites a discussion about the making of a colony and its social apparatus. However, the discussion about the circumstances that led to the colony's foundation has been typically relegated to the Roman expansion following the dissolution of the Latin League in 338 BC. The conclusion of the conflict between the Etruscans and the Romans (311–264 BC), in particular, spearheaded the establishment of colonies and led to *de facto* termination of Etruscan communities. A panoply of captured cities, *evocationes* of gods and triumphs in Rome is reported by Livy (9.32–46). However, Livy's notion of destruction needs to be treated with caution. Crucially, the Etruscan defeat at Sentino in 295 BC and a fully-fledged expedition in 294 BC against Rusellae, a community lying some 44 km to the northwest of Cosa, represented the watershed for the tightening of Roman pressure in this region. The following years, as reported by Livy, sanctioned the demise of Etruscan communities with a host of yearly campaigns: Tarquinia (281 BC), Vulci (280 BC), Volsinii (280 BC), and Caere (273 BC) are the landmark events in the defeat of the Etruscans. Overall, it is safe to infer that, with Vulci defeated, the district fell under the jurisdiction of Cosa. The survival of Vulci after the conquest has been greatly debated. Plausibly coerced into a *foedus*, and still under the rule of the aristocracy of old (*Satie*, *Tute* and the likes), the town was stripped of most of its landholdings. The end of activities at Ghiaccioforte and Doganella has been traditionally interpreted as evidence of the termination and dispossession enforced by the Romans in 273 BC (Ciampoltrini & Rendini 1992). The fact of the matter is that this pattern of interruption may not have been as pervasive as one may think. The settlements at Ghiaccioforte, Doganella and possibly Saturnia apparently underwent significant transformations, if not downright disappearance, but the evidence for their termination is tenuous at best. Sovana, for instance, is a conspicuous exception to this trend of widespread destruction: its constellation of 3rd–2nd century BC tombs, some of which of monumental character, namely 'Tomba dell'Ildebranda' and 'Tomba del Tifone', suggest a settlement continuum independent of the colonial reconfiguration of the region (Steingräber 2013, 665).

## 5.4. The early phases

But let us now return to the momentous days of Cosa's foundation and bring into sharper focus the actors involved. The discovery of one Etruscan inscription bearing the names of *Larthi* and *Sethre Auni* in the environs of the *Arx*, if anything, reminds us of the cultural landscape in which Cosa was founded (Bace 1983, 111–112; also Carandini & Cambi 2002).[6] This contested document has been discussed by a host of scholars, from Frank Brown himself to the late Mario Torelli. If anything, it proves, first, that the colony's landscape was lived and traversed by indigenous communities that preceded or coexisted with the arrival of the new settlers. Second, it may also indicate that the colony, enjoying Latin status, may have seemed particularly attractive to non-Romans, and thus accommodated local communities, whether Italic or Etruscan settlers. We can further pursue this avenue into the analysis of Cosa's settlers and their familiarity with the region by delving into the practicalities attended as the colony turned on its engines.

Other than defining the wall circuit and bringing together the hilltop and port settlements, the Cosa founders had to take on a more stringent task: providing the community of builders on the hilltop with water, a vital condition for the survival of the colony. Four major reservoirs of 800,000 l capacity each, cut out of the rock, built in polygonal masonry and heavily mortared rubblework finished with a thick coat of *cocciopesto*, punctuated three gates and the central plateau (Fig. 5.5). The establishment of these monumental features not only contributed to the harvesting of rainwater for all sorts of pressing needs, but also spawned the phenomenon of cisterns that in the following centuries peppered the site in the hundreds, big and small, public and private, becoming the cultural signature of this community, a pattern that is particularly visible in the insular Mediterranean. It is fair to say though, that the 3rd century BC was also a time demarcated by the appearance of greatly enhanced water systems in urban contexts that equally drew on centuries of water harvesting strategies. In cities, better than in any other context, a blend of grandeur, ingenuity, and opportunism drove the adoption of engineering arrangements that altered their respective landscapes and local socio-political relations. Cosa is an excellent case in point to demonstrate how water resources were stored, preserved, and delivered to local constituencies. How a disadvantaged community – it had neither a spring nor an aqueduct – effectively supplied its constituency with water and went as far as establishing baths in the early Augustan period, has been brought into focus by recent scholarship (De Giorgi 2018). More fundamentally, from the onset of the colony, cisterns became the architectural signature of the settlement; fall/winter rains and runoffs were the vital requisites for filling these features. But they were more than simple recipients of precipitation. Rather, they were part of a sophisticated retention system that secured a sufficient supply of water for each domestic units and public amenities. The procurement of adequate water supplies was an essential need for the Cosa occupants to survive the seasonal drought of the Tyrrhenian summers.

*Figure 5.5. Cosa: one of the four public reservoirs (photo by the author).*

The elucidation of the water management practices and how those practices evolved at Cosa are particularly critical for understanding the development of the ancient town. Why Cosa is located where it is, above and beyond the mantra of 'strategic purposes', has long been the crux of the problem. The absence of aqueducts, springs, or any other year-round water resource nearby that would sustain the community through the dry season has intrigued the scholars of Roman Republican history and archaeology. The role of paved and slightly canted surfaces, as well as conduits designed to shed seasonal runoff into the several large reservoirs throughout the town, continues to be argued. Nevertheless, new data makes it now possible to offer intriguing details about the development of the water system at Cosa, including the role of architecture and aspects of civic government. More subtly, though, the cisterns and their sophisticated impounding systems became the hallmarks of the town and punctuated its built environment in the following centuries, signalling, as they did, an incremental adjustment to overarching environmental conditions and demographic growth.

Cosa, however, was not alone in articulating effective, long-lasting strategies to offset meagre precipitation rates, or in showcasing sophisticated water retention

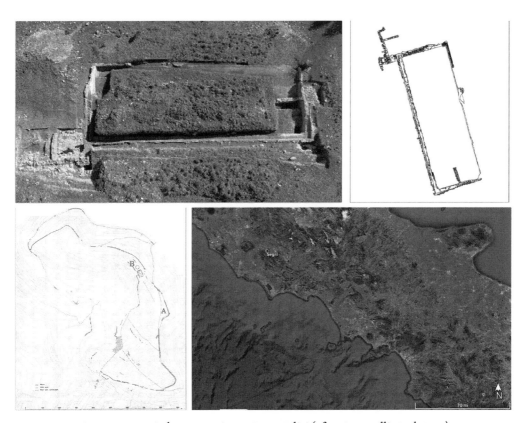

*Figure 5.6. Segni: the excavation at Prato Felici (after Ceccarelli et al. 2016).*

systems. A case in point is that of Segni, ancient Signa, in Latium, an early colony of Rome in the 6th century BC and presumably resettled in 495 BC. Here recent excavations in the area of Prato Felici have brought to light a monumental cistern of the second half of the 2nd century BC, built in solid *opus caementicium* and sheathed with hard signinum (Ceccarelli *et al.* 2016). The structure negotiated the perimeter of the walls and, considering the height and thickness, was designed to provide its growing community with a fresh reserve of water (well over 900,000 l) (Fig. 5.6). Amid the flurry of monumental buildings that transformed the townscape of Signa, the new cistern gestured at novel techniques of harvesting water, negotiating the slope of the hill, and replacing the obsolete concept of the round tholos cisterns, hitherto key to sustain the community. Where natural resources fell short, the hand of man brought about correctives. Lastly, moving south across the Italian peninsula, the remarkable 'vasche limarie' of Brundisium (another colony of the Middle Republic) and their complicated network of alimentation remind us of the scale of capital-intensive investment of the water infrastructure and its three historical phases of configuration. More fundamentally, these cisterns remind us of the evolution of Brundisium's water supply system, from the modest array of wells and pipelines of the 3rd century BC to a fully-fledged distribution network in the Trajanic period. Overall, above and beyond the great ingenuity and determination of these builders, these projects ostensibly demonstrate their builders' dexterity in both building long-term infrastructure and engaging it in local ecologies.

So far, the essay has showed that this currency of water capture, retention, and delivery was a common strategy both in central and southern Italy during the 3rd century BC in contexts of precarious water supply. But, zeroing back on Cosa, the first generation of the colony and its great investments did not produce the expected results. A rapid survey of archaeological and textual records of a set of colonies that either struggled or became deserted in the decades following their foundation opens new vistas into complicated narratives of settlement and downright abortive foundations (Laffi 2007). The seaports of Buxentum and Sipontum remind us of the frail nature of some of these colonial projects, a far cry from the picture of colonists happily trundling in their ox carts and spearheading the conquest of central Italy. Lukewarm interest in the colony of Cosa, presumably low economic returns, and a generation of young men lost to the Punic Wars may have impacted the demographics of the town. The town walls just described ostensibly encompassed an almost empty landscape. What is more, a few *heroa*, reminiscent of the mausolea of Anatolia

*Figure 5.7. Cosa: heroon on the 'Necropoli Orientale' (photo by the author)*

and North Africa and scattered in the countryside along the northeastern road and south of the *Arx*, were the isolated harbingers of a mortuary landscape that failed to materialize (Fig. 5.7) (Brown 1949; Ciampoltrini 1991). The mausoleum S-1, south of the *Arx*, is a gripping example of an austere, isolated tomb that gestures at the viewers and conveys the lofty aspirations of this community in its early days. Who were they? It may appear as though these individuals are more likely to be enterprising equestrians than people anywhere near the rank of senators. A handful of names are worth mentioning: Q. Salonius (of Etruscan extraction or exposure), the families of the Salvii and Tongilii, M. Larius, the artisan Marcus Cusonius, the Titii, and the entrepreneur Quintus Fulvius. Firm conclusions are of course limited. And, to give an idea on how little impact the colony had on its surrounding territory, it is worth noting that only two new farms are attested in the vast territory of Cosa (Carandini & Cambi 2002). Meanwhile, no durable houses were built: the construction of domestic units within the colony is not attested, based on the archaeological record, until the first quarter of the 2nd century BC.

During this phase of early recession, Cosa's narrative of settlement gets seemingly even more interlocked with that of her doppelganger, the elusive Etruscan settlement of Orbetello. Whether serving as *epineion* or not, this community did not fare well either after the 3rd century BC, slowly fading into disuse in less than a century, for reasons that are a matter of dispute. Our current research is testing the underwater sediments through their matrix and organic components (ostracods included), and it appears that a reduction of sea level and oscillations in the salinity may have adversely affected conditions of the lagoon, making the anchorage unserviceable. Recently, Paolo Liverani has moved forward this debate suggesting some compelling interpretative frameworks that help us model the relationship between Orbetello and Cosa (Liverani 2020, 136). In particular, he posits that the dialectic between the two sites may have followed the pattern seen at Volsinii and Falerii, with a similar interplay between *Vetus* and *Novus*, and the subsequent eclipse of the earlier settlement. In this vein, Orbetello, the putative 'Cosa *Vetus*', would have not only adumbrated the settlement that later occupied the Ansedonia hill, but also significantly contributed to its demography, thanks to a substantial transfer of population in 197 BC, an event that is textually documented (Livy 33.24. 8–9). Of course, these are hypotheses that, though suggestive, remain an argument from silence. But it is fair to say that it is the fluid nature of the colonization process, and notably the establishment of Latin colonies, known for their less regimented configuration and accessibility to non-Romans, that perhaps enabled the transfer of Orbetello's population to the colony of Cosa. As Liverani (2020, 137) remarks, Cosa in 197 BC was accorded the privilege to choose their second draft of colonists, and it stands to reason that they chose those they knew best. How Orbetello fared in the aftermath of these transformations we are not in the position to tell. A small, albeit elusive settlement lingered on in the following centuries, as suggested by tenuous signs of occupation in the area of the main sanctuary, today deeply buried under the Duomo (Calastri 2019). Not a whole lot of information, but enough to infer that Cosa indeed eclipsed Orbetello and offered a better anchorage, while presenting better opportunities to its stakeholders and community members.

## 5.5. The town plan

Cosa's development seized the opportunity of new forces and resources, ushering in a town plan that was not as rationally conceived as Brown had it. The appearance of monuments in the 2nd century BC need not to be taken up here, as it is documented by a wealth of scholarship (Brown 1980). Instead, I would like to focus on the eccentricities of Cosa's plan, as they vividly appear in the archaeological record. Our geophysical survey makes it plain that entire blocks of the town remained empty and created space for bouts of construction that never materialized. (Plate 5.1). The nature of the terrain hindered the development of the colony and limited the extent of a number of axes of traffic, thus presenting a picture that is at variance with the traditional view of Cosa. Street N near the bath and Street 6 were blocked by the superimposition of buildings. Street 7 is also a great case in point, as there is evidence of buildings that faced away from the *forum* and opened on streets that are clear examples of this trend. What is more, the rugged topography of the town had to be reckoned with. Street 5, for instance, long believed to be the backbone of the town, had a steep gradient that made it impossible for carts and heavy traffic to move between the northwestern gate ('Porta Fiorentina') and the *forum*.

The presence of a putative *horreum* and its adjacent small square next to the northwestern gate, however, are suggestive of the activities that unfolded on the fringes of the town and the priorities that dictated the partition of space. The *horreum*, initially interpreted as 'Temple A', was hastily investigated in 1972 (Brown 1984). Adjacent to the northwestern gate, the building lies on a 41.81 × 28.12 m terrace made of polygonal masonry linked to the 3rd-century BC fortification walls. Apparently, a system of storage rooms in the rear and possible *tabernae* on the wings articulated a space traversed by a drainage channel and accessed via a ramp, thus facilitating the movement of carts. The excavation, however, limited its inspection to partition walls and portico, glossing over key-issues such as the nature of the finds and phases of use. Furthermore, the field notes mention only in passing the presence of large, broken containers for the storage of foodstuff, failing to discuss the nature of the building. A small collection of 2nd- to 3rd-century AD ceramics offers a general snapshot of use. However, it stands to reason that the planning of the building and its realization harken back to the early days of the colony in the 3rd century BC. While the test-trenches excavated in 1972 could only partially reveal the exact configuration of the building, it nevertheless seems clear that a market adjacent to a main gate of the town was a key feature early on. It functioned as a portal to Cosa's vast territory and constituents, moving traffic to and from the town thanks to its easy access to the *via Aurelia*. It also cemented Cosa to its environs in economic and cultural terms. Grain and timber for ship construction may have been key commodities in the unfolding of these networks, and the metrical inscription of Titus Caesius Taurinus from Praeneste (CIL XIV 2852) is a good case in point. But in the 2nd century BC, the provision and transport of grain for the North Italian and Spanish campaigns would have provided economic opportunities for the community (Scott 2019). Perhaps, commercial areas as lenses can help us shift the pendulum away from the *via sacra* and the *Arx* and explore the foci that best capture the town and its development in the 2nd century BC, once conflicts were settled and the colony had to reinvent its identity.

Once again, our geophysical survey offers the possibility to corroborate this perspective. A substantial building lies northwest of the *forum*. It is approximately 48 × 78 m in size, with a large courtyard, portico, and rooms on its northwest and northeast sides. At the centre of the southeastern sector is also a rectangular feature. The monumental character of the building can be gleaned from the 0.9 m width of one of the walls that appears on the surface. What is more, the masonry consists of large rectangular limestone blocks, thus at variance with Cosa's ubiquitous 2nd century BC *opus incertum*. The location of the building is also of interest, both in terms of its positioning in relation to axes of traffic and the adjacent *forum*. In particular, it is served by Street O and thus easily accessible from the northeastern gate ('Porta Romana') which connected the site to the main arteries of traffic, to wit the *via Aurelia*, established in 241 BC, and the road that, following that eastern slope of the town, eventually merged with the port's road access. Overall, location, size, and accessibility make it plain that this establishment must have been included in the initial planning of the colony or in the extensive monumentalization of the town in the 2nd century BC. The function of the building, of course, is the issue, and we should bear in mind that this is but a rendition of a seemingly complicated edifice. Nevertheless, the presence of small units, plausibly *tabernae*, that is space for retail and commercial activities, may suggest a commercial space, and, in particular, the building that accommodated the daily practices and routines of the people who lived at Cosa. The most compelling example of a structure of this nature, albeit different in layout, is the early *macellum* and adjacent system of *tabernae* at Alba Fucens, another Latin colony founded in 303 BC. An early *macellum*, flanked by *tabernae* was located southeast of the *forum* and adjacent to the *basilica*. A commercial space is a desirable addition to the urban fabric at Cosa, and, more importantly, it would clarify the almost wholesale lack of *tabernae* from excavated houses, with the exception of the House of Diana and some of the so-called '*atria publica*' adjacent to the *forum*.

## 5.6. Conclusion

This history as so far revealed is at odds with the prevailing view that assumes a monolithic concept of foundation and a few *ad hoc* adjustments. Instead, this essay contends that the making of the colony was a fundamentally local enterprise, while the transfer of the Orbetello community not only injected new life, but also gave the opportunity to rethink the urban project and its sustainability. What is more, integrating the port and the commercial areas in new frameworks furthers our understanding of the colony and its genesis.

We are of course only at the beginning of work, and I suppose these projects could be viewed as merely a new coat of paint for an old house. But the returns Cosa has given to our knowledge of the archaeology of Roman Italy seem to me fully to justify their pursuit.

## Notes

1. Ciampoltrini & Rendini 1992, 996 on the apparent destruction of the site port site that may have occurred in the context of the 'Etruscan War'. Whether the apparent termination of the site was caused by violence or simple reorientation of the community remains to be established.
2. Valerius Maximus (1.6.7) and Julius Obsequens (*Prod.* 24) on the dire omens that framed the 137 BC expedition of C. Hostillius Mancinus, from the departure in Portus Herculis to the disaster of Numantia.
3. McCann 1987 offers a most comprehensive report of the port excavations. A personal communication by Claudio Calastri stresses the current sorry state of the site of the temple (not even the foundations of the buildings survive).
4. As indicated by the western embankment wall, 'P' and 'PW' for instance, two long retaining features that stabilised the steep hillside.
5. On-going research is designed to fully investigate these remains: Gilles Broacard and Jean-Philippe Goiran are my partners. Although it was stated that 'The sides of this natural fracture have been scarped along various sections to remove splintering and overhanging limestone' (McCann *et al.* 1987, 85), this seems hardly the case: the accurate, levelling of the vertical wall of rock has to be seen as a preparation for accommodating some kind of scaffolding or lifting apparatus.
6. While this heavily battered stone was found in a dump during the excavation of the temple of Jupiter, its lettering may hint a 3rd–1st-century BC origin, and possibly after the colonial *deductio.*

## Bibliography

Bace, E. J. (1983) *Cosa: Inscriptions on Stone and Brick-Stamps.* Ann Arbor, University of Michigan Press.

Bandalat, L., Posamentir, R., Rönnberg, M., Griese, S. & Hübner, C. (2019) Cosa revealed: Augustus, a new development, and the shape of an odd colony. In A.U. De Giorgi (ed.) *Cosa and the Colonial Landscape of Republican Italy (Third and Second Centuries BCE)*, 67–87. Ann Arbor, University of Michigan Press.

Barker, S., Bernard, S., Brennan, M., De Giorgi, A. U. & Fontana, G. (forthcoming) The Latin Colony of Cosa and its Fortifications. *Antiquity.*

Bispham, E. (2006) Coloniam deducere: how Roman was Roman colonization during the Middle Republic? In G.J. Bradley & J.-P. Wilson (eds) *Greek and Roman Colonization: Origins, Ideologies and Interactions*, 73–160. Swansea, Classical Press of Wales.

Bradley, G. (2006) Colonization and identity in Republican Italy. In G. Bradley & J.-P. Wilson (eds) *Greek and Roman Colonization: Origins, Ideologies and Interactions*, 161–187. Swansea, Classical Press of Wales.

Broadhead, W. (2008) Migration and hegemony: fixity and mobility in second-century Italy. In L. De Ligt & S. Northwood (eds) *People, Land, and Politics: Demographic Developments and the Transformation of Roman Italy, 300 BC–AD 14*, 451–70. Boston, Brill.

Brown, F. (1949) *Cosa I: History and Topography.* Rome, American Academy in Rome.

Brown, F. (1980) *Cosa: The Making of a Roman Town.* Ann Arbor, University of Michigan Press.

Brown F. (1984) The northwest gate of Cosa and its environs, 1972–1976. In *Studi di antichità in onore di Guglielmo Maetzke*, 493–498. Rome, Bretschneider.

Brown, F., Richardson, E. & Richardson, L. (1994) *Cosa III. The Buildings of the Forum: Colony, Municipium and Village.* Rome, American Academy in Rome.

Calastri, C. (2019) L'urbanistica antica di Orbetello. *L'Argentariana* 10, 2–10.

Carandini, A. & Cambi, F. (eds) (2002) *Paesaggi d'Etruria. Valle dell'Albegna, Valle d'Oro, Valle del Chiarone, Valle del Tafone. Progetto di ricerca italo-britannico seguito allo scavo di Settefinestre*. Rome, Edizioni di Storia e Letteratura.

Carlsen, J. (1984) Considerations on Cosa and Ager Cosanus. *Analecta Romana* 13, 49–58.

Castagnoli, F. (1956) La Centuriazione di Cosa. *Memoirs of the American Academy in Rome* 24, 147–165.

Ceccarelli, L., Cifarelli, F.M., Colaiacomo, F., Kay, S., Panzieri, C. & Smith, C. (2016) Il Segni Project: prima campagna di scavo. In G. Ghini, Z. Mari & A. Russo Tagliente (eds) *Lazio e Sabina 10*, 177–183. Rome, Quasar.

Ciampoltrini, G. (1991) La necropoli di Cosa. Ricerche e recuperi 1985–1991. *Bollettino di Archeologia* 7, 59–73.

Ciampoltrini, G. (2019) Archeologia urbana a Orbetello. In M. Cardosa (ed.) *Le antiche mura 'etrusche' di Orbetello*, 97–111. Orbetello, Effigi.

Ciampoltrini, G. & Rendini, P. (1992) Porti e traffici nel Tirreno settentrionale fra IV e III secolo a.C. Contributi da Telamone e dall'Isola del Giglio. *Annali della Scuola Normale Superiore di Pisa* III 22.4, 985–1004.

Coles, A.J. (2017) Founding colonies and fostering careers in the Middle Republic. *Classical Journal* 112.3, 280–317.

De Giorgi, A.U. (2018) Sustainable practices? A story from Roman Cosa (Central Italy). *Journal of Mediterranean Archaeology* 31(1), 3–26.

De Giorgi, A.U. (2022) Entrando a Cosa, dal Porto. In S. Quilici Gigli (ed.) *Entrando in Città*, 95–108. Rome, L'Erma di Bretschneider.

De Giorgi, A.U., Hobart, M., Ludke, M. & Scott, R.T. (2023) Cosa during Late Antiquity. In R. Rao & S. Sebastiani (eds) *Mediterraneo Toscano II. Archaeological Landscapes of Late Antique and Early Medieval Tuscia*, 126–140. Turnhout, Brepols.

Dyson, S.L. (1978) Settlement patterns in the Ager Cosanus: the Wesleyan University Survey, 1974–1976. *Journal of Field Archaeology* 5(3), 251–268.

Erdkamp, P. (2011) Soldiers, Roman citizens and Latin colonists in Mid-Republican Italy. *Ancient Society* 41, 109–146.

Fentress, E. (ed.) (2003) *Cosa V. An Intermittent Town*. Ann Arbor, University of Michigan Press.

Fentress, E. & Perkins, P. (2016) Cosa and the Ager Cosanus. In A.E. Cooley (ed.) *A Companion to Roman Italy*, 378–399. Chichester, Wiley-Blackwell.

Guidoboni, E. (ed.) (1989) *I terremoti prima del Mille in Italia e nell'area mediterranea*. Bologna, SGA.

Hanson, J. & Ortman, S. (2017) A systematic method for estimating the populations of Greek and Roman settlements. *Journal of Roman Archaeology* 30, 301–324.

Laffi, U. (2007) *Colonie e municipi nel mondo romano*. Rome, Edizioni di Storia e Lettratura.

Levi, D. (1927) Esplorazione archeologica nell'agro Cosano. *Studi Etruschi* 1, 477–485.

Liverani, P. (2020) Displacements. Riflessioni conclusive di metodo. In M.C. Biella (ed.) *Displacements. Continuità e disconitunità urbana nell'Italia centrale tirrenica*, 135–141. Rome, Quasar.

McCann, A.M., Bourgeois, J., Gazda, E., Oleson, J.P & Lyding Will, E. (eds) (1987) *The Roman Port and the Fishery of Cosa*. Princeton, Princeton University Press.

Rathbone, D.W. (1981) The development of agriculture in the 'Ager Cosanus' during the Roman Republic: problems of evidence and interpretation. *Journal of Roman Studies* 71, 10–23.

Rattighieri, E., Rinaldi, R., Bowes, K. & Mercuri, A.M. (2013) Land use from seasonal archaeological sites: the archaeobotanical evidence of small Roman farmhouses in Cinigiano, South-Eastern Tuscany – Central Italy. *Annali di Botanica* 3, 207–215.

Rodenwaldt, E. & Lehmann, H. (1961) *Die antiken Emissare von Cosa-Ansedonia, ein Beitrag zur Frage der Entwässerung der Maremmen in etrusckischer Zeit*. Heidelberg, Springer.

Sadori, L. (2018) The Lateglacial and Holocene vegetation and climate history of Lago di Mezzano (central Italy). *Quaternary Science Reviews* 202, 30–44.

Scott, R.T. (2019) Cosa: how perfect! How come? In A.U. De Giorgi (ed.) *Cosa and the Landscape of Republican Italy (Third and Second Centuries BCE)*, 21–29. Ann Arbor, University of Michigan Press.

Scott, R.T., De Giorgi, A.U., Cha, C. & Posamentir R. (2021) Cosa excavations: new interpretative frameworks. In S. Sebastiani & C. Megale (eds) *Mediterraneo Toscano. Paesaggi dell'Etruria romana*, 207–218. Turnhout, BREPOLS.

Steingräber, S. (2013) Worshiping with the dead: new approaches to Etruscan Necropoleis. In J.M. Turfa (ed.) *The Etruscan World*, 655–670. London and New York, Taylor and Francis.

Stek, T.D. & Pelgrom, J. (eds) (2014) *Roman Republican Colonization: New Perspectives from Archaeology and Ancient History*. Rome, Palombi.

Termeer, M.K. (2015) *Latin Colonization in Italy before the End of the Second Punic War: Colonial Communities and Cultural Change*. Groningen, University of Groningen.

Will, E.L. & Warner Slane, K. (2019) *Cosa: the Roman and Greek Amphoras*. Ann Arbor, University of Michigan Press.

# Chapter 6

## The archaeology of Fregellae: an update

### Francesca Diosono

> You take delight not in a city's seven or seventy wonders,
> but in the answer it gives to a question of yours.
> — Italo Calvino, *Invisible Cities*

## 6.1. Introduction

The aim of this paper is to give a general overview of the current state of our knowledge of the Latin colony of Fregellae, including some new data that have emerged in ongoing research, albeit in the necessarily limited space available. As part of the commission received in 2011 from Filippo Coarelli to edit the excavations of the temples in the *forum* and along the *via Latina* (Battaglini *et al.* 2019) and of the 18 *domus* on Decumanus I (currently being published) conducted between 1980 and 2009 by the University of Perugia, I examined and reorganised all the documentation and coordinated the study of the structures and materials found. Moreover, thanks to the collaboration of the *Soprintendenza, Belle Arti e Paesaggio per le Province di Latina e Frosinone* (SABAP Latina Frosinone), I was also able to access their archives to study the data contained therein.

Situated in *Latium Adiectum* in a strategic position along the *via Latina*, the colony of Fregellae (Fig. 6.1) was one of the most flourishing Italian cities of its time. Its trade occurred both by land and by river along the route connecting Rome to Capua and along the valleys of the rivers Sacco and Liri, ending at the Minturnae seaport. Founded by Rome in 328 BC to control the territory of Fabrateria disputed between the Volscians and Samnites, it was conquered by the latter in 316 BC and then re-founded by Rome between 313 and 312, together with the foundation of Interamna Lirenas, while the *via Latina* was being extended to Capua (an examination of all relevant ancient sources can be found in Coarelli 1998; Rawson 1998; Maiuri 2009; Balbo 2016; Laffi 2017). For a long time Fregellae represented for Rome a stronghold and one of the most devoted and loyal colonies; the wealthy local aristocracy was proud of its military and political role, stopping Pyrrhus' advance in 280 BC and Hannibal's in

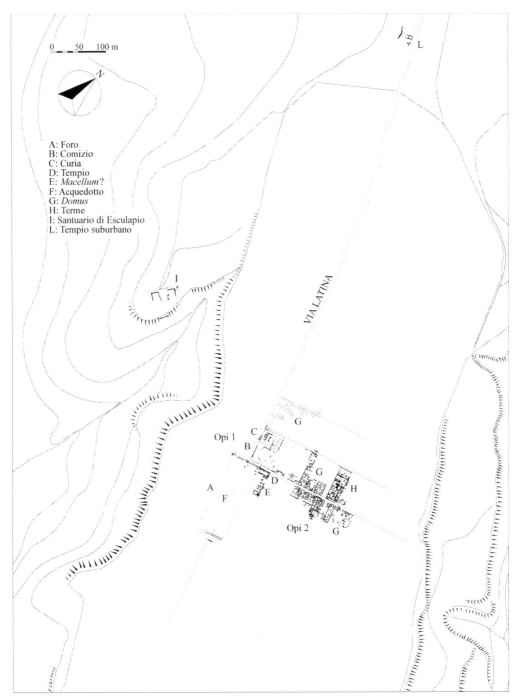

Figure 6.1. General plan of the excavations carried out at Fregellae by the University of Perugia between 1978 and 2009 (Battaglini 2019, 13, fig. 1).

211 BC, acting as the leader of the Latin colonies hostile to the Carthaginian general in 209 BC. The knights of the *turma fregellana* also took part in the war against Antiochus III of Syria (194–189 BC). The town was besieged and destroyed in 125 BC by Rome itself for its claim to extend Roman citizenship rights. This exemplary punishment entailed the deportation to Rome of the most influential citizens to be tried and sentenced to death and the performance of the rite of *devotio* on the defeated enemy town (as happened to Veii, Corinth and Carthage: Macrob. *Sat.* 3.9), with the demolition of all buildings, public and private, the cutting of water channels and the throwing of salt onto the fields.

A vexed question is whether or not building materials were recovered from the now-destroyed Fregellae for the construction of the new colony of Fabrateria Nova, founded nearby in 124 BC. This is likely to have been the case, but it has left no particularly obvious traces. Roman soldiers plundered the town as spoils of war before destroying it and, as we shall see later, there are archaeological contexts of destruction that appear to be intact and not disturbed by later interventions. In addition, no material datable to a period significantly later than 125 BC has been found that would attest to a renewed frequentation of the urban area. The importance of Fregellae for Roman archaeology thus lies in its being a closed context, at least in its urban area, where life stopped in 125 BC and never resumed. The study of building techniques, architectural solutions, and material culture more generally may thus allow a better understanding of their chronology.

## 6.2. The territory

The territory on which Fregellae was established was inhabited, even before Volscian domination, by people whose material culture and religious conceptions were akin to the Latin world, even though at present it is still not possible to link them to a specific Italic population. Their settlement is indicated by votive offerings found in the area of the suburban temple on the *via Latina* and by ceramic materials, especially bucchero and bucchero-type pottery, found in secondary deposition in various excavation contexts within the town, all datable between the last quarter of the 7th and the 5th centuries BC. Furthermore, an antefix featuring the head of Silenus and dated to the 5th century BC (Fig. 6.2) attests the presence of a sacred building in the sector of the *domus* north of the *Comitium* (Diosono 2019a, 97–101). The 4th century BC represents a hiatus in the occupation of the plateau, where clashes took place between the Volscians and Samnites, while two strongholds on high ground surrounded by polygonal walls controlled it: that of Rocca d'Arce to the north, on the right bank of the Liri, and that of Falvaterra to the south, on the left bank (the latter still unpublished, see Diosono 2019a, 100). The colony was founded by Rome immediately east of the Liri, hence the reason for the dispute with the Samnites. The fertile and well-connected territory of the colony must have been extensive, broadly

*Figure 6.2. Antefix with the head of Silenus dating at 5th century BC from the urban area of Fregellae (Diosono 2019a, 98 fig. 3).*

corresponding to the territories of the two modern municipalities of Arce and Ceprano.

In previous centuries, fortuitous discoveries and excavations were made in search of archaeological evidence. Between 1978 and 1984, the University of Cambridge, under the direction of Michael Crawford and in collaboration with the University of Perugia, carried out surveys in the area with targeted trenches, the results of which have been partially published (Crawford 1981; 1983; 1984; 1985; 1987a; 1987b; Crawford & Keppie 1984; Crawford *et al.* 1985; 1986). Further surveys were conducted by other research groups (Nicosia 1979; Malandrino 1991; Monti 1998). Various hypotheses on the centuriation were also made (Monti 1992).

After the destruction of the town in 125 BC, its territory was referred to as *Fregellanum* in the sources and must have still been inhabited and productive: a periodic market was held there at a temple (Strabo 5.3.10), and a villa from the imperial period has also been excavated there (Betori 2009). Currently, the project 'A Landscape of Conflict: Battlefield Archaeology in the Territory of Ancient Fregellae / Modern Ceprano (FR, Lazio, Italy)' directed by Dominik Maschek is seeking traces of the siege of the town. The conservation activities conducted by the *Soprintendenza* have also, in recent years, brought to light other evidence, coeval or subsequent to the colony (Molle & Marandola 2016; Molle *et al.* 2016).

## 6.3. The town

### 6.3.1. Planning and organization

Between 2004 and 2005 a short geophysical prospection project conducted by the British School at Rome led to a reconstructive hypothesis of the layout of the wall circuit (Ferraby *et al.* 2008), which still needs to be verified in the field. Conventionally, the plateau, naturally delimited by differences in elevations, continues to be identified with the urban area. It is crossed longitudinally by the *via Latina* (corresponding to the present 'Via di Opi') on a northwest–southeast axis, which constitutes the town's *cardo*, on which the three *decumani* known so far are set perpendicularly. However, our knowledge of the town is still too limited to attempt a reconstruction of its urban fabric. In addition to the excavated buildings presented in this chapter, we only know that the regular distance between the three *decumani* leads to the formation of elongated *insulae*. Jeremia Pelgrom (2008) has tried reconstructing the town's layout by replicating the same house module and extending it in order to outline various *insulae* within the hypothesised town area. In fact, the *domus* excavated so far seems to present at least two different dimensional modules, both attested in the group of *domus* on Decumanus I. Consequently, smaller and larger houses do not seem to have belonged to distinctive quarters linked with the different status of the residents and were in fact grouped together. As for the preliminary settlement operations, it seems that, in a phase preceding the construction of the buildings, wells were dug at several points of the urban area, even though many of them went permanently out of use at the time the *domus* were built.

### 6.3.1. The forum

Excavations in the *forum* area were conducted by the University of Perugia in the 1980s–90s. A general, if partial, synthesis of the results has been published (Coarelli 1998), together with a recent in-depth study of the small temple at the northeast corner of the square, built at the time of the foundation of the colony and redecorated in the 2nd century BC (Battaglini *et al.* 2019). The excavations also brought to light the *curia/comitium* complex (almost completely spoliated after 125 BC), a double row of pits on the two short sides of the square, a fountain, a large underground hydraulic canal running lengthwise and a building on the east side that was identified at the times as a *macellum*. A survey carried out in 2004–05 by the University of Perugia in collaboration with the British School at Rome revealed the presence of at least one other public building with rich architectural terracotta decorations on the southwest side of the *forum* (Ferraby *et al.* 2008). Due to the shallow depth at which the ancient remains are buried and the fact that the *forum* is located on the highest point of the plateau, the preservation of the structures has been severely compromised in recent years, even following the excavations, by agricultural works and building activities, whether authorised or not. North of the *comitium* is a residential complex named 'domus of Opi 1' in the excavation documentation of the University of Perugia, which has never been the subject of systematic study.

### 6.3.2. The Sanctuary of Aesculapius

In 1975, a landslide affected a side of the hill on which the Sanctuary of Aesculapius stood and on which the loading basin of a still functioning power station was built. The landslide brought to light approximately 3,000 artefacts, including many fictile votive offerings, which were recovered under the direction of Anna Gallina Zevi, officer of the *Soprintendenza* (this material remains unpublished). Some architectural elements and building materials had already been found in 1927.

From 1978 and 1984 the area of the Sanctuary was excavated by the University of Perugia (from 1978 to 1980 by the University of Cambridge too). Although the results of this operation were published as a volume (Coarelli 1986), this only included the materials from the 1978 excavation campaign, with the rest remaining almost entirely unpublished. Conservation activities, which I conducted under the direction of Alessandro Betori at the time when the power station was being expanded, led to the discovery of further material from the Sanctuary scattered in the plain to the southwest (also unpublished).

The attribution of the largest known sacred complex in the Latin colony to Aesculapius has not been questioned so far (Lippolis 2009; Känel 2015) and is based on the discovery of inscriptions referring to the god and his *paredra* Salus. The extra-urban complex stood on high ground to the west of the town, overlooking it from above, facing southeast. The presence of large block-built retaining walls on the side of the hill could suggest its interpretation as a terraced sanctuary. A sizable drainage channel for water flowing down the valley was also found. The hypothesis that downhill from the temple stood a theatre facing the town has so far found no support in the field. The temple had a transverse *cella*, leaning against a portico on three sides, and had two building phases (280–240 BC and 180–150 BC), of the oldest of which only few walls and the *thesaurus*, of Greek rather than Roman type (Martín Esquivel & Diosono 2019, 335), remain.

### 6.3.3. *The suburban temple along the via Latina*

Following looting activities in the 19th century, the first materials related to the temple were documented in 1990 when works linked with the widening of 'Via di Opi' (which, as mentioned, roughly follows the ancient route of the *via Latina*) damaged its front. Subsequently, geophysical prospection and two excavation campaigns (2002 and 2004) were there carried out by University of Perugia. All materials and data have recently been published (Battaglini *et al.* 2019). The temple stood just outside the northern entrance to the town and its architectural features and cultic materials have led to it being attributed to the cult of Bona Dea. Like almost all buildings from Fregellae, it also features two decorative phases: one relating to the years when the colony was established and the other to the 2nd century BC. It must have stood near a spring, which dried up following the construction of the A1 motorway, which heavily modified the surrounding landscape. The various drains found in the temple area must have been connected to this spring and the ritual use of its water.

### 6.3.4. *The Baths*

The Baths (the large building at the top right in Fig. 6.3) were excavated by the University of Perugia under the coordination of Vassilis Tsiolis and Giovanna Battaglini from 1996 to 2001, when their presentation as a museum was initiated, with further works carried out between 2007 and 2009. The excavation of the thermal building was then completed in 2017, as part of restoration activities, promoted by Carlo Molle (SABAP Latina Frosinone) and directed by me in the field. The results are presented here for the first time (in a necessarily condensed format) together with the subsequent new reconstructive hypothesis. The subject of preliminary publications, most of which have dealt with architectural aspects (Tsiolis 2001; 2006; 2008; 2013;

Coarelli 2004; Vincenti 2008; 2012), the Baths have so far been described as having two building phases, the first datable to the last 30 years of the 3rd century BC and the second to the first quarter of the 2nd century BC (Tsiolis 2013, 105). This chronology is based on a thorough architectural analysis, but not on the materials found during the various stratigraphic excavations, which have only been studied to a small extent (Pedroni 1997; Diosono 2008; 2017) and are in fact completely unpublished.

The first phase is mainly visible at the front of the Baths, which faces the Decumanus I, due to excavations which took place in the 19th century, if not before, and which completely destroyed the second phase (above it) in order to reach valuable artefacts further below. Evidence of this are the terracotta telamons that ended up in the Campana collection and then in the Louvre (Hausmesser 2018), as well as the other eventually walled-up in the church of Ceprano (Monti 1998, 92, pl. XVI.10). These upheavals have thus allowed modern excavation to proceed to a considerable depth in a fairly large sector, revealing several rooms whose floor level is similar to that of

*Figure 6.3. General plan of the sector of the Baths and of the* domus *east of the Forum (illustration by D. Lanzi & M. Moreno Alcaide).*

the oldest phase of the *domus* I.7 across the street (also presented in the museum). Deep soundings excavated in 2007 revealed a furnace further north that can also be attributed to the first phase (Tsiolis 2013, 96, 104–105, referred to as 'saggio N' instead of 'saggio *alfa*'), which is thus much larger than initially assumed, even though its overall dimensions are not known at present.

The second phase extends from Decumanus I, which it faces as in the previous phase, to Decumanus II. The entrance is monumental, with four half-columns leaning against pillars set on the sidewalk, which supported a roof decorated with architectural terracottas. There was also a side access, with a narrow passageway running outside the east side, with a threshold opening into Room 13 (Figs 6.3–6.4), the excavation of which is discussed below. The west side of the Baths was instead adjacent to a *domus* that has not been investigated, but which was seen during the modern roofing of the Baths. The foundations in limestone blocks are all that remains of the front part, whereas the rest of the complex features rich floors and some structures such as bathtubs with furnaces, seats covered in *cocciopesto* and *labra* supports. The rooms were vaulted with a system of curved tiles on ribs (Tsiolis 2001). The walls were probably made of unfired clay (mudbrick), as were

*Figure 6.4. Orthophoto of the 2017 excavation area taken at the end of the campaign: Room 13 (top) and Room 14 (bottom) (photo by the author).*

those of the various *domus*, which was likely the case also in the earliest phase of this building.

The part of the second phase displayed in the museum does not include the entire building: the northern sector, probably consisting of service rooms, is not visible, but was located on a higher terrace supported by a low polygonal retaining wall. The stratigraphy associated with the second phase was better preserved away from Decumanus I, and this made it possible to investigate, in several places, the destruction contexts datable to 125 BC together with what was sealed beneath them (Diosono 2017). The area excavated in 2017 (Fig. 6.4) is in the northeast sector of the museum part of the Baths, below the modern roof. The subject of repeated excavations by the University of Perugia (1997, 2007, and 2008), these rooms have not been assigned a name. In conformity with the previously published plans of this building, the northernmost is here referred to as Room 13 and the southernmost as Room 14.

Room 13 yielded a layer with a high concentration of materials, which was also below the column shaft that was later relocated on its stylobate in the 2007 restoration. Its limits are defined to the north, by the polygonal wall that supports the northern sector of the Baths; to the east, by the perimeter wall in limestone blocks from the second phase of the baths, on which the already mentioned external access opens, framed by two long perpendicular jambs; to the west and south, by wall sections consisting of a stone plinth surmounted by fractured tile remains (originally likely supporting earthen walls), featuring later additions in reused blocks and a small dolium (filled with ash). The stratigraphy also shows destruction and levelling activity for the construction of a third phase in this sector, also evident in Room 14 and in the open space to the west of Rooms 13 and 14. The polygonal wall would also seem to belong to this third phase, because its clay foundation is at a higher height than the structures of the second phase.

Room 14, to the south of the previous room, is defined, to the east, by the eastern limestone block wall of the second phase of the Baths; to the south, by the wall of the *alveus* of the eastern sector, also belonging to the second phase of the Baths. However, it has no clear boundary with the adjacent area to the west, excavated in 2007, except for the presence of a large third-phase pillar. Beneath the destruction layer of 125 BC (made up of collapsed earthen walls with some building material), this room also shows traces of a third phase: there is evidence of flooring preparation on which fragments of burnt tufa blocks and fragments of *cocciopesto* had accumulated; these look like components of the *alvei* already known from the Baths and appear to be demolished parts of a structure exposed to strong heat and covered with hydraulic *cocciopesto*. Underneath the floor preparation lay the beaten earth of the second phase, in which evidence for the removal of drains and some *dolia* partly inserted into the ground was evident. Thus, it seems that Room 14 changed its function in the third phase: the level was raised, one of the large pillars was constructed, and waste building materials were piled up there, probably related to the maintenance of the thermal facilities. The earlier phase identified during this excavation seems to correspond with what is traditionally referred to as the second phase of the Baths.

The 2017 excavation thus calls into question the two-phase chronology of the Baths proposed so far in the published studies, adding a third one, as suggested by the stratigraphy and the sequence of structures, at least in the northern sector. But regardless of this last excavation campaign, work during the construction of the museum between 2007 and 2008 had already highlighted inconsistencies with the reconstructions then proposed and that have continued to be proposed, even in relation to the front. Indeed, an analysis of the various levels of visible structures and floors shows that the building layout and sequence is much more complex than the plans and analyses published to date.

Figure 6.5. General view from the southeast of the front of the Baths as it appears in the Archaeological Park. A: Floors of the first phase; B: foundation blocks of internal walls attributed to the second phase; C: floors of the second phase; D: level of the entrance of the second phase; E: foundation blocks of the east perimeter wall of the second phase; F: floor of undetermined phase; G: excavation area of 2017 (graphic editing by the author).

In fact, even by looking at the structure as it is visible today (Fig. 6.5), one can see several inconsistencies with the published version:

- The floor in *cocciopesto* decorated with tesserae F lies on a layer of clay about 1 m thick covering the floors of the first phase A, but is at a lower level than the second phase C. Indeed, the floor F does not have a relationship of continuity with any feature of the second phase, whose access walkway (as indicated by the sidewalk D in which the bases of the frontal semi-column are preserved) and internal walkway (as indicated by all preserved floors C) are at the same level.
- The foundation limestone blocks B visible in the front part of the Baths and assigned to the second phase are settled on the floors A of the first phase (and in some cases cut them) and on the remains of stone wall structures. The blocks B are placed not only at a lower level than floor F but also at a lower level than the second phase floors C. In fact, at least a 40 cm thick layer of clay lies between the *cocciopesto* floor C and the upper surface of these blocks B. Some of these alignments of blocks B fit within this (later) clay layer, which prepares the second phase floors C and which probably covers other blocks placed along the same alignment, but not visible. Since the walls in blocks B are inserted into and covered by the same thick layer of clay on which the second phase floors C rest, the stratigraphy shows that they do not belong to the same building phase. The walls in blocks B are therefore more likely to be connected to the building phase relating to the floor F than to that of the floors C.

- The wall E in tufa and limestone blocks, interpreted as the east perimeter wall of the second phase, rest on that 40 cm layer of clay which covers the first phase floors A and rests at a higher elevation than the second phase internal walls B. This would create an unlikely construction solution, in which the perimeter walls, which bear more weight, are placed at an higher elevation (and on a layer of clay) than the inner walls B, which rest on floors A (the latter covered by the clay on which wall E rests). It is thus likely that walls E and B did not belong to the same phase, rather wall E goes with floors C (second phase) and walls B with floor F (intermediate phase between the first and second).

In summary, while the northern sector of the Baths shows a period of reorganisation subsequent to the second phase and prior to the destruction of 125 BC, the southern sector points to a planimetric and structural reorganisation intermediate between the first and the second phases, whose plan and interpretations should, therefore, be revised. The above discussion highlights how the dossier of the Baths, their different building phases, reconstructive plans, and functional interpretations of the rooms must be tackled anew, combining a planimetric study conducted on the three dimensions with that of the numerous materials found in the stratigraphy.

### 6.3.5. *The domus on Decumanus I*

Between 1980 and 1999 the University of Perugia team excavated 18 *domus* on Decumanus I (Fig. 6.3) and worked on the Archaeological Park, under the coordination of Paolo Braconi and Giovanna Battaglini. Between 2000 and 2009, these activities were exclusively related to the preparation of the museum and restoration of the structures within the Archaeological Park, which include some of the *domus* on Decumanus I (the others were re-interred) and the Baths (preliminary publications: Coarelli 1998; Battaglini & Diosono 2010; Känel 2010; Battaglini & Braconi 2019). A volume soon to be published by the *Accademia dei Lincei* (Diosono *et al.* forthcoming) will include extensive discussion of the size-modules attested for these houses, their different internal organisation linked to the various forms of use of the different spaces, the two building phases identified and their chronology, the construction techniques, the rich decoration, and aspects of the domestic cult. Even though it is not possible to discuss here the content of unpublished studies by others (which I have access to in my role as volume editor), it seems reasonable to briefly summarise one of the lines of research that I have personally contributed to.

The excavation of these *domus* has shed new light on the domestic sphere and daily life of a period of Roman history in which they are not particularly well known. In fact, many of the contexts excavated at Fregellae are well preserved and relate to the time of the destruction of the *domus*, as well as the other buildings in the town, in 125 BC. The study of the finds (preliminary publications: Guidobaldi 1989; Diosono 2008; 2019b; Diosono *et al.* 2019a) was carried out by also considering, when stratigraphically reliable, their spatial location. We were thus able to reconstruct a definite picture of the materials present in various houses at the time of their collapse (clearly following a general sacking of the town by the Roman army). The opportunity to analyse in great detail the material culture from various dwellings made it possible to note similarities and differences in the eating and consumption habits of the different households. Given the profound connection that links the sphere of food and nutrition with the cultural identity of an individual or a community, as well as with the expression of social and economic relations, this analysis allowed me to better understand the varied complexity of the inhabitants of this ancient town. Indeed, food represents a substantial part of a society's daily activities and is also one of the most conservative. From the study of how food and drink are preserved, prepared, and consumed, much can be understood about the inhabitants of a settlement, relating, of course, to the trade networks that guarantee the supply of imported products. In colonial areas or, more generally, any area where social groups and individuals of different origin coexist, this kind of study may help to illuminate their interactions and transformations.

The quantitative study of the finds in the different *domus* allows us to state that in the 2nd century BC different culinary and cooking practices typical of the Roman-Latin area, as well as of Magna Graecia and southern Italian regions, coexisted at *Fregellae*. At the same time, the ceramic material used for cooking and eating was almost exclusively of local production (Borgers & Diosono forthcoming). Different food customs therefore coexisted within the same house, either because people with different habits lived there or because a hybrid cuisine had developed at the intersection of the different traditions.

On the one hand, as attested by the presence of forms and types of kitchen pottery of a different tradition than those widespread in the area under examination, it is possible to hypothesise the presence of individuals and family units of non-Latin origin within the Latin colony. On the other hand, over time and through cohabitation, the dietary customs of the first generations of colonists began to incorporate other culinary traditions introduced by the arrival of new inhabitants of other origins, so that the town began to produce and use local pottery suitable for these different recipes. The material culture effectively confirms what is reported in historical sources, which describe Fregellae in the 2nd century BC as characterised by a massive immigration of Italics (e.g. Livy (41.8.8) writes of 40,000 Samnites and Pelignians present in the town in 177 BC). Names of Italic origins are also found stamped on locally produced black-glazed pottery (Nonnis 1998; Diosono et al. 2019b, 215–218). This immigration appears to have been generally characterised by a peaceful integration between the various elements, old and new, of the urban body (Coarelli 1991; 1998, 38–39), even though, over time, the Fregellan aristocracy tended to move to Rome, whilst the inhabitants began to request the granting of Roman citizenship as a way of distinguishing themselves from the newcomers.

The multiformity and cultural complexity of Fregellae are also evidenced by other aspects of the material culture: the contacts and familiarity with the Greek and eastern world (already indicated by the early cult of Aesculapius) are attested by Greek craftsmen active in the town or by decorative themes inspired by that world (Coarelli 1998; Känel 2010; 2019; Vincenti 2021) and also by the good quantity of Greek pottery found, consisting in particular of amphorae. They also help us to identify material traces of another fact reported in the sources and so far probably underestimated, namely the arrival of 200 families of Punic aristocracy in 202 BC, hostages after the battle of Zama, who asked to reside here and not in Rome (Nep. *Annib*.7.2–3). Their presence is made tangible, among other things, by the sheer quantity of amphorae of Punic production that have been found in Fregellae. Their number is absolutely above average when compared to other centres in inland Italy of the same period, and they furthermore attest that contacts with Punic territories continued even after the fall of Cartage in 146 BC.

## Bibliography

Balbo, M. (2016) La rivolta di Fregellae nel 125 a.C. *Mediterraneo Antico* 19, 253–262.

Battaglini, G. (2019) Il tempio del foro: le indagini archeologiceh e le strutture. In G. Battaglini, F. Coarelli & F. Diosono (eds) *Fregellae. Il tempio del Foro e il tempio suburbano sulla via Latina*, 9–17. Rome, Giorgio Bretschneider.

Battaglini, G. & Braconi, P. (2019) Dalla tegola al mattone. Laterizi sperimentali a Fregellae. In J. Bonetto, E. Bukowiecki & R. Volpe (eds) *Alle origini del laterizio romano. Nascita e diffusione del mattone cotto nel Mediterraneo tra IV e I secolo a.C.*, 495–506. Rome, Quasar.

Battaglini, G. & Diosono, F. (2010) Le domus di Fregellae: case aristocratiche di ambito coloniale. In M. Bentz & C. Reusser (eds) *Etruskisch-italische und römisch-republikanische Häuser*, 217–231. Wiesbaden, Reichert.

Battaglini, G., Coarelli, F. & Diosono, F. (2019) (eds) *Fregellae. Il tempio del Foro e il tempio suburbano sulla via Latina*. Rome, Giorgio Bretschneider.

Betori, A. (2009) Villa con impianto termale in località Sant'Angelo al Cannuccio, Ceprano (FR). In R. Padovano (ed.) *Sorgenti e terme nella Valle del Sacco*, 339–344. Padua-Rome, Esedra.

Borgers, B. & Diosono, F. (forthcoming) Organising the production of cooking ware at Fregellae, southern Lazio (Italy), between the 4th – 2nd centuries BC. In *Technology, Crafting and Artisanal Networks in the Greek and Roman World*. Berlin, De Gruyter.

Coarelli, F. (1986) (ed.) *Fregellae II. Il santuario di Esculapio*. Rome, Quasar.

Coarelli, F. (1991) I Sanniti a Fregellae. In *La romanisation du Samnium aux IIe et Ier siècles av. J.C.*, 177–185. Naples, Centre Jean Bérard.

Coarelli, F. (1998) La storia e lo scavo. In F. Coarelli & P.G. Monti (eds) *Fregellae I. Le fonti, la storia, il territorio*, 29–69. Rome, Quasar.

Coarelli, F. (2004) Le terme di Fregellae. In G. Ghini (ed.) *Lazio e Sabina 2*, 73–76. Rome.

Crawford, M.H. (1981) Archaeology and history at Fregellae. In G. Barker & R. Hodges (eds) *Papers in Italian archaeology II. Archaeology and Italian Society. Prehistoric, Roman and medieval studies*, 197–201. Oxford, British Archaeological Reports.

Crawford, M.H. (1983) Excavations at Fregellae 1981. *Archeologia laziale* 5, 84–87.

Crawford, M.H. (1984) Scavi a Fregellae 1982–1983. *Archeologia laziale* 6, 133–136.

Crawford, M.H. (1985) Excavations at Fregellae 1984. *Archeologia laziale* 7, 112–118.

Crawford, M.H. (1987a) Excavations at Fregellae 1978–1985. An interim report on the work of the British team, Part IV. The resistivity survey. *Papers of the British School at Rome* 55, 75–77.

Crawford, M.H. (1987b) Prospezioni a Fregellae. *Archeologia laziale* 8, 299–301.

Crawford, M.H. & Keppie L. (1984) Excavations at Fregellae, 1978–1984. An interim report on the work of the British team. *Papers of the British School at Rome* 52, 21–35.

Crawford, M.H., Keppie, L. & Vercnocke, M. (1985) Excavations at Fregellae, 1978–84. An interim report on the work of the British team, Part II. *Papers of the British School at Rome* 53, 72–96.

Crawford, M.H., Keppie, L., Patterson, J. & Vercnocke, M. (1986) Excavations at Fregellae, 1978–1984. An interim report on the work of the British team, Part III. The Territory. *Papers of the British School at Rome* 54, 40–68.

Diosono, F. (2008) Materiali e modelli orientali nella colonia latina di Fregellae (Ceprano/Arce, FR). *Rei Cretariae Romanae Fautorum Acta* 40, 393–396.

Diosono, F. (2017) Un denario di L. Calpurnio Pisone Frugi (RRC 340/1) da Fregellae. Considerazioni su emissioni gentilizie e riforma semionciale. *Annali Istituto Italiano di Numismatica* 63, 135–162.

Diosono, F. (2019a) Il tempio suburbano sulla via Latina e la costruzione del paesaggio sacro della colonia di Fregellae: culto e cultura materiale. In G. Battaglini, F. Coarelli & F. Diosono (eds) *Fregellae. Il tempio del Foro e il tempio suburbano sulla via Latina*, 95–110. Rome, Giorgio Bretschneider.

Diosono, F. (2019b) *Siamo quello che mangiamo. Pratiche alimentari e identità dalle domus di Fregellae*. In M. Cipriani, E. Greco, A. Pontrandolfo & M. Scafuro (eds) *Dialoghi sull'Archeologia della Magna Grecia e del Mediterraneo, vol. I*, 139–146. Salerno, Pandemos.

Diosono, F., Caselli, A., Consigli, S., de Minicis, M., Forcatura, V., Lanzi, D., Sepiacci, S., Staiano, S. & Tiburzi, N. (2019a). Living in *Fregellae*: pottery from the *domus*. In A. Peignard-Giros (ed.) *Daily Life in a Cosmopolitan World. Pottery and Culture during the Hellenistic Period*, 551–562. Wien, Phoibos.

Diosono, F., Ceccaccio, M. & Seccaroni, E. (2019b) *La ceramica a vernice nera*. In G. Battaglini, F. Coarelli & F. (eds) *Fregellae. Il tempio del Foro e il tempio suburbano sulla via Latina*, 211–249. Rome, Quasar.

Diosono, F., Battaglini, G., Braconi, P., Coarelli, F. & Moreno Alcaide, M. (eds) (forthcoming) *Fregellae. Le Domus del quartiere ad Est del Foro*. Rome, Giorgio Bretschneider.

Ferraby, R., Hay, S., Keay, S. & Millett, M. (2008) Archaeological survey at Fregellae 2004–2005. In C. Corsi & E. Polito (eds) *Dalle sorgenti alla foce. Il bacino del Liri- Garigliano nell'antichità. Culture, contatti, scambi*, 125–131. Rome, Quasar.

Guidobaldi, M.P. (1989) Le anfore della colonia latina di Fregellae. In *Amphores romaines et histoire économique. Dix ans de recherche*, 600–601. Rome, École française de Rome.

Hausmesser, L. (2018) Les statues en terre cuite de la collection Campana. La multiplication des Atlantes. *Comptes rendus des séances de l'Académie des Inscriptions et Belles-Lettres* 162.1, 365–386.

Känel, R. (2010) Bemerkungen zum Terrakotta-Bauschmuck hellenistischer Wohnhäuser in Mittelitalien. In M. Bentz & C. Reusser (eds) *Etruskisch-italische und römisch-republikanische Häuser*, 263–271.Wiesbaden, Reichert.

Känel, R. (2015) Das Aesculapius-Heiligtum in Fregellae und sein Bauschmuck aus Terrakotta. In T. Stek & G.-J. Burgers (ed.) *The Impact of Rome on Cult Places and Religious Practices in Ancient Italy*, 67–95. London, Institute of Classical Studies.

Känel, R. (2019) Der sog. Thvma-Meister. Beobachtungen zur Aktivität eines griechischen Koroplasten in Fregellae. In P. Lulof, I., Manzini I. & C. Rescigno (eds) *Deliciae fictiles 5. Network and Workshops. Architectural Terracottas and Decorative Roof Systems in Italy and Beyond*, 377–386. Oxford, Oxbow Books.

Laffi, U. (2017) Italici in colonie latine e latini in colonie romane. In M. Chelotti, M. Silvestrini & L. Todisco (eds) *Itinerari di Storia. In ricordo di Mario Pani*, 51–61. Bari, Edipuglia.

Lippolis, E. (2009) L'Asklepieion di Fregellae. Architettura, esigenze rituali e forme di ricezione del culto ellenistico in ambito centro-italico. In E. De Miro, V. Calì & G. Sfameni Gasparro (eds) *Il culto di Asclepio nell'area mediterranea*, 145–157. Rome, Gangemi.

Maiuri, A. (2009) Deductio-deletio. Strategie territoriali di Roma repubblicana. Il caso Fregellae. *Studi e Materiali di Storia delle Religioni* 75, 89–116.

Malandrino, P. (1991) Ceramica a vernice nera di Fregellae. *Terra dei Volsci* 1, 16–32.

Martín Esquivel, A. & Diosono, F. (2009) Materiali numismatici. In G. Battaglini, F. Coarelli & F. (eds) *Fregellae. Il tempio del Foro e il tempio suburbano sulla via Latina*, 329–339. Rome, Quasar.

Molle, C. & Marandola, S. (2016) Un tratto della Via Latina e un sepolcreto tra Fregellanum e Fregellae (Ceprano, Frosinone). In Ghini, G., Mari, Z. & Russo Tagliente, A. (eds) *Lazio e Sabina 11*, 185–192. Rome, Quasar.

Molle, C., Persichini, S. & Pietrafesa, D. (2016) Ricerche archeologiche nell'ager Fregellanus. In G. Ghini, Z. Mari & A. Russo Tagliente (eds) *Lazio e Sabina 10*, 213–218. Rome, Quasar.

Monti, P.G. (1992) Un nuovo contributo alla ricostruzione della centuriazione romana nel Lazio meridionale. Il caso dell'agro fregellano e fabraterno. *Terra dei Volsci* 1, 14–21.

Monti, P.G. (1998) *Carta archeologica del territorio*. In F. Coarelli & P.G. Monti (eds) *Fregellae I. Le fonti, la storia, il territorio*, 81–111, Rome, Quasar.

Nicosia, A. (1979) *Ceramica repubblicana nella media valle del Liri. Quaderni del Museo Civico di Pontecorvo* 1, 23–41.

Nonnis, D. (1998) *Appendice epigrafica e prosopografica*. In F. Coarelli & P.G. Monti (eds) *Fregellae I. Le fonti, la storia, il territorio*, 77–78, Rome, Quasar.

Pedroni, L. (1997) *Tessere plumbee dalle terme di Fregellae (Arce, FR). Bollettino di Numismatica* 28/29, 203–210.

Pelgrom, J. (2008) Settlement organization and land distribution in Latin colonies before the Second Punic war. In L. de Ligt & S. Northwood (eds) *People, Land, and Politics. Demographic Developments and the Transformation of Roman Italy 300 B.C.-A.D. 14*, 333–372. Leiden, Brill.

Rawson, E. (1998) Fregellae: fall and aurvival. In F. Coarelli & P.G. Monti (eds) *Fregellae I. Le fonti, la storia, il territorio*, 71–76, Rome, Quasar.

Tsiolis, V. (2001) Las termas de Fregellae. Arquitectura, tecnología y cultura balnear en el Lacio durante los siglos III y II a.C. *Cuadernos de Prehistoria y Arqueología* 27, 85–114.

Tsiolis, V. (2006) *Fregellae. Il complesso termale e le origini degli edifici balneari urbani nel mondo romano*. In M. Torelli & M. Osanna (eds) *Sicilia ellenistica, consuetudo italica. Alle origini dell'architettura ellenistica d'Occidente*, 243–255. Rome, Edizioni dell'Ateneo.

Tsiolis, V. (2008) *Modelli di convivenza urbana. Fregellae e la questione dell'introduzione delle pratiche termali nel Lazio meridionale*. In C. Corsi & E. Polito E. (eds) *Dalle sorgenti alla foce. Il bacino del Liri-Garigliano nell'antichità. Culture, contatti, scambi*, 133–143. Rome, Quasar.

Tsiolis, V. (2013) The baths at Fregellae and the transition from Balaneion to Balneum. In S.K. Lucore & M. Trümper (eds) *Greek Baths and Bathing Culture. New Discoveries and Approaches*, 89–111. Leuven, Peeters.

Vincenti, V. (2008) Pavimenti dalla prima fase delle terme di Fregellae (FR). Cenni preliminari. In C. Angelelli & C. Cecalupo (eds) *Atti del XIII Colloquio dell'Associazione italiana per lo studio e la conservazione del mosaico*, 407–418. Rome, Quasar.

Vincenti, V. (2012) I pavimenti della seconda fase delle terme di Fregellae (FR). Cenni preliminari. In C. Angelelli, M.E. Erba, D. Massara & E. Zulini (eds) *Atti del XVII Colloquio dell'Associazione italiana per lo studio e la conservazione del mosaico*, 277–288. Rome, Quasar.

Vincenti, V. (2021) Artigiani greci a Fregellae (FR) in una domus di epoca ellenistica? Particolarità delle tecniche esecutive. In C. Angelelli & C. Cecalupo (eds) *Atti del XXVI Colloquio dell'Associazione italiana per lo studio e la conservazione del mosaico*, 225–238. Rome, Quasar.

# Chapter 7

## *One should always dress like a marble column (Jackie Kennedy-Onassis): new insights on the urbanism of Alba Fucens*

### Cécile Evers

## 7.1. Localisation

Alba Fucens is a town located in the present-day Abruzzo region, in the ancient territory of the *Aequii*, on the border with the *Marsi*, at the foot of the Apennines, with the mighty silhouette of Monte Velino towering up at an altitude of nearly 2,500 m north of the town. It is situated along the *via Valeria* (Van Wonterghem 1983; 1991), the continuation of the *via Tiburtina*, 68 miles (100 km) east of Rome on a hilltop 1,022 m above sea level, and 300 m higher than the (agricultural) plain around it (Plate 7.1). Easy to access and even easier to defend, it strategically controls the Fucine lake basin and all the roads passing through this major hub of Central Italy, connecting Etruria to Campania and Rome to the Adriatic coast.

## 7.2. A brief history

Alba was established as a Latin colony in 303 BC, at the end of the Second Samnite War, to control the newly conquered territories (De Visscher 1960, 7–12; Mertens 1981, 7–13). The large number of 6,000 colonists was settled (Livy 10.1) in this kind of autonomous city state. It kept a strong bond with its mother city and continued to be a staunch ally of the Romans during the Republic. In 211 BC, during the Second Punic War, when Hannibal made a bold march on Rome in an attempt to liberate Capua, besieged by the Roman legions, and set up camp just four miles away from the City, it was the only colony that responded to the Roman's cry for help. The *Albenses* did immediately send 2,000 men to defend the city walls (App. *Hann.* 39). Hannibal left five days later. Exhausted by the wars though, Alba sided with the 11 colonies that refused to send new troops in 209 BC and was obliged to do so in 204 BC, but with a contingent twice as numerous as a punishment. Built as an impregnable stronghold, it

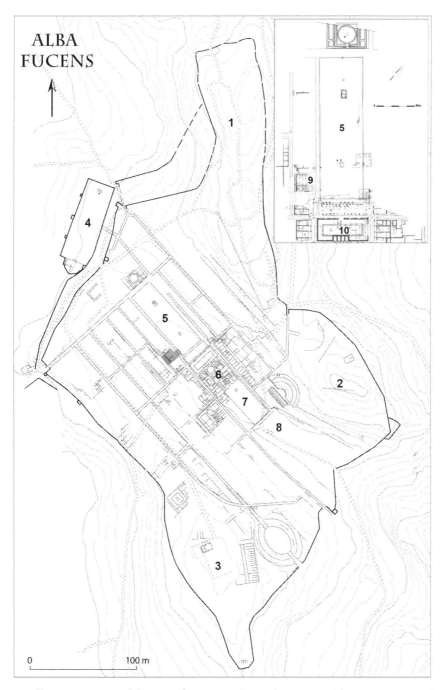

*Figure 7.1. Alba Fucens. Map of the town (J. Mertens & S. Delcros, copyright ULB CReA-Patrimoine).*
*1. San Nicola 2. Pettorino 3. San Pietro 4. Northern Terrace 5. Forum 6. Piano di Città 7. Sanctuary*
*of Hercules 8. Southern Piazza 9. New Belgian excavations 10. Basilica.*

was conveniently used to host important state prisoners, such as the dethroned kings Syphax of Numidia (203 BC), Perseus of Macedonia (168 BC), and Bituitus of the Arverni (121 BC). During the Social War (91–89 BC), the inhabitants of Alba, although in the middle of the territory of the insurgents (*socii*) and besieged by them, stayed faithful to the Roman Republic (Livy *Per.* 72). In 89 BC, the consul L. Porcius Cato died next to the Fucine lake during an attempt to retake the territory of the Marsi. But the war was over for the allied forces and Alba, like many other cities, benefited from the *Lex Iulia de civitate Latinis danda* (90 BC) and subsequently became a *municipium* of Roman citizens, administered by a board of four elected magistrates, the *quattuorviri* – two *iure dicundo* and two *aediles* (Letta 2019; 2021, 268). The peace was short. During the Civil Wars of the 1st century BC, the town found itself again on the front line of hostilities. In 78 BC Cornelius Scipio entrenched himself in the town against Sulla. The town was besieged and taken, Scipio killed (Coarelli 1998). Alba sided with Caesar in 49 BC and later with his heir Octavian, choosing wisely on both occasions. Caesar had great plans for the draining of the nearby Fucine lake, but his assassination stopped everything (Suet. *Iul.* 44.5). Augustus could not afford to follow suit, but Claudius did, in line with his policy to take over the dictator's infrastructure projects (Letta 1994, 203). Claudius tried to control the water level – and gain fertile land – by having an impressive drainage tunnel (5.6 km long) dug into the hill of Monte Salviano, allowing the overflow to be discharged into the Liri river. According to Suetonius, the works took 11 years (between AD 41 and 52) and employed 30,000 workers. But the result was not satisfactory and the first inauguration ceremony a disaster (Plin. *HN* 36.24.124; Tac. *Ann.* 12.56–57; Suet. *Claud.* 20–21.32; Cass. Dio 60.11.5, 61.33.3–5). The lake seems to have been finally successfully drained by Hadrian (SHA *Hadr.* 22.13), with the works having been completed in AD 149 (under Antoninus Pius), leaving only the central part, mostly what is today called the 'Bacinetto' underwater (D'Amato 1980, 155, fig. 22; Letta 1994, 210; 2019, 358–359). Large tracts of agricultural – and very fertile – land were gained, benefitting the economy of Alba and of the smaller local towns (esp. Marruvium). Tetrarchic portraits (De Ruyt 1982, 34–42 cat. 14–18, pl. IX–XI; LSA-1045–1049) and a milestone bearing the clumsily erased name of Magnentius (AD 350–351) (De Ruyt 1982, 156–160 cat. 190, pl. LIII; Van Wonterghem 1983, 10–11, fig. 8; EDR078542; HD002781; EDCS-13900464) testify to the wealth of the town during the late 3rd and 4th centuries AD. The last known inscription mentioning works (doors) on a public building dates from AD 362 (CIL IX 3921; Letta 2012a, 20, 41 cat. 35; EDR185085; EDCS-14804951). The last literary source is from Procopius (*Goth.* 2.7, 25.34), who wrote that the army of the *magister militium* John, sent by Justinian to help Belisarius besieged in Rome by the Ostrogoths, overwintered in Alba in AD 537, if we assume that the localisation in Picenum is wrong.

## 7.3. General topography

The settlement, on the Alba hill, is shaped like an elongated lozenge (1,150 m long × 675 m wide) (Fig. 7.1) (Mertens 1969, 37–118; 1981; 1988; Ceccaroni 2006). There are three summits: the San Nicola hill (1,016 m a.s.l., commonly interpreted as the old acropolis, where the medieval village, Alba Vecchia – destroyed by the lethal 1915 earthquake [Galadini 2022, 15–19] – was situated), the Pettorino (990 m a.s.l., with a temple) and the San Pietro Hill (992 m a.s.l., with a temple reused as a church). The central valley lying in between them, *c.* 100 m wide, contains the main public buildings of the town. Oriented northwest–southeast, it follows a downward slope (from 960 to 949 m a.s.l.), beginning, at the highest end, with the Northern Terrace (a *campus*), followed by the *forum*, then the downtown area (the Piano di Città with *macellum*, baths and *tabernae*), the Sanctuary of Hercules and, finally, a square with an exedra and a temple probably dedicated to eastern deities at the lowest point. The houses were built on the upper terraces flanking the valley and the main temples on the hilltops, with the notable exception of the Sanctuary of Hercules. The whole town (*c.* 34 ha) is defended by an impressive wall in polygonal masonry, almost 3 km long.

## 7.4. The archaeology of Alba Fucens

### 7.4.1. *The main stages of urbanisation according to Joseph Mertens*

But Alba wasn't built in one day. The chronological sequence of the urbanisation is quite intricate (Mertens 1988; 1991; Lackner 2008, 20–26).

- Stage A (3rd century BC)
  - **A.1:** The first works are of a definite military nature: the defence walls in cyclopean masonry bear witness to the town's original function as a fortress in newly conquered territories. Their chronology has been partly revised by Daniela Liberatore (Liberatore 2004, 41–109, 129–134). The initial defensive circuit was constructed at mid-slope, following the orography, and included the Alba Vecchia, Pettorino and probably San Pietro hills. The walls were built according to what Giuseppe Lugli calls the 'seconda maniera', sometimes quite fine, made of medium-sized blocks. They were obviously repaired, improved, provided with a tower and new gates during their long life (Liberatore 2004, 129 [phases e–g], 130–131 [phases II–IV]).
  - **A.2:** The drainage of the area was indispensable, as the main part of the town lies in a small valley, functioning as an alluvial basin. Like in Rome, where the area of the *forum* could only be used after the construction of the *Cloaca Maxima*, the Roman engineers built early on a large drain that runs the length of the town, and numerous canalisations, all of which have been explored, cleared and mapped by our team of archaeo-speleologists since 2010 (Vrielynck *et al.* 2013; 2015; Vrielynck 2017; partly used by Rose 2018, 115–148). The sewerage system of the town is indeed quite impressive and very complex, mirroring the urbanistic evolution of the colony. Almost every *taberna* is also provided with a well and some quite large ones have been found, even recently, like the one in the sanctuary of Hercules, in front of the *sacellum* (Ceccaroni 2013, 261–271). Water was plentiful, even before the Augustan (?) construction of the aqueduct (Rose 2018, 47–113). Geological soundings in the southern part of the square

of the of Herculean complex have shown that this valley bottom area was an inhabitable marshland before the drainage works and levelling works carried out by the Roman colonists (Galadini 2013; Russo *et al.* 2022, 3).

- **A.3:** Urban planning: construction of the terrace walls, levelling of the *forum* area (and of the further squares?), construction of the necessary administrative buildings (*comitium* and *curia, forum,* plus the sacred Herculean complex). Forum and *comitium* were built on 'virgin' soil. An orthogonal plan is laid out in the central valley, with parallel and perpendicular streets oriented by the *via Valeria* ('Via del Miliario'). The *insulae* follow this pattern, are oblong, c. 30–40 m wide and 80–110 m long. Most of the official buildings are built along this axis (*comitium, forum, basilica, macellum,* Herculean complex). On both sides of this political-administrative zone, a long row of shops with a portico in front of them are aligned. The orthogonal plan is also visible in the structures (*domus publicae*) underneath the *basilica* (built during the first half of the 2nd century BC). Even on the central-eastern slope, all the oldest buildings are set in the orthogonal plan, which was kept during the whole lifespan of the town. The main temples, on the Pettorino and San Pietro hills, were also constructed during the 3rd century BC.
- Stage B (2nd century BC): the town is monumentalised according to Hellenistic models. Part of this monumentalisation, i.e. the terracing of the hill slopes leading to the temples, the Basilica, porticoes of the Herculean sanctuary, porticoes on the streets, as well as the paving of the streets, are dated by Mertens to the 2nd and beginning of the 1st centuries BC, but following the original pattern which must have been clearly delineated on the ground.
- Stage C (after the destructions of the civil wars): the town is completely reconstructed.
- Stage D (2nd century AD): embellishment of the public and private buildings.
- Stage E (from the 3rd century AD onwards): decline.

### 7.4.2. The Belgian excavation

The site has been excavated by a Belgian team since 1949, at the initiative of Fernand De Visscher with the help of Franz De Ruyt, then mostly under the archaeological direction of Joseph Mertens from 1950 until 1991 (Mertens 1969, 7–36; Campanelli 2006; De Ruyt 2006; Strazzulla 2006). In 2006/07, following an exhibition held at the Academia Belgica in Rome and in the Brussels Art & History Museum, the Italian archaeological authorities (*Soprintendenza per i Beni Archeologici dell'Abruzzo*) launched a new ambitious research program and generously invited Belgian archaeologists to join them. What began as a small-scale training excavation has become more and more professional, collaborating with specialists in various fields, from archaeozoologists to restorers, epigraphists and archaeo-speleologists. Pending the final publication, this essay will offer a summary of some of our more significant discoveries. Our team from the Université Libre de Bruxelles (CReA - Patrimoine), together with the Royal Museums of Art and History, has been excavating and studying the southwestern zone of the *forum* for 10 campaigns since 2007.

### 7.4.3. *The forum*

This part of the town had been partly scrutinised by Joseph Mertens in the 1950s–60s and by Jean Ch. Balty at the beginning of the 1960s, but large-scale excavations were impossible as the terrain was still in private hands. In the early 1950s, Mertens, in his attempt to understand the layout of the public square, dug a series of trenches in the *forum* (Fig. 7.1: 5). He later increased the number of trial trenches, including a long one (in 1971) that crossed the square from east to west (Mertens 1977, 256–260, figs 4–5). Two small monuments, the 'tempietto' and a monumental base, were found in its central part (Mertens 1969, 97, map III.B and C). The *comitium* stands to the north of the square, probably with the *curia* behind it (Mertens 1968; 1969, 98–101, fig. 32a, map III.F, map IV), as in the contemporary colonies of Cosa and Paestum (Balty 1991, 168–178). On the southern side, stands the *basilica* (Mertens 1969, 63–65, fig. 11, map II.L), a later addition, preceded by a portico (the *diribitorium*) (Mertens 1969, 92–96, figs 23–24; Gros 1996, 210; Liberatore 2004, 110–122). The square itself is 171.68 m long (with the porticoes), the paved *platea c.* 142 × 43.50 m (46.5 m according to Strazzulla *et al.* 2012, 170). It was supposedly flanked on both long sides by a row of *tabernae* along a portico opening on the 'Via del Miliario' (on the western side) (Mertens 1981, 40 fig. 29; 1988, 103 fig. 21; 1991, 111 fig. 12).

### 7.4.4. *The Schola*

But the long sides of the *forum* had not been systematically studied. Only one room, cut by a trench in 1960, was excavated by J. Ch. Balty in 1961 (Fig. 7.2: 4) (Mertens 1969, 90–91, pl. 33a, map III.H; Balty 1991, 195–196, fig. 117; Bollmann 1998, 42 cat. A.66, fig. 52; Wohlmayr 2004, 149–150, fig. 22; Evers & Massar 2012, 115–116, fig. 2). It opens onto the western portico of the *forum*, about 3.7 m wide, which runs along the 'Via del Miliario' (probably the extension of the *via Valeria*). Its dimensions (5.45 × 10.20 m) are similar to the module used for the shops in the southern part of the town (5.10–5.50 × 9–12 m). These same measurements, it should be noted, were used for the shops surrounding the *forum* of the contemporary colony of Paestum, founded in 273 BC (Greco & Theodorescu 1987, 19; Pesando 2012, 206–208). The presence at the back of the room of a platform with a column in Teos marble (*marmo africano*) supporting a white marble Corinthian capital (Galadini 2006, 134, fig. 100) suggests that it was a small *sacellum*, perhaps used by a *collegium*. The rich decoration of the interior, made up of *opus sectile* on the floor and marble panelling on the walls (*crustae*), seems to confirm this identification and certainly rules out the idea of a commercial space.

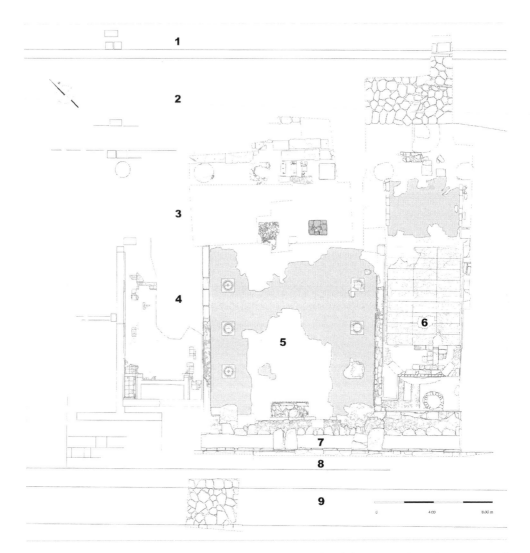

Figure 7.2. Alba Fucens. Rooms along the southwestern side of the Forum (S. Delcros, copyright ULB CReA-Patrimoine). 1. Platea of the Forum 2. Via Valeria / del Miliario 3. Porticus 4. Schola 5. 'Columnar Hall' 6. 'Marble Room' 7. Sewer 8. Terrace wall 9. Via Nova.

### 7.4.5. The new Belgian excavations

These are located north of the last shops of the 'Via del Miliario', below a trial trench of the 1950s, and directly south of the *Schola* (Fig. 7.2). The aim was to ascertain if the regular colonial grid and rows of *tabernae* of the southern part of the town could be found around the *forum*, and to clarify the chronological sequence of the constructions. We excavated part of the upper terrace, and on the *forum* level, two rooms, the portico and part of the road (the continuation of the *via Valeria*) to the pavement of the square.

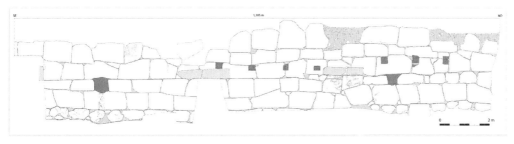

*Figure 7.3. Alba Fucens. Terrace wall (S. Connor & C. Pion, copyright ULB CReA-Patrimoine).*

### 7.4.5.1. The upper terrace

On the upper terrace, a paved street runs parallel to the extension of the 'Via del Miliario' (Fig. 7.2: 8–9) (Evers & Massar 2013, 298–299). It corresponds to the one identified during various surveys in the 1950s and named *via Nova* (De Visscher & De Ruyt 1951, 76–77). It measures *c.* 2.4 m in width – approximately 8 feet (for this module for secondary roads see Chevallier 1972, 96) – and its curbstones are still preserved. It continues behind the *tabernae* facing the *diribitorium* and joins the perpendicular 'Via dell'Elefante'. Its surface, free of any trace of car ruts on this section, is cambered for drainage, rainwater flowing through lateral openings into a storm drain.

### 7.4.5.2. The terrace wall

The terrace retaining wall is built in a superb polygonal masonry (Figs 7.2: 8; 7.3) (Evers & Massar 2013, 299–300, fig. 3). Two series of square recesses, placed in a horizontal line, were carved at the back of the Columnar Hall. They may have served as sockets for the beams supporting a floor or for another kind of structure above the sewer. A quadrangular opening can be seen behind each room: the outlet of the culvert of the upper terrace. Only the southern *diverticulum* was used, as can be seen from the traces of wear and tear and the limescale deposits on the wall. The opening had been blocked by fragmentary architectural elements (a marble frieze, a column shaft). We excavated it over a length of 6 m. An ancient collapse prevented us from going any further. The bottom is covered with *bipedales* whose width corresponds exactly to that of the collector. The northern canal, on the other hand, stops at a short distance from the opening (60 cm). It had never been used, and its bottom has not been protected by ceramic tiles or covered with mortar.

### 7.4.5.3. The sewer

The rainwater flows into a large collector at the foot of the terrace, 1.7 m high and 0.8 m wide, also built in polygonal masonry (Figs 7.2: 7; 7.4: on the left). It was strangely not recognised during Mertens' trial trenches of the *forum* or Balty's excavation of the *Schola*, although De Visscher identified it at the back of the *tabernae* A and B (De Visscher *et al.* 1954, 347, fig. 21, 354). Most of the cover slabs had been taken away during Antiquity, with just the ones in continuation of the perpendicular walls of

*Figure 7.4. Alba Fucens. Columnar Hall (copyright ULB CReA-Patrimoine).*

the original *tabernae* left in place. The fill was a treasure trove and presented, at the southern end, a wonderful section containing datable material – *terra sigillata chiara*, both African and imitations (*c.* AD 360–450) – in a destruction layer (Evers & Massar 2012, 127–129). A double-faced official inscription in white marble, evidently coming from a public building, has been found at the bottom. The front side probably dates from the 1st century AD, the back to the 3rd century AD (Evers & Massar 2012, 126, figs 18–19; CIL IX 7933).

### 7.4.5.4. The Columnar Hall

A first room was discovered, directly south of the *Schola*, measuring 12.5 m deep (13.4 m to the terrace wall) and 11.4 m wide, i.e. double the usual module (Figs. 7.2: 5; 7.4) (Evers & Massar 2012, 116–121, figs 6–12; 2013, 301–304, figs 4–5). The partition wall with the *Schola*, constructed in *opus testaceum* and *opus incertum* was found thrown to the ground by an earthquake. Only a few shreds are still standing on a base of large *opus quadratum* blocks. The *opus testaceum* is made of tiles cut in a triangle (Lugli 1957, 569). One of these bears the stamp CORD(VS), another the name Q. Naevius Hybrida, probably attesting to the fact that the factory (*figlina*) belonged to the family of Q. Naevius Cordus Sutorius Macro (21 BC – AD 38), the praetorian prefect of Tiberius and Caligula, originally from Alba, where he sponsored an important building activity (De Visscher 1957a; 1957b; PIR², N12; Eck 2000). Several of these stamped tiles had been found in the earlier excavations (Buonocore 1994) and one, on a fragmentary terracotta pipe sadly out of context (in colluvial deposits), recently by the team from the University of Foggia that opened up an excavation right in front of us on the other long side of the Forum (Liberatore 2018).

Two rows of columns punctuated the internal space. There were originally at least three on each side (the southwestern base was despoiled during antiquity), placed very close to the walls (85 cm). The location of a fourth column can still be guessed at along the back wall. Only the plinth with the base, carved in one piece with the inferior part of the first drum of the columns (*immoscapo*), is preserved. The shafts, cable-fluted in their lower third, then fluted (20 flutes), rest on precisely carved Attic bases made of high-quality local limestone. They supported elegant Corinthianizing capitals with acanthus leaves in the style of the Forum of Augustus (Pensabene 2019, 172–173, figs 24–25). The overall height of these columns (including base and capital) must have approached 5.4 m (18 feet) (Wilson Jones 2000, 143–156). Three smaller capitals indicate the existence of a higher order or, perhaps, of a baldachin-like structure at the back of the room, like in the *Schola*, or may have been reused during a late phase (other architectural parts were found in the collapse of the northern partition wall). Following a canonical Corinthian model, they are very close to mid-Augustan examples and to the capitals of the larger columns reused in the Alban San Pietro church (Pensabene 2019, 173–174, fig. 26). The reworking of the southern bases, provided with large notches roughly carved with a pick, testifies to a partitioning in perishable material linked to a change of function of the room during a Late Antique phase (stables?). Two of the columns from the nave of the San Pietro church, placed at the entrance of the apse, carved in local limestone, are almost identical in their components (base with *immoscapo*, shaft) and size to the ones from the Columnar Hall, although bearing canonical Corinthian capitals. Pensabene (2019, 168–173, 8s 8d, figs 6, 18, 20) suggests that not all of the capitals of the room may have been Corinthianizing.

The floor is covered with a plain white mosaic, made up of cuboid tesserae (height: 3 cm; width: 1 cm) embedded vertically in the laying mortar. This particular technique, known as *a denti di cavallo* ('horse's teeth'), is used when the soil is not very stable, either due to its sandy nature or, as it is probably the case here, to the presence of underground water. Numerous repairs and restorations are visible, made necessary by slow ground movements that have strongly deformed the floor. Even before the earthquake that put an end to its use, the room no longer seems to have been used. Underneath the collapsed wall, we found that it had been despoiled and abandoned for quite a long time: the columns were incomplete, one base had been stolen, the pavement was quite wavy. We found nothing except bones from butchered animals (dated by C14 analysis between AD 324–438 and 376–437).

The fragments of the north wall still retained parts of their painted decoration. Large elongated rectangular panels with a red background decorated with marine animals (dolphin and *ketos*) alternate with small vertical panels with imitations of giallo antico plaques. The poor state of preservation makes stylistic analysis difficult. However, it is possible to propose a chronological range between the beginning of the 2nd and the end of the 3rd century AD.

The square plan of the room, with the columns very close to the walls, evokes the Corinthian *oecus* of Vitruvius (*De arch.* 6.3.9; Gros 2001, 62–65), as it is still visible in some houses of Pompeii, such as the House of Meleager (VI.9.2) or the House of the Labyrinth (VI.11.8–10). This type of impressive construction, covered with a barrel-vaulted ceiling, could be suitable as a reception hall, either municipal (for the civil or religious authorities) or for a *collegium*.

This *oecus* was built after a complete reorganisation of the original colonial modular structure: the architects destroyed the old partition between the two *tabernae* – of which we found the foundations – and rebuilt the eastern limit of the sewer, originally in polygonal masonry, thinning it out to create a square internal space. The construction of a monumental entrance on the *Forum* portico, transforming its original design, enhanced even more the importance of this impressive room.

### 7.4.5.5. The Marble Room

A second room was cleared south of the Columnar Hall (Figs 7.2: 6; 7.5–7.6). With dimensions of 5.5 × 11 m, it follows a module similar to that of the *Schola* and of most of the shops in the lower part of the town, along the 'Via del Miliario' and the 'Via dei Pilastri', namely half that of the Columnar Hall. The hall is wide open on the portico of the *forum* (Evers & Massar 2012, 121–125, figs 13–17; 2013a, 304–308, figs 6–8).

*Figure 7.5. Alba Fucens. Marble Room (copyright ULB CReA-Patrimoine).*

From the entrance onwards (where the threshold has been stripped in ancient times), the floor is paved, over a length of *c.* 6.4 m with a succession of three parallel rows of nine slabs of bardiglio nuvolato marble, each measuring 1.60 × 0.7 m. They are 3–4 cm thick and laid upon a bed of 15 cm of very hard pink mortar. Only one of them, at the entrance of the room, had been despoiled. Some piecing is apparent where the slabs were put in place with a crowbar: small triangular or trapezoidal pieces fill the gaps around the angles of some plaques. Several contiguous slabs present a kind of mirror image design: they were sawn from the same block and placed like the leaves of an open book. Two slabs on the southwestern side exhibit traces of a formidable

*Figure 7.6. Alba Fucens. Marble Room. Reconstitution of the marble cladding of the southern wall (phase II) (copyright ULB CReA-Patrimoine).*

impact, with radiating cracking, probably caused by the earthquake that destroyed the Columnar Hall. This kind of flooring is typical of imperial public buildings (Olevano 2001; 2005). Along the walls, a sloppy border, clearly a renovation, is formed by small tiles in bardiglio and pavonazzetto.

Where the bardiglio pavement ends, a semicircular wall, razed to the ground, is visible. It originally formed an apse, as in the sanctuary of the *Augustales* of Misenum (De Franciscis 1991; Bollmann 1998, 356–363 cat. A.50, pl. 8.1–2), and was also possibly provided with a bench along the wall. The apse was reinforced at the back by two retaining walls abutting on the sewer. The floor was paved, maybe in a later phase, with a rich *opus sectile*, laid on a rather powdery greyish mortar and composed of rectangular and square slabs of various marbles: giallo antico, pavonazzetto, alabastro listato, bardiglio, breccia corallina (?) and white marble. The apse was later demolished, the room enlarged, and the *opus sectile* extended and repaired, mainly using salvaged slabs, some still bearing fragmentary inscriptions. The materials used include white marble, bardiglio, alabaster, rosso antico, and pavonazzetto.

The three walls of the room were lavishly decorated with marble veneer. Although the general structure of the revetment is coherent, one recognises quite a lot of disparate marble components. The lower part of the walls is covered with long slabs of bardiglio and cipollino to a height of about 27.5 cm. In some places, they are replaced by salvaged elements: white marble friezes, superimposed mouldings in pavonazzetto, or even an inlaid slab of rosso antico. They are topped by cornices in rosso antico and white marble, about 5.5 cm high and protruding by *c.* 1 cm. Some of these white marble mouldings still have remnants of red paint, testifying to the desire to imitate the Cap Tenaros marble. Above this cornice, and set back from the base, some fragments of alabastro fiorito plaques are still in place. They were framed by vertical bands of cipollino, *c.* 7.5 cm wide. Hundreds of marble fragments have been studied and recomposed to comprehend the original structure of the parietal decoration and its various repairs (Fig. 7.6). At least four rosso antico capitals and their bases were recovered from the room, but also later pavonazzetto imitations. The parietal decoration loosely follows a structure attested in Herculaneum, in the *oecus* 18 of the House of the relief of Telephos (Guidobaldi *et al.* 2014, cat. 45, 87–90, pls 157–160), but also on the *forum* of Cumae (Nuzzo 2010, 384 fig. 9). It can also be found on the façade of the three 'municipal buildings' on the small southern side of the *forum* of Pompeii (Balty 1991, 72, fig. 47). It is, though, especially close to the one in the Alban *Schola* (Balty 1991, 196, fig. 117).

The room presents a different archaeological situation from its neighbour: after the earthquake, the rubble was removed and the room repaired and reused. We found it filled with a detrital layer dating from AD 380–430. The presence of an apse, razed to the ground in a later phase, as well as the lavish decoration of the floors and walls, suggest that this room may have served as a *sacellum* for a college, perhaps that of the *seviri Augustales*, of which there is so much epigraphic evidence in Alba Fucens (Devijver & Van Wonterghem 1984–1986, 165–166; Buonocore 1995, 127).

No inscription or imperial image confirm this hypothesis, but many rooms with an apse and marble decoration on the floor and walls have been identified as seats of *Augustales* associations: we can mention the one in the southern area of the *forum* of Roselle (Bollmann 1998, 415–418 cat. A.74, fig. 28), those around the *forum* (northwestern and southeastern corners) and the ancient *Piscina Publica* of Paestum (Greco & Theodorescu 1987, 23–24, figs 2.1–2, 13; Bollmann 1998, 389–391 cat. A.57, fig. 50, pl. 12.2) and, especially, the one on the *forum* of Tibur (Bollmann 1998, 378–380 cat. A.74, ill. 41). Let us also remember that many *collegia* of the Republican period linked to a specific divinity, such as the *Mercuriales* of Paestum or the *Herculanei* of Tibur, were associated with the imperial cult from the Augustan period onwards (Bérard 2012, 90–92).

### 7.4.5.6. The well

Behind the apse, a well with a diameter of 1 m and a depth of 5 m was excavated in 2010 (Evers *et al.* 2013). The water appeared at a depth of 1m. This anaerobic environment has allowed the preservation of a diverse and interesting organic material: wood, leather, sponge, fruit cores and shells, etc. The material, both ceramic and numismatic, indicates a date of the main filling at the time of the emperors Claudius or Nero; the upper part kept on being used until the 3rd century AD, when it was definitely closed.

### 7.4.5.7. The portico and the street

Both rooms opened onto a deep portico (equal to the width of each room), each circular column base – *c.* 130 cm in diameter (4.5 feet) – standing in front of the partition walls between the rooms (Fig. 7.2: 2–3) (Evers & Massar 2013, 309–311, figs 9–11). This system was reorganised when the *oecus* was constructed: the central column was taken away and replaced by a pair of (probably Corinthian) columns placed on a square plinth (side of 108 cm, with the trace of a 90 cm circular base on top), creating a monumental entrance. A short flight of stairs separated the higher colonnaded passage from the street (the continuation of the 'Via del Miliario'). It had been completely despoiled in front of the Marble Room but is still partly preserved further north. The street, *c.* 16 feet wide (double the *via Nova*), is paved and in fine condition, although its western edge has been torn away. It bears deep ruts, testifying to its use for carts, right next to the *Forum* square and in front of its side porticoes, which is surprising to say the least. One would indeed expect animal-driven vehicles to be banned from the *forum*, like in Pompei and so many other Roman towns. To the east, the curbstones towards the *forum* square have been preserved, but the paving of the latter has unfortunately been despoiled.

   This system of a colonnaded street is similar to the situation downtown (Mertens 1969, 19), although on a grandiose scale: if the intercolumniation is the same (complying with the modular system of the *tabernae*), the width of the walkway under the portico is double the size. Even the *via Valeria* is broader along the *Forum*. The importance of the public square, the centre of the town's political life, is thus effectively highlighted (see, already, De Visscher *et al.* 1954, 353). Strangely, no continuation of the 'Via dei Pilastri' was found on the eastern side of the square, nor by Mertens nor by the team of the Foggia University (Strazzulla *et al.* 2012), although traces of the portico still exist.

The floor of the portico in front of the Marble Room is paved with an extremely worn white mosaic of a technique similar to that of the Columnar Hall. A simple geometrical pattern, made of black tesserae, acts as a kind of 'doormat' located at the boundary between the portico and the lower street area. Over time, both this motif and the rest of the mosaic carpet have undergone numerous alterations and restorations. It had been strengthened by a border of small stone slabs placed longitudinally in the continuation of the walls, effectively separating this space from the rest of the portico, that probably fell into disuse after the destruction of the Columnar Hall.

### 7.4.5.8. The Fasti Albenses

Lying on the portico mosaic in front of the Marble Room, we found a layer of destruction with the remains of two structures: to the south, a vertical construction in *opus testaceum*, perhaps a statue base, and to the north a mass of white plaster on which inscriptions were painted in rustic capitals. After a thorough excavation and the discovery of a fragment mentioning the Calends of May, we realised that it was the remains of a large calendar, painted on stucco, that must have originally covered an area of no less than 10 m$^2$ (Fig. 7.7). The hundreds of fragments were laying directly on the mosaic in a heap, in no apparent order – except for one large plaque. Their rear side shows the imprints of bricks, traces of the wall that supported it.

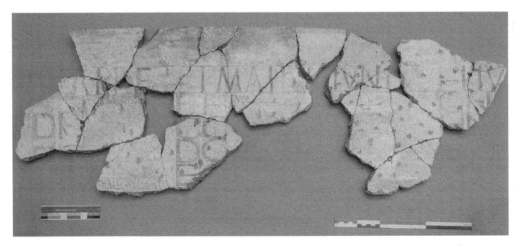

Figure 7.7. *Alba Fucens.* Fasti Albenses. *Upper part with the calends from April to July (copyright ULB CReA-Patrimoine).*

The calendar was thus stripped off a wall – probably to reuse its bricks – and thrown away on the portico. A second layer of white stucco, extremely thin (less than 1 cm thick) and badly preserved, with some rare traces of engraved letters, still covered some fragments. The whole surface of the original calendar bears pick marks made to facilitate the adhesion of the upper layer of stucco. This second phase has helped save some of the painted letters from decay, allowing us to carry out a painstaking work of cleaning, consolidating, gluing, photographing, drawing, and reconstructing the structure. Cesare Letta and Patrick Tansey have been deciphering and interpreting the whole document (Letta 2013; 2014; Evers & Massar 2014; Tansey 2018), with a final publication due in 2025.

Most of the document consists of a post-Julian calendar, with the 12 columns of the months. Underneath this, a strip contains the names of the dedicators (magistrates), followed by columns listing the pairs of consuls of the Roman Republic and the beginning of the Empire (*Fasti Consulares*). The whole text (412 × 232 cm), written in red letters on white stucco, is framed by a large border in green paint. We cannot be sure of its original location, as it was found in a secondary context. Although one might be tempted to place it under the *forum* portico, on the facade wall of the Marble Room, two arguments contradict this: the room was probably never closed by a brick wall and the opening would have been too narrow, not allowing the space for a door. The fragility of the stucco and painting (*a secco*) must also be stressed: it had to have been placed in an enclosed space. The Columnar Hall, although further from the discovery spot of the *Fasti*, presents similar problems: it looks as if it had never been closed by a solid wall, and the calendar would have been difficult to read behind the columns. The only place where it can have been exhibited, close to where it was dumped, is the northern wall of the Marble Room, above the veneer plinth. This emphasizes once more the official character of this space.

## 7.5. Conclusions

The *forum* of the colony, indispensable for its functioning as a town, must have been planned at the very beginning. The structuring of the valley had to be dealt with first. The retaining walls of the terraces (those identified in the 1950s and the one presented here) as well as the sewer, in polygonal masonry, which shape the slopes around the *forum* square, testify to one of the earliest urbanisation phases of the town, still in the 3rd century BC, with adaptations during the 2nd century BC. The structuring of the adjoining regular modules is contemporary, as we can deduct from the discovery of the base of the original partition wall, constructed in polygonal masonry, in the middle of the Columnar Hall, underneath its mosaic. The same division in modules is still visible on the terrace wall, with recesses dug out at two different levels – corresponding to the two original rooms. The culverts were also already planned in the construction of the terrace walls, even if not all of them were finally used.

It is more difficult to define a function for these rooms during this first phase. They were probably initially simple shops, as Bollmann had proposed in a very theoretical way in her study on the Roman *scholae* (Bollmann 1998, 113–122) following in any case the 'colonial' module also used in Paestum (about 5.5 × 11 m). The commercial function would later be relegated to the lower part of the town. The presence of the well at the bottom of the Marble Room, an essential element found in all the shops of Alba south of the *basilica*, provides the only trace of this first use.

We have until now no real chronological data for the construction of the *forum* portico. We can probably follow Mertens' proposal of a 2nd–1st centuries BC Hellenistic style upgrading of the town, attested for the construction of the *basilica* and the renovation of the Herculean complex, but no architectural element of the columns is preserved (except a base with fluted drum on the eastern side, in front of the *taberna* III, if in place (Di Cesare & Liberatore 2017, 19–20, figs 18–19)). The only assurance we have is that the building of the entrance of the Columnar Hall replaced the original rhythm of the colonnade.

Mertens recognised a monumental transformation of Alba at the end of the Republic. Our research has particularly highlighted this phenomenon. The Columnar Hall underwent a major restructuring: initially formed by two units of colonial module, it was unified by destroying the partition wall, and a Corinthian *oecus* was built, a hall whose square proportions were obtained by moving the back wall of the hall (eastern wall of the sewer) backwards (the polygonal wall was destroyed and replaced by a thinner one). A white mosaic was then laid on the floor, and probably on the whole length of the portico in front of the three rooms. It has only been preserved in front of the Marble Room (with a reinforcing border), the unit that had the longer life during the Late Empire. A monumental entrance – with two Corinthian columns – was built as an entrance to the Columnar Hall, removing the column that faced the partition wall of the two original spaces. The recent study by Patrizio Pensabene has shown that the Attic column bases date from a model created just after the second triumvirate. Indeed, if we read the ancient sources – Appian (*Sam.* 45.1, 47.1) and Cicero (*Phil.* 3.6–7, 4.5–6, 14.31) in particular – we do realise how closely the future Augustus was linked to Alba. As soon as he returned from Epirus with the news of Caesar's death, Octavian took on Mark Antony and sought to hire soldiers. It was at this point, in 44 BC, that the First Martian Legion defected from Mark Antony and rallied to the young Caesar, moving to Alba Fucens. And it is there that they confronted the forces of Mark Antony who had rushed there to bring them back to order and had to return to Rome empty-handed. Octavian joined them in Alba, with the rest of his troops (almost five legions by then), and wrote to the Senate, who congratulated him. This position of strength prevented Antony from having him designated *hostis publicus*. Augustus will no doubt have never forgotten the loyalty of the *Albenses*. The town already had a special link with Caesar, who was patron of the municipium (De Visscher 1964) and, if we do not yet have an inscription linking Augustus directly to the town, we do have one dedicated to his grandson Lucius Caesar as patron of the colony (Letta 2012b).

These three rooms on the western side of the *forum*, along the *via Valeria* and close to the *basilica* and the *diribitorium*, had, in my opinion, official or semi-official functions from the end of the Republic onwards. The Marble Room has a similar plan to that of the *Schola*, with almost identical dimensions and a very similar floor and wall layout. The rich decoration is not suitable for a shop. The materials used, such as rosso antico, giallo antico and pavonazzetto, were some of the most expensive marbles of the Empire. The dais at the back of one room and the apse in the other indicate their use as a *sacellum*, although it is not possible to identify the deities honoured. The very structure of the three rooms, with no counter or back room, does not show any indication of a commercial function. On the contrary, both their layout and their location make them particularly suitable for public or semi-public functions, probably related to colleges. The incredible richness of the decoration of the Marble Hall and the *Schola*, the presence of a floor made of large slabs of bardiglio, the remains of an official inscription and, above all, the presence of the town's calendar, bear ample witness to this. Like in so many Italian cities, the Augustan Age was a turning point in their urbanism. The commercial functions of the *tabernae* were probably banned from the *Forum* area and relegated to the south. The *Schola* became a small *sacellum*, and the Columnar Hall was built, maybe as an official banqueting hall for the town's magistrates or for a *collegium* (*Augustales*?). The Marble Hall may have functioned as an *Augusteum* and was the repository of the official calendar of the town. The rooms were even more embellished during the Claudio-Neronian epoch, with a lavish display of marble veneer. The testament of Macro and the draining of the Fucine lake had brought new wealth.

After the Julio-Claudian period, the rooms continued to be used and restored. A major restructuring of the Marble Hall, during which the apse was razed to the ground and a new *opus sectile* laid, took place at a still undetermined period (possibly in the 3rd century AD, if an inscription and a series of coins can be linked to this event). The walls of the Columnar Hall were also redecorated in the 2nd or 3rd century AD. Its floor gradually deteriorated though, and it lost its representative function to become a stable, and maybe a butcher shop (rests of slaughtered animals dating from the *c.* AD 400). After an earthquake that put an end to the town's prosperity, it was despoiled and abandoned, while the Marble Room was cleared and restored. It too finally fell into disuse, its marble veneer slowly falling on the floor, before being recovered by a detrital fill dating from *c.* AD 380–430, then by the thick layer of colluvium that covered the whole town during the early Middle Ages and forced the inhabitants to seek higher ground (Galadini *et al.* 2012). The only ancient structure with no archaeological layer on top is the *via Valeria*, that continued to be used for several centuries after the abandonment of the *forum*.

## Acknowledgements

Our research in Alba Fucens would never have been possible without the constant support of Emanuela Ceccaroni and of the various *Soprintendenti* of the Abruzzo Region and, since 2022, of the *Direzione dei Musei d'Abruzzo* (Federica Zalabra) and of the *Direzione Generale dei Musei* (Massimo Osanna). The funding has been generously provided by the Université Libre de Bruxelles and the Fonds National de la Recherche Scientifique. My sincerest thanks to all.

## Bibliography

Balty, J.Ch. (1991) *Curia Ordinis: recherches d'architecture et d'urbanismes antiques sur les curies provinciales du monde romain.* Brussels, Académie Royale de Belgique.

Bérard, F. (2012) Épigraphie latine du monde romain. *Annuaire de l'École pratique des hautes études (EPHE), Section des sciences historiques et philologiques* 143, 90–95.

Bollmann, R. (1998) *Römische Vereinshäuser. Untersuchungen zu den Scholae der römischen Berufs-, Kult- und Augustalen-Kollegien in Italien.* Mainz am Rhein, Ph. von Zabern.

Buonocore, M. (1994) Lateres signati regionis IV. In *Epigrafia della produzione e della distribuzione*, 361–369. Rome, École française de Rome.

Buonocore, M. (1995) Per uno studio sulla diffusione degli \*Augustales nel mondo romano: L'esempio della 'Regio IV' augustea. *Zeitschrift für Papyrologie und Epigraphik* 108, 123–129.

Campanelli, A. (2006) Cinquant'anni di ricerche. In A. Campanelli (ed.) *Poco grano molti frutti. 50 anni di archeologia ad Alba Fucens,* 22–33. Rome, Academia Belgica – Brussels, Musées Royaux d'Art et d'Histoire. Chieti – Sulmona, Synapsi edizioni.

Ceccaroni, E. (2006) La colonia latina. In A. Campanelli (ed.) *Poco grano molti frutti. 50 anni di archeologia ad Alba Fucens,* 57–65. Rome, Academia Belgica – Brussels, Musées Royaux d'Art et d'Histoire. Chieti – Sulmona, Synapsi edizioni.

Ceccaroni, M. (2013) Alba Fucens: gli interventi della Soprintendenza per i Beni Archeologici dell'Abruzzo nell'isolato in via del Miliario e nel piazzale del santuario di Ercole. *Rendiconti della Pontificia Accademia Romana di Archeologia* 85, 245–277.

Chevallier, R. (1972) *Les voies romaines.* Paris, Armand Colin.

Coarelli, F. (1998) Lépide et Alba Fucens. *Revue des Études Anciennes* 100.3–4, 461–475.

D'Amato, S. (1980) *Il primo prosciugamento del Fucino.* Avezzano, Centro Studi Marsicani.

De Franciscis, A. (1991) *Il sacello degli Augustali a Miseno.* Napoli, Arte Tipografica.

De Ruyt, Cl. (2006) Perché Alba Fucens ? In A. Campanelli (ed.) *Poco grano molti frutti. 50 anni di archeologia ad Alba Fucens,* 41–45. Rome, Academia Belgica – Brussels, Musées Royaux d'Art et d'Histoire. Chieti – Sulmona, Synapsi edizioni.

De Ruyt, Fr. (1982) *Alba Fucens III. Sculptures d'Alba Fucens (pierre, marbre, bronze). Catalogue raisonné.* Brussels, Institut historique belge de Rome; Rome, Academia Belgica

Devijver, H. & Van Wonterghem, Fr. (1984–86) Un 'curator arcae sevirum' ad Alba Fucens. *Ancient Society* 15–17, 165–166.

De Visscher, F. (1957a) La carrière et le testament d'un préfet du prétoire de Tibère. *Bulletin de l'Académie Royale de Belgique (Classe des Lettres)*, 5ᵉ série, 42.5, 168–179.

De Visscher, F. (1957b) L'amphithéâtre d'Alba Fucens et son fondateur Q. Naevius Macro, préfet du prétoire de Tibère, *Rendiconti Accademia Nazionale dei Lincei. Classe di scienze morali, storiche e filologiche Serie VIII,* 12.1–2, 39–49.

De Visscher, F. (1960) L'histoire d'Alba Fucens. In *Alba Fucens. Découverte d'une cité romaine des Abruzzes.* Catalogue d'exposition. Brussels, Palais des Beaux-Arts.

De Visscher, F. (1964) Jules César patron d'Alba Fucens. *L'Antiquité Classique* 33.1, 98–107.

De Visscher, F. & De Ruyt, Fr. (1951) Les fouilles d'Alba Fucens (Italie Centrale) en 1949 et 1950. *L'Antiquité Classique* 20, 47–84.

De Visscher, F., De Ruyt, Fr., De Laet, S. & Mertens, J. (1954) Les fouilles d'Alba Fucens (Italie Centrale) de 1951 à 1953. *L'Antiquité Classique* 23, 331–402.

Di Cesare, R. & Liberatore, D. (2017) The tabernae of Alba Fucens. *Fasti On Line Document & Research* 379, 1–26.

Eck, W. (2000) s.v. Naevius II.3. *Der Neue Pauly* 8, 690.

Evers, C. & Massar, N. (2012) IIIviri iure dicundo ponendum curaverunt. Réflexions sur quelques monuments du forum d'Alba Fucens. In J.Ch. Balty (ed.) *Belgica et Italica. Joseph Mertens: Une vie pour l'archéologie. Alba in excelso saxo. Obscura incultis Herdonia ab agris,* 113–128. Brussels-Rome, Institut historique belge de Rome.

Evers, C. & Massar, N. (2013) Découvertes archéologiques récentes à Alba Fucens. La zone sud-occidentale du forum. *Rendiconti della Pontificia Accademia Romana di Archeologia* 85, 295–313.

Evers, C. & Massar, N. (2014) *Fasti Albenses:* il contesto archeologico. In R. Paris, S. Bruni & M. Roghi (eds) *Rivoluzione Augusto. L'imperatore che riscrisse il tempo e la città,* 86–89. Rome-Milan, Electa.

Evers, C., Massar, N. & Vrielynck, O. (2013) Alba Fucens (Massa d'Alba, AQ). South-western side of the Forum. Campaign 2010. *Quaderni di Archeologia d'Abruzzo* 2, 475–478.

Galadini, F. (2006) Le evidenze del terremoto tardoantico. In A. Campanelli (ed.) *Poco grano molti frutti. 50 anni di archeologia ad Alba Fucens,* 130–139. Rome, Academia Belgica – Brussels, Musées Royaux d'Art et d'Histoire. Chieti – Sulmona, Synapsi edizioni..

Galadini, F. (2013) Il Piano della Civita pre-Alba Fucens. Indicazioni da sondaggi geognostici nel settore meridionale dell'area archeologica. *Rendiconti della Pontificia Accademia Romana di Archeologia* 85, 279–293.

Galadini, F. (2022) Ruins and remains as a background: natural catastrophes, abandonment of medieval villages, and the perspective of civilization during the 20th century in the central Apennines (Abruzzi Region, Central Italy). *Sustainability* 14.15, 1–43.

Galadini, F., Ceccaroni, E., Falcucci, E. & Gori, S. (2012) Le fasi di colluviamento tardoantiche nel Piano della Civita e la fine della frequentazione dell'abitato di Alba Fucens. In J.Ch. Balty (ed.) *Belgica et Italica. Joseph Mertens: Une vie pour l'archéologie. Alba in excelso saxo. Obscura incultis Herdonia ab agris,* 187–199. Brussels-Rome, Institut historique belge de Rome.

Greco, E. & Theodorescu, D. (1987) *Poseidonia – Paestum III. Forum nord.* Rome, École française de Rome.

Gros, P. (1996) *L'architecture romaine. Du début du IIIe siècle av. J.-C. à la fin du Haut-Empire. 1. Les monuments publics.* Paris, Picard.

Gros, P. (2001) *L'architecture romaine. Du début du IIIe siècle av. J.-C. à la fin du Haut-Empire. 2. Maisons, palais, villas et tombeaux.* Paris, Picard.

Guidobaldi, F., D'Amico, A., Lugari, A., Guzzo, P.G. & Guidobaldi, M.P. (2014) *Mosaici antichi in Italia: Regione prima Ercolano.* Pisa, Fabrizio Serra editore.

Lackner, E.-M. (2008) *Republikanische Fora.* München, Biering und Brinckmann.

Letta, C. (1994) Rileggendo le fonti antiche sul Fucino. In E. Burri & A. Campanelli (eds) *Sulle rive della memoria. Il lago Fucino e il suo emissario,* 202–212. Pescara, Carsa edizioni.

Letta, C. (2012a) Museo del Fucino in Avezzano – Il Lapidario. Schede. In F. De Sanctis, R Del Monaco, A. Saragosa & D. Villa (eds) *L'Aia dei Musei,* 16–46. Avezzano, Associazione Culturale Antiqua.

Letta, C. (2012b) Il Collegium ararum luciarum di Alba Fucens: un'eco della morte di Lucio Cesare? In H. Solin (ed.) *Le epigrafi della Valle di Comino. Atti dell'ottavo convegno epigrafico cominese,* 89–103. San Donato Val di Comino, Associazione 'Genesi'.

Letta, C. (2013) Prime osservazioni sui Fasti Albenses. *Rendiconti della Pontificia Accademia Romana di Archeologia* 85, 315–335.

Letta, C. (2014) *Fasti Albenses.* In R. Paris, S. Bruni & M. Roghi (eds) *Rivoluzione Augusto. L'imperatore che riscrisse il tempo e la città,* 80–85. Rome-Milan, Electa.

Letta, C. (2019) Mutamenti istituzionali nei municipi dell'Itali nella prima età imperiale: il duovirato a Marruvium e l'emissario claudiano del Fucino. In N.J. Andrade, C. Marcaccini, G. Marconi & D. Violante (eds) *Roman Imperial Cities in the East and in Central-Southern Italy,* 349–363. Rome, L'Erma di Bretschneider.

Letta, C. (2021) L'epigrafia di *Marsi* ed *Aequi* nel Supplementum di *CIL* IX. *Epigraphica* 83, 259–269.

Liberatore, D. (2004) *Alba Fucens: studi di storia e di topografia.* Bari, Edipuglia.

Liberatore, D. (2018) Bolli dell'officina di Q. Naevius (Hybrida?) a Alba Fucens. *Zeitschrift für Papyrologie und Epigraphik* 206, 241–254.

Lugli, G. (1957) *La tecnica edilizia romana. Con particolare riguardo a Roma e Lazio.* Rome, G. Bardi.

Mertens, J. (1968) Il foro di Alba Fucens. *Notizie degli Scavi di Antichità* 22, 205–217.

Mertens, J. (1969) (ed.) *Alba Fucens I. Rapports et études.* Brussels, Institut historique belge de Rome; Rome, Academia Belgica.

Mertens, J. (1977) La stratigraphie et l'évolution planimétrique du centre monumental d'Alba Fucens et de *Herdoniae.* In P.-M. Duval & Ed. Frézouls (eds) *Thèmes de recherches sur les villes antiques d'Occident,* 253–264. Paris, Éditions du Centre Nationale de la Recherche Scientifique.

Mertens, J. (1981) *Alba Fucens di Massa d'Albe. 30 anni dopo.* Brussels, Centre belge de recherches archéologiques en Italie centrale et méridionale.

Mertens, J. (1988) Alba Fucens. *Dialoghi di Archeologia* 3.6.2, 87–104.

Mertens, J. (1991) Alba Fucens: à l'aube d'une colonie romaine. *Journal of Ancient Topography* 1, 93–112.

Nuzzo, E. (2010) Subtilitas Phlegrea. Nota sulla formazione del linguaggio architetonico a Cuma in età augustea. *Mélanges de l'École française de Rome. Antiquité* 122.2, 377–398.

Olevano, F. (2001) Per un studio tipologico delle pavimentazioni a lastre marmoree omogenee. In A. Paribeni (ed.) *Atti del VII colloquio dell'Associazione italiana per lo studio e la conservazione del mosaico,* 549–555. Ravenna, Edizioni del Girasole.

Olevano, F. (2005) Pavimenti a lastre marmoree omogenee da Pompei ed Ercolano. In C. Angelelli (ed.) *Atti del X colloquio dell'Associazione italiana per lo studio e la conservazione del mosaico,* 137–146. Tivoli, Scripta Manent.

Pensabene, P. (2019) Alba Fucens: il reimpiego a S.Pietro e le 'normalizzazioni' dell'ordine corinzio in età augustea e nel medioevo. *BABESCH. Annual Papers on Mediterranean Archaeology* 94, 161–182.

Pesando, F. (2012) Nuove ricerche nell'isolato della Domus di Via del Miliario. In J.Ch. Balty (ed.) *Belgica et Italica. Joseph Mertens: Une vie pour l'archéologie. Alba in excelso saxo. Obscura incultis Herdonia ab agris,* 201–211. Brussels-Rome, Institut historique belge de Rome.

Rose, D. (2018) *Studi sull'opera poligonale tra alta Valle del Salto e Fucino. L'acquedotto e la cloaca maxima di Alba Fucens.* Rome, Quasar.

Russo, G., Ceccaroni, E., Conte, A.M., Medeghini, L., De Vito, C. & Mignardi, S. (2022) Archaeometric study on Roman painted terracottas from the Sanctuary of Hercules in Alba Fucens (Abruzzo, Italy). *Minerals* 12, 346, 1–12.

Strazzulla, M.J. (2006) Agli inizi della ricerca. In A. Campanelli (ed.) *Poco grano molti frutti. 50 anni di archeologia ad Alba Fucens,* 35–39. Rome, Academia Belgica – Brussels, Musées Royaux d'Art et d'Histoire. Chieti – Sulmona, Synapsi edizioni.

Strazzulla, M.J., Di Cesare, R. & Liberatore, D. (2012) Alba Fucens: saggi di scavo nel settore sud-orientale dela foro. In J.Ch. Balty (ed.) *Belgica et Italica. Joseph Mertens: Une vie pour l'archéologie. Alba in excelso saxo. Obscura incultis Herdonia ab agris,* 161–186. Brussels-Rome, Institut historique belge de Rome.

Tansey, P. (2018) *Notabilia Varia* in the *Fasti* of Alba Fucens. *Studi Classici e Orientali* 64, 199–269.

Van Wonterghem, Fr. (1983) La Via Valeria nel territorio di Alba Fucens. *Acta Archaeologica Lovaniensia* 22, 3–38.

Van Wonterghem, Fr. (1991) La viabilità antica nei territori di Alba Fucens e Carseoli. *Il Fucino e le aree limitrofe nell'antichità,* 423–440. Avezzano, Archeoclub d'Italia.

Vrielynck, O. (2017) Le réseau d'égouttage antique d'Alba Fucens (Italie, Abruzzes): recherches archéologiques 2010–2015. *Bulletin de la Société Spéléologique de Namur*, 46–59.

Vrielynck, O., Dulière, E. & Denis, M. (2013) Alba Fucens (Massa d'Albe, AQ). Recherches sur les égouts. *Quaderni di Archeologia d'Abruzzo* 2, 488–492.

Vrielynck, O., Denis, M. & Funcken, L. (2015) Alba Fucens (Massa d'Albe, AQ). Le réseau d'égouttage, campagnes 2012 et 2013. *Quaderni di Archeologia d'Abruzzo* 5, 97–98.

Wilson Jones, M. (2000) *Principles of Roman Architecture.* New Haven and London, Yale University Press.

Wohlmayr, W. (2004) *Kaisersaal. Kultanlagen der Augustalen und munizipale Einrichtungen für das Herrscherhaus in Italien.* Wien, Phoibos Verlag.

### Website References

EDCS: https://db.edcs.eu [accessed 29 January 2023]
EDR: http://www.edr-edr.it [accessed 29 January 2023]
HD: https://edh.ub.uni-heidelberg.de [accessed 29 January 2023]
LSA: http://laststatues.classics.ox.ac.uk [accessed 29 January 2023]

# Part III

Not your standard Roman town

# Chapter 8

# From sanctuary to settlement: mapping the development of Lucus Feroniae through geophysical prospection

*Stephen Kay, Sophie Hay & Christopher Smith*

## 8.1 Introduction

This paper presents the results of a new study of the site of Lucus Feroniae (Capena, Lazio) through geophysical prospection. The research builds on a long-term study of Roman urbanism in central Italy through non-invasive survey techniques led by the British School at Rome which commenced with the investigation of Falerii Novi (Keay *et al.* 2000) and Otricoli (Hay *et al.* 2013) as part of the Roman Towns Project. Subsequently, the research extended to include earlier Etruscan centres including Vulci (Sabatini *et al.* 2021), Acquarossa and Spina (Kay *et al.* 2020). On the left bank of the River Tiber, centres were investigated in the Sabina (Forum Novum) as well as in the Abruzzo, with an extensive survey of Iuvanum and smaller-scale investigations of Peltuinum (Hay 2015) and Alba Fucens (Hay 2014). The surveys used a variety of non-destructive techniques, principally geophysical prospection, as a means to examine and develop an understanding of a wide range of urban sites, aiming to investigate and challenge some of the traditional models of ancient urban planning.

The fieldwork at Lucus Feroniae was undertaken over the course of three seasons (June 2013, May 2015, and March 2017), comprising an extensive magnetometry survey of areas within the modern archaeological park and immediately to its south and west (Fig. 8.1). These results were then used to direct more detailed Ground-Penetrating Radar (GPR) surveys, initially with two test areas within the modern park and subsequently a large area to the south.

Situated within the modern-day *Provincia di Roma*, approximately 28 km to the north of Rome, the town of Lucus Feroniae falls within the *ager Capenas*. The site was first discovered in 1953 and subsequently investigated by the *Soprintendenza Archeologia, Belle Arti e Paesaggio per l'area metropolitana di Roma, la Provincia di Viterbo e l'Etruria Meridionale*. The site lies in an open area which gradually slopes east towards

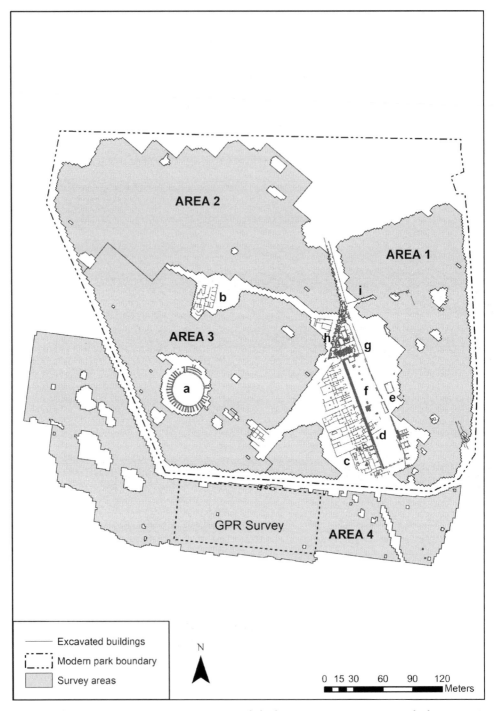

*Figure 8.1. The survey areas at Lucus Feroniae and the known monuments: A. Amphitheatre; B. 'Via Capenate baths'; C. 'forum baths'; D. Hellenistic structures; E. Altar to Feronia; F. forum; G. basilica; H. Augusteum and Republican temple; I. temenos.*

the Tiber flood plain and the river beyond. A series of hills rise to the northwest (Mt S. Lorenzo, Mt Ruzzola, Mt Belvedere), with access to the north limited by a complex of ridges that lie beyond modern day Fiano Romano (Jones 1962, 189). Approximately 8 km to its north runs the Fosso Pantanelle, flowing from the base of Mt Belvedere southeastwards onto the Tiber flood plain, and to the south flows the Fosso di Gramiccia. The town itself lies at an important intersection between the 'Via Capenate' and 'Via Tiberina'. Today a large portion of the land surrounding the site is agricultural, with most of those areas surveyed now open grassland, although to the east much was lost during the construction of the *Autostrada del Sole*.

## 8.2. Historical background

Lucus Feroniae has a deep but interrupted history (Russo Tagliente *et al.* 2016; Benedettini & Moretti Sgubini 2019; also Gazzetti 1992; Torelli *et al.* 2018). The discovery of the earliest cremation necropolis in southern Etruria, with 12 individuals for the 13th and 12th centuries BC, raises important questions about the way this site operated in the economy of the late Bronze Age (Trucco *et al.* 2014; also Fuminante 2014), and the extent to which any notion of the importance of the site may have survived into the next phase of activity which is visible in the archaeological record, from the 6th to 4th centuries BC.

Unfortunately, all this material is found in disturbed contexts, so detail is missing. Small fragments of architectural terracottas suggest the possibility of the built environment. Standard and miniature pottery, especially relating to food and perfume, including imports from western Greece, Attica and Etruria, terracotta figures, and bronze figurines from northern and southern Etruria, Umbria, and Latium, all suggest a sanctuary site, and one which attracted worshippers from some distance, or at the least, attracted those who had the capacity to acquire goods from a distance. The bronzes included a deer, a haruspex, a warrior, individuals in the pose of offering, and *kouros* and *kore* figures. There were also personal ornaments including ones produced as far afield as the Balkans and Near East. Similar finds have been made in Falerii Veteres. There are numerous connections also with the Abruzzo and Adriatic coast (Russo Tagliente *et al.* 2016, 23–26).

Both architectural and votive evidence, again scattered, shows an increase in activity in the 3rd century BC. It would appear that the sanctuary was significantly wealthy (see Torelli *et al.* 2018). This may have attracted one of the most famous incidents in the history of the sanctuary, a sack by Hannibal's troops in 211 BC. Livy (26.11.8–10) tells us that the sanctuary contained much gold and silver, dedicated by the people of nearby Capena and surrounding peoples, who offered their first-fruits. The importance of the sanctuary is also indicated in a passage of Dionysius of Halicarnassus (3.32.1–3). Although perhaps anachronistically placed in the reign of Tullus Hostilius, Dionysius claims that the sanctuary was a meeting point for Romans and Sabines, that it gathered merchants, artisans and farmers, and its fairs were the most celebrated in Italy. Epigraphical attestations also survive on bases of dedications, and it seems clear that pottery (especially *vernice nera*) was being produced on the site for dedication and export, as well as arriving from further afield. Also visible on site is coinage, especially from Campania, along with rings and seals, some dating back to early phases of the site (Russo Tagliente *et al.* 2016, 29–70).

The sack was highly profitable, but seems to have elicited some religious concerns. Livy (13.83–91) says that out of religious concern, the soldiers left heaps of bronze behind; Silius Italicus (*Pun.* 13.81–93) reports that Hannibal forced the soldiers to despoil the site (the story was clearly told by Coelius Antipater: FRHist 15 F25). A bronze *brocca*, found in a tomb in Capena, dedicated to Numisius Martius, has been thought to be an example of such abandoned booty (Ferrante 2008). As an omen of the following year showed, the sanctuary cannot have been totally destroyed, since Livy (27.4.14–15) reports the portent of statues sweating blood. Early 2nd-century BC architectural terracottas provide evidence for the rebuilding or restoration of the temple, which was struck by lightning in 196 BC (Livy 33.26.8).

It is likely that much of the archaic structure of the site disappeared in a major restructuring in the 2nd century BC, which created a substantial area of regular building not far from the temple. Local stone was used in *opus incertum*. Who was living here? Food containers with inscribed individual names, all male, might suggest cult personnel, but this phase remains obscure (Russo Tagliente *et al.* 2016, 71–74).

Later in the 2nd century BC, Lucus Feroniae experienced another substantial transformative moment, with a major reconstruction which was funded by one Cnaeus Egnatius, who left a major inscription on the site, probably relating to the repaving of the area. This reconstruction produced a new temple on a substantial podium with an octastyle portico in the Corinthian order. This sits within a large piazza of three *actus* in size (3/8 of a hectare), which is set within the road network around the site, notably the *via Campana*, which also passes through the grove of Dea Dia (Scheid 1976).

The Egnatius who was the dedicator of this complex was styled praetor, and it is possible to identify him with Cn. Egnatius praetor in the mid-140s BC, who served in Macedonia, and was a signatory to a *senatus consultum* relating to Corcyra (SEG III 451). That inscription tells us that he belonged to the Stellatina tribe, which included nearby Capena (Taylor 1960, 275; Brennan 2000, 225).

However, the Egnatian complex appears to have been left unfinished and possibly spoliated, perhaps in the course of the battles between Marius and Sulla. A colony was placed here and has been most recently dated by Stanco to the early 1st century BC, although its name, Colonia Julia Felix Lucoferensis shows it also received a veteran colony of the triumviral period (Keppie 1983). Nearby centuriation will be associated with one or other phase of this colonial settlement. Its first magistrates may have been the *duoviri quinquennales* C. Didius and M. Vettius, whose inscription is found on a reused votive base (CIL I 3338b = AE 1983 401). In architectural terms we see a new *forum*, a *sacellum* of Salus Frugifera, and a *basilica*, which may have used columns from the temple of Feronia.

The Egnatian family's commitment to the sanctuary, whether or not this relates to an early 1st century BC putative colony, may also have been commemorated in coinage from 75 BC by C. Egnatius Maximus. Crawford identified a female figure on the coins as Libertas with a *pileus*, but the recent interpretation would favour Feronia, who does appear, but named, on early Augustan coins by the low-born Turpilianus (Crawford 1975, 405–406; on Turpilianus see Wallace-Hadrill 1986, 78). The Egnatii survived the Sullan period, but were destroyed in Octavian's proscriptions, and it is very likely that at this stage the nearby villa passed from this family to the Volusii. Marzano suggests that one of the main operations of the Volusii may have been the production of lime, and a large lime production area was indeed found just 1 km away (Marzano 2007). Another aspect of the economy of the site is the port at Baciletti, probably the portus Curensis, which offered a connection to the Tiber.

That the triumviral or post-Actium colony provoked controversy is evident from a passage in the writings of the Roman land surveyors, where Julius Frontinus notes flaws in the maps (*Lib. Colon.* T 37–38).

The Augustan period sees another restructuring of the area, with a new pavement, walkways, honorific statues, a small temple of Salus, and a *sacellum* to the *Genius Coloniae*. The Egnatian inscription is covered over. Stanco (2016) notes the decline in inscriptions to Feronia, and suggests that the cult was in terminal decline, replaced by Salus Frugifera and the imperial cult. Interestingly, the road system remains core to the urban layout. A dam and aqueduct ensured the supply of water.

After the death of Augustus, the Volusii marked their gratitude with a temple to the Divus Augustus on the site of the building which had possibly been the *basilica*. Their own villa was intimately connected to the larger site, but it was not the only one in the area, and all were clearly productive, starting in the later 2nd century BC, and renovated around the time of Actium (Russo Tagliente *et al.* 2016; doubts over the hypothesis of an ergastulum at the Villa of the Volusii have been raised by Marzano 2007, 140–148).

The complicated imperial history of the site sees various interventions, for instance under Caligula and Trajan, which can be traced in the significant remains of sculpture, largely of the imperial family. The site acquires two sets of baths which continue into Late Antiquity, and a Trajanic-Hadrianic amphitheatre. In the 3rd century AD, two ornamental entrances are created for *ludi iuvenum Romanorum Lucoferoniensium* (Stanco 2016). These games included ones associated with the birthday of Rome, 21 April. However, the inhabited area of the town which had flourished between the 1st and 2nd centuries AD, with some impressive mosaics and the enrichment of significant villas around the site, including the Villa of the Volusii, begins to decline, possibly as agricultural production is concentrated in the imperially owned Fundus Flavianus (Russo Tagliente *et al.* 2016). Restorations are scarce, and the area is gradually abandoned between the 4th and 6th centuries AD, although there was a short-lived Christian community there, who may have repurposed public buildings as churches, with nearby tombs. No bishopric was ever founded, and the community seems to have moved to the nearby Castellum Scoranum (Gazzetti 1992).

## 8.3. The Cult of Feronia

Varro clearly attributes Feronia to a group of Sabine deities (Varro *Ling.* 5.74; Di Fazio 2012, 2013). Schulze insisted on the Etruscan aspect of the cult, but this was part of his over-emphasis on the Etruscans throughout (Schulze 1904). However, it was also an ancient idea; Cato the Elder (FRHist 5 F69) claimed the cult was founded by young men sent to Capena from Veii (even though his name, Propertius, is Umbrian). In fact, the cult is widely spread across a wide swathe of central Italy up to the head of the Adriatic in one direction and across to Sardinia in the other. Feronia was also celebrated in the Campus Martius at Rome, where she was adopted by the later 3rd century BC (even though the cult of Feronia may have been 'evoked', some effective doubts have been raised by Stek 2009, 31; see also Di Fazio 2013, 20–23). Her cult outside Rome is said to be as old as the Roman kings, but certainly continues well into the empire. Her characteristics are highly varied. She is often found paired with a male deity, and it is possible we see a divine couple, Jupiter Feretrius and Juno Feronia. At some point, Feronia is associated with slaves and freedom – slaves were set free in her shrine near Terracina (Serv. *Aen.* 8.564). This has led to the identification of female figures with the *pileus* as Feronia, critically on coinage (par. 8.2).

Aside from these considerations, it appears that Feronia tended to be worshipped in groves and associated with sanctuaries with wide audiences. If this is correct, we can think about the possibility of Feronia having roles related to commerce and boundaries, at any rate, to general principles which allow this divinity to be assimilated to cults across the marketplaces of Italy. At this point the argument becomes somewhat speculative and theological.

For our purposes the most significant issue perhaps is to ask what kind of settlement Lucus Feroniae was. Its function as a meeting place, and the accumulation of wealth in the sanctuary seems directly related to the worship of Feronia, though we perhaps should see this as a symbiotic relationship. We cannot trace elite appropriation of the sanctuary before the Egnatian phase in the later 2nd century BC, but from this point onwards, the singular importance of Feronia to the site seems to be at least diluted and possibly in rapid decline. Conversely, the space becomes open for other display, both religious and secular. The role of Lucus Feroniae as a centre for games associated closely with Rome may be taken to track deeper shifts in the expression of how a node of interaction might work.

## 8.4. The geophysical surveys

Over the course of the three field seasons, magnetometry and GPR survey were carried out covering those areas accessible both within the archaeological park and directly surrounding it to the south and southwest. A local grid system was established using a Total Station and GPS, delineating a series of 30 × 30 m grids orientated at an approximate 45° angle to the excavated structures. The magnetometry survey was conducted using two Bartington Grad601 dual probe fluxgate gradiometers, with data collected at a sample interval of 0.25 m along 0.5 m traverse intervals. A GPS was used to record local topography and to accurately map the excavated roads and structures. The GPR survey was used to target areas where the results of the magnetometry were either unclear or where they suggested a deeper, more complex stratigraphy. It was undertaken using a GSSI SIR 3000 with a single channel 400 MHz antenna, with data collected at traverse intervals of 0.25 m. Two small test areas within the archaeological park were initially surveyed followed by a larger area outside of the park to the south, covering approximately 1 ha.

### 8.4.1. Magnetometry survey

The magnetometry survey at Lucus Feroniae covered an area of 12.5 ha (Fig. 8.2). The features are described by area (Fig. 8.1) in the section below, as a range of subsurface anomalies were recorded across the study area.

#### 8.4.1.1. Eastern area (Area 1)

Situated along the eastern limits of the modern archaeological park, directly to the east of the forum and the 'Via Tiberina', Area 1 covered approximately one fifth of the total area surveyed (Fig. 8.1). Despite several areas of localised magnetic disturbance to the north and east, the results of the magnetometry were generally clear, with a series of archaeological features identified across the area (Fig. 8.2).

Starting in the north of Area 1, of particular interest are two groups of strong, parallel positive anomalies within fairly distinct regions, each displaying a series of regular and evenly distributed circular positive anomalies between them. The first area, situated directly to the east of the 'Via Tiberina' and appearing to respect the northern limits of the sanctuary, contains a series of 15 positive linear anomalies running approximately northeast–southwest (Fig. 8.3: 1). Each of these anomalies is approximately 0.9 m in width, occurring at regular intervals of *c.* 5 m. Given their signal strength and nature, these anomalies almost certainly represent filled cuts in the underlying shallow bedrock. The circular positive anomalies, measuring approximately 1 m in diameter and occurring at regular intervals of *c.* 6 m between these linear features, probably also represent cuts in the bedrock. The second region, separated from the first by an area of *c.* 5 m devoid of features (possibly a trackway), has a similar arrangement of linear and circular positive anomalies. The linear features, orientated northwest–southeast and at intervals of approximately 2.7 m, measure *c.* 0.6 m in width. The positive circular anomalies measuring approximately 0.8 m in diameter and occurring at intervals of *c.* 1.5 m between these linear anomalies, may again represent filled circular cuts.

A possible interpretation for the series of trenches and pits visible in the data across these two regions is agricultural activity. In terms of chronology, it would appear that the features respect a large rectilinear feature directly to the south and west. Measuring approximately 23 × 127 m and running parallel to the *forum*, this feature perhaps represents a part of the sanctuary. Similarly, to the south of these, two

Key

⌐ ¬
⌐ _ ¬ Lucus Feroniae archaeology park

──── Excavated Structures

nT/m
+

0   30   60      120
                    Metres

N

B _ S _ R
BRITISH SCHOOL
AT ROME

*Figure 8.2. Magnetometry survey of Lucus Feroniae.*

*Figure 8.3. Schematic interpretation of the Magnetometry survey.*

parallel linear anomalies (Fig. 8.3: 2) have a north–south alignment and are associated with an area of magnetic disturbance. From a study of archival photographs and documentation, these appear to relate to a pathway or railway line installed during the 20th century excavations at the site, leading to a spoil heap. At the southern end of this feature, a cistern, also recorded during 20th-century excavations, is visible in the results (Fig 8.3: 3), possibly connected to a wider network of water channels which extends to the north and west. A series of structures were recorded immediately to the east of the temple and altar, even though the disturbance from the excavations and the dumping of spoil has masked some of the features (a fence around the area prevented the extension of the survey). Finally, at the very southern extent of the survey, the magnetometry recorded a series of buildings clustered around the southeast corner of the forum (Fig. 8.3: 4).

### 8.4.1.2. Northern area (Area 2)

Situated to the north of the 'Via Capenate' the area comprises approximately 3 ha and lies between the northern edge of the modern archaeological park and the partially excavated road (Figs 8.1 and 8.2). The continuation of the 'Via Capenate' is clearly visible running east–west across the western part of the survey area (Fig. 8.3: 5), continuing beyond the archaeological park as evidenced by aerial photographs of the site. As in Area 1, an area of probable agricultural activity can be identified, taking the form of a series of parallel positive linear anomalies likely again representing trenches dug into the bedrock (Fig. 8.3: 6).

Of particular interest in relation to these areas of agricultural activity are a series of possible cisterns located across Area 2 (Fig. 8.3: 7). Several features appear to be directly connected to a series of negative linear anomalies radiating outwards at approximate right angles to the features, similar to those seen in Area 1. It is possible that these anomalies relate to an irrigation system linked to the agricultural activity, although since they appear to cut across the area of cultivation activity this may indicate that they post-date the agricultural trenches.

The majority of this area appears devoid of any distinct structures, with just a grouping of features at the junction of the 'Via Capenate' and 'Via Tiberina', close to the Augusteum. The final anomaly of interest (Fig. 8.3: 8) is recorded as a strong, rectangular positive anomaly. It may represent a cistern or a large solid foundation; the internal area has a lower magnetic field at the centre, perhaps indicating a change in construction material.

### 8.4.1.3. Central area (Area 3)

Situated to the south of the 'Via Capenate' between the *forum* and the southern and southwestern limits of the archaeological park, Area 3 constitutes approximately 25% of the total area surveyed. The results in Area 3 display a higher degree of disturbance caused by modern activity – most notably to the south of the 'Capenate baths' and to the west of the amphitheatre, most likely related to spoil from excavations. Multiple dipolar striations are also visible running approximately northwest–southeast across this area, again most likely linked to modern agricultural activity at the site. The most significant features in the results from this area are the predominantly negative linear anomalies identified in the eastern part of Area 3. Extending south from the 'Via Capenate' is a strong double negative anomaly (Fig. 8.3: 9), probably walls, which appear to delineate a series of divided open spaces backing onto an area of intense building activity identified in the magnetometry results flanking the 'Via Tiberina'. Within this area of activity, various positive and negative linear anomalies have been identified, probably representing the continuation of domestic structures that radiate out from the *forum*. Of particular interest are two dipolar anomalies in two of these open spaces, similar in form and signal strength to kilns. It may also be possible, therefore, that these open spaces were used for production.

The southeastern corner of Area 3 was less affected by modern activity at the site and is dominated by a large rectilinear structure (Fig. 8.3: 10) measuring approximately 22 × 12m. The structures appear to continue beyond the eastern limit of the survey expanding outwards from the *forum* area.

### 8.4.1.4. Southern area (Area 4)

Area 4 covers approximately one quarter of the total area surveyed. Large parts of this area were inaccessible during data collection due to thick vegetation and high levels of surface water. There was also a substantial quantity of modern interference in this area, relating to abandoned construction work, archaeological excavations, and refuse disposal.

The central section of Area 4 contains a wealth of previously unknown archaeological features, revealing the continuation of the 'Via Tiberina' (Fig. 8.3: 11) and a further two possible roads branching off the 'Via Tiberina'. A large number of rectilinear features are visible along both roadsides, and given their form most likely represent domestic structures, suggesting a reasonably dense occupation through the central part of this area. In general, the strong negative linear anomalies appear to represent walls whilst the positive anomalies within the groups of these negative linear features may represent floor surfaces or accumulation of fired material such as roof tiles.

From an interpretation of the anomalies, it is possible to identify a number of potential separate structures which extend away from the central road. Several groups of individual rooms are identifiable through a number of interconnecting features (Fig. 8.3: 12). Of further interest, however, are a series of four, parallel, negative linear anomalies to the east of the 'Via Tiberina', measuring 11 to 29 m in length and orientated approximately northwest–southeast. The appearance of these anomalies and the relatively quiet nature of the open areas between them, are similar to the anomalies identified in the eastern part of Area 3. It is possible, therefore, that these linear features represent similar dividing structures designed to demarcate individual open spaces such as gardens, courtyards or areas utilised for some form of production.

### 8.4.2. *Ground-penetrating radar survey*

Following the initial magnetometry survey in 2013, two small test areas of targeted GPR survey were conducted within the park in 2015 to compare with the results of the magnetometry as well as to apply GPR in an area where there was significant magnetic disturbance. The technique offers an increased resolution, as well as being less affected by ambient noise, and the possibility to assess anomalies at a range of depths. The data were collected in a regular series of parallel traverses at a distance of 0.25 m with varying lengths. The test grids provided useful additional detail to the magnetometry, in particular in the area towards the *forum* where spoil had been deposited from previous excavations.

The magnetometry survey immediately to the south of the archaeological park indicated a dense occupation alongside the 'Via Tiberina' leading south from the *forum*. Following the tests within the park, a central area of 143 × 60 m was therefore investigated with GPR. The results indicate a complex range of interlocking features that appear to define elements of an urban settlement focused around an area approximately 80 m wide that runs in a northeast–southwest direction. The results of the GPR survey indicate an approximate depth of features ranging 0.3 to 1 m, after which there is the underlying bedrock.

The majority of the high amplitude anomalies indicate brick or stone-built walls that suggest a substantial level of preservation. In a central area, a feature in the magnetometry results is shown in greater clarity and linearity (Fig. 8.4: 1), suggesting a square form, perhaps a central courtyard with a number of regular adjacent rooms.

Of particular interest are five long parallel features (Fig. 8.4: 2) aligned in a southeast direction away from the central concentration of features. These also coincided with features recorded by the magnetometry. The regularity and amplitude of these features suggests a solid construction, even though the features do not appear to join to the east. It is possible that these are some form of land division as noted elsewhere in the hinterland of Lucus Feroniae (Gazzetti 2016, 145). Other regular features were recorded by the GPR in the central eastern area indicating an orientation along a secondary road leading to the northwest (Fig. 8.4: 3).

The GPR anomalies that are described are in the central part of the survey area with relatively few features recorded either to the east or west, suggesting a concentration alongside the central road that traverses the survey area.

## 8.5. The sacred woodland

The combined geophysical surveys at Lucus Feroniae have revealed previously unknown large parts of the site, tracing a settlement that appears to stretch along the principal throughfares and which is centred around the sanctuary and *forum*.

An element of particular interest are the regularly spaced anomalies (Fig. 8.3: 1) to the immediate north of the excavated temple and altar. The proximity to the sacred

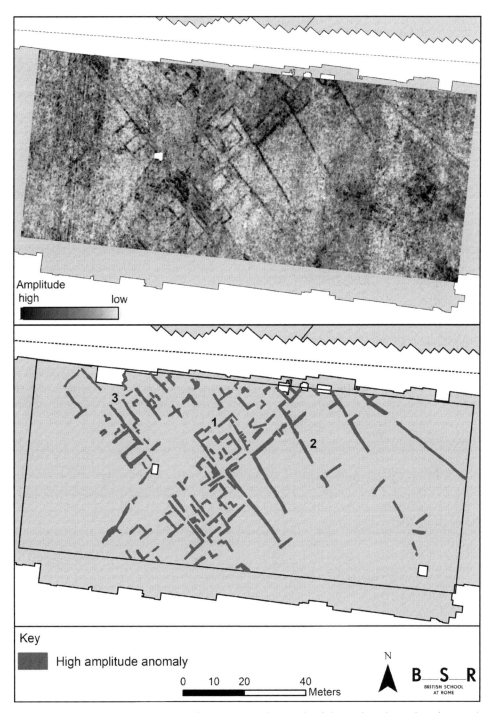

Figure 8.4. The Ground-Penetrating Radar survey to the south of the archaeological park: GPR data at an estimated depth of 0.5 m (top) and interpretation of high amplitude features (bottom).

area and the lack of construction, especially in an area close to the 'Via Tiberina', are perhaps indicators that the area was respected in antiquity. The form of the geophysical anomalies has parallels with agricultural activity, with the long features potentially filled trenches and the circular cuts filled pits suggesting the possibility of vine trenches and tree holes. This hypothesis is supported by nearby excavations on the 'Via Tiberina' (at km 19.5), where, together with 10 burials, 21 pits and 9 channels were identified, interpreted as pits for fruit trees and channels for irrigation (Di Nardo & Iorio 2016).

The distribution of these anomalies has very strong similarities with those of vine trenches. To the southeast of Rome, in the area of Tor Pagnotta, a large number of parallel trenches were excavated on the same northeast–southwest alignment, measuring 0.7–0.8 m in width and at distance of 3.7 m (Santangeli Valenzani & Volpe 1980). The features at Lucus Feroniae are similar in width (approximately 0.9 m) with a row separation of 5 m, still, however, greater than that indicated by Columella (*De arboribus* 4.3). There are few parallels with magnetometry surveys of these forms of features in central Italy, even though one example from nearby Musarna (Viterbo) recorded channels 0.85–0.95 m in width and at an average spacing of 6.6 m (Broise & Jolivet 1995). Whilst the width and spacing of the anomalies would appear to fit the hypothesis of a vineyard, these are also interspersed with regular circular features, interpreted as pits, measuring approximately 1 m. A hypothesis is that these are pits for trees cut into the bedrock, as recorded elsewhere near Lucus Feroniae (Di Nardo & Iorio 2016, 154). The spacing of these in a vineyard may reflect the use of interplanted cultivation with the planting of fruit trees or the arbustum technique where vines are intercropped with other plants and encouraged to climb tress (Dodd 2022, 453). One argument against the possible interpretation of this as a vineyard is that this area on the right bank of the Tiber was less suitable for the cultivation of vines (Santangeli Valenzani & Volpe 2012, 62), even though this may also reflect patterns of modern urban development and these features being recognised in the archaeological record.

A further aspect to consider regarding these geophysical anomalies is the proximity to the sanctuary of Lucus Feroniae. As noted above, Feronia tends to be associated with sacred woodlands and, indeed, trees had a sacred character in ancient Italic religions (Coarelli 1987). The interpretation as these features forming part of a sacred woodland around the sanctuary has been put forward by Del Lungo (2019), interpreting these geophysical features as part of a woodland around the temple. A parallel can be drawn with the *lucus* identified at the sanctuary of Jupiter at Gabii. Excavations around the temple identified 70 pits measuring 1.2 to 1.3 m (compared with 1 m at Lucus Feroniae). These have been interpreted as pits for fruit trees that formed a sacred woodland, whereas the *templum* was considered a free area in the centre of the woodland itself (Coarelli 1987).

## 8.6. The settlement of Lucus Feroniae

The settlement of Lucus Feroniae went through several phases of restructuring and urban development over the course of its history. From the initial foundation of the sanctuary in the 6th century BC (Russo Tagliente *et al.* 2016, 4) archaeological evidence attests major rebuilding in the 2nd century BC, as well as other interventions such as the repaving paid by Cnaeus Egnatius (par. 8.2). Following its designation to colony status in the early 1st century BC, further transformation is recorded in the Augustan period as well as later in the Trajanic-Hadrianic period (such as the amphitheatre), and even later with the construction of a bath complex in the Late Antique period. Whilst many of these phases may be recorded in the geophysical survey, these can only be untangled through excavation. However, it is clear that the settlement had a change, perhaps in the 1st century BC, shifting from the site of a sanctuary to the role of small town, a change tied to the worship of Feronia. However, despite this transition, the settlement appears to have maintained its original concentration along the two principal roads and, on the basis of the visible archaeological record and geophysics, appears to be dominated by public buildings with less private space, a phenomenon of small towns seen elsewhere in central Italy (for example Forum Novum, Amiternum, Iuvanum). From its origins as an Italic sanctuary, Lucus Feroniae appears to have later taken on the role of administrative centre with public buildings grouped around the *forum* and which served the needs of a dispersed population in the immediate hinterland. The geophysical survey results appear to indicate that the settlement was less dense beyond the excavated baths to the west along the 'Via Capenate'. Furthermore, previous field walking to the west also confirmed a lack of pottery scatters (Jones 1962, 196–197). However, several villas have been recorded in its immediate hinterland, one of which (Volusii Saturnini), built around 50 BC, appears to have belonged to Q. Volusius who, as previously noted, financed a temple to the Divus Augustus (Marzano 2007, 371). It would seem apparent therefore, at least by the early Imperial period, that the role of Lucus Feroniae had changed, as it served an economy centred around agricultural production with a small population living within the actual town.

## Acknowledgements

The survey at Lucus Feroniae was undertaken thanks to the kind permission of the *Soprintendenza Archeologia, Belle Arti e Paesaggio per l'area metropolitana di Roma, la Provincia di Viterbo e l'Etruria Meridionale* and supported by the then Soprintendente Dott.ssa Alfonsina Russo, as well as Dott. Gianfranco Gazzetti and Dott.ssa Francesca Guarneri. The surveys were generously funded by a grant from the De Hann Foundation to the British School at Rome. The geophysical surveys and earlier fieldwork reports, upon which this paper draws, were carried out by a joint team from the British School at Rome and the Archaeological Prospection Service of Southampton (APSS) including Matthew Berry, Sophie Hay, Alice James, Stephen Kay, and Eleanor Maw.

# Bibliography

Benedettini, M.G. & Moretti Sgubini, A.M. (2016) Il santuario capenate di Feronia la ripresa delle indagini. In A. Russo & F. Guarneri, F. (eds) *Santuari mediterranei tra Oriente e Occidente: interazioni e contatti culturali*, 171–180. Rome, Scienze e Lettere.

Brennan, T.C. (2000) *The Praetorship in the Roman Republic*. Oxford, Oxford University Press.

Broise, H. & Jolivet, V. (1995) Bonification agraire et viticulture antiques autour du site de Musarna (Viterbo). *Atlante Tematico di Topografia Antica* 4, 107–116.

Coarelli, F. (1987) *I santuari del Lazio in età repubblicana*. Rome, Nuova Italia Scientifica.

Crawford, M.H. (1975) *Roman Republican Coinage*. Cambridge, Cambridge University Press.

Del Lungo, S. (2019) Il *lucus* e il tempio: il destino di Lucus Feroniae tra tarda Antichità e alto Medioevo. Alcune questioni aperte. In M.G. Benedettini & A.M. Sgubini Moretti (eds) *Un grande santuario interetnico: Lucus Feroniae scavi 2000-2010*, 197–211. Pisa, Edizioni ETS.

Di Fazio, M. (2012) I luoghi di culto di Feronia. Ubicazioni e funzioni. *Annali della Fondazione per il Museo Claudio Faina* 19, 379–408.

Di Fazio, M. (2013) *Feronia. Spazi e tempi di una dea dell'Italia centrale antica*. Rome, Quasar.

Di Nardo I. & Iorio, V. (2016) Le necropoli. In A. Russo Tagliente, G. Ghini & L. Caretta (eds) *Lucus Feroniae. il santuario, la città, il territorio*, 153–154. Rome, Scienze e Lettere.

Dodd, E. (2022) The archaeology of wine production in Roman and pre-Roman Italy. *American Journal of Archaeology* 126.3, 443–480.

Ferrante, C. (2008) Una brocca di bronzo con dedica a Numisius Martius dalla necropoli delle Saliere a Capena. *Cahiers du Centre Gustave Glotz* 19, 7–25.

Fulminante, F. (2014) *The Urbanization of Rome and Latium. From the Bronze Age to the Archaic Era*. Cambridge, Cambridge University Press.

Gazzetti, G. (1992) *Il territorio capenate*. Rome, Quasar.

Gazzetti, G. (2016) Centuriazione e organizzazione del territorio. In A. Russo Tagliente, G. Ghini & L. Caretta (eds) *Lucus Feroniae. Il sanctuario, la citta, il territorio*, 145–148. Rome, Scienze e Lettere.

Hay, S. (2014) Geophysics projects. *Papers of the British School at Rome* 82, 324–327.

Hay, S. (2015) Geophysics projects. *Papers of the British School at Rome* 83, 294–298.

Hay, S., Keay, S. & Millett, M. (2013) *Ocriculum (Otricoli, Umbria): an Archaeological Survey of the Roman Town*. London, British School at Rome.

Jones, G.D.B. (1962) Capena and the Ager Capenas. *Papers of the British School at Rome* 30, 116–207.

Kay, S., Pomar, E. & Hay, S. (2020) Spina revisited: the 2008 geophysical prospection in the light of the excavation results. *GROMA Documenting Archaeology* 5, 1–16.

Keay, S., Millett, M., Poppy, S., Robinson, J., Taylor, J. & Terrenato, N. (2000) Falerii Novi: a new survey of the walled area. *Papers of the British School at Rome* 68, 1–95.

Keppie, L. (1983) *Colonisation and Veteran Settlement in Italy, 47-14 B.C.* London, British School at Rome.

Marzano, A. (2007) *Roman Villas in Central Italy. A Social and Economic History*. Leiden & Boston, Brill.

Russo Tagliente, A., Ghini, G. & Caretta, L. (eds) (2016) *Lucus Feroniae. Il santuario, la città, il territorio*. Rome, Scienze e Lettere.

Sabatini, S., Göransson, K., Gustavsson, A., Kay, S., Pomar, E., Selsvold, I. & Webb, L. (2021) History and archaeology at Vulci: old evidence and new data from a geophysical investigation in the urban area. *Bollettino di Archeologia On Line* 12, 5–33.

Santangeli Valenzani, R. & Volpe, R. (1980) Tentativo di ricostruzione di una sistemazione agricola di età repubblicana nei dintorni di Roma. *Archeologia Classica* 32, 206–215.

Santangeli Valenzani, R. & Volpe, R. (2012) Paesaggi agrari della viticoltura a Roma e nel suburbio. In A. Ciacci, P. Rendini & A. Zifferero (eds) *Archeologia della vite e del vino in Toscana e nel Lazio*, 61–69. Florence, All'Insegna del Giglio.

Scheid, J. (1976) Note sur la Via Campana. *Mélanges de l'École française de Rome. Antiquité* 88.2, 639–668.

Schulze, W. (1904) *Zur Geschichte lateinscher Eigennamen*. Berlin.

Stanco, E.A. (2016) 'Lucus Feroniae', Due Monumenti: Il 'Ponderarium' e Il 'Ludus Iuvenum.' *Zeitschrift Für Papyrologie Und Epigraphik* 200, 531–543.

Stek, T. D. (2009) *Cult Places and Cultural Change in Republican Italy: a Contextual Approach to Religious Aspects of Rural Society after the Roman Conquest.* Amsterdam, Amsterdam University Press.

Taylor, L.R. (1960) *The Voting Districts of the Roman Republic.* Rome, American Academy in Rome

Torelli, M., Moretti Sgubini, A.M., Benedettini, M.G., Serafin, P., Carini, A., Ligabue, G. & Perrone, N. (2018) Scavo negli anni Duemila nel santuario capenate di Feronia: un primo bilancio dello stato della ricerca. *Annali della Fondazione per il Museo Claudio Faina* 15, 125–136.

Trucco, F., D'Ercole, V. & Cavazzuti, C. (2014) L'introduzione del rito incineratorio in Etruria meridionale la necropoli dell'età del Bronzo recente di Lucus Feroniae. In R. Zaccagnini & L. Mercuri (eds) *Etruria in Progress: la ricerca archeologica in Etruria meridionale*, 24–29. Rome, Gangemi.

Wallace-Hadrill, A. (1986) Image and Authority in the Coinage of Augustus. *Journal of Roman Studies* 76, 66–87.

# Chapter 9

## Septempeda: integrated approaches for revealing a 'small town' in Picenum

### Frank Vermeulen

### 9.1. Introduction

Scholarly research of the past two decades has convincingly demonstrated that a substantial majority of towns in Roman Italy, with their roots in the mid- or late Republican period, probably measured less than 20 ha, and can thus be described as 'small towns'. While there was some urban growth in the Imperial period, these basic parameters of urbanism did not fundamentally change: most urban settlements in Roman Italy remained relatively small (de Ligt 2012; Flohr 2021, 40; broader discussion of this phenomenon in Sewell 2016; de Ligt and Bintliff 2019; Vermeulen 2023). Although criteria guiding the recognition or bestowal of 'town status' differ from period to period and from region to region, however small, the settlements considered here are, they functioned in principle during at least one period of their existence as urban entities with a form of civic autonomy. In terms of physical appearance some of the elements that should or could be present for a settlement to belong to this category, whatever its size, are: a defended urban core, an internal street network, distinctive functional zones, a range of building types (both private and public), elite housing, a range of workshops and some craft industry, forms of monumentality, various types of epigraphy, and large organised cemeteries. It is perhaps not recommended to propose a strict minimum size, as in most cases the archaeological record does not permit a reliable estimate of their exact size in a given period of time, nor of the number of houses which existed simultaneously during their heyday. Nevertheless, much enhanced topographical research on ancient urban centres with some form of continuity of life, as well as increasing use of modern techniques of urban survey on partly or fully abandoned town sites, are starting to be convincing regarding town size estimates and the full deciphering of the physical constituents of Roman cities. Especially greenfield sites, where the ancient Roman population had partly or often completely abandoned their original urban area to move to more secure locations elsewhere, have in recent years demonstrated to be very suited to a more holistic approach to ancient urbanism. The general refinement of landscape-based strategies, widely employing techniques such as geophysical prospections, aerial photography, remote sensing, and GIS-based topographic analysis, allows now the fine-grained cartography required to bring out the necessary details of full urban layouts of Roman towns in Italy (Keay *et al.* 2000; Guaitoli 2003; Johnson and Millett 2012; Vermeulen *et al.* 2012; Verdonck *et al.* 2020).

The wide variety of regional trajectories visible in the urbanism of Roman Italy, between mid-Republican times and the Early Empire, shows that the historical evolution of urban settlement systems and their great variety of urban forms, can only be understood by examining a whole series of region-specific factors. Climatic and environmental factors, economic relationships between cities and their hinterlands, hierarchical relationships between cities, and communication and interactions between cities belonging to the same regional system, all influence the chances for small towns to arise and survive. Determining factors such as the geographical distribution of agricultural or mineral resources, the connectivity of the area with the Mediterranean Sea or with navigable river systems, the density and quality of the road system or the specific ethnic and social composition of the autochthonous population before Roman dominance are all factors that influence the nature of the urban network further developed by Rome.

A good example of the resulting urban diversity within a specific regional context is the urban network and evolution in central-Adriatic Italy, where the ancient regions of the *ager Gallicus* (later 'Adriatic Umbria') and Picenum are located (Fig. 9.1). Today, quite satisfying and reliable information about urban site size and layout, and sometimes even early town development, can be found in a series of deserted towns in this region, where almost 50% of the Roman town sites were partly or totally abandoned or displaced after the Roman Imperial period. The strategy of extensive non-invasive survey was introduced here from 2002 onwards by a Ghent University team under my direction, in particular in the town sites of Potentia, Ricina, Trea and Septempeda (Vermeulen *et al.* 2017). The approach has since then been applied by several teams intensively surveying and studying abandoned Roman towns and their hinterlands in the region (e.g. Suasa, Ostra, Sentinum, Forum Sempronii, Tifernum Mataurense), which before 2000 were known only via a few excavated 'windows' in their sometimes ill-defined town areas. A whole series of these partially or fully abandoned Roman towns are now being uncovered via intensive total surveys, integrated into apposite excavations in carefully selected areas. Such well-integrated strategies mean that it is now not only possible to obtain good information about their size, general internal organisation, and functions during their heyday in the early Imperial period, but sometimes also to gain a better understanding of the early phases of town formation, and of certain changes and sometimes radical shifts in the urban development of these centres. One of the town centres, studied intensively over the past years, Septempeda, deserves further attention, as it might be a good case study for the phenomenon visible in a whole series of small towns spread over Italy, deviating somehow from the canonical model of the Roman town concept.

## 9.2. Septempeda, a road settlement disguised as a town

The site of Septempeda (within the modern province of Macerata, Marche) grew from its probable origin as a mid-Republican village into a Roman town along a *diverticulum* of the *via Flaminia* linking the consular road from Nocera Umbra through the valley of the River Potenza to Ancona and the Adriatic coast. The ancient Roman site is located at some 50 km inland from the Adriatic coast and lies directly north of the river, on a flattish to slightly sloping river terrace (Fig. 9.1). The former urban area also enclosed a small hill stretching immediately north of this terrace. Today arable land prevails here, as the site was abandoned in early medieval times and its remaining population moved to an upland location in nearby San Severino Marche. A small rural church and a few modern houses are the only constructions in the now legally protected archaeological park, whose limits coincide more or less with the abandoned Roman town area.

Excavations during the 20th century uncovered here an almost complete Imperial Roman bath complex, scanty remains of at least two Early Imperial *domus*, some stretches of the street system, and several elements of the town defences, including parts of the town wall, and two monumental gates in the southwest and east sides of the wall circuit (Landolfi 2003; Landolfi & Perna 2004). Late Republican and Imperial period finds near and outside the town walls comprise small groups of Roman burials located near the main outgoing roads west and east of the town centre and parts of a large pottery workshop outside the presumed western gate. Scant historical and written data on the origin of the agglomeration suggest that the core of this urban settlement was a roadside settlement, still called *oppidum* in the *Liber Coloniarum* (Blume *et al.* 1848, 253). When Roman and Latin colonists settled here in the late 3rd or early 2nd century BC, as a result of the *Lex Flaminia*, the place most likely received the status of *praefectura*, while it became a *municipium* only around the mid-1st century BC (Paci 1999; Sisani 2006). The recent archaeological investigations (below) show that status promotion was preceded a few decades earlier by the erection of a monumental town wall, incorporating the habitation nucleus near the river and the adjoining small hill into an enclosed irregular area of approximately 15 ha. The still ill-understood old settlement core along the east–west-oriented *via Flaminia per Picenum Anconam* certainly comprised a late Republican artisanal unit that produced black gloss ceramics, while certain reused architectonic decoration fragments found in the later bath complex suggest the existence of a late Republican sacred building nearby, perhaps to be identified with the temple for the goddess Feronia (CIL IX 5711; Landolfi 2003, 58–59). That one of the gates belonging to this wall, in the southwest of the town, was built over a series of 2nd century to early 1st century BC graves, demonstrates the spatial expansion of the settlement by the beginning of the last

*Figure 9.1. Septempeda located within the major network of Roman roads and towns in central Adriatic Italy during the Early Imperial period (D. Taelman).*

century before our era. It looks as if a former burial area was by this time incorporated in a now larger and better structured settlement with urban features.

While the 20th-century excavations and the study of antiquarian collections of sculpture and epigraphy from the territory of Septempeda (Marengo 1996; Landolfi 2003) revealed some essential information about the ancient town, most of the urban topography remained to be discovered. This was not helped by the almost silent ancient written sources about the town, or by the fact that no above-ground traces of its architecture remain visible today. Since 2004, however, the urban site has been the object of more systematic archaeological investigations, using a range of techniques currently employed for urban surveys and topographic studies on greenfield sites in the Mediterranean.

On the one hand, a programme of non-invasive prospection allowed the team from Ghent University to take a sturdy grip on the internal organisation of the urban topography of this Roman town (Vermeulen *et al.* 2017, 126–127; Vermeulen & Taelman forthcoming). The main field operations of the Belgian archaeologists so far include feature detection and monitoring with oblique and low altitude aerial photography, geophysical prospection of the whole town site using magnetic, georadar, and earth resistance methods, some limited artefact surveys, and the study of the recently available high resolution satellite imagery and LiDAR data of the area. Systematic aerial photography of the site in different seasons between 2004 and 2021, using traditional small aeroplanes and drones, and normal as well as near infrared photography, allowed the Ghent team to map a whole series of distinct crop marks in fields of alfalfa herbs covering large parts of the intramural areas. The interpretative mapping identified many elements of the urban street network (Fig. 9.2), the *forum* with part of its monumental buildings, many structures belonging to housing sectors, parts of the circuit wall and towers, a previously unknown gate (southeast gate), and an impressive monumental complex with porticoes outside the eastern gate. From 2010 to 2021 a multi-method geophysical research strategy was undertaken, comprising principally magnetometry and earth resistance prospection. Both methods combined covered an area of *c.* 15 ha, comprising 80% of the intramural space and some areas outside the walls (Plate 9.1). Tests with additional geophysical techniques aimed at obtaining even more precision for some of the detected structures comprised a small georadar survey and a few ERT profiles (disappointing GPR results, probably due to the clay-rich content of the soil, prompted us to quickly abandon this technique, while the time consuming ERT profiles were only applied near specific areas, such as the formerly excavated baths and the newly discovered western gate). The results from these geophysical operations not only made it possible to confirm or help to interpret some of the structures discovered by aerial photography, but also allowed the detection of significant new traces pertaining to houses, streets, and the towns defences. All newly mapped traces from aerial photography and geophysics were subsequently confronted with, or enhanced by, generally available remote sensing material, such as vertical aerial photography, LiDAR coverage and some commercially available satellite imagery.

On the other hand, a whole series of targeted stratigraphic excavations and trial trenches, dug under the supervision of the *Soprintendenza Archeologia Belle Arti e Paesaggio delle Marche* between 2004 and 2018, and a focused augering campaign by the Ghent team in 2021, allowed some of the older excavation data and the gradually revealed remote sensing evidence to be verified (Vermeulen *et al.* 2020; Vermeulen and Taelman forthcoming). The best stratigraphic opportunities were offered by some development-led archaeology resulting from interventions aimed at enhancing the modern infrastructure of the Municipality of San Severino. Although

*Figure 9.2. View in the summer of 2021 on a clear linear cropmark in alfalfa grass; in the background the Ghent University augering team investigates specific features (photo: F. Vermeulen).*

the locations of most of these were not the result of deliberate archaeological choices, the outcome of these excavations (covering a total of some 1,250 m²) allowed us to compare stratigraphic data with the results from remote sensing operations. They not only helped verifying some of the older ill-documented excavations, but allowed us to discover a whole series of new structures pertaining to the town defences, and architectural features in several intra- and extramural areas. They added very valuable information about the dating, depth, and character of the presumed archaeology, confirmed or changed many hypotheses, and also provided a good sample for the study of the material culture of this town. The additional hand-augering campaign (34 cores) on a north–south section of the urban area and on a series of features, improved our understanding of the near-surface geology, the geomorphological situation, and the evolutionary history of the site, and helped with verifying the nature, depth and date of particular features detected by geophysical and aerial survey.

It is no surprise that the resulting map of the ancient town, combining all legacy and newly obtained structural data, illustrates the *forma urbis* during its phase of main floruit, the early Imperial period. Even if several elements (town wall, *forum*, main streets, etc.) were no doubt planned here in late Republican times, it can be expected that parts of the intramural architecture and some elements of the street system were gradually altered throughout the centuries. Nevertheless, for our broad understanding of the local urbanism at Septempeda we now possess a very valuable basic overview, that we can synthesise briefly here (Plate 9.2).

The monumental town wall, built in *opus quadratum* technique with local sandstone blocks, is on average *c.* 2 m wide and approximately 1.5 km long. Its irregular pentagonal circuit incorporates most of the habitation nucleus laid out on the almost flat terrace north of the River Potenza. It also incorporates a small hill, perhaps in order to create an extra element for defence and visual control, but at the same time allowing space for a kind of *arx*, as is well known from many a Republican town in Italy (e.g. Cosa). Stratigraphic excavations near the eastern gate in 2018 showed that the sandstone wall was flanked on its inner side by an earthen bank (*agger*) 9–10 m wide, probably bordered on the town side by a small wall or ditch. Bank and ditch were confirmed by remote sensing in several areas of the circuit, respectively by aerial photography in the eastern part of the wall circuit and by a deep profile earth resistance prospection (ERT) near the western gate. It is not yet clear when exactly the town wall construction should be dated to, but suggestions have been made of a date connected with events a few years after the Social War, such as an intervention by Sulla who settled the veterans of war operations in Picenum (e.g. at Auximum) in their region of origin shortly after 90 BC. This chronology is currently the most likely option (Perna 2012, 386–387) not contradicted so far by the stratigraphic data and the few finds associated with the wall construction.

The wall had at least five monumental entrance gates (east, southeast, north, west, and southwest), two of which – the southeast and west gates – are only known by way of remote sensing, whilst another one – the north gate – remains somewhat hypothetically positioned on the map. Apart from the towers connected with the gates – the west, southwest and east gate each with two towers, the southeast gate with only one – a series of isolated towers was also found, creating a defendable wall circuit with strongpoints at more or less regular distances varying between 50–90 m. Most of the towers are round, with a diameter of some 7.5 m, but near the southeast gate a rectangular tower was constructed, indicating maybe a later date and addition to the defensive system. The two gates connected with the main central east–west street of the town were no doubt the most important ones, as they ultimately connected Septempeda with Rome (west gate) and Ancona (east gate). The excavated southwest gate, which possibly gave access to a necropolis and maybe to a crossing (bridge?) over the River Potenza, was also equally impressive (Fig. 9.3). All four discovered gates are of the so-called courtyard type, with an inner courtyard with the axis of the court extending perpendicularly inward from the line of the wall. Outwards, the three main courtyard gates were half closed by an additional stretch of wall joining two flanking towers, thus creating a very defendable semicircular or pear-shaped concave outer space. This central court gate system developed in the 4th century BC in Greece and the Hellenistic East, and gradually spread to the Italian peninsula through Magna Graecia (Winter 1971, 217–219). From the 2nd century BC

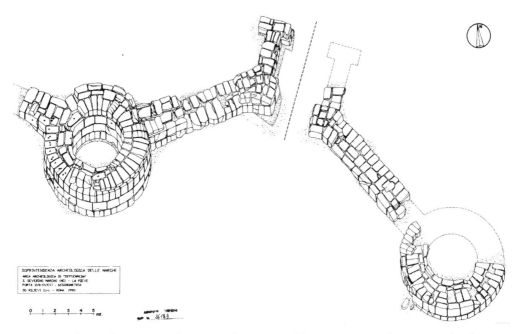

*Figure 9.3. The southwest gate of Septempeda, excavated between 1971 and 1995, provides the most complete picture of the monumental gates of the town* (Soprintendenza Archeologia Belle Arti e Paesaggio delle Marche).

onwards these types of gates are often flanked by one or two towers (Brands 1988, 148) and the specific disposition of the towers creating a semicircular to pear-shaped space outside the gate was introduced in Italy in a series of late Republican cities built by Rome, in particular under the reign of Sulla (Perna 2012).

The amazingly detailed aerial and geophysical imagery of broad linear traces interpretable as buried streets allows us to map large parts of the town's street system. These features were confirmed in several places by stratigraphic observations (excavations and augerings) of the still-existing streets, both inside and outside the wall circuit. The present evidence indicates that, at least during the early Empire, many streets were paved, and that they had an average width of no more than 4 m. The street system of a Roman town is partly conditioned by the need for connections with its territory, and with the world beyond its borders, and partly by the planning of the urban centre itself. In Septempeda the east–west oriented *diverticulum* linking the *via Flaminia* at Nuceria (Nocera Umbra) with the Adriatic coast became the conditioning factor, as it was from the street village around this *decumanus maximus* that the urban reality emerged. This east–west street gave access to far away Rome and to Ancona, to adjoining coastal areas and to other towns in or near the Potenza valley, such as Camerinum, Matilica, Trea, Ricina, and Potentia. Other internal streets were connected to the three remaining gates, giving access to the agricultural areas to the north of town, to cemeteries, and to the valley floor and the presumed river crossing in the south, beyond which other nearby towns, such as Tolentinum and Urbs Salvia could easily be reached. Although the urban planning does not seem to have involved a very strict orthogonal street system, and the network of streets might have grown rather gradually, there was surely an intention to create a series of axes parallel to the central road, and a few perpendicular connections to ensure easy access all around. This evolution must be seen in association with the demographic bloom of the settlement from the 1st century BC onwards, when living quarters perhaps gradually filled the intramural space once the town wall was built.

It is likely that simultaneously with the creation of the wall circuit and some of the main street arteries, a *forum* was developed in the very centre of the settlement, along the *decumanus maximus*. The insertion of such a public centre in the late Republican roadside settlement of Septempeda can, together with the completion of the wall circuit, be seen as crucial for the effort during the 1st century BC to convey the idea of a town. It demonstrates the adaptation of Italic population centres to the new standards of the Roman way of life and surely promoted the acculturation of the local population. It is probably here that cults for the gods Feronia and Jupiter, both attested by inscriptions (Marengo 1996), and later for the Emperor, must have concentrated their activity. But it was also a market centre, well connected to the road system, and the focus for the whole surrounding territory, as well as the place for the legal, political, and cultural matters of the community. The precise location of the *forum* of Septempeda was only discovered in 2009, as a result of the integration of aerial photography with geophysical prospections. Its plaza, identified immediately north of the main *decumanus*, was recognised as a rectangular square of at least 60 × 30 m, positioned with its longitudinal axis perpendicular to this street. The square was at some point in time surrounded by a series of public buildings and monuments, such as a possible *basilica* to the north, the (excavated) bath complex to the west, and perhaps several temples and *tabernae* to the east. The area immediately south of this *forum* and the central east–west street was partly occupied by a series of rich *domus* as the old excavation evidence suggests. Although there is still a lack of precise chronological information about the different buildings surrounding the *forum*, it can be presumed on the basis of parallels in the region that the period between the last decades of the 1st century BC and the 2nd century AD were the main phases of dynamic transformations and of monumentalisation of this urban centre. The excavated bathhouse may have been one of the latest additions to this public area, as it was probably built in the first decades of the 1st century AD. There is evidence that it might have been (partly?) in use until the early 5th century AD.

The character and evolution of housing in Septempeda is still difficult to trace, as no fully excavated houses are known so far. Thanks to discoveries in the 1920s and 1970s in an area to the southwest of the *forum*, where four mosaic floors and the remains of painted stucco were found and minimally documented, and, more recently, due to the integration of aerial photography, geophysics, and targeted augering, it is now possible to map parts of houses in almost all intramural sectors of the town. Very provisional data indicates that the richer and larger ones, belonging to the *domus*-type that emulates Hellenistic and central Tyrrhenian residences, are mostly to be found near the central area, especially near the *forum* and along the main *decumanus*. They are characterised by their elongated rectangular shape, a certain symmetry, the presence of an *atrium* surrounded by rooms at the centre, and often one or more *peristilia* towards the back. Excavation and augering evidence suggest the use of solid building materials, and sometimes more luxurious mosaic floor decorations in several houses. Of course, smaller houses, or combinations of simple housing with typical economic urban infrastructure (e.g. shops, workshops) must also have been present, but these are more difficult to identify among the ephemeral evidence of crop marks.

Finally, our surveys and the excavations have demonstrated that certain extramural parts of Septempeda were the subject of urban expansion and growth. Immediately outside the western gate an elongated area with production facilities (e.g. pottery workshops) exemplifies the need for late Republican to early Imperial productive areas to shift away from the public centre. Such a move of artisanal/economic activities towards the edges of the urban area is probably also part of a gentrification of the spaces surrounding the *forum*, increasingly occupied by high-status residences. Further down the road to the west several organised burial areas were discovered, reaching areas along the linear road trace at more than 1 km outside the gate. A large necropolis was partly studied between the arterial roads that leave the town through the west gate and the southwest gate. A strong visibility was likely guaranteed to the necropolis by the passage of the important *diverticulum* of the *via Flaminia*, today largely covered by the modern valley road. A majority of the excavated burials date to the 1st–2nd centuries AD, and at least some tombs on the roadside had a monumental character.

While typical buildings for games and spectacles such as a theatre or an amphitheatre, have not been detected in Septempeda, we can now attribute a partly similar function to the monumental precinct found outside the town wall near the eastern gate. Here a large open square (of approximately 12,000 m²) delimited by the town wall and with porticoes on at least two sides was first detected by aerial photography and later identified as a probable *campus* (Vermeulen *et al.* 2020). Partial excavation of its main central structure, an open-air swimming pool (30 × 15 m), allowed us to date the building of this sports complex to the 1st century AD. The original meaning of the word *campus* is that of a free and flat space, used as a multifunctional public area with a civic purpose: the physical training and armed exercises by the young citizens of a community took place here. This physical training, in particular arms drill, horse riding, and swimming, but also gymnastics and other sports, was supposed to complete their intellectual training (Borlenghi 2011). The *campus* was also one of the main public spaces intended for the community, where each person had the opportunity to take care of their body, to devote themselves to exercises, to walk, and to socialise in the shade of trees or under sheltering porticoes. In a relatively small town like Septempeda, the presence of such a complex may have also replaced the need for a more monumental, but also more expensive, amphitheatre building.

## 9.3. Conclusion

From *c.* 90 BC to the reign of Augustus, the aftermath of the Social War and the visit of Caesar to the region of Picenum, triggered strong integration of the slowly developing central-Adriatic region with the 'Roman system'. The earlier colonisation and urbanisation waves of Romans and Latins on and near the Adriatic coast during the 3rd and 2nd centuries BC were now followed by an accelerated urbanism through municipalisation and the settlement of new colonists in many settlements of the interior lands (Vermeulen 2017). This phenomenon, which has many parallels in other regions of peninsular Italy, produced in the central Adriatic region a more or less artificially created 'finalised' urban landscape with a high density of small to medium-sized towns interlinked by roads. Many pre-Roman hilltop centres and other less successful former central settlements of indigenous origin lying away from the new arteries began to be gradually and definitively abandoned. The small number of pre-Roman centres that survived paled into insignificance compared to the successful coastal Latin and Roman citizen colonies and to the quite evenly spread new small towns in the interior valleys that often grew out of *praefecturae* thanks to an intense injection of people from Rome or the Tyrrhenian region.

This process of town formation, stimulated by Rome along the major roads and their *diverticula*, often following the valley corridors, was very much a key feature of Roman urbanism during the late Republic, when the mobile elite involved in the creation of new architecture in Italy, partly inspired by the Hellenistic example, transformed the geography and created monuments for the future in the form of towns. Interesting locations along the road and river network, where settlers and viritane colonists from Latium started to congregate, created optimal conditions for the decisive step towards urbanism. As in many other situations, the case of Septempeda in the central Potenza valley seems to exemplify a model of gradual replacement of a former fortified Italic village. In this particular case, the Picene hilltop site of Monte Pitino, located some 7 km to the east of the new Roman roadside town in the valley floor lost its prime importance during this process, and was ultimately abandoned (De Neef & Vermeulen 2020).

Interestingly, archaeological evidence from Septempeda suggests that the start of this process came a few decades before the municipalisation of the region, and therefore one can assume that other (partly strategic) reasons, such as the settlement by Sulla of veterans in this area, could explain the earlier transformation from flourishing roadside village into a real town with imposing walls and gates. The further monumentalisation of this small town in the century following its promotion is then probably the result of further economic and demographic success, stimulated by a healthy competition between communities in the same region and the aspirations of local elites for *urbanitas* and career promotion. The economic base of such an inland small town, located in a fertile and diverse settlement areas on the crossroads of the rolling hills of Marche and its Apennine upland, was overwhelmingly agrarian. Like many others, this centre presented a model of 'urban governance' over rural resources. Urban elites received a disproportionate share of rural income and spent it mostly on urban goods and imported luxuries; taxes paid by country-dwellers financed urban amenities. Cities depended on the surplus of their countryside, but land management strategies served urban elites and policies. An additional impulse given to such a centre was possibly also the settling of a large number of veterans there during the Triumvirate and the early Augustan reign. The further development of the *forum*, set in the centre of the town, with its plaza surrounded by a set of public and sacred buildings, such as probably a *basilica* and a *curia*, a few temples, rows of *tabernae* and a bathhouse, can be linked to this event. That probably under the reign of Augustus a large *campus* was built outside the town walls, near the eastern town gate, might be another indication that veterans were deeply involved in the construction of new buildings and the development of public infrastructures in Septempeda. From then onwards the small town, strategically located on an economically relevant route between the Tiber valley, the Apennine mountains and the Adriatic Sea, was fully equipped to surf on the waves of relative prosperity and stability that characterized the larger part of the first two centuries of our era.

## Acknowledgements

We are very thankful to Dr Tommaso Casci Cecacci, responsible of this area for the *Soprintendenza*, for allowing us to study the archive data from previous excavations carried out at the site of Septempeda.

## Bibliography

Blume, F., Lachmann, K. & Rudorff, K. (eds) (1948) *Gromatici veteres. Die Schriften der römischen Feldmesser*. Berlin, Georg Reimer.

Borlenghi, A. (2011) *Il campus. Organizzazione e funzione di uno spazio pubblico in età romana. Le testimonianze in Italia e nelle province occidentali*. Rome, Quasar.

Brands, G. (1988) *Republikanische Stadttore in Italien*. BAR International Series 458. Oxford, British Archaeological Reports.

de Ligt, L. (2012) *Peasants, Citizens and Soldiers: Studies in the Demographic History of Roman Italy 225 BC–AD 100*. Cambridge, Cambridge University Press.

de Ligt, L. and Bintliff, J. (eds) (2019) Introduction. In L. de Ligt & J. Bintliff (eds) *Regional Urban Systems in the Roman World, 150 BCE – 250 CE*, 1–34. Leiden/Boston, Brill.

de Neef, W. & Vermeulen, F. (2020) A view from the hills. Investigating protohistoric phases in the longue durée of the Potenza Valley (Marche, Italy). In M. Dabas, S. Campana & A. Sarris (eds) *Mapping the Past. From Sampling Sites and Landscapes to Exploring the 'Archaeological Continuum'*, 53–66. Oxford, Archaeopress.

Flohr, M. (2021) Beyond Pompeii and Ostia: commerce and urban space in Roman Italy. In F. Vermeulen & A. Zuiderhoek (eds) *Space, Movement and the Economy in Roman Cities in Italy and Beyond*, 39–67. London, Routledge.

Guaitoli, M. (ed.) (2003) *Lo sguardo di Icaro. Le collezioni dell'Aerofototeca Nazionale per la conoscenza del territorio*. Rome, Campisano Editore.

Johnson, P.S. & Millett, M. (eds) (2012) *Archaeological Survey and the City*. Oxford, Oxbow Books.

Keay, S., Millett, M., Poppy, S., Robinson, J., Taylor, J. & Terrenato, N. (2000) Falerii Novi: a new survey of the walled area. *Papers of the British School at Rome* 68, 1–93.

Landolfi, M. (2003) *Il Museo Civico Archeologico di San Severino Marche*. San Severino Marche.

Landolfi, M. & Perna, R. (2004) Septempeda. In G. Paci, G.M. Fabrini & R. Perna (eds) *Beni Archeologici della Provincia di Macerata*, 89–91. Pescara, Carsa.

Marengo, S.M. (1996) Septempeda. *Supplementa Italica* (n.s.) 13, 193–228.

Paci, G. (1999) Dalla prefettura al municipio nell'agro Gallico e Piceno. In A. Rodríguez Colmenero (ed.) *Los orígines de la ciudad en el Noroeste Hispánico*, 55–64. Lugo, Deputación de Lugo.

Perna, R. (2012) Nascita e sviluppo della forma urbana in età romana: alcuni casi nelle città delle Regiones V e VI. In G. De Marinis, G. M. Fabrini, G. Paci, R. Perna & M. Silvestrini (eds) *I processi formativi ed evolutivi della città in area adriatica*, 375–399. Oxford, Archaeopress.

Sewell, J. (2016) Higher-order settlements in early Hellenistic Italy: a quantitative analysis of a new archaeological database. *American Journal of Archaeology* 120.4, 603–630.

Sisani, S. (2006) *Umbria, Marche*. Roma/Bari, Laterza.

Verdonck, L., Launaro, A., Vermeulen, F. & Millett, M. (2020) Ground-penetrating radar survey at Falerii Novi: a new approach to the study of Roman cities. *Antiquity* 94, 705–723.

Vermeulen, F. (2017) *From the Mountains to the Sea. The Roman Colonisation and Urbanisation of Central Adriatic Italy*. Babesch Supplement 30. Leuven/Paris/Bristol, Peeters Publishers.

Vermeulen, F. (2023) Le porte delle città romane nell'Italia centrale adriatica: metodi invasivi e non invasive. *Atlante Tematico di Topografia Antica* 33, 203–218.

Vermeulen, F. & Taelman, D. (forthcoming) Septempeda: Integrating Non-invasive Surveys, Legacy Data and New Stratigraphic Evidence in the Mapping of a Roman townscape in Picenum. In *Festschrift Simon Keay*.

Vermeulen, F., Burgers, G.J., Corsi, C. & Keay, S. (eds) (2012) *Urban Landscape Survey in Italy and the Mediterranean*. Oxford, Oxbow Books.

Vermeulen, F., Van Limbergen, D., Monsieur, P. & Taelman. D. (eds) (2017) *The Potenza Valley Survey (Marche, Italy). Settlement Dynamics and Changing Material Culture in an Adriatic Valley between Iron Age and Late Antiquity*. Academia Belgica. Studia Archaeologica 1. Rome, Editorial Service System.

Vermeulen, F., Casci Ceccacci, T. & Cilla, G. (2020) Scoperta di un campus extra-murale nella città romana di Septempeda (Picenum). *Archeologia Aerea* 14, 33–47.

Winter, F.E. (1971) *Greek Fortifications*. London, Routledge & Kegan Paul.

# Part IV

Roman towns in the *longue durée*

# Chapter 10

# Lunae: new perspectives from recent archaeological fieldwork

*Simonetta Menchelli, Paolo Sangriso,*
*Silvia Marini & Rocco Marcheschi*

## 10.1. Lunae: an overview

*Simonetta Menchelli*

Lunae was founded in 177 BC as a Roman colony in a problematic district because of Ligurian resistance (about this people: De Marinis & Spadea 2007; Paltineri 2018). Rome had to conquer them in order to continue the unification of the Italian peninsula (Terrenato 2022, 214, 134–135) and facilitate its ongoing expansion towards the northwestern Mediterranean. In fact, the port of this district was used by the Romans even before the foundation of the colony: from *Lunae Portus* in 195 BC the consul Cato sailed for Spain against the Carthaginians (Livy 34.8.4).

This territory was in a strategic position because it could easily be reached from the south, along the coastal axis that would become the *via Aurelia Nova*, built in 200 or 144 BC, as an extension of the *via Aurelia Vetus* from Pisa to the north (Coarelli 1985, 23). Moreover, Lunae was connected, through an efficient road and river network, both to Parma (and therefore to the Po Valley) and to Luca, the Latin colony founded in 180 BC, also with an anti-Ligurian function (Fig. 10.1). In the early 2nd century BC, many military actions in this district were documented by Livy (34.56.1 [193 BC]; 39.32.2 [185 BC]). In 180 BC Rome managed to deport 48,000 Ligurians to Samnium, and therefore the colony of Lunae could be founded, with 2,000 settlers each receiving a plot of 51.5 *jugera* (Livy 41.13.4; Coarelli 1985, 29).

Lunae can be included in the 2nd century BC 'maritime experimental' type of colony, that maintained the usual plan of a military fort (Fig. 10.2) (particularly necessary because the Apuanian Ligurians were only definitively defeated in 155 BC by M. Claudius Marcellus), but having an agrarian character: many more settlers compared to the 'traditional' 300 colonists and with very large allotments to compensate for the risk (Salmon 1969; Gros & Torelli 2007, 182–183; Pelgrom & Stek 2014b, 14–15). In the

*Figure 10.1. Lunae in its geographical context (drawing by Rocco Marcheschi)*

town's foundation phase, interaction between the local people and the elite (Lippolis 2016; Terrenato 2022) is barely perceptible, given the disruptive intervention of Rome, although cultural exchanges are documented in numerous graves identified in this territory (Menchelli *et al.* 2021a).

The wall circuit was 560 m north–south by 440 m east–west, enclosing an area of more than 24 ha: therefore, Lunae was a settlement of medium dimensions, more or less equal or larger than many 3rd–2nd-century BC Roman colonies along the Tyrrhenian and Adriatic coasts (Pelgrom & Stek 2014a; 2014b; Van Limbergen & Vermeulen 2017, 181–183). The town walls today are completely buried, but they have been identified by aerial photography and, in some parts, by archaeological excavations (Pasquinucci & Menchelli 2023). The plan shows an indentation in the southeastern sector of the wall circuit, recorded in historical cartography at least from the second half of the 18th century. In the relevant literature, this indentation has always been considered an adaptation to the shoreline, but recent geoarchaeological research has proved that it was due to the presence of a palaeo-riverbed of the Parmignola stream (Bini *et al.* 2013) today represented by a canal not surprisingly called 'il canale dei grandi muri'.

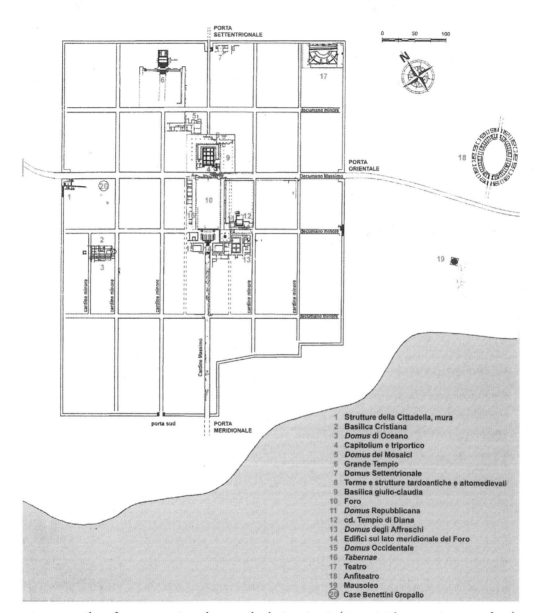

*Figure 10.2. Plan of Lunae, Soprintendenza Archeologica Liguria (Gervasini & Mancusi 2016, 84, fig. 3).*

Our Luni-Porta Marina Project (Menchelli *et al.* 2021c) deals precisely with the southeast quarter of the town, immediately to the east of the *cardo maximus*, and near this indentation and 'Porta Marina' (i.e. 'Porta Meridionale' on Fig. 10.2; see also Fig. 10.3). We chose this area, firstly, because it had never been investigated before neither by 19th-century archaeologists nor in contemporary times, and, secondly, because of its strategic location for studying the connections between Lunae and its harbour system, which from the mid-1st century BC was of great economic importance since becoming the trading centre of the white Apuanian marble (Paribeni & Segenni 2015).

According to Strabo's description (5.2.5), this harbour system was large and made up of various basins, and in fact the geoarchaeological investigations have identified, in the southeast sector of the town, a large inlet with a deep draft, and therefore particularly suitable for the *naves lapidariae*, while a river port has been located to the west for lower tonnage ships (Bini *et al.* 2013).

Considering the town's urbanistic development, the most ancient settlement in Lunae has been identified in some archaeological trenches below the *Capitolium* and the *tabernae* (C, D, E) in the western portico of the *forum*. This settlement dates back to the late 3rd to early 2nd century BC and consisted of huts featuring clay and straw walls with curved-tiled roofs. It also included some fireplaces and pits interpreted as garbage dumps, and a hole containing Graeco-Italic amphorae fixed vertically, most probably for libation offerings. Moreover, a stockade consisting of east–west-oriented double poles was brought to light: most probably it had defensive functions, or it may have been meant to separate the different housing sectors (Rossignani *et al.* 2002). Naturally, it is difficult to establish whether this settlement preceded the foundation of the colony, when *portus Lunae* was utilised by military expeditions, or if these huts were the temporary dwellings of the colonists before the construction of the town. In any case, it is significant that this first settlement is close to the main 'junction' (*diverticulum*) connecting to the via Aurelia Nova, and this is where the central area of the town would develop shortly afterwards (Pasquinucci & Menchelli 2023, 196).

Moving on to the foundation of the colony, it is obvious that the wall circuit was built at the same time as the founding of Lunae in 177 BC, followed by the most significant civil and religious buildings (the *forum*, the *Capitolium* and the Great Temple dedicated to Luna, Apollo, and either to Dionysus or to the Genius of the Roman People) (Durante & Gervasini 2000, 60–70). Burial rituals of dogs identified both below Taberna E in the *forum* (an entire skeleton deposited in two *ollae*) and in the northeastern sector of the town, where the theatre would later be built (two burials of dogs in pits) also refer to the initial phases of the colony (Gervasini 2020). Given that these graves were respectively placed in the most ancient settlement of *Luna* and at a short distance from the southeast corner of the walls, their meaning is evident: dogs, a symbol of purification, were considered protectors in the transitional and transformational phases (from enemy territory to conquered territory, from outside to inside, from the world of the living to the world of the dead). Similar dog burials to protect the town walls have been documented in the colonies of *Ariminum* (268 BC), Paestum (273 BC) and perhaps Saena Julia (Gervasini 2020).

Being a 2nd-century BC colony, Lunae could have been endowed with a *forum* as early as its initial phases: it had elongated dimensions and it was lined by *tabernae*, according to a late 4th-century BC successful model, most probably derived from the *forum Romanum* (Lackner 2008, 117, 356–357; Sewell 2014, 127–129).

The *decumanus maximus* replaced the above-mentioned sideway of the *via Aurelia Nova* which entered the town through the eastern gate and continued northwards from the western gate. The *cardo maximus* was the main road between Lunae's northern *suburbium* and its harbour area, but it was divided into two sectors (the northern and the southern) by the *Capitolium-Forum* block. Although in this period the square grid pattern was spreading (Gros & Torelli 2007, 179–184), as documented in the nearby colonies of Parma (183 BC) and Luca (180 BC), Lunae had *insulae* with the traditional rectangular form and a constant width (2 *actus* = 240 *pedes* = 70 m), while their length varied: it was 90–95 m, and 71, 120, 140 m respectively north and south of the *decumanus maximus* (Durante 2001a). Most probably, this town plan was the most suitable for the Lunae's topographical context which, as we have seen, was affected by the proximity of its harbour system and of the palaeo-riverbed of the Parmignola stream.

In the late 2nd/early 1st century BC the *Capitolium* was rebuilt, and in this period some of the rich *domus* of Lunae, which would characterise the townscape until the late Roman period, started to be constructed (Durante 2010). Regarding this topic, our project made a significant contribution to the knowledge of the urban planning of Lunae by bringing to light Domus A and Domus B in the Porta Marina quarter (par. 10.2).

## 10.2. The late Republican *domus* in the Porta Marina quarter

*Paolo Sangriso*

The sector of the *insula* excavated in the Porta Marina quarter is occupied by two *domus* (A–B) (Fig. 10.3) featuring a long period of use (from the Republican period to the early 8th century AD) with important building transformations (Domus A was partially occupied by a workshops and Domus B by Temple C). As in other cases in Lunae, the two *domus* shared the east–west perimeter wall: *parietes communes* have been found in the 'Domus Repubblicana' and in the late Republican phase of the 'Domus degli Affreschi' (Durante & Landi 2001, 22 n.17; Ghedini 2012, 324–325). Given its planimetric, organisational and decorative characteristics, Domus B is of remarkable interest not only for its structural evidence, but also for its position in the Lunae plan, providing new data for discussing the organisation of the space within the town (Fig. 10.3 and Plate 10.1B). The cross-referencing of excavation data (pottery, fresco fragments, and floor decorations) allows us to place the construction of Domus B between 70 and 50 BC (Menchelli *et al.* 2021c, 371–380) and the organisational scheme fits the type with *atrium* (B4, about 160 m²) (Gros 1997, 913 n. 101, 917–918 n. 110), but already featuring a peristyle of considerable size with a central columned area and a *nymphaeum* (B12), a probable *triclinium* (B5) and at least one reception room (B8) (Rinaldi 2012, 71–95).

*Figure 10.3. The Porta Marina quarter of Lunae: Domus A, Domus B and Temple C (drawing by Rocco Marcheschi).*

Lacking traces of pillars around the *impluvium*, the *atrium* can be considered of Tuscanic style, as documented in other *domus* in Lunae ('Domus degli Affreschi' / first phase: Zaccaria Ruggiu 1983, 16; 1991, 99; 'Domus Occidentale'/second phase and 'Domus degli Affreschi' (Zaccaria Ruggiu 1983, 26; 1991, 102; Durante 2001a, 281; Bueno 2012b, 335). The *atrium* was flanked (Vitr. *De arch.* 6.31.1–2; Gros 1997, 905–908) by two *alae* (B1, B9a) and four *cubicula* (B2–3, B10, B11). The basin of the *impluvium* would have been completely removed by the construction of Temple C (par. 10.3) and, underneath it, there are no traces of either a cistern or channelling systems (an element common to all the *domus* investigated to date in Lunae: Durante 2001b, 277, n. 26). It is worth noting the presence, in axis with the *impluvium* basin, of a plinth most probably intended to support the *cartibulum* (Zaccaria Ruggiu 1995, 349–382, esp. 364). On its eastern side, the *atrium* was flanked by a *tablinum* (B7) and by the corridor (B6) leading into the peristyle (B12), which presents a slightly offset plan to the north with respect to the front of the Domus B, thus occupying a sector expected, by symmetry, to belong to the Domus A. Its central area, having brick columns covered with stucco, in the Byzantine/Lombard period was used as a necropolis (at the moment four tombs have been brought to light: Menchelli *et al.* 2022).

The pavements of the *domus* are of a remarkable quality, starting with the mosaic of the *fauces,* in black and white rows of adjacent squares, delineated and divided by their diagonals (Balmelle *et al.* 1985, pl. 17c, 48). This geometric motif is connected, by means of a wide white band, with the figured mosaic leading into the *atrium*. This is formed by a band of rectangles with arched structures surmounted by T-shaped merlons which accommodate – on a white background – ships with their masts laid-down (Plate 10.1A): most probably this mosaic represented *navalia* (Vincenti 2001). The floor of the *atrium* continued with an elegant orthogonal punctuation of white marble cubes on a black background field (Gervasini *et al.* 2021), its floor continuing from *ala* B1 and cubicle B2. *Ala* B1 preserves part of the mosaic threshold and its preparation in the southern part, while the northern one is paved with a *cocciopesto* floor without inserts. Cubicle B2, having a marble-based cement floor, was only accessible from room B1. The organisation of these two lateral rooms is also reflected in the southern side, where the division between rooms B9a and B9b is indicated not only by the different floors (B9a having mosaic in alternating black and white isosceles triangles with preparatory drawing preserved on the cement base: Balmelle *et al.* 1985, pl. 17c, 48), but also by an east–west wall that separated them. Given the presence of Temple C, we cannot hypothesise the relationship between room B9a and room B10, but since room B9b can only be reached through the threshold connecting it with room B10, most probably, by symmetry with the northern side, room B10 was entered through room B9a.

The floor of cubicle B10 is lost, while B9b retains flooring evidently related to its function. The latter room was paved in *opus sectile*: only the mortar imprints remain, indicating an orthogonal composition of adjacent squares and rhombuses bordered by rows of tiles, framed by a pink local limestone frame. The northeastern corner of the room, aligned with the threshold in the southwestern corner, is instead paved with a marble-based cement having coloured inserts; linear traces of mortar identified on this small square space suggest that it could be utilised for a fixture or housing a piece of furniture, which we obviously cannot identify.

The *tablinum* (B7) has a black-and-white mosaic floor with a central pseudo-emblem surrounded by a scale motif, bordered by a double red and black frame, with vine shoots and vine leaves in the corners (Gervasini *et al.* 2021). The corridor (B6), paved in *cocciopesto* without inserts, led into the peristyle with a marble-based cement floor with red and blue coloured inserts. The likely *triclinium* (B5) was most probably paved like room B2 and opened onto the peristyle. Room B8, also opened onto the peristyle, presents an *opus sectile* floor with a perspective cube motif consisting of three-coloured rhombuses in local limestone having a central pseudo-emblem in a geometric pattern; this motif is bordered by a series of alternating coloured tiles; a further sequence of square tiles with embedded square elements in alternating colours continues up to the western wall with a marble band.

The decorative apparatus of the *domus* obviously corresponds to the organisation of the housing spaces, and therefore, although excavations are still ongoing, we can present some considerations on this topic. The *navalia* mosaic, at the end of the entrance corridor, indicates the source of the *dominus'* wealth, while the presence of the *cartibulum*, in axis with the *impluvium* basin and the *tablinum*, seems to be a clear reference to the traditional values of the Roman house. The characteristics of the rooms gravitating around the *atrium* permit us to consider this sector not completely 'public' but to distinguish between different degrees of this definition.

In fact, while the *tablinum* is an open and visible place of power and communication, a first degree of privacy is given by cubicle B2, accessible only from *ala* B1, which is also open onto the *atrium*. A completely private or very exclusive access can be attributed to the rooms on the southern side of the *atrium: ala* B9a was most probably transformed into a vestibule for cubicle B10, which guaranteed the only way into cubicle B9b. In this room the restricted access and the characteristics of the floor (featuring a funnel-shaped perspective given by the different sizes of the rows of tiles) suggest an optical pathway tied to the likely furniture originally present in the northeastern corner, which perhaps contained/represented sacred, or in any case very intimate, elements shared by the inhabitants of the Domus B (Bueno 2012c; Bassani 2012). Corridor B6, on the northern side of the *tablinum*, gave access to the peristyle, which was overlooked by room B5, most probably used as a *triclinium*, and by room B8 that, given its large size and high-quality floor decoration, can be interpreted as a reception room (without excluding the *triclinium* function) where the *dominus* could receive important guests in a private and pleasant hall, open onto the colonnaded space of the peristyle.

So many floor typologies, its complex plan, the respect for tradition (given the most probable presence of the *cartibulum*) identify Domus B as a high-quality building, in no way inferior to the contemporary *domus* facing the *forum* and therefore an expression of the same social class. The presence of such *domus* along the *cardo maximus* prompts some reflections about the urban structure of Lunae. Given the small size of the town, if members of the local elite built their *domus* not only on the *forum* but also along the *cardo maximus*, we can assume that the latter (which, through the southern gate, came from the port area, the most representative site of the town's wealth) was also considered part of the centre. From this point of view, the area around this axis would almost take on the role of the 'town's *atrium*', where the protagonists of its economic development appear and present themselves, and the mosaic with the *navalia* would be its most obvious symbol.

## 10.3. The temple in the Porta Marina quarter and the early imperial age in Lunae

*Rocco Marcheschi*

In the first century AD, the Domus B in the Porta Marina quarter underwent a fundamental rebuilding and the small Temple C was constructed on this site. The new building, whose structures are preserved at the foundation level, has a rectangular plan (7.4 × 9.9 m) divided into two rooms (Fig. 10.4A). For its installation, a single rectangular cut affected the mosaic floor of the *atrium*, part of the *impluvium* and the rooms on the south side of the *domus*. It was a small tetrastyle temple, prostyle or *in antis*, probably built on a podium and accessible, via a staircase, on the west side (Menchelli *et al.* 2021c, 381–383). Along with the construction of the temple,

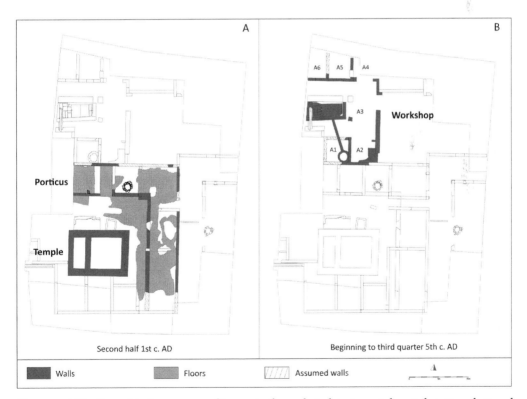

*Figure 10.4. The Porta Marina quarter of Lunae in the early to late imperial period. A: Temple C and its porticus. B: workshop (drawings by Rocco Marcheschi).*

a series of building interventions reconfigured the plan of the rooms of the *domus* located along the north and east sides of the *atrium*: the inner walls of the rooms were razed to the ground; the entrances to the *atrium* (B1, B6, B7) and to the peristyle (B12) were closed.

After these operations, the floors were raised using different building materials resulting from the spoliation of the *domus*. The renovation of the rooms located along the north and east sides of the *atrium* created an uninterrupted space (4.30 m wide), probably a *porticus*, that skirted the temple and the square that surrounded it (Menchelli *et al.* 2021c, 395). The imposing work thus defined an open area, between the temple and the *porticus*, probably paved in marble (*c.* 5.4 m wide on the north side and *c.* 2.7 m on the east side). The refurbishment of the *domus* and the construction of the temple were brought to completion as a unitary project, to be dated in the second half of the 1st century AD (Menchelli *et al.* 2021c, 381, 391–395).

We have no evidence of similar operations in the southern rooms of the *domus*, that are still being excavated, and in the western sector, which have been deeply altered by post-depositional phenomena. At the moment, we can propose two different solutions about the plan of the *porticus* on the southern side. In this regard, the information provided by the southern perimeter wall of the *domus* is decisive: it was dismantled in ancient times, but its traces along the southern side of cubicle B9 are about 5.4 m away from the temple. Assuming that the temple had been erected in the centre of the available space, according to a principle of symmetry, two reconstructive hypotheses are possible: (1) the southern arm of the *porticus* could have been extended beyond the southern wall, involving the structures of another building, still to be identified; (2) more likely, the temple did not display any portico on the southern side, which was therefore closed by the perimeter wall of Domus B.

It is still not clear how – along the eastern side of the temple – the *porticus* was connected with the *cardo maximus* which, by then, was colonnaded (Durante & Gervasini 2000, 35). At the same time, we still have to understand whether, and in which way, the peristyle of the *domus* was involved in the renovation of the eastern sector of the building. In any case, we know that the east–west perimeter wall shared by Domus A and B defined the northern limit of the religious complex, and it was respected as a demarcation line between two properties until Late Antiquity.

The construction of Temple C is part of a phase of growth and urban development of the Roman colony, documented by the building activity that involved the public and private spaces of the town from the Julio-Claudian period, that has frequently been related to the lucrative marble economy (Gervasini 2015). It was from this moment onwards that the vast programme of monumentalisation of the town centre was progressively implemented, starting with the *forum*, which was paved, and its porticoes rebuilt in marble (Durante 2001a, 18). Meanwhile, the theatre was built in the northeastern corner of the colony's plan (Berton *et al.* 2020; Fig. 10.2: 17). A building, perhaps the *curia*, was erected in the middle of the southern side of the *forum* and it was flanked by two quadrangular squares, paved in *opus sectile* (E$_1$, the

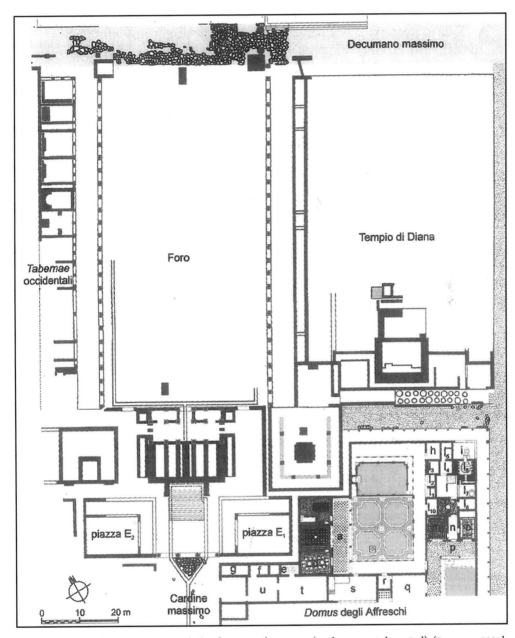

*Figure 10.5. The* forum vetus *and the* forum adiectum *(early Imperial period) (Durante 2001b, 291, fig. 16).*

eastern one; $E_2$, the western one) (Durante 2003, 142–144, with bibliography; Fig. 10.5). The 'area con fontane', in the southeastern sector of the *forum*, can be attributed to this phase; it was communicating to the north with a meeting room, possibly the seat of the *collegium* of *Augustales* (Rossignani 1995, 443) (Fig. 10.5).

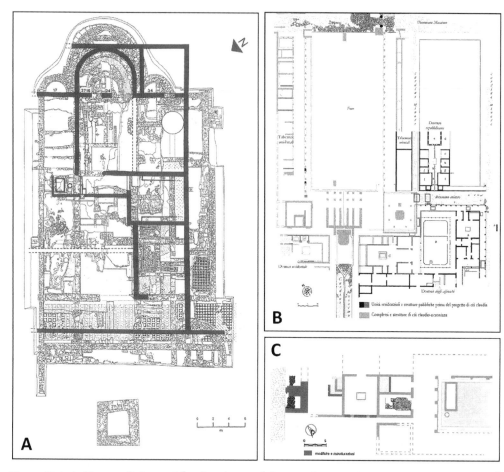

*Figure 10.6. A: 'Domus di Oceano' (early 5th c. AD) (Lusuardi Siena & Sannazaro 1995, 213 fig. 5).
B: The* forum *and the* domus *overlooking it (late-Republican period) (Durante 2001b, 273, fig. 2).
C: 'Domus settentrionale' (Durante & Gervasini 2000, 71, fig. 39).*

In the Claudian age, a large porticoed square was built alongside the *forum vetus*
and housed, along the southern side, a single-cell temple on a *podium*, called 'Tempio
di Diana', modelled on the imperial *fora* in Rome (Durante & Landi 2001, 33–41). On
the opposite side of the *forum adiectum*, the *basilica* was built in the same phase,
incorporating the eastern arm of the portico of the *Capitolium* (Rossignani 1995,
450–451) (Fig. 10.5).

The rich *domus* provides further elements to define the framework of renovation
that affected Lunae from the Julio-Claudian age onwards. The construction of the
'Domus settentrionale', located near the northern gate of the town walls, is dated to
the end of the Tiberian period. It presents a vast residential wing gravitating around
the peristyle; all the rooms were paved in *opus sectile* (Ghiotto 2012a; Fig. 10.6C). The
coeval 'Domus di Oceano', in the western sector of the town, displayed a series of

rooms opening onto a Tuscanic *atrium* paved in grit and polychrome marble *scutulae* (Bueno 2012b). This renovation frenzy also involved the 'Domus degli Affreschi', located near the southeastern corner of the *forum*, which can be traced back to the same chronological horizon. The *domus*, realised through the acquisition of several residential units, was made of two areas connected by porticoes and gardens (Bueno 2012a) (Figs 10.5 and 10.6B).

As it has been pointed out, this vast building programme affecting the political centre of Lunae (and of many other towns in Italy) entailed the expropriation of sectors of *domus* located near the *forum* (Facchinetti 2016): for example the construction of the *forum adiectum* cancelled the 'Domus repubblicana' built on the east side of the *forum vetus* (Ghiotto 2012b). Square $E_1$ and the 'area con fontane' were built on the 'Domus degli Affreschi' rooms overlooking the forum (Durante 2003, 142–143). Square $E_2$ obliterated part of the western rooms in the 'Domus occidentale', built close to the southwestern sector of the forum during the 1st century BC (Bueno 2012c).

Temple C was not necessarily linked to this phenomenon: its modest dimensions and marginal position, even if placed along the *cardo maximus*, suggest that it was not involved in the general building frenzy that aimed at constructing remarkable public buildings in the *forum* area, which in turn required the acquisition, and in some case the expropriation, of private property. Considering the temple's poor state of preservation, the lack of decorative elements and the absence of epigraphic documentation, we cannot identify the deity to whom it was dedicated. In any case, the temple's dimensions and the careful renovation of Domus B seems to indicate that it could have belonged to a *collegium*: in fact, its similarities, both structural and topographical, with the temple of the *fabri tignarii* in Ostia (Menchelli *et al.* 2021c, 384–385) have already been recognised. Therefore, the temple may have been built by a *collegium* or a private individual connected to it, most probably a member of the local elite (about which see in general Cafaro 2022). In this regard, the mosaic with *navalia* (par. 10.2), can suggest that the wealth of the owner of Domus B derived from maritime trade and/or shipbuilding. Albeit more than a century had passed since the construction of the *domus*, it seems at least intriguing to suppose a link between a professional association of traders or shipbuilders and one of the members of the family which formerly owned the *domus* from the late Republic. Perhaps even the individual who promoted the construction of the temple belonged to a *collegium* or was a patron of the association and donated the space and/or built the temple at his own expense.

## 10.4. The decommissioning of Temple C within the town's historical context

*Silvia Marini*

The stratigraphy of the temple complex, directly covered by agricultural layers, does not allow us to reconstruct its phases and identify the moment of its decommissioning. This structure, like the adjacent ones, is indeed only preserved at the level of its foundation, due to the intensive spoliation of building material that affected the area from Late Antiquity up to modern times, and also to the agricultural works in the 18th and 19th centuries. However, the excavations which involved the southern area of Domus B with the *porticus* surrounding the temple, and those in the area between the Domus A and Domus B, allow us to frame the final phase of the structure within the town's historical context.

In the area to the south of Domus B, an accumulation of ceramic sherds for drainage attributable to the Byzantine period has been identified. It covered the southern perimeter wall of Domus B, which was affected by spoliation. The *porticus* of the temple rested on this perimeter wall up to its foundation.

The northern wall of the *porticus* instead reused the perimeter wall separating Domus A and Domus B. The former presents traces of a fire (remains of burnt and collapsed roof beams on *atrium* A3) that can be dated to the last decades of the 4th century AD, probably resulting from the earthquake that has been documented in several areas in the town. In general, collapsed structures linked to a seismic event followed by fires have been identified along the southern sector of the *decumanus maximus*: the earthquake is documented, for example, in the house known as 'del piccolo dolio', which presents traces of fire and of the first floor collapsing onto the ground floor (Durante & Landi 2010, 161). Relevant evidence, even though less marked, is also present in the 'Domus di Oceano', whose destruction its materials seem to date to the end of the 4th century AD (Lusuardi Siena & Sannazzaro, 1995, 196–197).

The honorary base of the *Consularis Tusciae et Umbriae* Lucilius Constantius, datable to after AD 366 and probably placed in the *Capitolium*, is the latest document of an intervention in the public and religious areas of the town (Durante 2001b, 21), which should not have been of particular interest in the late 4th century AD. In fact, a little further north, the rubble of the Great Temple was found in a fallen position and not removed after the earthquake, with the columns of the eastern portico all collapsed in the same direction. Most probably, even the removal of the marble pavement in the *forum* area and of other architectural elements was connected with this crisis (Durante 2001b, 23).

Returning to the area of 'Porta Marina', the perimeter wall common to Domus A and Domus B, which constituted the north side of the temple's *porticus*, was stripped to the foundation, like its southern analogue, except in the western sector. In this latter sector, in fact, the wall was preserved and a small round cistern was built on it: it belonged to a workshop, most probably for washing fabrics, installed on Domus A around the mid-5th century AD. (Fig. 10.4B). This workshop included a large pool that reused the enlarged *impluvium* of Domus A (Menchelli *et al.* 2021b, 268). The marble slabs used to extend the surface area of the *impluvium* may have come from the paving of Temple C or its access staircase. Therefore, we can assume that materials were recovered from the *porticus* wall to be employed in the construction of the workshop once the temple had lost its sacral function. On the other hand, the search for building material does seem to have involved either the temple's plinth (whose foundation was brought to light intact) or the internal structure of the *porticus*. Most probably, the base of the temple was still used as a dwelling, shelter or otherwise, so that the surrounding space was not affected by the spoliation operations that affected the perimeter wall.

From the late 4th century AD onwards, the disinterest in the town's public and religious buildings became tangible. At this time, a bath likely related to the nearby 'Domus dei Mosaici' was built reusing part of the north branch of the *porticus* of the *Capitolium*, thus closing off access to the sacred area from that side. The bath was built precisely by reusing fragments of architectural decoration and statues recovered from the dismantling of the public area (Durante 2010, 45–46).

At the same time or a few decades later, the 'Domus dei Mosaici' was restructured: it came to occupy areas previously belonging to public buildings (such as the *basilica* and the *porticus* around the *Capitolium*) and featured the conspicuous mosaic representing the *Circus Maximus* (Lusuardi Siena 1985, 304).

In the last decades of the 4th century AD the 'Domus di Oceano' (Fig. 10.6A) was still being endowed with a series of large and well decorated rooms, including a hall connected to an *exedra* with a balustrade and a room with masonry benches along three sides (Lusuardi Siena & Sannazzaro 1995, 198). Next to the hall with an *exedra*, another large hall was later built, characterised by a poorer pavement and connected to a smaller room (Lusuardi Siena & Sannazzaro, 1995, 199). The entire complex (apsidal hall, room with benches, smaller room) was still in use in the late 4th to early 5th century AD, as indicated by numismatic evidence (Lusuardi Siena 1985, 306): it may have been a *domus ecclesiae* in use between the earthquake which damaged the *domus* and the construction of the first church of Lunae in the 5th century AD (Lusuardi Siena & Sannazzaro, 1995, 200–205). In this church the plinths of the columns reused marble bases probably removed from the *triporticus* surrounding the *Capitolium*: one of these bases, dated to the second half of the 4th century AD, provides a *terminus post quem* for the construction of the church (Lusuardi Siena & Sannazzaro, 1995, 193), a chronology confirmed by the materials found in the abandonment layers of the *domus* (Lusuardi Siena 1985, 306).

The general situation documented in Lunae, together with the stratigraphy of our excavations, allows us to hypothesise a decline in interest and a progressive abandonment of Temple C during the 4th century AD. This event was certainly influenced both by the Christianisation process (a diocese is attested at Lunae in the 5th century AD: Lusuardi Siena 2003, 197) and by the Theodosian edict of AD 380 (Menchelli *et al.* 2021c). Most probably, Temple C, like the adjacent Domus A, suffered damage during the earthquake that occurred at the end of the 4th century AD and, like the other religious buildings in the town, was not repaired, its space being repurposed with part of its building materials being reused (as indicated by the excavation results).

From at least the mid-5th century AD onwards, the town organised its political and religious structures around the bishop's chair: the construction of the Byzantine fortress, which would enclose all the religious buildings between the late 6th and the early 7th century AD (Cagnana *et al.* 2021, 206–208), sanctioned the definitive deconstruction of the Roman town's plan.

## 10.5. Some concluding remarks

*Simonetta Menchelli, Paolo Sangriso, Silvia Marini & Rocco Marcheschi*

In conclusion, the town's urban evolution can thus be outlined in a diachronic perspective, even though we must admit that our knowledge of Lunae remains partial: we are only informed about the top of society, that is the group most associated with public buildings and the remarkable *domus*. Throughout the Roman period much of the Lunae's society continues to escape us: not only the dwellings of the first colonists, but also later middle-class houses are yet to be identified. Even so, the restudy of the published documentation identified a specimen of a small house near the western gate featuring an upper floor in *opus craticium* (Durante 2001a, 64). This may well represent the first clue that a less elite quarter may have been located in the western sector of Lunae, crossed by the minor *cardo* that connected the town with its port system through the south gate (i.e. 'porta sud' on Fig. 10.1).

Furthermore, we now need to look for Lunae beyond its town walls: as it is often the case in Roman towns, the urban settlement further extended outside the colonial walls. In the north sector, immediately west of the northern gate, the Great Baths building (featuring two *piscinae*, many rooms and *opus sectile* floors) was brought to light in the late 19th century and then reburied for preservation. In the eastern sector, apart from the amphitheatre built along the sideway of the *via Aurelia Nova* in the 1st–2nd centuries AD, some structures have been partially excavated, whereas investigations in the western sector have offered very limited results. Moreover, at the moment there is no evidence for reconstructing the harbour system with, presumably, its *horrea*, all the facilities necessary for the handling of the marble, and the *scholae* of the various *collegia*, some of which are epigraphically attested (*fabri tignarii*: CIL XI 1355; *dendrophori*: CIL XI 1355; *centonarii*: CIL XI 1354; Cafaro 2022).

In conclusion we hope that our project, which include systematic GPR (Adriano Ribolini, University of Pisa) and aerial photography campaigns (Giuseepe Ceraudo and Veronica Ferrari, University of Salento: Menchelli *et al.* 2022), will very soon provide new data about Lunae's urban development, inside and outside its walls.

## Bibliography

Balmelle, C., Prudhomme, R. & Morricone Matini, M. L. (1985) *Le décor géométrique de la mosaique romaine: répertorire graphique et descriptif des compositions linéaires et isotropes.* Paris, Editions A&J Picard.
Bassani, M. (2012) *Ambienti e spazi cultuali.* In F. Ghedini & M. Annibaletto 2012 (eds) *Atria longa patescunt. Le forme dell'abitare nella Cisalpina romana,* 111–134. Rome, Quasar.

Berton, M., Gervasini, L. & Mancusi, M. (2020) Le indagini archeologiche 2014. In L. Gervasini & M. Mancusi (eds) *Il teatro romano di Luna*, 28–52. Genoa, Sagep Editori.

Bini, M., Brückner, H., Chelli, A., Gervasini, L., Mancusi, M. & Pappalardo, M. (2013) *Portus Lunae*. Dati per la ricostruzione paleogeografica del paesaggio costiero dell'alto Tirreno. Il progetto di ricerca geoarcheologica. In *Archeologia in Liguria* n.s. 4, 11–26.

Bueno, M. (2012a) Luna 5. In F. Ghedini & M. Annibaletto 2012 (eds) *Atria longa patescunt. Le forme dell'abitare nella Cisalpina romana*, 333–334. Rome, Quasar.

Bueno, M. (2012b) Luna 6. In F. Ghedini & M. Annibaletto 2012 (eds) *Atria longa patescunt. Le forme dell'abitare nella Cisalpina romana*, 335. Rome, Quasar.

Bueno, M. (2012c) *Spazi riservati*. In F. Ghedini & M. Annibaletto 2012 (eds) *Atria longa patescunt. Le forme dell'abitare nella Cisalpina romana*, 97–110. Rome, Quasar.

Cafaro, A. (2022) Un'indagine sul notabilato di *Lunae*: i duoviri. In A. Vanni Desideri (ed.) *Le periferie e il centro. Studi di storia ed epigrafia dell'Italia romana*, 21–35. Fucecchio, Edizioni dell'Erba.

Cagnana, A., Gandolfi, D., Lambiti, F., Landi, S., Mancusi, M., Parodi, L. & Tiscornia, I. (2021) *La costruzione della fortezza bizantina di Lunae (SP)*. Archeologia Medievale 47, 187–211.

Coarelli, F. (1985) La fondazione di *Lunae*, problemi storici ed archeologici. *Quaderni Centro Studi Lunensi* 10, 17–36.

De Marinis, R. & Spadea, G. (eds) (2007) *Ancora su I Liguri: Un antico popolo europeo tra Alpi e Mediterraneo*. Milan, Electa.

Durante, A.M. (ed.) (2001a) *Città Antica di Luna. Lavori in corso*. La Spezia, Luna Editore.

Durante, A.M. (2001b) Edilizia privata a Luna. Note a margine di recenti scoperte. In M. Verzar & M. Bass (ed.) *Abitare in Cisalpina. L'edilizia privata nelle città e nel territorio in età romana*, 269–295. Trieste, Editreg.

Durante, A.M. (2003) L'edilizia privata a Lunae. Trasformazioni di un modello urbanistico. In J. Ortalli & M. Heinzelmenn (eds) *Abitare in città. La Cisalpina tra Impero e Medioevo*, 141–152. Wiesbaden, Reichert.

Durante, A.M. (2010) L'area capitolina e i settori di indagine. In *Città antica di Luna*, 11–29. Genoa, Fratelli Frilli Editore.

Durante, A.M. & Gervasini, L. (2000) *Lunae. Zona archeologica e Museo Nazionale*. Rome, Istituto Poligrafico dello Stato.

Durante, A.M. & Landi, S. (2001) Luna. Un Foro di età imperiale. In E.M. Vecchi (ed.) *Da Luna alla Diocesi*, 15–64. La Spezia, Edizioni Giacché.

Durante, A.M. & Landi, S. (2010) Lunae, Ortonovo (SP). Case Benettini Groppallo. *Archeologia in Liguria* n.s. 2, 157–178.

Facchinetti, G. (2016) Esproprio o donazioni? Dalla proprietà privata a quella pubblica nella documentazione archeologica dell'Italia settentrionale. In C. Chillet, M.-C. Ferriès & Y. Rivière (eds) *Les confiscations, le pouvoir et Rome de la fin de la République à la mort de Néron*, 69–394. Bordeaux, Ausonius éditions.

Gervasini, L. (2015) *Lunae e il marmo*. In E. Paribeni & S. Segenni (eds) *Notae lapicidinarum*, 35–41. Pisa, PUP.

Gervasini, L. (2020) La deposizione rituale dei cani. In L. Gervasini & M. Mancusi (eds) *Il teatro romano di Luna*, 53–56. Genoa, Sagep Editori.

Gervasini, L. & Mancusi, M. (2016) Aggiornamenti lunensi. Studi e ricerche. *Quaderni Centro Studi Lunensi* n.s. 10, 69–100.

Gervasini, L., Landi, S. & Sangriso, P. (2021) *Domus dell'area 1000 (Insula XXVIII)*. In L. Gervasini & S. Landi (eds) *Mosaici antichi in Italia. Regione settima. Luna*, 237–248. Pisa, Istituti Editoriali e Poligrafici.

Ghedini, F. (2012) *Soluzioni e modelli abitativi tra tarda repubblica e tardo impero*. In F. Ghedini & M. Annibaletto (eds) *Atria longa patescunt. Le forme dell'abitare nella Cisalpina romana*, 291–332. Rome, Quasar.

Ghiotto, A.R. (2012a) Luna 1. In F. Ghedini & M. Annibaletto (eds) *Atria longa patescunt. Le forme dell'abitare nella Cisalpina romana,* 328. Rome, Quasar.

Ghiotto, A.R. (2012b) Luna 3. In F. Ghedini & M. Annibaletto (eds) *Atria longa patescunt. Le forme dell'abitare nella Cisalpina romana,* 330–331. Rome, Quasar.

Gros, P. (1997) *Vitruvio. De architectura.* Turin, Einaudi.

Gros, P. & Torelli, M. (2007) *Storia dell'Urbanistica. Il mondo romano,* New ed. Rome-Bari, Laterza.

Lackner, E.M. (2008) *Republikanische Fora.* Munich, Biering & Brinkmann,

Lippolis, E. (2016) La città in Italia tra modelli ellenistici e politica romana. L'italia Centrale e la creazione di una koiné culturale? In M. Aberson, M.C. Biella, M. Di Fazio, P. Sánchez & M. Wullschleger (eds) *I percorsi della'Romanizzazione,* 201–247. Bern, Peter Lang.

Lusuardi Siena, S. (1985) Lo scavo della cattedrale di Lunae (SP). Notizie preliminari sulle campagne 1976–1984. *Archeologia Medievale* 12, 303–311.

Lusuardi Siena, S. (2003) Gli scavi della Cattedrale di Lunae. In M. Marcenaro (ed.) *Roma e la Liguria Maritima. Secoli IV-X,* 195–202. Bordighera, Istituto di Studi Liguri.

Lusuardi Siena, S. & Sannazzaro M. (1995) Gli scavi nell'area della cattedrale lunense. In G. Cavalieri Manasse & E. Roffia (eds) *Splendida Civitas nostra,* 191–216. Rome, Quasar.

Menchelli, S., Bulzomì, F. & Marini, S. (2021a) Topografia e Topologia: la documentazione funeraria nei paesaggi liguri ed etruschi fra Romanizzazione e Tardo-antico. *Studi Classici e Orientali* 67, 159–197.

Menchelli, S., Genovesi, S. & Marcheschi, R. (2021b) Luni tardoantica. Il quartiere presso Porta Marina: continuità e cambiamenti nel sistema insediativo. In I. Baldini I. & C. Sfameni (eds) *Abitare nel Mediterraneo tardoantico,* 268–271. Bari, Edipuglia.

Menchelli, S., Sangriso, P., Cafaro, A., Marini, S. & Marcheschi, R. (2021c) Lunae. Gli scavi nel quartiere di Porta Marina. *Rendiconti della Pontificia Accademia di Archeologia* 92, 369–415.

Menchelli, S., Ferrari, V., Sangriso, P., Marini, S. & Marcheschi, R. (2022) Nuove ricerche a Luni. Il contributo dei recenti scavi e delle indagini aereotopografiche. In M.L. Marchi, G.Forte, D. Gangale Rosoleo & I. Raimondo (eds) *Landscape 2,* 85–95. Venosa, Osanna Editore.

Paltineri, S. (2018) The Ligurians. In G.D. Farney & G. Bradley (eds) *The Peoples of Ancient Italy,* 673–700. Berlin, De Gruyter.

Paribeni, E. & Segenni, S. (eds) (2015) *Notae lapicidinarum.* Pisa, PUP.

Pasquinucci, M. & Menchelli, S. (2023) Entrando nelle città dell'Etruria/Tuscia. Assetti topografici e percezioni antiche: Populonium, Volaterrae, Pisae, Luna. *Atlante Tematico di Topografia Antica* 33, 193–201.

Pelgrom, J. & Stek, T.D. (2014a) *Roman Republican Colonization. New Perspective from Archaeology and Ancient History.* Rome, Palombi Editori.

Pelgrom, J. & Stek, T.D. (2014b) Roman colonization under the Republic: historiographical contextualisation of a paradigm. In J. Pelgrom & T.D. Stek (eds) *Roman Republican Colonization. New Perspective from Archaeology and Ancient History,* 10–44. Rome, Palombi Editori.

Rinaldi, F. (2012) Ambienti di rappresentanza. In F. Ghedini & M. Annibaletto (eds) *Atria longa patescunt. Le forme dell'abitare nella Cisalpina Romana,* 71–95. Rome, Quasar.

Rossignani, M.P. (1995) Foro e Basilica a *Lunae.* In M. Mirabella Roberti (ed.) *Forum et basilica in Aquileia e nella Cisalpina romana,* 443–459. Turin, Arti Grafiche Friulane.

Rossignani, M.P., Bruno, B. & Locatelli, D. (2002) Insediamenti ed economia nell'area di Portus Lunae nella prima metà del II sec.a.C. *Africa romana* 14, 753–765.

Salmon, E.T (1969) *Roman Colonization under the Republic.* London, Thames & Hudson Ltd.

Sewell, J. (2014) Gellius, Philip II and a proposed end to the 'model-replica debate'. In J. Pelgrom & T.D. Stek (eds) *Roman Republican Colonization. New Perspective from Archaeology and Ancient History,* 125–139. Rome, Palombi Editori.

Terrenato, N. (2022) *La Grande Trattativa.* Rome, Carrocci Editore.

Van Limbergen D. & Vermeulen F. (2017) Topographic gazetteer of Roman towns in Picenum and eastern Umbria et ager Gallicus. In F. Vermeulen *From the Mountains to the Sea*, 165–202. Leuven, Peeters.

Vincenti, V. (2001) Il motivo degli edifici ad archi nei mosaici antichi. In A. Paribeni (ed.) *Atti del VII Colloquio dell'Associazione Italiana per lo Studio e la Conservazione del Mosaico*, 61–74. Ravenna, Edizioni del Girasole.

Zaccaria Ruggiu, A. (1983) La casa degli Affreschi a Lunae: fasi edilizie per successione diacronica. *Quaderni del Centro Studi Lunensi* 8, 3–38.

Zaccaria Ruggiu, A. (1991) Abitazioni private e spazio pubblico: il caso di Lunae e di Conimbriga. *Rivista di Archeologia* 15, 97–110.

Zaccaria Ruggiu, A. (1995) *Spazio privato e spazio pubblico nella città romana*. Rome, École française de Rome.

# Chapter 11

## Interamna Lirenas: how special?

*Alessandro Launaro*

### 11.1. Introduction

Many ancient towns have enjoyed a long life, often reaching well beyond Antiquity. When this has happened, it has been primarily on account of the continued relevance they enjoyed as the world around them changed. Many, however, failed to keep up with such transformations and were eventually abandoned, never to be occupied again. While the memory of their former existence began to fade, some of them acquired a new purpose as vast sources of building materials ready to be extracted and (re)used elsewhere: the more accessible the site, the more systematic, thorough, and prolonged these 'extractive activities' turned out to be. Once this had ceased, debris was spread over to level the ground and many of these sites were eventually reclaimed for agriculture ('greenfield sites'). The site of an ancient town is often given away by the enduring presence of some notable ruins, usually associated with those monumental features which are indicative of its original status.

Interamna Lirenas (Southern Lazio, Central Italy) is one Roman town, which, on the other hand, disappeared almost completely from sight (Fig. 11.1), its memory mostly preserved in the modern name of the area (Contrada Termine, today part of the Municipality of Pignataro Interamna). By the time modern scholarship began to take a more systematic interest in it, it offered such an underwhelming spectacle that archaeologists were quickly convinced of its early decline and fundamentally backwater character (par. 11.2). However, as it has been the case for several other 'greenfield sites' (e.g. Falerii Novi: Millett, this volume; Septempeda: Vermeulen, this volume), since 2010 our understanding of Interamna has been profoundly affected by the systematic and extensive application of non-destructive archaeological techniques, particularly geophysical prospection and the study of the plough soil assemblage (Launaro and Millett 2023), enhanced by targeted excavations (Bellini *et al.* 2014a, 2017, 2018, 2019, 2020; Ballantyne *et al.* 2015, 2016; Goddard *et al.* 2022; forthcoming). This approach has since revealed an urban plan sprawling over 24 ha

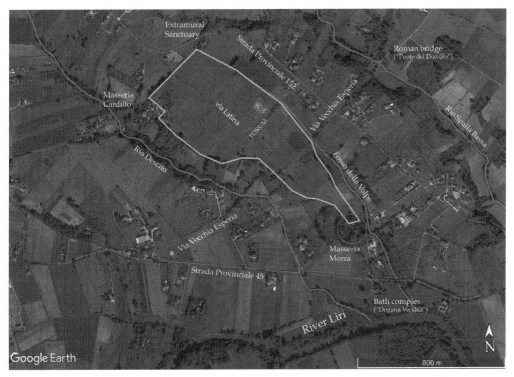

*Figure 11.1. The site of Interamna Lirenas and its environs (image from Google Earth, retrieved on 28/05/2021; 41°25'35.22"N / 13°45'11.82"E).*

and featuring a hitherto unknown level of urban complexity. Furthermore, it has produced clear evidence of sustained growth from the mid-Republican to early Imperial period, with no real signs of either contraction or decline until the later part of the 3rd century AD.

If these discoveries have prompted a specific reconsideration of the archaeology of this town, their implications are in fact broader. As it will be shown, the historical trajectory of Interamna appears to have significantly diverged from traditional narratives about the development of Roman Italy in the Imperial period, long-assumed to have been characterised by stagnation and decline (e.g. Giardina 1997, 233–264, as such referred in Patterson 2006, 2, 265). Therefore, the problem is whether Interamna should be considered a special case in Antiquity (i.e. representative of itself only) or rather an average community in Roman Italy whose nature and trajectory have been more comprehensively revealed by archaeology than it is usually the case. This chapter will thus provide an overview of the results of 13 years of archaeological fieldwork at Interamna, and how these may contribute to a reappraisal of the long-term development of Roman urbanism in Italy.

## 11.2. Interamna Lirenas in context

The site of Interamna Lirenas occupies a southern spur of a river terrace in the middle of the Liri Valley, a fundamental route of communication across Central Italy in any period. About 1 km long, roughly triangular in shape, the spur is oriented northwest–southeast and extends towards the meandering course of the River Liri (ancient *Liris*), only few hundred metres away. Flat on top, it features rather marked slopes on its sides (especially the southwestern one) and towers over the plain below from a relative height of 30 m (60 m a.s.l.). Gifted with a well defensible site, Interamna was placed at a strategic crossroad in the landscape (Fig. 11.2): the *via Latina*, which constituted the main axis of the urban settlement, here approached the course of the Liri (navigable at the time), where it was joined by a road running along the valley bottom (from the northwest, today corresponding to the *Strada Provinciale 45*) and another one crossing over the river itself (to the south), before further proceeding to the southeast (towards Teanum, in Campania) (Launaro and Millett 2023, 5–7). The site represented a bridgehead along the left bank of the river Liri and lay within a territory which, in the latter part of the 4th and the early 3rd centuries BC, was crucially involved in the confrontation between Romans and Samnites.

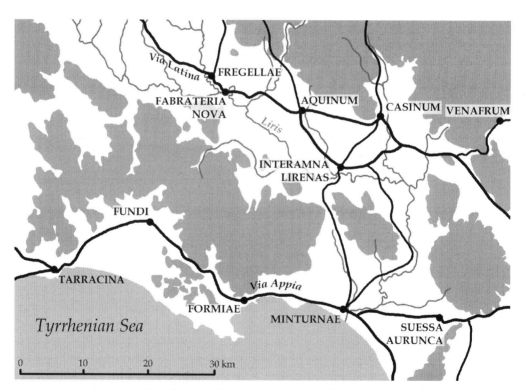

*Figure 11.2. Settlement and road networks in the lower Liri Valley in Antiquity (dark grey areas = over 1,000 m a.s.l.).*

Such character is well reflected in the available textual evidence, which for long has represented the main source of information about Interamna (Launaro and Millett 2023, 7–10). Ancient authors mentioned Interamna in passing, primarily due to its participation in broader events of the Republican period: its foundation as a Latin colony in 312 BC in the context of the Samnite Wars (Livy 9.28.8; also Diod. Sic 19.105.5, Vell. Pat.1.14.4.); its role as a (wavering) ally of Rome during the Second Punic War (Livy 27.9.7, 27.10.10, 29.15); the Triumviral settlement of veterans in its territory (Cic. *Phil.* 2.105; also *Lib. Col.* L 234.18–20 = C 182.36–37). By the time of the Principate, Interamna had comprehensively ceased to play any part in the main narrative of Roman history and, as such, it disappeared from it. Epigraphic evidence partly compensated for this lack of information, even though it projected the image of a town soon bypassed by the main road network (Wightman 1994, 31–32; also Ceraudo 2004; 2007), and which, albeit acting as a venue for local periodical markets (*Inscriptiones Italiae* 13.2.49–50), may have struggled financially such as to require direct supervision from a *curator rei publicae* at the turn of the 3rd century AD (CIL X 4860). After all, Interamna is notably absent from the relevant sections of both the *Tabula Peutingeriana* (Segmentum V) and the *Itinerarium Antonini* (302.1–304.4). Besides, we are told that an otherwise 'collapsing' bath complex was maintained and kept in operation only thanks to generous benefactions from members of the *gens Sentia* (M. Sentius Crispinus and M. Sentius Redemptus) between the 3rd/4th and the early 5th centuries AD (CIL X 5348–5349).

Considering the scarcity of visible material remains across the site, it should not surprise that the first modern archaeological studies of Interamna tended to see it flourish in the Republican period, only to begin a process of inexorable decline soon afterwards. Michelangelo Cagiano de Azevedo (1947, 9–10), implicitly subscribing to a long-established view that interpreted colonies as *propugnacula imperii* (Cic. *Leg. agr.* 2.27), linked the fortunes of Interamna to the military and strategic role it played while Rome was consolidating its hold over Italy. According to Filippo Coarelli (1982, 215) the centre was eventually 'absorbed' by nearby Aquinum, likely becoming one of its *vici*. The first systematic analysis of the plough soil assemblage over the urban area, carried out by Canadian archaeologists in 1978–83 and primarily focussed on the distribution of fineware and amphorae potsherds, appeared to confirm these interpretations: the area of occupation would have peaked (*c.* 30 ha) around the late 2nd to early 1st centuries BC, only to have shrunk dramatically (*c.* 10 ha) by the 1st century AD, and even further later on (Hayes & Wightman 1984, 138, fig. 2, 140–145, 148). The obvious contrast between Interamna and its neighbouring towns in terms of archaeological remains ('city walls are not definitely attested at Interamna, which also lacks theatre and amphitheatre') and surviving inscriptions ('Interamna has only one quarter to one fifth of the number found in the town and territories of Aquinum and Casinum') only reinforced this view (Wightman & Hayes 1994, 35). Admittedly, one dissonant interpretation was put forward by Gaetano Lena (1982, 60–61), a local scholar whose own analysis of the plough soil assemblage dated the peak of urban occupation to the Imperial period (dismissed by Hayes & Wightmen 1984, 145 n.9).

## 11.3. The Interamna Lirenas Project

### 11.3.1. *Research framework*

What made Interamna Lirenas so unpromising and somewhat underwhelming is exactly what brought our team from the University of Cambridge to Contrada Termine. Looking for a 'greenfield site' where to pursue the non-destructive survey approaches that had been successfully applied in the Tiber Valley and elsewhere (Millett 2013; Keay & Millett 2016), we were drawn there by the ideal conditions the site offered for both geophysical prospection (almost unencumbered by later buildings and comprehensively accessible) and systematic surface collections (fields being periodically ploughed with optimal visibility) (Bellini *et al.* 2014b, 262). After all, notwithstanding its possible decline in the Imperial period, early modern wanderers had indeed recorded the presence of numerous ruins across the site (Notarjanni 2016 [1814], 41–42; Romanelli 1819, 384), with some of the paved streets being still visible (and in use!) in the 1940s (Cagiano de Azevedo 1947, 24). If Interamna had indeed experienced an early decline as previous scholarship had argued, it would have still presented a rare opportunity to map a Republican urban layout little affected by later developments (an almost 'closed context', akin to Fregellae: Diosono, this volume). However, there were already good reasons to believe that this may have not been the case.

First, just outside town, downhill from the main settlement, next to a likely crossing over the River Liri, stood the remains of a large room in *opus listatum/ vittatum*, featuring a groin vault and two apses. Known locally as 'Dogana Vecchia', it was badly damaged during the Second World War and only the lower part is still preserved today. Notwithstanding the lack of any specific features normally found in association with bath complexes (e.g. *tubuli*, *suspensurae*), Cagiano de Azevedo (1947, 10, 24–28) was minded to interpret this structure as what was left of the building repeatedly restored by the *gens Sentia* (par 11.2), taking it as an indicator of Interamna's flourishing between the end of the 4th and the beginning of the 5th century AD. But this late vitality, not impossible after a prolonged period of decline, clearly contrasted with the results of the Canadian survey (par 11.2). As it happens, a quick reanalysis of the Canadian dataset highlighted possible flaws in its original interpretation, somewhat misrepresenting the widespread presence of early – and even late – Imperial finds across the site (Bellini *et al.* 2014b, 259–260).

These preliminary considerations convinced us that a systematic reappraisal of the archaeology of Interamna was indeed fully warranted. While a full-coverage geophysical prospection may have well revealed the (still-buried) urban layout, we were also aware that knowledge of commonware pottery had very much improved since the 1980s. Due to their local/regional distribution, commonwares were likely to provide more reliable evidence of occupation compared to finewares and amphorae, whose access/supply had been significantly affected over time by their increasingly overseas origin (Bellini *et al.* 2014b, 267–269). To further enhance these activities, we carried out a systematic field survey in the surrounding territory (2010–14: preliminary results discussed in Launaro & Leone 2018; Launaro 2019, 123–132) and launched a series of targeted excavations around the *forum*.

### 11.3.2. Geophysical prospection

The extent of the surface scatters in the plough soil provided a good indication of the (maximum) extent of the urban area of Interamna Lirenas. Except for a group of houses located at the northwestern and southeastern ends of the spur (Masseria Cardillo and Masseria Morra respectively), the rest of the site consisted of a series of open agricultural fields, whose easy accessibility made it possible to carry out a full-coverage geophysical prospection of the site (24.3 ha in total) with both fluxgate gradiometry and ground-penetrating radar (GPR). The fluxgate gradiometry (2010–12) and the initial targeted application of GPR (2012–14) were carried out in collaboration with the British School at Rome (BSR) and the Archaeological Prospection Services of Southampton University (APSS), under the supervision of Sophie Hay. The main GPR survey was carried out in partnership with Lieven Verdonck and Frank Vermeulen from Ghent University (2015–17), part of a larger project involving similar work at the site of Falerii Novi as well (Millett, this volume). The results of all these activities have been comprehensively presented and thoroughly discussed in a recent monograph (Launaro & Millett 2023, 39–104). The following discussion will draw attention to some relevant features of the ancient town which the geophysical prospection has revealed (Plate 11.1).

One of the most striking aspects of the town is certainly its dense occupation. Except for some marginal sectors featuring few (if any) geophysical anomalies interpreted as buried structures, the built area is generally packed with a wide array of private and public units. Most domestic units (84%) tend to be relatively small (190 x House I: <500 m²), but are widely interspersed with fewer larger ones (25 x House II: 500–1,000 m²; 5 x House III: > 1,000 m²), thus showing no noticeable sign of zoning or separation according to social status (a pattern which is well-attested at those Roman towns, like Pompeii and Herculaneum, whose plan is comprehensively known: Wallace-Hadrill 1994, 75–78). Furthermore, a series of 19 sizable 'courtyard buildings', mostly located at a distance from the *forum*, may represent service structures (*horrea, macella, scholae*) as well as apartment blocks (or indeed both, especially if they had featured an upper floor). A preliminary comparison with the new plan of Falerii Novi (Millett *et al.* forthcoming; also Millett, this volume) is proving helpful. Even though the intramural area of Interamna (*c.* 23 ha) was considerably smaller than that of Falerii (*c.* 31 ha), it did harbour a much larger proportion of smaller domestic units (House I) and about six times the number of 'courtyard buildings', possibly indicating a higher population density and an even larger population overall. Although its higher population density (90 inhabitants/ha) may have represented a response to spatial constraints imposed by the topography, it is in fact more or less in line with independent estimates which have been put forward for Roman urban settlement of middling size (Millett 2013, 37–39; Hanson & Ortman 2017, 314–319; also Russell & De Simone this volume). In short, from a demographic point of view, Interamna appears to have been hardly special.

However, one of the problems with this kind of population estimates is that they tend to refer to the 'peak' of occupation, invariably assuming the entirety of the urban area to have been comprehensively occupied at some point in time. This lack of chronological/spatial dimension is admittedly problematic but can be effectively balanced out with a systematic study of the plough soil assemblage (e.g. Vaccaro 2013). Taking the spread of well-dated commonware pottery to provide a reliable diachronic indication of occupation levels across the site (par. 11.3.1), it was possible to map how the urban area of Interamna may have developed in the Roman period (Fig. 11.3). Its initial occupation appears to have been rather limited, clustered around the *forum* area and few satellites spots within the plateau (possibly involving as few as 200 families out of an initial colonial contingent of 4,000). This may be explained by considering that a larger number of colonists than normally assumed may have been settled in the *ager* (Launaro 2019, 126). Besides, the nefarious impact of the Samnite siege (294 BC) and the passage of Hannibal's army (211 BC) must have seriously disrupted the development of the Latin colony in its crucial, initial phase (Launaro & Millett 2023, 90–91). But the situation began to improve soon afterwards, and urban occupation may have indeed reached its maximum extent by the 1st century BC (as originally argued by Hayes & Wightman 1984). However, this trend continued until the early 3rd century AD, with a population likely peaking in the 1st–2nd centuries AD (Launaro & Millett 2023, 69–80, 97–99).

This trajectory appears to defy traditional expectations about Interamna – and many other towns in mid-Imperial Italy. This requires some explanation, particularly in consideration of the apparent sidelining of this community as indicated by the later course of the *via Latina* (established in the Augustan period: Ceraudo 2004, 155–156; 2007, 105–110), which effectively bypassed Interamna, in favour of a more direct link between Aquinum and Casinum (a situation later reflected in both the *Tabula Peutingeriana* and the *Itinerarium Antonini*) (par. 11.2). If the later course of the *via Latina* undoubtedly provided a more expedient route for long-distance journeys through the Liri Valley (i.e. the kind of travel which *itineraria* were arguably for), this does not imply that the existing communication network had ceased to exist. On the contrary, large and important centres like Aquinum (Ceraudo, this volume) and Casinum may have relied on this secondary network to further connect with the rest of the valley and, most importantly, the River Liri itself. After all, if the Emperor Claudius had indeed considered redirecting the waters from the Fucine Lake into the Liri not only to reclaim good agricultural land, but also to make it *even more* navigable (Dio Cass. 60.11.5), it stands to reason that the river represented a very important waterway across that part of Central Italy, linked with the important port of Minturnae and, through it,

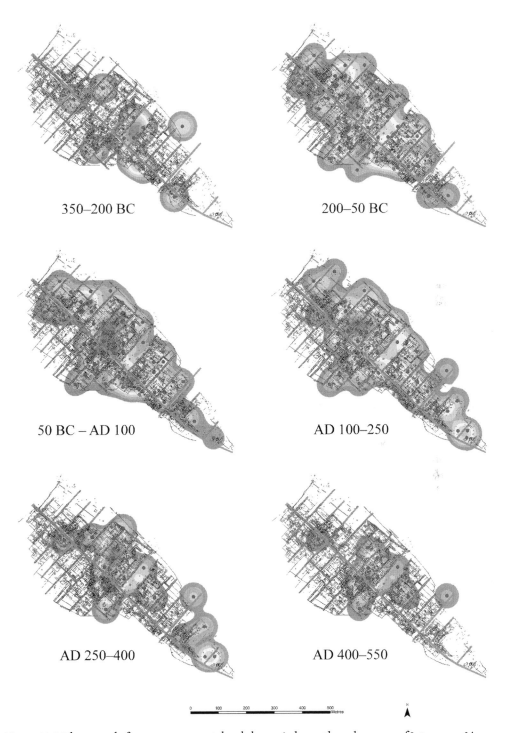

350–200 BC

200–50 BC

50 BC – AD 100

AD 100–250

AD 250–400

AD 400–550

*Figure 11.3. The spread of commonware potsherds by period over the urban area of Interamna Lirenas (as modelled in Launaro & Millett 2023, 72–77 figs 4.22-27).*

the Mediterranean (Guidobaldi & Pesando 1989, 44, also n. 49). If one considers this extended and integrated communication network, the place of Interamna acquires renewed centrality: not only it was the only town located along the course of the Liri between Fabrateria Nova and Minturnae, but it was well connected to both Aquinum (earlier route of the *via Latina*) and Casinum (road leading northwards, today known as 'Via Vecchia Esperia', and passing on the bridge over the Rio Spalla Bassa, the so-called 'Ponte del Diavolo: Fig. 11.1).

These considerations may go some way towards explaining the considerable presence of those 'courtyard buildings' which, as it has been suggested, may have represented apartment blocks as well as *horrea*, or even *macella* (see above; see Plate 11.1). If their number appears excessive for a middling town like Interamna, it would be much more explicable had the town represented a trade hub within the valley, in service to larger centres like Aquinum and Casinum. That Interamna played such a crucial role is indicated by the fact that its name features in two separate lists of periodical market venues (*nundinae*), meaning that it likely acted as a link between two (largely independent) regional market circuits, the only town in the Liri Valley known to have done so (Launaro & Leone 2018, 325–326). A large open space (*c.* 0.5 ha) at its southeastern end has been interpreted as a *forum pecuarium* (Launaro & Millett 2023, 66). This likely played a part in the wool trade, which represented a fundamental resource across the region more generally, and at Interamna specifically (Launaro & Leone 2018, 326–327).

More recently, Interamna's direct link with the river has found further confirmation thanks to a GPR survey of the area of 'Dogana Vecchia' (Fig. 11.1), near the present course of the Liri (Launaro & Verdonck forthcoming). The preliminary interpretation of the geophysical anomalies has revealed the presence of a temple (whose remains may have been seen by Notarjanni 2016 [1814]: 42), a possible bath complex (distinct from the remains which Cagiano interpreted as such), and – more significantly – a sizable *horreum*. All things considered, these structures likely formed part of the river port of Interamna, whose main period of operation (as tentatively indicated by the plough soil assemblage) is currently attested between the late 1st century BC and the 4th century AD. By intercepting – and enabling – an intense traffic between the centres of Aquinum and Casinum to the north and Minturane and the Tyrrhenian coast to the southeast, Interamna likely offered a diverse range of opportunities to many, something which may well explain its population levels and dense occupation over a prolonged period (2nd century BC to 3rd century AD). Remarkably, the scale and significance of these activities would be completely lost were we to exclusively rely on the presence of finewares and amphorae imported from overseas (Launaro & Leone 2018, 335–337).

Interamna was thus a lively node in a local/regional network which the town supported and – no less importantly – benefitted from. Without this awareness, it would be impossible to explain the hitherto unknown urban monumental character as revealed by the geophysical prospection. Two intramural sanctuaries dominated the lower plain and the course of the Liri to the southeast, their position consonant with a Hellenistic architectural tradition well-attested both in Italy and abroad (Gros & Torelli 2007, 193–196; Yegül & Favro 2019, 96–110). Similarly, along the northwestern side of the town, a roofed theatre (par. 11.3.3) towered over an open terrace (an elegant garden?), enhancing its visibility from the road running on the parallel spur immediately to the northeast (today *Strada Provinciale 152*). Remarkably, notwithstanding the relevance of the *via Latina* as the backbone of the urban layout, the town's most impressive public buildings were located away from it, invariably facing outwards, as if to convey a sense of the opulence and success of that community to those approaching it from any side (Launaro & Millett 2023, 97). But Interamna did not merely offer a spectacle to outsiders: at least one secure *macellum* and three bath complexes served its own population. Of the latter group, the largest one is likely the one maintained and renovated by members of the *gens Sentia* (Launaro 2019, 132; Launaro & Millett 2023, 101; *pace* Cagiano de Azevedo 1947, 10, 24–28). Conditions may have significantly changed from the 3rd century AD onwards, involving a significant if gradual reduction of both the urban area (Fig. 11.3) and the underlying population, a process apparently mirrored in the countryside (Launaro 2019, 130–132). Nevertheless, that the town continued to exist as a civic centre of some relevance well into the 5th century AD is indicated by that late act of *euergetism* from a wealthy *patronus* (M. Sentius Redemptus, in AD 408). This represents a rather unusual case among the towns of southern Latium in this period (Savino 2005, 187–188), made even more remarkable by the fact that, although the *gens Sentia* was probably from Atina (Wightman & Hayes 1994, 43), they had clear interests at Interamna. One cannot but wonder if Interamna's privileged relationship with the River Liri, an important waterway whose existence did not require the same level of maintenance or investment as the road network clearly did, may have had a part in slowing down and delaying the town's decline and abandonment (Savino 2005, 66–70).

### 11.3.3. Excavation

Since 2013, guided by the results of the geophysical prospection, targeted excavations around the *forum* area have brought to light a series of public buildings and some remarkable epigraphic evidence whose nature and chronology have significantly added to our understanding of Interamna Lirenas and its development. But geophysical prospection did not merely identify the most promising sectors in which to open our trenches. It rather provided invaluable information about both their immediate and broader context, making it possible to widen the reach of our interpretation in ways that would not be possible in the absence of such (detailed) data about what it is still buried (and invisible).

The earliest well-dated structures brought to light belong to a *porticus* built in the early 2nd century BC, which was eventually razed to make room for the theatre towards the end of the 1st century BC (Bellini *et al.* 2019). A small section of the covered walkway (featuring a width of *c*. 6 m) was uncovered underneath the *postscaenium* of

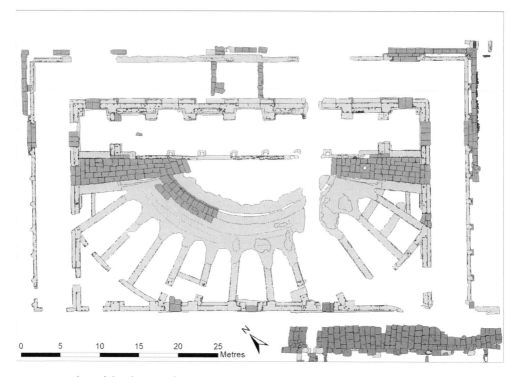

*Figure 11.4. Plan of the theatre of Interamna Lirenas, including remains of the Republican* porticus *uncovered under the* postscaenium, *as revealed by the excavation (2013–22).*

the theatre (Fig. 11.4). It likely extended further in both directions, its continuation to the Southwest having been entirely removed (including foundations) when the (lower) *cavea* was excavated. It is defined by two linear parallel structures in *opus quadratum* (local travertine): the one to the northwest was open, featuring descending steps and a series of columns/pilasters (as indicated by their foundations), whereas the one to the southeast corresponded to a perimeter wall which closed the building on that side. Whatever complex it may have been originally part of, the *porticus* was located quite centrally, but notably away from both the *via Latina* and the *forum*, along the northeastern limit of the settlement. This situation strikingly resonates with the one already recorded for the intramural sanctuaries (and their likely *porticus*) which have been identified along the southwestern edge of town (par. 11.3.3).

An adaptation of the Greek *stoa*, the *porticus* was being adopted by Roman architecture at about the same time, especially in its more 'functional' versions closely associated with trade and other business activities (Davies 2017, 128–132). But precocious examples of this architectural type were to be found outside Rome too, notably at Minturnae, where a *porticus duplex* (190–174 BC) was built along the *via Appia*, immediately outside the western gate of the original *castrum*

(Guidobaldi & Pesando 1989, 50–51). What may have acted as the model for the *porticus* at Interamna is less relevant than its early date, which is contemporaneous with precocious developments elsewhere. Besides, a preliminary study of the early (Republican) phase of the *basilica* (see below) recorded same building technique and materials as those employed in the *porticus* (Goddard *et al.* 2022, 345–346; forthcoming), thus suggesting that both buildings may have formed part of a contemporary monumental development. All things considered, whatever the actual scale of the troubles experienced by Interamna during the 3rd century BC, this community had begun to flourish soon after the end of the Second Punic War, likely seizing the unprecedented opportunities that the conquest of the Mediterranean offered to both Romans and their Italian allies.

The next major urban transformation took place between the end of the 1st century BC and the early decades of the 1st century AD. Hardly a surprising outcome when considering the development of Roman urbanism in Italy (Gros & Torelli 2007, 243–270), this discovery actually defied traditional expectations about Interamna, a town long assumed to have been already declining by the beginning of that period (par. 11.2). Building activities associated with this phase tend to feature same techniques (mainly *opus reticulatum*, complemented with *opus testaceum*) and building materials (*cubilia* made of local travertine). The earlier *basilica* at the northern corner of the *forum* was demolished to (and largely including) foundation level, being replaced by a new structure (c. 26 × 19 m) (Fig. 11.5) (Bellini *et al.* 2020, 365–367; Goddard *et al.* 2022, 345–346). This building presented a rather standard plan, whose internal layout was defined by a series of 14 columns. The excavation confirmed these columns to have been made of bricks and decorated with a thick layer of stucco featuring 24 flutes (as typical of the Ionic/Corinthian order which was popular at the time).

The sector immediately to the north of the *forum* underwent an even more significant redevelopment: two *insulae* were merged (by closing off the road running behind the *basilica*), earlier buildings were knocked down (including a *porticus*: see above) and a large terrace was created (supported by a solid retaining wall: Bellini *et al.* 2020, 367). The resulting platform was then occupied by a theatre (c. 55 × 31 m), whose *cavea* was contained within a rectangular roofed hall (c. 45 m × 26 m) (Bellini *et al.* 2017; 2018). Roofed theatres, albeit not unknown in Italy, did represent a relatively rare occurrence (in general Sear 2006, 119–185). Acoustically better performing than their more traditional, open-air counterpart, they presented their own structural challenges (in general Izenour 1993). It certainly made sense to advertise the clear monumental ambition of this project (and the notable wealth which had made it possible) by giving it pride of place on a purpose-built stage (the terrace): anyone traveling along the alternative route of the *via Latina* few hundred metres away would have linked this with the ambition and resources of the citizens of Interamna – and of their wealthy and powerful *patroni* too.

What the excavation has brought to light mirrors what else we have since learned about the place which Interamna occupied within a political network which

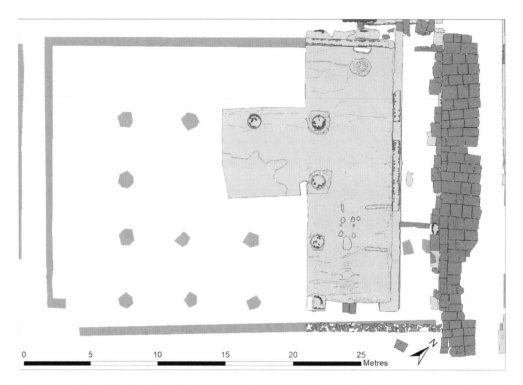

*Figure 11.5. Plan of the basilica of Interamna Lirenas as revealed by the GPR prospection (2015–17) light grey) and excavation (2019–22).*

extended across the region, including Rome. Not only a reappraisal of a well-known inscription has confirmed that Julius Caesar had been *patronus municipi* in 46 BC, but the excavations themselves have uncovered new epigraphic evidence that matches and enhances our renewed narrative of the development of the town (Launaro & Patterson 2020). A member of the local *gens Novia* (M. Novius Tubula) likely began a senatorial career by being elected as a plebeian tribune in the time of Augustus, celebrating this achievement by donating an inscribed sundial to its hometown. The construction of the theatre itself likely benefitted from the generosity of a wealthy freedman of the Sulpicii Galbae, a certain Anoptes, whose name may have featured on the *frons scaenae* itself. The fact that the interests of this powerful and wealthy family primarily concentrated along the coast between Terracina and Puteoli, passing through Minturnae, provides a suggestive indication of the place which Interamna occupied within the political and economic geography of the region between the late Republican and early Imperial periods.

What the excavation reveals about later phases is heavily affected by significant post-abandonment disruptions. Dating any development to the mid-to-late Imperial period is thus rather challenging. The *basilica* certainly received a new concrete floor, but the associated stratigraphy has not yet revealed an absolute chronology for this intervention. The *frons scaenae* of the theatre was certainly transformed at a later period, with the addition of elements in *opus testaceum* whose characteristics (e.g. the increased thickness of the layer of mortar) may find some correspondence with examples dated to the 3rd century AD (Lugli 1957, 611–621, also tav. CLXXI fig. 3). That the theatre was still in operation in this period (and possibly after) seems indicated by the fact that M. Sentius Crispinus had been awarded the honour of a *bisellium* (double seat at the theatre) at some point between the 3rd and 4th centuries AD (par. 11.2).

On the other hand, the excavation has been quite informative about the post-abandonment phase. In line with earlier interpretations, it seems likely that the increased level of disruption, conflict and general insecurity associated with the Greco-Gothic War (AD 535–554), and not experienced in the area since the time of Hannibal, had prompted the last remaining inhabitants to abandon the town, probably already deserted by the time of the Lombard invasion of the late 6th century AD (Launaro & Millett 2023, 101). The earliest archaeological sign of abandonment may indeed be represented by some skeletal remains radiocarbon dated to 588–704 cal AD at 83.8% probability (LTL21908 – 1381+45BP). These belonged to a 30/40-year-old woman, whose burial cut through what was left of the marble floor of a building of uncertain function located at the southwestern corner of the *forum* (Goddard *et al.* 2022, 347). Additional juvenile burials are attested at this spot, one of which has been radiocarbon dated to 994–1155 cal AD at 95.4% probability (LTL20241A – 977±40 bp) (Bellini *et al.* 2020, 367). These latter activities may well have taken place at the time when the theatre was undergoing a systematic and thorough process of spoliation (as indicated by the presence of few fragments of *ceramica a bande rosse* tentatively dated to the 10th–12th centuries AD). This process is attested across the trenches more generally and resulted in a large quantity of debris being accumulated everywhere. Later on, this material was spread over: the area was levelled by filling any hollows (e.g. the theatre's *cavea*) so as to create an even surface suitable for arable agriculture (although few remains of modest height must have remained partly visible across the plateau).

## 11.4. Conclusions

Our understanding of Interamna Lirenas has profoundly changed. Whether our insights can be used to develop any more general consideration about the development of towns in Roman Italy depends on how representative we consider this case to be. Interamna's trajectory for the period up to and including the 1st century AD now hardly stands out compared to our expectations for most other Italian towns over the same period. Clear signs of expansion in the 2nd century BC and, even more so, in the time of Augustus and the early Imperial period, are well-known phenomena. The significance of Caesar's patronage of Interamna in 46 BC should not be overstated: although only three other towns are currently known to have boasted such privilege

(Alba Fucens, Bovianum and Vibo Valentia), significantly more probably did so (Caesar needed to consolidate his network of political support as widely and thoroughly as possible across Italy, especially at such a critical time). What really defies expectation is the lack of visible crisis and the apparent continuity in the 2nd and 3rd centuries AD. Again, this is not unheard of (Russell & De Simone, this volume), but it is something which we would have remained ignorant about Interamna had it not been for the study of commonware pottery as evidence of local/regional networks.

That Italy and its towns had been experiencing a precocious crisis during the 2nd century AD, somewhat prefiguring and anticipating the more general crisis of the 3rd century AD, has been predicated on a very specific interpretation of the earlier period. For a long time, the success (and wealth) of Italian communities in the late Republican period has been attributed to their elites' ability to fully exploit the unprecedented business opportunities resulting from a combination of most favourable market conditions across the Mediterranean and the widespread availability of (cheap) slave labour. This would have led to the development of an intensive agricultural system centred on cash crops (wine, olive oil) and so closely reliant on such specific conditions as to be fundamentally inflexible (i.e. the so-called 'villa economy': Launaro 2015). As such it could have not survived the maturation of the empire and the rise of the provinces (less favourable market conditions), let alone the decline in the supply of the essential slave labour (as the empire stabilised and military campaigns became much rarer) (Giardina 1997, 233–264; also Carandini 1989). The crisis of Italian agriculture and overseas exports could not but have a negative feedback effect on the wealth of the Italian landed elite and their ability to invest and take a direct interest in towns and their communities. On the other hand, Italian towns would have been effectively sidelined as the flow of trade and wealth between Italy and the rest of the Mediterranean had fundamentally changed. In other words, the success of Italy and its towns has for long been understood as a function of its participation in long-distance Mediterranean trade.

However, it is precisely this emphasis which is probably unwarranted. It has been shown that overseas demand for the products of such an intensive, export-oriented, slave-based agriculture was relatively limited even at its peak (Launaro 2017, 96–102). Thanks in no little part to the wealth generated by military campaign overseas and the varied range of business opportunities which they had created, the Roman and Italian elites took on themselves to invest in their towns, triggering a process which turned Italy into one of the most urbanized regions in the Roman world (Gros & Torelli 2007, 181–198). The supply of this growing urban demand (including – but not limited to – Rome) likely came to represent a solid and vast market for Italian agriculture, largely independent of changing patterns across the empire. Given the variety and fragmentation of the Italian landscape, an integrated communication network must have played an effective and essential role in guaranteeing a comprehensive supply of these communities (especially when located further away from the coast, and thus less likely to be able to intercept the flow of provincial goods to Rome). The local and regional nature of these networks may well explain their limited archaeological visibility if only (imported) finewares and amphorae are considered diagnostic (Launaro & Leone 2019).

All things considered, Interamna was never 'special'. Between the late Republican and early Imperial period, it enjoyed that same growth that is attested at many other Italian towns. On the other hand, its unexpected continuity in the mid-Imperial period may reflect conditions that were much more widespread across Italy than traditionally acknowledged. What, if anything, makes this site somewhat special is how comprehensively its archaeology has been revealed (Launaro & Millett 2023, 107–108): none of the approaches, methodologies and techniques employed there are new, but their systematic combination and scale of application have allowed a remarkably holistic (re)appraisal of a Roman town in Italy. This research has indeed shown the immense informative potential of 'greenfield sites', even those – like Interamna – which may look the most underwhelming on the surface. It is precisely their marked accessibility and, therefore, suitability for the application of a wide array of extensive survey techniques and approaches which holds the greatest potential. Indeed, more integrated studies like this one will hopefully follow, expanding our dataset of Roman towns – both in Italy and beyond – whose plan and full range of material culture are comprehensively known and understood.

## Acknowledgements

The Interamna Lirenas Project is run by the Faculty of Classics of the University of Cambridge in close collaboration with the *Soprintendenza Archeologia, Belle Arti e Paesaggio per le Province di Frosinone e Latina* and the *Comune di Pignataro Interamna*, in partnership with the British School at Rome (since 2010) and Ghent University (2015–17). Fieldwork has been made possible by generous support from the Faculty of Classics, the Arts and Humanities Research Council (AH/M006522/1), the *Comune di Pignataro Interamna*, the McDonald Institute for Archaeological Research, the British Academy, the Leverhulme Trust and the Isaac Newton Trust.

## Bibliography

Ballantyne, R., Bellini, G.R., Hales, J., Launaro, A., Leone, N., Millett, M., Verdonck, L. & Vermeulen, F. (2016) Interamna Lirenas. *Papers of the British School at Rome* 84, 322–325.

Ballantyne, R., Bellini, G.R., Launaro, A., Leone, N. & Millett, M. (2015) Interamna Lirenas. *Papers of the British School at Rome* 83, 299–302.

Bellini, G.R., Hay, S., Launaro, A., Leone, N. & Millett, M. (2014a) Interamna Lirenas. *Papers of the British School at Rome* 82, 327–331.

Bellini, G.R., Launaro, A. & Millett, M. (2014b) Roman colonial landscapes: *Interamna Lirenas* and its territory through Antiquity. In J. Pelgrom & T. Stek (eds) *Roman Republican Colonisation: New Perspectives from Archaeology and Ancient History*, 255–275. Rome, Palombi Editori.

Bellini, G.R., Launaro, A., Leone, N., Millett, M., Verdonck, L. & Vermeulen, F. (2017) Interamna Lirenas. *Papers of the British School at Rome* 85, 321–324.

Bellini, G.R., Launaro, A., Leone, N., Millett, M., Verdonck, L. & Vermeulen, F. (2018) Interamna Lirenas. *Papers of the British School at Rome* 86, 303–306.

Bellini, G.R., Goddard, D., Grünwald, D., Launaro, A., Leone, N. & Millett, M. (2019) Interamna Lirenas. *Papers of the British School at Rome* 87, 333–336.

Bellini, G.R., Goddard, D., Grünwald, D., Launaro, A., Leone, N., Millett, M. & Pantano, W. (2020) Interamna Lirenas. *Papers of the British School at Rome* 88, 365–368.

Cagiano de Azevedo, M. (1947) *Interamna Lirenas vel Sucasina*. Rome, Istituto di Studi Romani Editore.

Carandini, A. (1989) L'economia italica fra tarda repubblica e medio impero considerata dal punto di vista di una merce: il vino. In M. Lenoir, D. Manacorda & C. Panella (eds) *Amphores romeines et histoire ´economique: dix ans de recherche*, 505–521. Rome, École française de Rome.

Ceraudo, G. (2004) La via Latina tra Fabrateria Nova e Casinum: precisazioni topografiche e nuovi spunti metodologici. *Archeologia Aerea* 1, 155–181.

Ceraudo, G. 2007. Miliari della via Latina nel territorio di Aquino. In A. Nicosia & G. Ceraudo (eds) *Spigolature Aquinati: Studi storico-Archeologici su Aquino e il suo territorio*, 105–119. Aquino, Museo della Città.

Coarelli, F. (1982) *Lazio*. Bari, Laterza.

Davies, P.J.E. 2017. *Architecture and Politics in Republican Rome*. Cambridge, Cambridge University Press.

Giardina, A. (1997) *L'Italia romana. Storie di un'identità incompiuta*. Rome-Bari, Laterza.

Goddard, D., Launaro, A., Leone, N., Millett, M. & Pantano, W. (2022) Interamna Lirenas. *Papers of the British School at Rome* 90, 345–348.

Goddard, D., Launaro, A. & Leone, N. (forthcoming) Interamna Lirenas. *Papers of the British School at Rome* 91.

Gros, P. & Torelli, M. (2007) *Storia dell'urbanistica. Il mondo romano*, New Ed. Rome-Bari, Laterza.

Guidobaldi, M.P. & Pesando, F. (1989) La colonia *civium romanorum*. In F. Coarelli (ed.) *Minturnae*, 35–66. Rome, Nuova Editrice Romana.

Hanson, J.W. & Ortman, S.G. (2017) A systematic method for estimating the populations of Greek and Roman settlements. In *Journal of Roman Archaeology* 30, 301–324.

Hayes, J.W. & Wightman, E.M. (1984) Interamna Lirenas: risultati di ricerche in superficie 1979–1981. In S. Quilici-Gigli (ed.) *Archeologia Laziale VI*, 137–148. Rome, Consiglio Nazionale delle Ricerche.

Izenour, G.C. (1993) *Roofed Theatres of Classical Antiquity*. New Haven, Yale University Press.

Keay, S. & Millett, M. (2016) Republican and early Imperial towns in the Tiber Valley. In A.E. Cooley (ed.) *A Companion to Roman Italy*, 357–377. Malden-Oxford, Wiley-Blackwell.

Launaro, A. (2015) The nature of the villa economy. In P. Erdkamp, K. Verboven & A. Zuiderhoek (eds) *Ownership and Exploitation of Land and Natural Resources in the Roman World*, 173–186. Oxford, Oxford University Press.

Launaro, A. (2017) Something old, something new: social and economic developments in the countryside of Roman Italy between Republic and Empire. In T. de Haas & G. Tol (eds) *The Economic Integration of Roman Italy: Rural Communities in a Globalizing World*, 85–111. Leiden and Boston: Brill.

Launaro, A. (2019) Interamna Lirenas – a history of 'success'? Long-term trajectories across town and countryside (4th c. BC to 5th c. AD). In A.U. De Giorgi (ed.) *Cosa and the Colonial Landscape of Republican Italy (Third and Second Century BC)*, 119–138. Ann Arbor, University of Michigan Press.

Launaro, A. & Leone, N. (2018) A view from the margin? Roman commonwares and patterns of distribution and consumption at Interamna Lirenas (Lazio). *Journal of Roman Archaeology* 31, 323–338.

Launaro, A. & Millett, M. (2023) *Interamna Lirenas: a Roman Town in Central Italy Revealed*. Cambridge, McDonald Institute for Archaeological Research.

Launaro, A. & Patterson, J. (2020) New epigraphic evidence from the Roman town of Interamna Lirenas (Central Italy). *Epigraphica* 20, 213–241.

Launaro, A. & Verdonck, L. (forthcoming) The river-port of Interamna Lirenas.

Lena, G. (1982) Interamna Lirenas: note di topografia antica. *Quaderni Museo Civico Pontecorvo* 2, 57–75.

Lugli, G. (1957) *La tecnica edilizia romana.* Rome, G. Bardi.

Millett, M. (2013). Understanding Roman towns in Italy: reflections on the role of geophysical survey. In P. Johnson & M. Millett (eds) *Archaeological Survey and the City*, 24–44. Oxford, Oxbow Books.

Millett, M., Launaro, A., Verdonck, L. & Vermeulen, F. (forthcoming) *Falerii Novi: the Ground-Penetrating Radar Survey of the Roman town.* Cambridge, McDonald Institute for Archaeological Research.

Notarjanni, F.A. (2016 [1814]) *Viaggio per l'Ausonia.* Latina, Atlantide Editore.

Patterson, J.R. (2006). *Landscapes and Cities. Rural Settlement and Civic Transformation in Early Imperial Italy.* Oxford, Oxford University Press.

Romanelli, D. (1819) *Antica Topografia Istorica del Regno diNapoli, Parte Terza.* Naples, Stamperia Reale.

Savino, E. (2005) *Campania tardoantica (284-604 d.C.).* Bari, Edipuglia.

Sear, F. (2006) *Roman Theatres. An Architectural Study.* Oxford, Oxford University Press.

Vaccaro, E. (2013) Re-evaluating a forgotten town using intrasite survey and the GIS analysis of surface ceramics: Philosophiana-Sofian (Sicily) in the longue durée. In P. Johnson & M. Millett (eds) *Archaeological Survey and the City*, 107–145. Oxford, Oxbow Books.

Wallace-Hadrill, A. (1994) *House and Society in Pompeii and Herculaneum.* Princeton, Princeton University Press.

Wightman, E.M. (1994). Communications. In J.W. Hayes & I.P. Martini (eds) *Archaeological Survey in the Lower Liri Valley, Central Italy*, 30–33. Oxford, Tempus Reparatum.

Wightman, E.M. & Hayes, J.W. (1994) Settlement patterns and society. In J.W. Hayes and I.P. Martini (eds) *Archaeological Survey in the Lower Liri Valley, Central Italy*, 34–40. Oxford, Tempus Reparatum.

Yegül, F. & Favro, D. (2019) *Roman Architecture and Urbanism: from the Origins to Late Antiquity.* Cambridge, Cambridge University Press.

# Chapter 12

# A town and its road: Aeclanum on the *via Appia*

*Ben Russell & Girolamo F. De Simone*

## 12.1. Introduction

Aeclanum lies in the district of ancient Hirpinia, a hilly region that still to this day constitutes a key corridor across the southern Apennines between the Tyrrhenian and Adriatic coasts of the Italian peninsula (Fig. 12.1). Hirpinia was gradually brought under Roman control following the construction of the *via Appia* through its heart in the 290s BC and the establishment of the colony at Beneventum, on its northern fringes, in 268 BC (on the *Hirpini*: Poccetti 2021). The earliest material culture recovered at Aeclanum dates to before this, perhaps as early as the 5th century BC, though we have only limited evidence for the character of the site prior to the 1st century BC. By this date, Aeclanum had certainly developed into an urban centre with a wall circuit. Following its capture by Sulla in 89 BC it became a Roman *municipium* and was later integrated into the *Regio II Apulia et Calabria*, as the westernmost town in the region. *Aeclanum* was promoted to colonial status relatively late, under Hadrian in AD 120 (as *Colonia Aelia Augusta Aeclanum*), and finally developed into an important Christian bishopric between the 4th and 7th centuries AD.

The site of Aeclanum covers *c.* 21 ha and the centre of this is now protected as a *parco archeologico* in Passo di Mirabella, within the territory of the Municipality of Mirabella Eclano (which preserves the name of the ancient town). Standing remains of substantial structures are still visible on site, though much of the town remains unexcavated. In 2016, new excavations and survey work at the site were initiated as a collaboration between the Apolline Project, the University of Edinburgh, the *Soprintendenza Archeologica, Belle Arti e Paesaggio per le Province di Salerno e Avellino* and the *Comune di Mirabella Eclano*, in association with the British School at Rome.

This paper will examine what the work at Aeclanum since 2016 reveals about the urban topography of the town and its development and relative prosperity over the *longue durée*. The *via Appia* has a key role to play in this story, but so too does the position of the town in its wider landscape: Aeclanum owed its prominence not to its size but its location, as an interconnected road station and the centre of a thriving

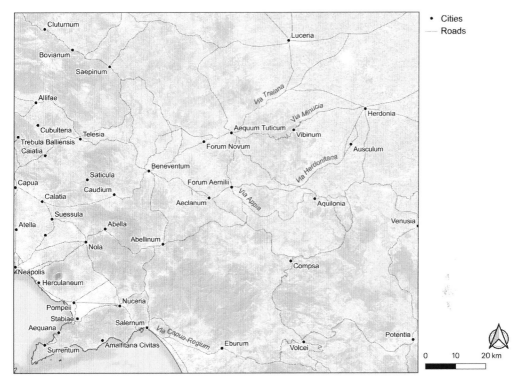

*Figure 12.1. Map of the territory between Neapolis and Venusia, showing known Roman roads and cities (image: G.F. De Simone).*

local territory (see Fig. 12.2). Aeclanum lay directly on the *via Appia*. Cicero stayed in the town twice while travelling along the Appia (*Att.* 7.3; 16.2), and it is listed on the Antonine Itinerary and shown on the *Tabula Peutingeriana*. The road brought a steady flow of people through the town, travellers' requirements providing opportunities for local businesses. The road also made Aeclanum a commercial hub for its wider territory and the most visible, and visited, centre in the local landscape. It attracted the attention of local elites keen to make their beneficence visible in the urban core, where everyone passing along the *via Appia* could witness it. As a result, Aeclanum has a monumentality and epigraphic record disproportionate to its relatively small size (Evangelisti 2017; and on this point, Camodeca 2021, 90).

## 12.2. The lie of the land

The Apennine mountain range presents a longstanding challenge for travel across the Italian peninsula. From the broad *ager Campanus* and the plains around Vesuvius, two primary routes are available across the Apennines. The first of these is through the treacherous *Furculae Caudinae*, which were used by the *via Appia*. The second is

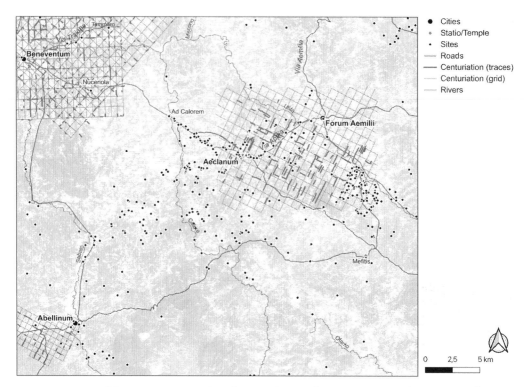

*Figure 12.2. Map of the territory around Aeclanum, showing known Roman roads, cities, smaller sites and evidence for centuriation (image: G.F. De Simone).*

a narrow mountain pass leading toward Abellinum, which is utilised by the modern motorway. Beyond the formidable limestone peaks of Taburno, Partenio, and the Picentini mountains, the topography is characterised by the rivers Sabato, Calore, Ufita, and Ofanto, which create valleys and many low hills, with a scattering of a few rocky peaks impeding efficient travelling. Located between the valleys of the rivers Calore and Ufita is Aeclanum. To the east of the town the landscape is dominated by the Daunian mountains, an irregularly shaped chain of hills and low mountains (on average *c.* 1000 m a.s.l.), and by the extinct volcano Vulture, before the land opens up to the extensive plains of Puglia.

In the Roman period an intricate system of roads developed to connect the two coasts of the Italian peninsula and facilitate travel across this difficult landscape. The town of Beneventum served as a primary transport hub in the west of the region. The town was a pivotal point on the *via Appia*, which then proceeds towards the southeast, passing through Aeclanum before reaching Venusia, on the edge of the plain (Fig. 12.1). The *via Traiana*, a later addition to the network, originated in Beneventum and was directed towards the northeast, passing through Aequum Tuticum before reaching Herdonia, again situated on the plain (Ceraudo 2012; 2015). The remaining components of the network consisted of secondary roads, which ran between the *via Appia* and the *via Traiana* and connected key settlements, such as the *via Herdonitana*, which connected Aeclanum to Herdonia, and the *via Aemilia*, linking Aequum Tuticum to Forum Aemilii.

Within this road network, Aeclanum was the largest town after Beneventum, from which it could be reached within two days by oxcart. The town was also well connected to several secondary routes, including a well-known drovers' path for sheep (Abete 2017, 31–34). Aeclanum's territory probably covered a sizeable portion of the territory southeast of Beneventum. The *Liber Coloniarum* (1.210.4–6 L; 2.261.5–8 L) reports the assignment of *centuriae* of 240 *iugera* (*c.* 60 ha), with a module of 20 × 24 *actus*, probably connected to the establishment of a colony under Hadrian. Based on aerial photographs and cartography, a sizeable centuriation grid (27° NE) of *c.* 15,200 ha between the rivers Calore and Ufita has been identified (Fig. 12.2; Ditaranto 2017). These *centuriae* probably only encompass a fraction of the territory of Aeclanum, which potentially reached as far as the River Calore to the west, or even beyond. This hypothesis is reinforced by the identification of material culture and pottery fabrics found in Taurasi, to the west, indicating close ties to Aeclanum rather than Abellinum. Under such circumstances, the territory of Aeclanum might have spanned 19,000–32,000 ha.

The clay hills of this region, interlayered with volcanic debris and carved by the rivers, were perhaps as fertile in antiquity as they are today. Currently grain and vineyards cover most of the land, while olive groves are also present; forests in the territory continue to be exploited for timber, while oxen and sheep still play a prominent cultural role. While the archaeological evidence remains incomplete, it nevertheless aligns with this picture and suggests that the area achieved a measure of self-sufficiency in terms of agricultural output.

## 12.3. Archaeological and historical background

Prior to the 1st century BC, we know little about the settlement at Aeclanum, and it is unclear whether the *via Appia* was constructed to pass through a pre-existing foundation or whether the presence of the road encouraged occupation of the site. A small sanctuary of Mefitis just to the north of the town was probably active in the 2nd century BC and several Oscan inscriptions can be associated with it (Sgobbo 1930; Colucci Pescatori 1991, 113; Poccetti 2021, 39). Little has been found in the area of the town itself, however, other than some scattered pottery of the 5th century BC (Parise Badoni 1969, 100). Several architectural terracottas, found near the early Christian basilica at the site, used to be thought to date to the Hellenistic period and so provide evidence for high-end building in this period (Sgobbo 1930), but they have recently been redated to the second half of the 1st century BC at the earliest and could be Augustan or later (Frese 2012). Terracing activity in the Roman period may well have removed early structures at Aeclanum. However, it is also possible that the site only developed an urban character in the late 2nd and 1st centuries BC, paralleling patterns elsewhere in Samnite regions (Tagliamonte 1996, 160). Isayev (2013, 21) notes that there is no mention of Aeclanum in Livy's account of the Hannibalic Wars, suggesting it did not exist or was unimportant.

Aeclanum is first mentioned in the historical sources by Appian, who documents Sulla's assault on the town in 89 BC (*B Civ.* 1.51). He tells us that the town had become a focal point of resistance to Sulla, who captured it by burning down its wooden walls. The fact that Aeclanum had a wall circuit, albeit a wooden one, indicates that the site had an urban character at this date. The town was also clearly influential in the region: Sulla makes an example of Aeclanum because he knows other towns in the region will pay attention.

The rest of what we know of 1st-century BC Aeclanum comes from the epigraphic record. Despite the punishment meted out by the Sullan forces, the town was immediately made a Roman *municipium* and inscribed in the Cornelia tribe (unlike most of the region of Hirpinia, which was enrolled in the Galeria tribe: Camodeca 2021, 92; Avagliano 2021, 330–332). This somewhat surprising turnaround in fortunes might be explained by the presence of prominent citizens of Aeclanum on the Sullan side, notably Minatus Magius, the great-grandfather of the historian Velleius Paterculus and a famous general who had raised a legion in Hirpinia in support of Sulla (Vell. Pat. 2.16.1; Salmon 1989, 232–233).

In the wake of its sack, Aeclanum experienced a wave of reconstruction, as outlined in four key inscriptions. A dominant player in this process was Gaius Quinctius Valgus, the notorious Sullan supporter (Salmon [1989, 230] calls him 'Sulla's greedy henchman'), who held various magistracies in towns across Campania, including Casinum and Pompeii, in the aftermath of the civil wars (CIL X 852 = ILS 5627 [Pompeii]; CIL X 5282 = ILLRP 565 [Casinum]). At Aeclanum he is recorded as *patronus municipii* (CIL IX 1140–1141 = ILLRP 523 = ILS 5318). This same text tells us that, along with two of the appointed *quattuorviri*, Valgus paid for the construction of new walls, gates, and towers. These other *quattuorviri* were Aulus Patlacius and Marcus Magius Syrus, the latter being probably the son of Minatus Magius, mentioned above. The second relevant inscription mentions two other individuals similarly paying for walls and towers as well (AE 1997, 393; Sgobbo 1931, 397–399, 402; Gregori & Nonnis 2013, 510, no. 22). To these two we can add a third inscription, reused in the walls of Frigento cathedral but probably from Aeclanum, which connects Valgus also to a *forum, porticus, curia* and cistern (CIL $I^2$ 3191 = ILLRP 598). A final text notes that another *quattuorvir*, Marcus Palius, paid for another *porticus* and an arch (CIL $I^2$ 3192 = ILLRP 599). We will return to some of these individuals below.

Of the various Late Republican structures mentioned epigraphically the only one that remains visible above ground is the wall circuit (marked on Figs 12.3 and 12.4). This encloses an area of just over 21 ha and the construction technique of the walls, where it can be observed, is a crude form of limestone *opus reticulatum*, which is not inconsistent with a 1st-century BC date (Avagliano 2021, 332). Until recently the

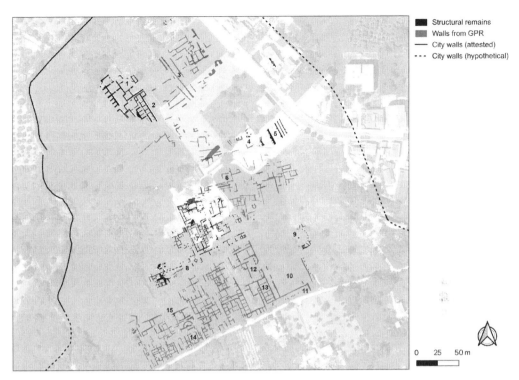

Structural remains
Walls from GPR
—— City walls (attested)
- - - City walls (hypothetical)

0    25    50 m

*Figure 12.3. Plan of the excavated structures and walls identified in the GPR survey in the centre of Aeclanum (image: G.F. De Simone).*

*forum* at Aeclanum – presumably the one mentioned in the inscription above, unless it was moved – was also unknown, but our geophysical survey at the site has now pinpointed a location, as will be discussed below.

We know more archaeologically about Aeclanum in the Imperial period. Most of the standing remains still visible at the site (indicated in black on Fig. 12.3) date to the 2nd century AD or later. The bulk of these were uncovered during the systematic and large-scale excavations carried out in the 1950s–60s under the direction of Giovanni Onorato and then in the following decades by Gabriella d'Henry (Onorato 1960; Colucci Pescatori & Di Giovanni 1999; Colucci Pescatori 2017). They include a residential area, comprising at least two large elite houses (the most complete the so-called 'Casa con peristilio': Fig. 12.3: 7), a *macellum* (Fig. 12.3: 9), bath complex (Fig. 12.3: 1), and the early Christian basilica (Fig. 12.3: 8). Industrial structures, including a kiln and a glass workshop, were added to the residential area in Late Antiquity (Lombardo 1977, 815–816). More recently, excavations along the *via Appia* to the southeast of the town have uncovered several suburban buildings and tombs (Di Giovanni 1996, 250–253; Colucci Pescatori 2017, 175; 2021, 185), as well as extensive Roman and Late Antique cemeteries (Lo Pilato 2005; Lambert *et al.* 2015). In 2005 significant work was carried out in and around the early Christian basilica (Lo Pilato 2010). And between

*Figure 12.4. View of the site of Aeclanum from the southwest (image: J. Souček).*

2006 and 2009, excavations at the entrance to the archaeological park also discovered various public structures (Fig. 12.3: 5), tentatively identified as part of a *porticus* and a *nymphaeum* and assumed therefore to be connected to the *forum*. Behind the façade of the presumed *nymphaeum* was found a headless imperial statue, thought originally to be Marcus Aurelius but now published as Domitian, as well as a series of marble architectural elements dating to the Julio-Claudian period (Mesisca *et al.* 2013; Avagliano 2017; De Simone & Russell 2019a, 337, fig. 1).

## 12.4. New work on the urban plan

Despite considerable excavation at the site up to 2009, there remained significant gaps in our knowledge of the urban topography of Aeclanum prior to the start of the current project. The exact course of the *via Appia* through the town had not been verified through archaeology (assumed course: Ditaranto 2013, 54, fig. 1; Lo Pilato 2019, 163, fig. 2). The layout of the wider street network had also not been clarified. The precise locations of the *forum*, of any temples or larger entertainment structures – such as theatre or amphitheatre – were also unknown. Of the structures partially uncovered during excavation, several were of uncertain function: the supposed *porticus* and *nymphaeum* complex uncovered in 2006–09, for example, and the series of rooms comprising the lower story of a building with apsidal wall adjacent to the baths (Fig. 12.3: 2). Other structures, while their function was apparent, had unclear layouts or chronological phasing and required further investigation.

Work at Aeclanum between 2016 and 2019 concentrated on a combination of targeted excavation and larger scale geophysical survey. The latter focused on three zones of the town, with a view to connecting areas of earlier interventions and understanding how the street system and built environment interacted with the unusual topography of the town (Strapazzon *et al.* 2017). Trenches were opened in four sectors, where it was thought stratified deposits could be uncovered and the phasing of structures revealed:

1. Sector A (Fig. 12.3: 4–5): the area of the structures previously described as a *porticus* and *nymphaeum* close to the entrance to the archaeological park, which we were able to identify as the location of the town's theatre (Trenches 1 and 5).
2. Sector B (Fig. 12.3: 1–3): the northern area of the town, where the baths excavated by Onorato are located and which we refer to as the 'North Baths' of the town (Trenches 2–4 and 7), as well as the area to the west of these where the line of a major roadway was visible on the geophysics (Trench 12).
3. Sector C (Fig. 12.3: 6–8): the residential zone in the centre of the town, next to the modern site office, where the early Christian basilica has been excavated (Trenches 6, 8, 14–15).
4. Sector D (Fig. 12.3: 9–15): the central-southern district, where the *macellum* was located and the geophysics now enables the identification of both the *forum* and a series of residential blocks stretching to the west (Trenches 9–11, 13, 16).

### 12.4.1. Site topography

Understanding the urban layout of Aeclanum is complicated by the site's topography. The town occupies the point at which a spur of land projects westwards from the main northwest–southeast ridge along which the *via Appia* ran in antiquity. The northeastern half of the town is constructed along the top of this northwest–southeast ridge, while the southern part of the town occupies the westward spur (Fig. 12.4). The northwestern quarter of the town, in contrast, drops away sharply. A number of long terrace walls must have been constructed in the Roman period to ensure that the public structures built up on the top of the two ridges did not slide down the hill to the northwest. Substantial terracing can still be noticed on the site along the western side of the North Baths and the central residential sector, across which the early Christian basilica was constructed (marked on Plate 12.1). A series of at least seven large buttress walls were also added to the western side of the North Baths to mitigate slippage. A further terrace wall of some description must have run roughly east–west along the northern side of the westward projecting spur that dominates the southern half of the town (marked as a dashed line on Plate 12.1). Indeed, a series of barrel vaults that are perhaps part of such a terrace are preserved in the farmhouse close to the westernmost tip of the town.

A terrace wall very likely also ran between the area of the North Baths and the central residential sector, but no traces of it survive. GPR survey of 890 m² of this area in 2016 identified evidence of substantial erosion, perhaps a landslide resulting from the collapse of this wall (Strapazzon *et al.* 2017, 244). The ends of walls can be seen on the geophysical results in this area, but their full extent cannot be determined (Fig. 12.3). GPR transects carried out over the lower, northwestern portion of the town in 2017 also failed to identify any structures in this area of the town, which seems to have been covered by several metres of soil eroded from the upper terraces of the site. That there certainly were structures on at least part of this lower terrace is confirmed by excavations in 2005 to the west of the early Christian basilica, where the walls of a *domus* with painted wall plaster were uncovered (Lo Pilato 2010, 356). Currently, however, we can reconstruct little of the urban plan in this part of the town and it is even possible that parts of the steep hillside here were never built on.

### 12.4.2. *The northern end of the town: the North Baths and a large public building*

In the upper part of the town, especially in the northern, central, and southern districts, the GPR survey was considerably more productive. In the northern area (Sector B), the GPR helped to clarify the arrangement of the structure(s) to the east and south of the North Baths (Fig. 12.3: 3). This complex was excavated by Onorato and probably dates to the 2nd century AD; it is the largest bathhouse in the town identified to date, covering an area of *c.* 1,400 m². To the east of the main rooms of the bathing complex the GPR indicated that there are no further structures, but rather an open space, perhaps a *palaestra*. The GPR also helped to make sense of the series of small rooms originally excavated by Onorato to the south of the baths, which are probably of the same date (Fig. 12.3: 2). Considering the topography of the site and the geophysical results it is now clear that these rooms comprise the basement story of a larger complex with a substantial apse at the centre of its western wall. At the level of the story above these small rooms the complex extended eastwards, like the baths, via an open space towards a pair of parallel north–south features, *c.* 5 m apart. This is evidently a second public building, with a substantial two-story building at its western end and an open *porticus*, in total measuring 64 × 39 m (Fig. 12.5). We have previously proposed that this was a cultic complex or possibly a *gymnasium*, given the proximity of the baths (De Simone & Russell 2018).

### 12.4.3. *The line of the via Appia and the location of the theatre*

The parallel north–south features to the east of the two complexes described above mark the foundations of a *porticus*, a fact confirmed by the excavations in Trench 12

*Figure 12.5. Computer reconstruction of the possible layout of the North Baths and adjacent public building at Aeclanum (image: J. Souček).*

(Fig. 12.3: 3). This *porticus* ran alongside the western side of a major north–south road, identified by the GPR survey and excavated in Trench 12. The North Baths and the public building to the south of it presumably faced on to this road. The alignment and width of the road, and the presence of the *porticus* running along its western side, strongly suggest that this is the *via Appia*. Where exposed in Trench 12, the road had been stripped of its paving, but a substantial stone-built drain, its vaulted covering still intact, ran along its western edge, immediately in front of the portico (De Simone & Russell 2019a, 338–339, fig. 2).

The line of this road can be traced on the GPR as far as the northeastern corner of the excavated residential sector. Here the GPR showed an area with a more irregular street network, which has been heavily damaged by deep ploughing (Strapazzon *et al.* 2017, 244). The carpark of the archaeological park also reduced the legibility of the results in this area, though to the northwest of the structures identified in 2006–09 as a *porticus* and *nymphaeum* (Fig. 12.3: 5), walls could be identified. A pair of parallel, curved walls with cross walls connecting them could be made out on the geophysics. Excavations in this area have since shown that the westernmost of these correspond to the outer wall of the *cavea* of a theatre, the stage building of which corresponds to the structure previously identified as a *nymphaeum* – the alternating *aediculae* and niches exposed in 2006–09 correspond to the façade of the *proscenium*. The architectural elements from this building, published already in 2013 and 2015, can be dated to the Julio-Claudian period (Mesisca *et al.* 2013; Mesisca 2015) and the complex seems to have remained in use until the 4th century AD (De Simone & Russell 2019b, 381–383). To judge from its plan, and especially the area of its *cavea* (*c.* 784 m$^2$), the theatre was probably designed to accommodate at least 2,200 people. The line of the *via Appia* could be traced as far as the rear of the theatre, where it either continued to the south or turned towards the southeast.

### 12.4.4. The forum and the southern area of the town

The most detailed GPR results came from the southern half of the town, in the area to the west of the *macellum* (Fig. 12.3: 9). This is the highest point in the town and seems to have been its civic core. Just to the west of the *macellum*, the GPR revealed a large open space, 28 × 75 m long (Fig. 12.3: 10). A test trench on the western edge of this space showed that this was originally a paved area, though the paving has since been stripped, leaving just the preparation surface behind. Such a large paved area can only be the *forum* of Aeclanum.

The *macellum* opens off the eastern side of the *forum* and can be dated to the first half of the 2nd century AD. It has an interesting form, with a circular internal courtyard ringed by rooms; the closest parallels are from Herdonia and Alba Fucens and are of similar date (De Ruyt 1983; Russell & De Simone 2020).

To the south of the *macellum* the GPR results reveal a probable road, flanked by a *porticus* to the east of it, which delineates the rest of the eastern side of the *forum*; this might be where traffic left the *forum* to join back on to the *via Appia*. A corresponding road seems to have run the full length of the western side of the *forum*. Along the southern edge of the *forum*, meanwhile, one side of a rectilinear building, at least as long (east–west) as the *forum* is wide, with an interior colonnade, is visible (Fig. 12.3: 11). This could be a further *porticus* or an enclosed public building, perhaps a *basilica*. The southern half of this complex lies under the modern access road that runs east–west through the site.

To the west of the *forum*, five evenly sized *insulae* were revealed. The first of these contained a small number of large buildings. The most northerly of these, which has two apsidal rooms, was probably a public bathhouse (Fig. 12.3: 12). If a *praefurnium* excavated in Trench 6 at the north end of this *insula* (which was originally interpreted as part of a domestic bath) was connected to these public baths, then this was a substantial complex, measuring *c.* 28 × 56 m. South of this is a rectangular structure broken up into smaller units by thin walls, perhaps foundation walls (Fig. 12.3: 13); the location of this structure would suggest either a civic or perhaps a commercial function (shops or a *horreum*?). One of the late Republican inscriptions noted above mentions a *curia* and this would be a logical location for it, but no certain identification can be posited on the basis of the GPR alone.

The next *insula* to the west contains a series of smaller structures. The southern half of the *insula* contains a building comprising a series of small rooms around a courtyard; those on the east side measure 4 × 5.5 m. This might represent a *horreum* or other storage or commercial building, comparable to the *horrea* identified at Interamna Lirenas on the basis of the geophysical survey there (Launaro, this volume). The structures in the northern half of this *insula* appear to be smaller units, perhaps houses or commercial structures. The third *insula* to the west of the *forum* contains a series of buildings of similarly uncertain function, though their arrangement suggests they are not public buildings.

More can be said about the fourth and fifth *insulae* to the west of the *forum*. No remains were identified in the GPR in the northern parts of these *insulae*. This is probably because the terracing structures over which the early Christian basilica was built, just to the north, turned to the west in this area, to align with the barrel vaults described above, which are further west. If this is correct then a substantial change in elevation probably occurred two-thirds of the way through these *insulae*, the original ground surface dropping away in those areas where the GPR results trail off. Some of the buildings in this part of the town seem to have been large and might even have had a public function: a large building with a courtyard and apse visible in the southeast corner of the fourth block to the west of the *forum* is particularly noteworthy (Fig. 12.3: 14). In 2019, Trench 16 was opened to test the GPR results in this southern sector of the town (Fig. 12.3: 15). An inner room of a large residence, filled by multiple phases of collapse, was exposed. Fragments of painted plaster in the collapse suggest this was a high-end *domus*, while the ceramics show it was probably destroyed by the earthquake of AD 346. It was impossible to expose the full height of the walls, but at a depth of 3 m the top of an arch was exposed, suggesting the walls continued further down.

## 12.5. Developments in Late Antiquity

The discussion above reveals how much our understanding of the urban plan of Aeclanum has improved since 2016. Excavations across the site have also added chronological depth to this picture, in particular with regard to Late Antique developments.

The AD 346 earthquake mentioned above appears to have been keenly felt at Aeclanum and ushered in an era of redevelopment (on this earthquake more generally: Galadini & Galli 2004). Unlike other towns in the region, in fact, Aeclanum seems to have generally prospered in the 4th and 5th centuries, at least up until AD 472, when ash from the so-called 'Pollena eruption' of Vesuvius blanketed the town. The bulk of our stratigraphic information from the excavation undertaken between 2016 and 2019 dates to the period AD 346–472. This evidence has been discussed in detail elsewhere (De Simone & Russell 2019b; Castaldo *et al.* 2023), but some of the salient features of Late Antique Aeclanum bear repeating here.

The impact of the AD 346 earthquake was detected archaeologically in all of the sectors of Aeclanum investigated via excavation. However, the response to the devastation varied across the site. Several buildings excavated were evidently destroyed in AD 346 and never rebuilt; they lay as ruins or piles of rubble. This was the case with the building – perhaps a house or commercial structure – uncovered in Trench 8, to the east of the previously excavated residential sector (Fig. 12.3: 6). This building had collapsed suddenly, its wall caving in before the roof fell on it (De Simone & Russell 2018). The elite house explored in Trench 16, as noted above, also never seems to have been rebuilt after the middle of the 4th century AD and this might be connected to the earthquake of AD 346.

Two large public buildings that were not abandoned after AD 346, but which did change function, are the theatre and the *macellum*. The theatre was certainly no longer in use and was in the process of being spoliated when ash from the AD 472 eruption fell on Aeclanum (on the ash found during excavation: Colucci Pescatori 2017, 174). How long before this date it had stopped to function as a theatre, however, is indicated by the discovery of domestic occupation layers in the substructures of the *cavea* (those identified by the GPR survey, mentioned above; Fig. 12.3: 4). The ceramics in these layers indicate that at least by the first half of the 5th century AD the substructures of the *cavea* were being lived in, and it is possible that the building stopped functioning as a theatre proper before this time (De Simone & Russell 2019b, 381–383). This picture is partly replicated in the *macellum*, where most of the structure seems to have been given over to domestic units after the 4th century AD (Onorato 1960, 28; Lombardo 1977, 814; Tocco Sciarelli 1999, 251), with occupation lasting even after AD 472 to judge from the ceramics (Castaldo *et al.* 2023). Just a single room in the northwest corner of the complex seems to have still acted as a commercial space, perhaps butcher's shop (Russell & De Simone 2020, 372).

Alongside signs of abandonment and the shifting functions of buildings, there is also evidence for renewed investment and reconstruction at Aeclanum. The North Baths were a major recipient of this investment. New marble floors and mosaics were laid out in the 4th or 5th century AD and a new pool was added to one side of the *frigidarium*. Another structure that seems to have been reconfigured and restored in this period is the large 'Casa con peristilio' in the centre of the town (Fig. 12.3: 7). Excavations in 2019 here showed that several of the walls were rebuilt with reused brick and tile in the late Roman period (Russell & De Simone 2020) and this restoration work might well have been connected to the building of the new Christian basilica adjacent to the *domus* (Fig. 12.3: 8). This new church, in fact, was built over the intersection of the streets beyond the southwestern corner of the house; its walls probably abutted those of the house. As Lo Pilato has noted (2010, 352), the road to the west of the 'Casa con peristilio' was blocked off by a wall in this later period and she has suggested that these developments were part of the creation of a sort of '*insula episcopalis*', centred on the new church in the town. If this is correct, then it is likely that the 'Casa con peristilio' was a key part of this new ecclesiastical core.

## 12.6. Three observations on urbanism at Aeclanum

### 12.6.1. *Urban arrangement*

New geophysical survey and excavation work at Aeclanum has helped to flesh out the urban plan of the site, even if very significant gaps remain. We now know where the *via Appia* entered and (approximately) left the town as well as much of its likely route through the site (Plate 12.1). The key late Republican and Imperial-era public buildings were aligned along a central spine, determined both by the topography of the site and the presence of the *via Appia*. Moving from north to south, a visitor passing along the *via Appia* would have encountered the North Baths and the public complex adjacent to them (on their right) then the theatre (on their left). It is probable that heavy, wheeled traffic would have turned to the southeast at the theatre – in order to bypass the *forum* – but anyone continuing further south would have found the *macellum*, a second set of baths, and probably the usual array of other civic buildings. We know little about the southeastern corner of Aeclanum, but the line of the *via Appia* can be traced via older excavations out of the town in that direction.

Substantial terracing was required to produce level ground on which these various public structures were constructed. The result was that, while the monumental façade of Aeclanum was oriented primarily inwards, towards traffic along the *via Appia*, this string of public buildings would also have dominated the skyline when viewed from the valleys to the east and, especially, to the west of the town, where the Calore River ran (Fig. 12.2). The town and its key public monuments, therefore, would have been visible from much of its territory.

### 12.6.2. *Size and status*

Aeclanum was never a large urban centre. At just over 21 ha, it lies on the cusp between de Ligt's categories of 'small town' (<20 ha) and 'medium town' (20–40 ha) (de Ligt 2012, 201). If we consider Aeclanum within the wider context of the Augustan *Regiones* I–II and perform a rank-size analysis, the town can be grouped with Fabrateria Nova, Acerrae, and Herdonia (<26 ha), while Telesia, Suessa, Minturnae (26–45 ha), Beneventum, and Neapolis (46–85 ha), and the large centres of Aquinum and Teanum Sidicinum (86–150 ha), can be grouped together in larger size rankings. For context, these can be compared to Ostia (154 ha), Capua (182 ha), and Rome (1,270 ha). If we take a subregional perspective, however, in the 750,000 ha centred on Aeclanum, the largest towns were Beneventum (46 ha) and Venusia (44 ha), with Aeclanum, Abellinum, and Herdonia acting as mid-rank centres (Fig. 12.1). Much smaller towns (such as Aequum Tuticum and Compsa) as well as smaller settlements and *mansiones* were interspersed between these centres. From this more focused perspective, Aeclanum was an important centre for a wide, lightly urbanised territory.

Calculating the exact population of Aeclanum is complicated by the fact that we simply have no idea what proportion of the town was occupied by housing. The domestic structures identified to date are largely elite *domus* and we have little information about where ordinary citizens lived. It seems probable that many of the *insulae* to the south of the *forum* contained housing, but we do not know whether the northwest area of the town was densely occupied or not; here the slope of the hillside now ranges between 13.5% and 15%. Despite uncertainties about the size of the inhabited area, we can estimate the urban population using density calculations derived from studies of Roman urban demography. Hanson shows that most studies of pre-industrial urbanism have identified typical population densities of between 100 and 500 inhabitants/ha (Hanson 2016, 55–66; also Wilson 2011, 176), with smaller towns tending to be less densely occupied. Hanson therefore proposes using a value of 100 inhabitants/ha for urban centres under 50 ha (Hanson 2016, 55–66). Millett has argued for 90–110 inhabitant/ha on the basis of the geophysical results at Falerii Novi (Millett 2012, 37–39), while a slightly higher average of 150 inhabitants/ha is used by de Ligt (2012, 233–235) in his analysis of central and southern Italy. If we take the area of Aeclanum as 21 ha, a density of 100–150 inhabitants/ha would result in a population of *c.* 2,100–3,150. If the steeply sloping northwestern part of the town was not occupied, we could reduce the overall area to 18 ha, resulting in a population of 1,800–2,700. Given the topography of the site, and the fact that some of it was probably not densely occupied, therefore, a population of *c.* 2,100 seems most plausible.

Despite its small size, Aeclanum was evidently a wealthy centre. Its public buildings were lavishly decorated with imported marble, which, given the location of the town in the centre of the Italian peninsula, implies serious investment of capital. This is most apparent in the theatre (on the marble of which: Mesisca *et al.* 2013; Mesisca 2015), but the *macellum* and the North Baths also features marble revetment and flooring (Astolfi *et al.* 2023). The site has also produced substantial quantities of statuary, including marble images of numerous emperors and members of the local elite (Avagliano 2021). Perhaps the most striking testament to the status of the town is its epigraphy. The number of inscriptions from the site – over 530 – is comparable to the total from much larger centres in the region and further south, such as Beneventum and Brundisium (Evangelisti 2017, 48–50). In a local context, it is particularly noteworthy that Aeclanum has produced roughly three times the number of inscriptions as Abellinum (a town that had become a colony over 200 years earlier) and far more 2nd–3rd-century AD inscriptions, in particular, are known from Aeclanum than Abellinum (Camodeca 2021, 90, 93).

Strikingly, investment in Aeclanum continued into Late Antiquity, when the town maintained the status it had enjoyed earlier. After the 3rd century AD, new investments came primarily via the *correctores*, the governors of *Apulia et Calabria*. But one final flourish of civic investment was provided, probably in the aftermath of the AD 346 earthquake, by one Umbonius Mannachius, who was honoured as *patronus* and *fabricator ex maxima parte etiam civitatis nostrae* (CIL IX 1362). New investment can be traced archaeologically on the site and fits into a wider pattern. We can compare the work carried out on the North Baths in the 4th century AD, for example, with the rebuilding of baths at other sites in central Italy in this period, largely funded by governors (Ward-Perkins 1984, 20–27; Christie 2006, 199; Soricelli 2009, 251–254; Underwood 2019, 39–41; De Simone and Russell 2019b, 379). At nearby Herdonia the baths underwent a similar transformation at this date (Leone *et al.* 2009; Volpe & Goffredo 2020, 66), while those at Venusia were expanded in the 4th century AD (Marchi 2010, 2). Despite these parallels, in its immediate vicinity, there are notable differences between the changes apparent at Aeclanum after AD 346 and those at Abellinum (Camodeca 2021, 90–94). At the latter, the baths never seem to have reopened after the AD 346 earthquake, while the large *domus* close to the town walls was broken up into smaller units, themselves mostly abandoned by AD 472 (Colucci Pescatori 1986, 126, 127–132). While the new ecclesiastical centre at Aeclanum grew up in the heart of the town, not far from the old *forum*, at Abellinum – as at Nola, to give a further example (Ebanista 2003) – religious life shifted outside the town to the church at Capo La Torre (Colucci Pescatori 2017, 169–170). Where Aeclanum became an important bishopric in southern Italy – producing the controversial Julian of Aeclanum in the early 5th century AD and sending a bishop to the Council of Constantinople as late as AD 536 (Rotili & Ebanista 2018, 54) – Abellinum struggled.

### 12.6.3. Territory and the members of the local elite

Aeclanum was seemingly a town that punched above its weight in terms of its public architecture and epigraphy. Where did this wealth come from? The presence of the *via Appia* must explain some of this. To some extent we might view Aeclanum as a town projected towards passing travellers. The North Baths and those to the west of the forum, visible on the GPR, were conveniently located, close to the line of the *via Appia*, similarly to many *mansiones* (Medri 2016). Beyond these public buildings, travellers would have required accommodation, food and drink, entertainment, and other transport-related services.

Beyond its role as a road station, most of the wealth in the town probably derived from its territory and especially its local elites. The prominence of the latter in the late Republican period has already been noted above. Minatus Magius had the influence and capital to raise a legion for Sulla in the 1st century BC, and his son was a prominent *quattuorvir*. While Gaius Quinctius Valgus invested heavily in the urban fabric of Aeclanum in the same period, he also seems to have benefitted from Sullan land confiscations to build up substantial estates in Hirpinia. This is a key point of Cicero's *de Lege Agraria Contra Rullum* (3.2.8), in 63 BC, in which he claims (presumably with a degree of exaggeration) that Gaius Quinctius Valgus, Publius Servilius Rullus' father-in-law, owned most of Hirpinia. Aeclanum also produced prominent members of the equestrian and senatorial classes in the 1st and 2nd centuries AD, as demonstrated by inscriptions from the site (Evangelisti 2014; De Carlo 2015, 175–183). Members of these families held magistracies and invested their money in the town and were rewarded for their efforts with public honours. They presumably had large estates in the area around Aeclanum, like Valgus had before them. This was a territory rich in timber, well-suited to all cultivations, and the raising of livestock. Aeclanum, while small, was a key central place in the wider region and highly visible; it was here that the members of the local elite invested their capital in order to ensure their own prominence in the monuments of the town. The size of these monuments, notably the baths but also the theatre – which seems to have been able to seat all of the likely adult urban population, while in other towns theatres generally accommodate about a third to a half (e.g. the theatre of Pompeii seats 3,100 out of a population of *c.* 9,600 inhabitants) – were presumably designed with the population of the territory in mind, as well as travellers along the *via Appia*.

## 12.7. Conclusions

There are clear parallels between Aeclanum and other 'small towns' on major roads. We can point to Ocriculum in Umbria, for instance. This small town again lay at the centre of a wealthy territory containing villa estates and was noted for its brick production and timber resources (Hay *et al.* 2013, 10, 153). Ocriculum was located both on the *via Flaminia* and adjacent to the River Tiber. Like Aeclanum, the urban plan of Ocriculum was heavily determined by the topography of the site, with its key public structures aligned on terraces dominating the *via Flaminia* as it passed through the town (Hay *et al.* 2013, 143). The local elites of the territory invested heavily in Ocriculum despite its small size, as shown by the fact that over 20% of the urban territory is devoted to public monuments and the town has produced a disproportionate quantity of high-end sculpture. A more local parallel is provided by Herdonia, a town of broadly similar size, which owed its Imperial-era prominence to another road, the *via Traiana*. Like Aeclanum the town prospered from the 2nd century AD and a degree of vitality can be traced into the 4th century AD (Volpe 2006, 562–564; Volpe and Goffredo 2020, 66). The town again suffered in AD 346 but key structures were rebuilt or repurposed, and signs of ruralization only appear after the end of the 5th century AD (Volpe 2006, 568–570; 2014; 1049).

Fruitful comparison might also be made with cities like Carsulae and Amiternum (recent work: Whitehead 2010; Heinzelmann & Buess 2022), and a range of other small towns in Italy. These small centres, like Aeclanum, prospered primarily due to their location. Despite its sack by Sulla, the construction of the *via Traiana* in the early 2nd century AD, and the pair of natural disasters that impacted the town in AD 346 and 472 (all events that could have negatively impact the town's development), Aeclanum remained a vital urban centre at the heart of a rich territory for at least six centuries. In the wider region, only Beneventum – which found a new lease of life under Lombard rule – shows greater continuity. Aeclanum was firmly rooted in both its fertile and potentially quite large local territory, populated by wealthy elites and agriculturally self-sufficient, as well as a diverse range of transport connections, the *via Appia* key among them. The construction of the *via Traiana* might have led to more long-distance traffic (Brundisium–Rome and *vice versa*) by-passing Aeclanum, but local and regional traffic would still have relied on the *via Appia*, while roads like the *via Herdonitana* bolstered this connectivity.

For a town so reliant on its road, it is apt that, when Aeclanum does eventually succumb and cease to function as an urban centre, its ruins are named with respect to their distance along this road. A document from the papacy of Gregory II, in the 8th century AD, describes the site simply as '*civitate diruta XV miliario apud Beneventanam civitatem*' (Kehr 1962, 106). This distance is eventually immortalised in the medieval name for the site: Quintodecimo.

## Acknowledgements

The fieldwork at Aeclanum was authorised by the *Soprintendenza Archeologica, Belle Arti e Paesaggio per le Province di Salerno e Avellino,* the most recent protocol number being 15906-P 11/06/2018. The geophysical survey and analysis of the results was undertaken by Guglielmo Strapazzon. Key assistance in the creation of the plans in Figs 12.1–3 and Plate 12.1 was provided by Josef Souček. Ben Russell's work on this contribution was completed during the tenure of a Philip Leverhulme Prize, for which he is grateful to the Leverhulme Trust.

## Rights Retention Statement

## Bibliography

Abete, G. (2017) *Parole e cose della pastorizia in Alta Irpinia.* Naples, Giannini.
Astolfi, M., Russell, B., Harrison, P., De Simone, G.F. & Mesisca, A. (2023) Marble at Aeclanum (Italy): new evidence from three public buildings. In A.B. Yavuz, B. Yolaçan & M. Bruno (eds) *ASMOSIA XII,* 175–183. Izmir, Dokuz Eylül University.
Avagliano, A. (2017) Ricontestualizzare la scultura romana in una città dell'Irpinia. Un loricato e alter statue onorarie da Aeclanum. *Archäologischer Anzeiger* 2017.2, 99–121.
Avagliano, A. (2021) La scultura romana di Aeclanum: un primo bilancio. In A. Visconti & M. Lanzillo (eds) *Studi sull'Irpinia antica,* 329–364. Naples, Tiotinx Edizioni.
Camodeca, G. (2021) Note sull'Irpinia in età romana. In A. Visconti & M. Lanzillo (eds) *Studi sull'Irpinia antica,* 89–130. Naples, Tiotinx Edizioni.
Castaldo, V., De Simone, G.F. & Russell, B. (2023) Sea or land? Trade from the coast to the fringes of Campania. In V. Caminneci, E. Giannitrapani, M.C. Parello & M.S. Rizzo (eds) *Late Roman Coarse Wares VI,* 88–100. Oxford, Archaeopress.
Ceraudo, G. (2012) Miliari della via Traiana in Hirpinia: un aggiornamento epigrafico e topografico. *Journal of Ancient Topography* 22, 95–106.
Ceraudo, G. (2015) La Via Appia (a sud di Benevento) e il sistema stradale in Puglia tra Pirro e Annibale. In *La Magna Grecia da Pirro ad Annibale,* 213–45. Taranto, ISAMG.

Christie, N. (2006) *From Constantine to Charlemagne. An Archaeology of Italy AD 300-800.* Farnham, Ashgate.

Colucci Pescatori, G. (1986) Osservazioni su Abellinum tardo-antica e sull'eruzione del 472 d.C. In C. Albore Livadie (ed.) *Tremblements de terre, éruptions volcaniques et vie des hommes dans la Campanie antique,* 121–141. Naples, Centre Jean Bérard.

Colucci Pescatori, G. (1991) Evidenze archeologiche in Irpinia. In *La romanisation du Samnium aux IIe et Ier s. av. J.-C.,* 85–122. Naples, Centre Jean Bérard.

Colucci Pescatori, G. (2017) Per una storia archeologica dell'Irpinia: dall'istituzione del Museo Irpino alle ricerche del secolo scorso. In V. Franciosi, A. Visconti, A. Avagliano & V. Saldutti (eds) *Appellati nomine lupi. Giornata internazionale di studi sull'Hirpinia et gli Hirpini,* 131–206. Naples, Università degli studi suor Orsola Benincasa.

Colucci Pescatori, G. (2021) Per una storia archeologica dell'Irpinia: dall'istituzione del Museo Irpino alle ricerche più recenti. In A. Visconti & M. Lanzillo (eds) *Studi sull'Irpinia antica,* 149–203. Naples, Tiotinx Edizioni.

Colucci Pescatori, G. & Di Giovanni, V. (1999) *Aeclanum.* Avellino, Sellino & Barra Editori.

De Carlo, A. (2015) *Il ceto equestre di Campania, Apulia et Calabria, Luncania et Bruttii dalla tarda Repubblica al IV secolo, Vol. I.* Rome, Edizioni Quasar.

de Ligt, L. (2012) *Peasants, Citizens and Soldiers. Studies in the Demographic History of Roman Italy, 225 BC-AD 100.* Cambridge, Cambridge University Press.

De Ruyt, C. (1983) *Macellum: marché alimentaire des romains.* Leuven, Université catholique de Louvain.

De Simone, G.F. & Russell, B. (2018) New work at Aeclanum (Comune di Mirabella Eclano, Provincia di Avellino, Regione Campania). *Papers of the British School at Rome* 86, 298–301.

De Simone, G.F. & Russell, B. (2019a) Excavation and survey at Aeclanum in 2018 (Comune di Mirabella Eclano, Provincia di Avellino, Regione Campania). *Papers of the British School at Rome* 87, 336–340.

De Simone, G.F. & Russell, B. (2019b) The late-antique eruption of Vesuvius in A.D. 472 and its impact from the Bay of Naples to Aeclanum. *Journal of Roman Archaeology* 32, 359–388.

Di Giovanni, V. (1996) Aeclanum romana. Le evidenze archeologiche. In *Storia illustrata di Avellino. L' Irpinia antica,* 241–256. Pratola Serra, Sellino & Barra.

Ditaranto, I. (2013) Aerotopografia e fotogrammetria finalizzata per la carta archeologica di Aeclanum. *Archeologia Aerea* 7, 53–64.

Ditaranto, I. (2017) Il contributo della fotografia aerea allo studio delle antiche divisioni agrarie in Irpinia orientale. *Archeologia Aerea* 11, 146–153.

Ebanista, C. (2003) *Et manet in mediis quasi gemma intersita tectis. La basilica di S. Felice a Cimitile: stora degli scavi, fasi edilizie, reperti.* Naples, Arte Tipografica.

Evangelisti, S. (2014) Le famiglie senatorie dei Betitii e degli Eggii di Aeclanum. In M.L. Caldelli & G.L. Gregori (eds) *Epigrafia e ordine senatorio: 30 anni dopo, vol. 2,* 635–52. Rome, Edizioni Quasar.

Evangelisti, S. (2017) Regio II. Apulia et Calabria. Aeclanum. Ager inter Compsam et Aeclanum. *Supplementa Italica* (n.s) 29, 37–251.

Frese, S. (2012) Due sime da Aeclanum. *Oebalus* 7, 75–85.

Galadini, F. & Galli, P. (2004) The 346 A.D. earthquake (central-southern Italy): an archaeoseismological approach. *Annals of Geophysics* 47.2/3, 885–905.

Gregori, G.L. & Nonnis, D. (2013) Il contributo dell'epigrafia allo studio delle cinte murarie dell'Italia repubblicana. In G. Bartoloni & L.M. Michetti (eds) *Mura di legno, mura di terra, mura di pietra: fortificazioni nel Mediterraneo antico,* 491–524. Rome, Edizioni Quasar.

Hanson, J.W. (2016) *An Urban Geography of the Roman World, 100 BC to AD 300.* Oxford, Archaeopress.

Hay, S., Keay, S. & Millett, M. (2013) *Ocriculum (Otricoli, Umbria: An Archaeological Survey of the Roman Town.* London, The British School at Rome.

Heinzelmann, M. & Buess, M. (2022) Prospezioni e scavi ad Amiternum. In R. Tuteri (ed.) *Amiternum da splendidissima civitas a parco archeologico*, 165–192. L'Aquila, Mac Edizioni.

Isayev, E. (2013) Italian perspectives from Hirpinia in the period of the Gracchan land reforms and the Social War. In A. Gardner, E. Herring & K. Lomas (eds) *Creating Ethnicities and Identities in the Roman World*, 9–32. London, Institute of Classical Studies.

Kehr, P.F. (1962) *Regesta Pontificum Romanorum, Italia pontificia. Vol. IX, Samnium - Apulia - Lucania.* Berlin, Weidmann.

Lambert, C., Lo Pilato, S., Lubritto, C., Ricci, P., Busiello, G. & Costa, R. (2015) La necropoli di San Michele ad Aeclanum: archeologia funeraria e studi paleonutrizionali. In P. Arthur & M.L. Imperiale (eds) *Atti del VII Congresso Nazionale di Archeologia Medievale (SAMI)*, 121–125. Florence, All'Insegna del Giglio.

Leone, D., Rocco, A. & Buglione, A. (2009) Dalle terme alle capanne. *Herdonia* tra fine V e VII secolo d.C. In G. Volpe & P. Favia (eds) *Atti del V Congresso Nazionale di Archeologia Medievale*, 83–92. Florence, All'Insegna del Giglio.

Lo Pilato, S. (2005) La necropolis tardoantica e l'insediamento altomedievale di Via San Michele a Mirabella Eclano (AV). *Archeologia Medievale* 32, 145–156.

Lo Pilato, S. (2010) Organizzazione e destrutturazione dell'insediamento di *Aeclanum*: considerazioni. In G. Volpe & R. Guiliani (eds) *Paesaggi e insediamenti urbani in Italia meridionale fra tardoantico e altomedioevo*, 349–365. Bari, Edipuglia.

Lo Pilato, S. (2019) Il primo Tratto Irpino della Via Appia. In M.L. Marchi (ed.) *Via Appia Regina Viarum. Ricerche, Contesti, Valorizzazione*, 153–185. Venosa, Osanna Edizioni.

Lombardo, L. (1977) Aeclanum. In *Locri Epizefirii*, 813–816. Naples, Arte Tipografica.

Marchi, M. L. (2010) Venosa. Nuovi dati sulla frequentazione tardoantica dell'area della SS. Trinità a Venosa. In G. Volpe & R. Guiliani (eds) *Paesaggi e insediamenti urbani in Italia meridionale fra tardoantico e altomedioevo*, 201–218. Bari, Edipuglia.

Medri, M. (2016) Lavarsi in viaggio e in albergo: alcune osservazioni sui balnea per i viaggiatori. In P. Basso & E. Zanini (eds) *Statio Amoena. Sostare e vivere lungo le strade romane*, 91–109. Oxford, Archaeopress.

Mesisca, A. (2015) I marmi colorati ritrovati nello scavo del ninfeo, ed erratici, a Aeclanum (Mirabella Eclano, Avellino, Italia). *Marmora* 11, 93–100.

Mesisca, A., Lazzarini, L. & Salvadori, M. (2013) Studio ed analisi archeometrica degli elementi marmorei ritrovati nel ninfeo romano di Aeclanum (Mirabella Eclano, Avellino, Italia). *Marmora* 9, 73–85.

Millett, M. (2012) Understanding Roman towns in Italy: reflections on the role of geophysical survey. In P. Johnson & M. Millett (eds) *Archaeological Survey and the City*, 24–44. Oxford, Oxbow Books.

Onorato, G.O. (1960) *La ricerca archeologica in Irpinia.* Avellino, Amministrazione Provinciale.

Parise Badoni, F. (1969) *La ceramica campana a figure nere.* Firenze, Sansoni.

Poccetti, P. (2021) Tradizioni di etnogenesi, 'identità italica' e assimilazione al mondo romano. In A. Visconti & M. Lanzillo (eds) *Studi sull'Irpinia antica*, 3–52. Naples, Tiotinx Edizioni.

Rotili, M. & Ebanista, C. (2018) Frigento e il suo territorio fra tarda antichità e medioevo: fonti scritte e testimonianze archeologiche. In A. Famiglietti (ed.) *San Marcino. Primo vescovo di Frigento tra storia e fede*, 47–86. Frigento, Tipolitoelle.

Russell, B. & De Simone, G.F. (2020) New excavations in the central and southern sectors of Aeclanum in 2019 (Comune di Mirabella Eclano, Provincia di Avellino, Regione Campania). *Papers of the British School at Rome* 88, 368–373.

Salmon, E.T. (1989) The Hirpini: *ex Italia semper aliquid novi*. *Phoenix* 43.4, 225–235.

Sgobbo, I. (1930) Monumenti epigrafici oschi scoperti ad Aeclanum. *Notizie degli Scavi di Antichità* 6, 400–411.

Sgobbo, I. (1931) La fortificazione romana di Aeclanum. In *Atti II Convegno di Studi Romani*, I, 394–402. Rome, Edizioni Cremonese.

Soricelli, G. (2009) La provincia del Samnium e il terremoto del 346 d.C. In A. Storchi Marino & G.D. Merola (eds) *Interventi imperiali in campo economico e sociale. Da Augusto al Tardoantico*, 245–262. Bari, Edipuglia.

Strapazzon, G., Russell, B. & De Simone, G.F. (2017) Integrating GPR and excavation at Roman Aeclanum (Avellino, Italy). In B. Jennings, C. Gaffney, T. Sparrow & S. Gaffney (eds) *AP2017: 12th International Conference of Archaeological Prospection*, 242–244. Oxford, Oxbow Books.

Tagliamonte, G. (1996) *I Sanniti: Caudini, Irpini, Pentri, Carricini, Frentani*. Milan, Longanesi.

Tocco Sciarelli, G. (1999) L'età tardoantica nelle province di Salerno, Avellino e Benevento. In *L'Italia meridionale in età tardoantica*, 243–266. Naples, Arte Tipografica.

Underwood, D. (2019) *(Re)Using Ruins: Public Buildings in the Cities of the Late Antique West A.D. 300–600*. Leiden/Boston, Brill.

Volpe, G. (2006) Città apule fra destrutturazione e trasformazione: i casi di *Canusium* ed *Herdonia*. In A. Augenti (ed.) *La città italiane tra la tarda antichità e l'alto Medioevo*, 559–587. Florence, All'Insegna del Giglio.

Volpe, G. (2014) Città e campagna, strutture insediative e strutture ellesiastiche dell'Italia meridionale: il caso dell'*Apulia*. In *Chiese locali e chiese regionali nell'alto medioevo*, 1041–1068. Spoleto, Centro Italiano di Studi sull'Alto Medioevo.

Volpe, G. & Groffredo, R. (2020) Reflections on Late Antique cities in *Apulia et Calabria* and in Southern Italy. In A. Carneiro, N. Christie & P. Diarte-Blasco (eds) *Urban Transformations in the Late Antique West: Materials, Agents, and Models*, 61–88. Coimbra, Imprensa da universidade de Coimbra.

Ward-Perkins, B. (1984) *From Classical Antiquity to the Middle Ages: Urban Public Building in Northern and Central Italy, A.D. 300–850*. Oxford, Oxford University Press.

Whitehead, J.K. (2010) The baths at Carsulae. Excavations and survey 2004–2008. *Fasti On Line Documents & Research* 187, 1–10.

Wilson, A.I. (2011) City sizes and urbanization in the Roman Empire. In A.K. Bowman & A.I. Wilson (eds) *Settlement, Urbanization, and Population*, 161–195. Oxford, Oxford University Press.

# Part V

Late Antiquity and beyond

# Chapter 13

## New archaeological perspective on Late Antique Aquileia

### Patrizia Basso

## 13.1. Introduction

Late Antiquity represents a crucial moment for the study of urban landscapes: the 4th and above all the 5th c. AD witnessed the decline of a long-stable empire and the onset of new historical processes that would lead to profound change, even to the physiognomy of the town. This was the result of the wars and the profound political and economic crisis that marked those years, but it was probably also linked to the period's decisive changes in the natural environment. Urban transformation in Late Antiquity will be approached in this essay through a privileged case, namely the town of Aquileia, near modern Udine, which in that period played a major political, military, and economic role. In those years, the town was a grand metropolis, the capital of *Venetia et Histria,* as well as the checkpoint on Italy's northeastern border and a supply point for the troops engaged on the *limes.* Therefore, it was an important Late Antique node for commercial traffic, as it had always been in previous phases of its history.[1]

In particular, in this paper I will present the results of an archaeological research project begun by the University of Verona in 2018, under my direction, in a field located in a southeastern sector of the town called, after its ancient owners, 'ex Fondo Pasqualis' (Plate 13.1).[2] Although our work is still ongoing, the excavation has already revealed very interesting data about the town in Late Antiquity – not just about the 4th century AD, a period, as is well known, of great vitality, but also about the lesser-known 5th century AD.[3]

In order to better understand these results, it would be useful to briefly contextualise our excavation in the historical and topographic framework of the town. As Livy writes (39. 55.4–6; 40.34; 41 and 43 *passim*), the colony at Aquileia was founded in 181 BC, after 12,000 Gauls invaded the border area between the respective territories of the Venetians, Gauls, and Istrians, where there had been a settlement since the

11th century BC and in particular a commercial emporium active between the 4th and 2nd centuries BC (Bandelli 1988; Chiabà 2009; Maselli Scotti 2009; Barca 2022). Like the pre-Roman centre, the new colony had a marked commercial character due to its geographical position, open to the Orient and the Mediterranean via the Adriatic but also to the Balkans and Continental Europe (Basso 2021, 182). The colony was built in an inland location, linked to the sea by a river about 50 m wide, identified as the *Natiso cum Turro* mentioned by Pliny (*HN* 3.126). Its right bank was home to a large river port, whose buildings were laid out in the middle of the 1st century AD (Plate 13.1: A). Over time, it grew to include ever-larger warehouses and ramps leading into the urban centre (Carre & Maselli Scotti 2001; Carre 2008; Maselli Scotti & Rubinich 2009, 103–106). At the end of the 4th century AD, the poet Ausonius celebrated it, along with the town walls, defining Aquileia to be *moenibus et portu celeberrima* (*Ordo nob. urb.* 9.64–72). Other, smaller docks have been hypothesised – thanks to geophysical analyses (Groh 2011) – to have been placed along the canals that surrounded Aquileia on the north and west sides, which would have provided a means of circumnavigating the town (Maggi *et al.* 2017).

Literary sources also emphasise the crucial role of Aquileia as a crossroads of trade, as can be read in a famous passage from Strabo (5.1.8), from the end of the 1st century BC, and in Herodian (8.2.3–4), from the 3rd century AD. 'Further confirmation comes from the numerous imported materials excavated in urban areas. These provide evidence of exchange not only with the nearby territories of *Noricum*, *Histria* and *Pannonia* but also with northeastern Europe, the Orient, Spain, and North Africa' (Basso 2021, 183).[4]

In addition to the port, Aquileia was progressively built up in the Republican and Imperial periods with typical public urban monuments, showing the monumental character of the town and its wealth over the centuries (Bertacchi 2003; Maselli Scotti *et al.* 2009; Tiussi 2009, 61–75). These works include the earliest town walls (Bonetto 2009, 83–85; Bonetto *et al.* 2019–2020) (Plate 13.1: M1 in yellow); the *forum* with the *comitium* (Plate 13.1: B), the *macellum* (Plate 13.1: C) and the *basilica* (Plate 13.1: D), built at the time of the town's foundation (Maselli Scotti *et al.* 2007; Maselli Scotti & Rubinich 2009, 93–98); the Augustan-age theatre (Ghiotto 2018; Ghiotto *et al.* 2020; 2021) (Plate 13.1: E); and the amphitheatre that, based on other excavations I recently directed, dates to the Claudian age (Basso 2018) (Plate 13.1: F). In the 4th century AD, as we will explain in more detail below, the town saw an 'urban revolution' (Sotinel 2005, 28; Tiussi & Villa 2019), with the construction of a *circus,* which was probably built during the Terarchy (Tiussi & Villa 2018; 2019, 117–124) (Plate 13.1: G); the huge *thermae* from the Constantinian age (Rubinich 2020; 2022; Rubinich & Braidotti 2021) (Plate 13.1: H); and the large market we are going to describe. This market, along with its large connected *horreum* for foodstuffs, constituted the town's new commercial centre despite the fact that the Republican/Imperial forum was still in use (Tiussi & Villa 2019, 98–101). It functioned throughout the 5th century AD, demonstrating the continuity of the town's role as a hub for travel and commerce in this period.

## 13.2. The University of Verona's research: methods and first results

Our excavation area (a surface area of 16,000 square metres) (Plate 13.1 and Fig. 13.1) had already been partially excavated in the 1950s by Giovanni Battista Brusin, then director of the Archaeological Museum of Aquileia, who was actively engaged in urban excavations (Bandelli 1990; Cigaina 2018; https://www.dizionariobiograficodeifriulani. it/brusin-giovanni-battista/). During his work in 'ex Fondo Pasqualis', Brusin identified three paved areas, interpreted as three market buildings, within a large commercial complex, as well as two parallel fortification walls, running along the north bank of the river Natissa, and two rooms with mosaic floors in the southeast corner of the central market (Brusin 1957; Basso forthcoming). Apart from these mosaics and the eastern market building, which was backfilled due to its poor state of preservation, the structures remain visible today in an archaeological area open to the public, managed by the Fondazione Aquileia (https://www.fondazioneaquileia. it/it/cosa-vedere/fondo-pasqualis-mercati).

Before the excavation, we studied Brusin's manuscripts and drawings along with a series of black and white photographs from the archives of the National Archaeological Museum of Aquileia (Basso forthcoming). This material allowed us to see that, despite

*Figure 13.1. Our excavation area: panoramic photograph. In the foreground, the structures uncovered by Brusin in the 1950s; on the bottom left, the house and the stable of the Pasqualis family; above, to the right, the basilica, and between the basilica and the excavation area is the location where a large, Late Antique horreum was identified, later reburied (thanks to Fondazione Aquileia).*

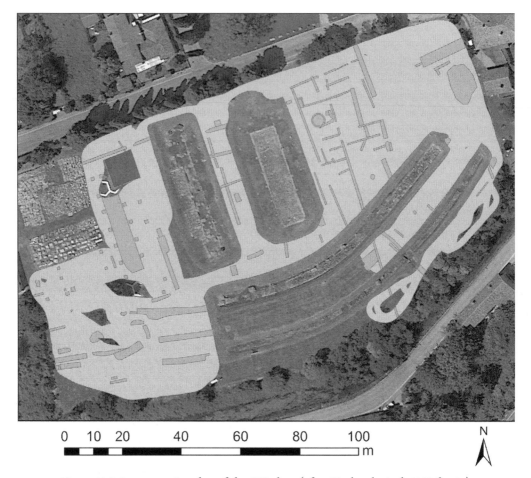

*Figure 13.2. Interpretative plan of the GPR data (after Verdonck et al. 2020 fig. 21).*

the large amounts of data gathered during those excavations, many questions remain unanswered about this area. In particular, Brusin was only able to excavate the eastern part of the land, because the owners did not want him to dig up a vineyard on the western side.

Another important approach used geophysical surveys. In 2018, Frank Vermeulen and his team (to whom I am very grateful) conducted a magnetometry and a georadar survey of the entire area, revealing some particularly clear anomalies such as a paved area surrounded by pillars located to the west of the structures excavated by Brusin (Verdonck *et al.* 2020) (Fig. 13.2). On the basis of these surveys and the archival documentation, in the four archaeological campaigns conducted so far, we have investigated both the walls and the market with the various excavation areas and trenches (Fig. 13.3A: excavation areas 1–5). Also, in order to reconstruct the natural environment, and in particular the course of the river, corings were taken from the south of the area (Fig. 13.3A: S1–S4). We also conducted botanical analyses on samples

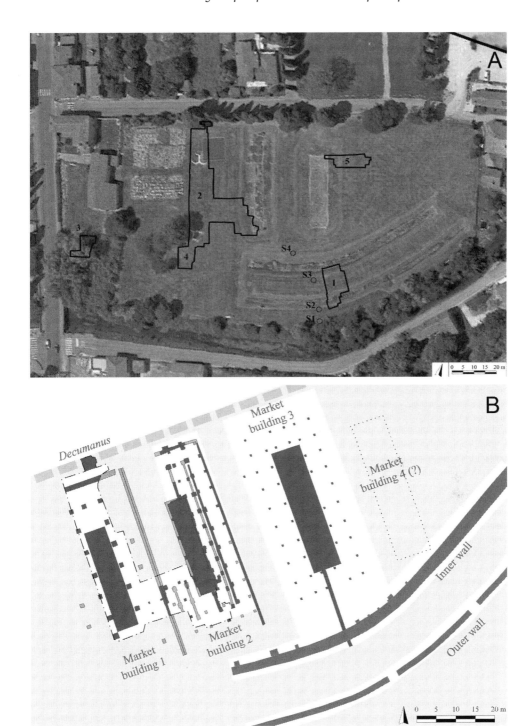

Figure 13.3. A: General view of the excavation areas and the corings made by University of Verona from 2018 until today (drone survey by Explora s.r.l.). B: Floor plan of the market buildings (in black the structures unearthed, in grey those hypothesized) (reworked by V. Grazioli).

drawn from the most complete stratigraphic section of the site, in the northern part of the field, as well as C14 analyses and archeozoological analyses, to supplement the data collected by Brusin at a time when such analytical approaches were not applied.

In this paper we focus on the Late Antique fortifications and market. However, we briefly mention the earliest structures brought to light by our excavations: some walls and pillars underneath the pavements of the market area and a quay by the bank of the Natissa brought to light at three points in the fortification's sector, from which there were some steps down to the river. The limited extent of the excavations, as well as groundwater that has risen since antiquity, prevent us from understanding these structures. However, even if the evidence is flimsy, it points to an earlier habitation in the area during the 1st–2nd centuries AD, which was unknown before our excavations (Basso & Dobreva 2020b, 8, 11–12; Basso *et al.* 2021b, 269).

### 13.2.1 The Late Antique fortifications

To study the fortifications, we excavated in three areas: the first between the inner and outer walls already brought to light by Brusin in the southern part of the field; the second further east, along the inner wall; the third near the ex Pasqualis house, where other excavations were conducted in 1993–1996 (Mandruzzato 1996; Basso & Dobreva 2020b, 11–13) (Fig. 13.3A: excavation areas 1, 4, 3).

The inner wall was very large (2.40–2.60 m), but only the foundations are preserved, because over time the wall was largely stripped of its stone (Fig. 13.4A). The foundations were constructed using numerous *spolia* recovered from other urban monuments and burial areas (honorary inscriptions, parts of moulded cornices, columns, funerary inscriptions: Buonopane forthcoming; Grazioli forthcoming). Of particular interest are two statue bases which probably come from the *forum*: they are dedicated to a senator *T. Caesernius Statius Quinctius Macedo Quinctianus*, who had a direct link with Emperor Hadrian, given that he was his *comes per Orientem et Illyricum* (Alföldy 1984, 96; Buonopane forthcoming). The wall stood above the quay by the bank of the Natissa, as mentioned above. That meant that the fortification used the river as a further defensive element, which functioned like the ditches that formed an integral part of other urban fortification systems.

The section of wall brought to light in our excavation area is topographically linked to many others uncovered in various parts of the town (Plate 13.1: M2, in red) and dated to around the end of the 3rd or the beginning of the 4th century AD (Villa 2004; Bonetto 2009; 2013; Buora 2016; Tiussi & Villa 2019). As mentioned above, all that remains of this wall are its foundations, so it has never been possible to estimate its elevation. So, we were particularly intrigued when we discovered a collapsed sector of its southern façade (5.5 × 5.3 m) (Fig. 13.5). This face, clearly detached from the core, perhaps due to a seismic event or some other violent occurrence, still presents an orderly succession of at least 30 rows of bricks, pebbles, and ashlar blocks. In the northern portion, a small rectangular slit with a semicircular brick ring is still visible

*Figure 13.4. A: the inner wall. B: the outer wall (photo by P. Basso).*

(Basso *et al.* 2021a, 96, figs 8–9; 2022, 91, fig. 7). This finding allowed us to estimate that the wall was about 11 m high (Delbarba 2021–22) (Fig. 13.8A).

Regarding its dating, Brusin's excavation trenches disrupted the relationship between the stratification and the wall, making it very hard to date. However, materials from the end of the 3rd and the beginning of the 4th centuries AD were collected in the layer that covered the fold of the wall. Diana Dobreva recognised African amphorae (*e.g.* African IID, the early version of Keay 25.1, Tripolitan II, Ostia IV.263) and common pottery (*e.g.* the Bierbrauer IIIc olla) (Basso & Dobreva 2020b, 16–18; Basso *et al.* 2022, 96–97).

Subsequently, at an as yet undetermined time in the 4th century AD, the Natissa shrank and its course moved further south, where it still runs today. Environmental analyses conducted in Aquileia suggest that the current of the Natissa was less strong toward the end of the 4th century AD.[5] But the movement of the riverbed was probably the result of artificial intervention. Indeed, during our excavation, four corings showed that the bank of the river was moved, carrying over a massive amount of debris (Basso *et al.* 2021b, 258, fig. 7; 2022, 92–93, fig. 8). Although it is too soon to come to any firm conclusions, it seems possible that we can connect these

*Figure 13.5. Collapsed sector of southern façade of inner wall (photo by P. Basso).*

findings to Ammianus Marcellinus's story (21.12.17) that during the siege of the town by Julian in AD 361 the river was diverted with great effort. This intervention had already been hypothesised in the port area, where several towers appear to have been constructed on the western bank of the river, which had evidently been moved before their construction. This reduced the width of the river, which, as has already been said, was probably originally around 50 m wide (Bonetto 2009, 90) (Plate 13.1: TTT2, TTT3, TTT4).

A new fortification, built about 12 m south of the inner wall, was much thinner (1.50 m) and was made with a core of irregular stone blocks. Its façade was composed of squared ashlar stones, bonded with abundant mortar (Fig. 13.4B) (Basso *et al.* 2021b, 257–259; 2022, 93–96). The wall was built on the above-mentioned highly inconsistent layer highlighted in the coring. Indeed, its construction required extensive land consolidation. On the southern side of the wall, a series of wooden piles was discovered, while on the northern side another row of wooden piles and some amphorae were brought to light (Basso *et al.* 2021b, 257–258, figs 5–6; 2022, 94–95) (Fig. 13.6). These poles were of oak, the most commonly used timber in the Roman age for public works in a damp environment, due to its robustness and resistance to moisture and xylophagous organisms (Basso *et al.* forthcoming). Moreover, below the wall, in a deep excavation carried out under very difficult working conditions due to the presence of a lot of rising groundwater, a bed of alder beams was brought to light (another wood widely used in wet environments) and below that we found a series of vertical poles and amphorae submerged vertically in the soil. Thanks to the amphorae recovered, studied by Diana Dobreva, the outer wall was dated to the first half of the 5th century AD (Basso *et al.* 2021a, 103, figs 19–20; 2022; forthcoming). The wooden poles, by contrast, are radiocarbon dated to before the amphorae: they were probably recycled from an earlier structure, perhaps related to a previous consolidation of the Natissa's bank. Dendrochronology unfortunately did not yield a more precise dating (Basso *et al.* forthcoming).

Brusin discovered three openings about 2–3 m wide on the excavated wall section, some 25 m apart from each other, one of which he more fully excavated. Our excavation focused on the analysis of another of these openings (the westernmost). At the southern-facing opening, we uncovered a wooden structure, consisting of three

*Figure 13.6. Amphorae and poles put in place for the construction of the outer wall (photo by P. Basso).*

parallel beams, at least 1.5 m long and 0.18 m thick, joined to six planks, at most 1.7 m long. At first, the structure was thought to be a pier for the river, but then the thinness of the planks, incompatible with the stresses produced by the weight of men and goods, as well as the fact that the wooden structure was the same width as the opening in the wall, led to the conclusion that this structure was probably a kind of closure system for that opening which had fallen from its original vertical position. The structure was radiocarbon dated (CEDAD-LTL19856A 1689 ± 45 BP, $\delta^{13}C$ (‰) 27.4 ± 0.4, 238AD (95.4%) 429AD), thus confirming the chronological framing of the wall in the first half of the 5th century AD (Basso *et al.* 2021b, 259–261, fig. 9; 2022; forthcoming). The stratigraphy of this area seems to suggest the presence of a narrow channel that branched off from the river to allow boats to enter the opening to unload goods.

To the north of the opening, the excavation revealed a ramp sloping in a north–south direction, with a slope of about 6–7 degrees, which seems to be connected at the north end with another passage running east–west (Basso *et al.* 2021b, 261–262; 2022, 95–96) (Fig. 13.8A). This was a system for offloading and transporting merchandise from the river to the market. There is no trace of openings for passage of merchandise in the inner wall in our excavated area, due to the later spoliation already mentioned, but a sector of the wall discovered further west than our excavation preserves one opening, about 2 m wide, as we discovered in archival documents (Basso *et al.* 2022, 104, fig. 22).

Only a part of the parapets of the ramp remains, consisting of some very large stone blocks (Basso *et al.* 2021b, fig. 12). The floor surface is missing, but in front of the opening it seems that it mainly consisted of wooden planks, since we found at least two lines of long iron nails. In the rest of the space, by contrast, the pavement was made of *cocciopesto* and rebuilt several times, as evidenced by the three surfaces identified (Basso *et al.* 2021b, 261, figs 10, 12, 13). Materials found in all these layers can be dated to the 5th century AD, demonstrating that the ramps and the opening were in use at that time (Basso & Dobreva 2020b, 19–20).

The frequent restoration of the floor opens new debate over what caused the deterioration of the space between the walls. Perhaps in the 5th century AD the natural environment or climate had changed? Future research and in particular the pollen analyses currently underway may provide the answers.

### 13.2.2 The Late Antique market

Immediately north of the inner wall, a monumental commercial complex was revealed, consisting of three or four large market buildings, one identified by our excavations and two or three by Brusin (the interpretation of the easternmost building as an additional commercial area remains uncertain, given that Brusin says that it was poorly preserved, without offering further data) (Basso *et al.* 2021b, 268–269, fig. 25). Over several years of excavation, we undertook two excavations to study two market buildings already discovered by Brusin (Fig. 13.3A: excavation area 2, 5). The complex was unitary, built on a very thick artificial fill, to raise the pavement in response to a rise of the water table. Materials collected in this level are being studied but seem to suggest that the two buildings date from the end of the 3rd and the beginning of the 4th century AD (Basso & Dobreva 2020a, 26–27).

The building here named 3 (Figs 13.3B and 13.7A) consists of a paved square, surrounded by two lines of stone bases with quadrangular holes in their surface, which probably held wooden poles (Basso *et al.* 2021b, 264, fig. 15–16) that supported a roof or canopy of some other light material, as proposed in the virtual reconstruction (Fig. 13.8B). A water channel runs around the northern sector, suggesting that 'messy' goods that required water, like fish and meat, were sold here. The animal bones found inside the small well located at the centre of this sector also confirm this hypothesis (Bandera forthcoming). The vast majority of these are from cattle, 85.2% of which show signs of butchery. Of particular interest is a scapula with a hole probably intended for suspension by a hook for the sale of the meat. A bear bone is also worth mentioning, possibly attesting to the presence of this animal as well in the diet of the time.

*Figure 13.7. A: the 'eastern' market building brougth to light by Brusin (building 3). B: the 'western' market building brought to light by Brusin (building 2). C: the new market building brought to light by our excavation (building 1) (photos by P. Basso)*

*Figure 13.8. A: 3D reconstruction of the two walls (Delbarba 2021-22). B: 3D reconstruction of the two market buildings brought to light by Brusin (2 and 3) and the* horreum *(by Nudesign; thanks to Fondazione Aquileia).*

The building named 2 presents a paved area, surrounded by a portico, which underwent various phases of structural change, as evidenced by the different rows of pillars brought to light by Brusin on the eastern side of the paved area (Basso *et al.* 2021b, 264, figs 17, 19) (Figs 13.3B and 13.7B). Perhaps on either side of the portico was a row of stores, as proposed in the virtual reconstruction (Fig. 13.8B).

One particularly important finding uncovered by our excavation (Figs 13.3A: excavation area 2; 13.3B and 13.7C) is a previously undocumented market building (named 1), corresponding to the previously mentioned geophysical anomalies (Basso *et al.* 2021b, 265–267). It was paved by Aurisina stones and in some cases by recycled architectural elements, such as a manhole. A kerb runs along the eastern limit of the paved area, on which are preserved some circular signs that we think were part of a *tabula lusoria,* where the market customers would have played games. On both sides of the paved area, six quadrangular pillars or reused columns emerged, corresponding to the geophysical anomalies. In our next excavation campaign, we plan to investigate them further. At this phase of the research, we think that this building, too, was surrounded by a portico.

To the east, the building was enclosed by a wall (Basso *et al.* 2021b, 264). The fact that it is adjacent to the wall that blocks off the western side of building 2 shows that the two buildings (1 and 2) sat side by side (Fig. 13.3B). The north wall of the complex was extensively despoiled over time. What remains, in building 2, is a section of the wall with external reinforcing pilasters, and, in building 1 just the wall's foundation. Between the wall and the paved area, a double entrance was identified, probably intended for chariots (traces remain of wheel ruts in the cocciopesto pavement) and pedestrians (Basso *et al.* 2021b, 267, fig. 24). This entrance was directly connected to the road that was discovered immediately north of the wall and that constituted one of the town's *decumani* (Plate 13.1: I; Fig. 13.3B): the excavation revealed several overlapping layers of pavement preparation starting from the early Imperial age up to the modern age (Basso *et al.* 2021b, 268, fig. 26–27).

Excavating the building, we identified a brick channel discharging water outside the complex, probably towards the Natissa, as well as one of the drains where water from the square drained into the channel (Basso *et al.* 2021b, 267, fig. 23). Brusin brought to light another similar channel connected to building 3 (Basso forthcoming) (Fig. 13.3B). In future excavations we will try to understand the relationship between this channel and the inner boundary wall. A photograph of Brusin's excavation in the 1950s, in the eastern border of the field, shows that in that portion of the wall there was a further channel that passed through it (Basso forthcoming). This would confirm the close architectonic, and therefore chronological, relationship between the squares and the internal wall. In fact, as has been said, the data gathered so far seem to date both constructions to sometime between the end of the 3rd and the beginning of the 4th century AD.

Judging from the piles of carbonised seeds found in the layers belonging to the era when a violent fire caused the abandonment of the market, it seems likely that buildings 1 and 2 were reserved for the sale of cereals. Archaeobotanical analyses conducted by Maria Bosco show that these cereals were mostly wheat and spelt and, to a lesser extent, barley and rye (Basso *et al.* 2021b, 265, fig. 20). These findings reveal some parts of the diet in this period. The discovery of cereals in buildings 1 and 2 and animal bones in building 3, as it has been said, attests to the differentiation of the commercial areas within a single structural complex.

We have not yet identified the east, west, and south perimeter walls of the complex (Fig. 13.3B). In addition, we do not know whether there was a north–south passage between buildings 2 and 3, or some other passages between all the buildings. So, as far as the market is concerned, there is still a lot of work to be done in future digs. However, based on the data so far obtained from excavations, archival research, geophysical surveys, cores, and analyses, our research is tracing a new physiognomy of Late Antique Aquileia, as I will explain in the next section.

## 13.3. Late Antique Aquileia

As mentioned above, the inner wall of our area was part of a large and solid urban fortification (Plate 13.1: M2, in red), built at the end of the 3rd and the beginning of the 4th century AD, in order to protect the town but also to strengthen its urban *dignitas* (Bonetto 1998, 190; Tiussi & Villa 2019, 93–97). Up to that time the Republican wall (Plate 13.1: M1. in yellow) would have remained in use. In fact, at the time of Maximinus the Thracian and his siege (AD 238) Herodian (8.2–4) described the walls as very old and in parts fallen into ruin (Bonetto 2009, 89). The new wall includes an urban area of about 83 ha, running along the river, which was used as an additional defensive element (Tiussi 2009, 77; Tiussi & Villa 2019, 93). Almost 4,000 m long, the wall is constructed from an enormous amount of building material, probably around 85,000 cubic metres (Basso *et al.* 2022, 107). The costs and difficulties of such an undertaking could perhaps explain the extensive use of spoliated materials observed along the entire perimeter (Bonetto 2009, 89; Tiussi & Villa 2019, 93).

Between the Tetrarchy and the Constantinian period, Aquileia witnessed a notable phase of urban monumentalisation, related to the economic and strategic role it played at that time (Tiussi & Villa 2019). Limiting ourselves to the southeast sector, the above-mentioned great *horreum* (66 × 88 m) (Plate 13.1: L) was modelled on those of Milan, built by Emperor Maximian: it consists of two large rectangular halls divided into naves by pillars and separated by an uncovered central area (Tiussi 2004, 299–300, fig. 17; Ventura 2013, 95; Tiussi & Villa 2019, 101). The discovery of cereals on the floor level testifies to the main use of the complex as a granary, probably intended to supply the army that had to be stationed there because of the threats on Italy's eastern borders (Mandruzzato & Maselli Scotti 1994; Tiussi 2009, 77; Basso *et al.* 2021b, 271–272).

Closely connected to this *horreum* was the large market that we have been excavating over the past few years, built, like the *horreum*, at the end of 3rd or the beginning of 4th century AD. This monumental commercial complex is evidence of Aquileia's important economic role during this phase of its history. North of the *horreum*, the first basilica (Plate 13.1: M) was built in the Costantinian age (to be precise, in the second decade of the 4th century AD) by bishop Theodore (Cuscito & Lehmann 2010; Villa 2012–13; Lusuardi Siena & Baratto 2013, 186–192; Novello *et al.* 2013), whose name is found in the centre of the magnificently preserved floor mosaics. The construction of these sacred and commercial structures shifts the urban centre of gravity from the *forum*, the heart of Aquileia in the Republican and Imperial periods, to this southwestern part of the town.

The area was still extremely vital in the first half of the 5th century AD, when a new fortification was built, probably at the behest of Theodosius II, who at that time controlled the fragile empire of the very young Valentinian III. The wall enclosed only the southern sector of Aquileia to protect this new centre of gravity of its urban life (Basso *et al.* 2022, 108–109; forthcoming) (Plate 13.1: M3, in green). For Aquileia, those years were difficult, not just because of internal politics, which saw the clash between Valentinian III and the usurper John, killed in the circus of the town (Procop. *Vand.* 1.3.9), but also because of the external threats from the Goths and a few years later from the Huns, which resulted in the conquest of the urban centre in AD 452. This second wall functioned as an ante-mural of the other, if we judge by examples from the eastern area of the Empire, particularly from Constantinople (Delbarba 2021–22; Basso *et al.* 2022, 109) (Fig. 13.8A). The presence of openings in this wall, which would have been related to a system of ramps identified between the two fortifications thanks to our excavation, attests to the close relationship that still existed between the river and the great market, with goods arriving along the Natissa and then being transported to the points of sale. In these years the abovementioned eastern port was probably replaced by new docks along the river in the southern sector of the town (Tiussi 2009, 81).

Throughout the 5th century AD, and therefore even after the siege by Attila, the market maintained its economic vitality (Basso *et al.* 2021b, 268). In fact, the material evidence from that period, studied by Diana Dobreva, shows that Aquileia was fully integrated into the Mediterranean trade network: the ceramics found in urban excavations dating to the second half of the 5th and the beginning of the 6th century AD are 84% amphorae, which attest to the importation of foodstuffs (oil, wine, and garum), and also fine tableware and oil lamps. The origins are mainly African but also Aegean and micro-Asian with a small percentage (2%) of ceramics of Southern Italic origin (Dobreva & Zago 2021; Basso *et al.* 2022, 110–112).

Many coins were found, as is typical in a commercial area, and most date from the 4th and 5th centuries AD. But what was exceptional was the discovery of a gold solid of Leo I, the first to be found at Aquileia. This finding attests to the circulation of precious metal coins on site in the second half of the 5th century AD and is extremely important evidence for market attendance.[6] Finally, the vitality of the area in this period is demonstrated by two floor mosaics identified by Brusin in the southeast corner of building 3, dated to the middle of the 5th century AD, although we do not yet know how exactly they fit into the broader context (Ghedini *et al.* 2017, 463–466; Basso *et al.* 2021b, 272, fig. 31).

The abandonment of the markets occurred in the first decades of the 6th century AD, when a violent fire caused the roof of the portico to collapse. The date is suggested by the materials uncovered in these layers and by radiocarbon dating carried out on some abovementioned cereal caryopses (Basso & Dobreva 2020b, 27; Basso *et al.* 2021a, 109; Dobreva & Zago 2021). The ramp discovered between the two boundary walls and used for the transport of goods from the rivers to the commercial squares, also fell into disuse in this period (Basso & Dobreva 2020b, 19).

In Aquileia, the poor evidence from the middle of the 6th century AD suggests a clear change in the function of the town during the Lombard period, when it gradually lost importance compared to the new centres of power such as Cividale del Friuli and later Udine. However, our research shows that people frequented the area even after the abandonment of the market. From the southeast to the northeast corner of building 1, excavations revealed a cut in the paving stones stratigraphically datable to between the second half of the 6th and the 7th century AD (Fig. 13.7C). Numerous postholes observed at the bottom suggest that this was the location of an enclosure or fence (Basso *et al.* 2021b, 269, fig. 28). But we will have to excavate the other half of the structure to get a better idea.

The presence of a number of graves, some of which Brusin discovered, attests to later frequentations. During our excavations, we identified five inhumations, without grave goods, splitting the stones of the Late Antique paved square. Dated between the 8th and 9th centuries AD, they could be related to a larger necropolis that was discovered around the basilica (Basso *et al.* 2021b, 269–270, fig. 29).

Then, apart from sporadic traces of life even in the Middle Ages, when the area – like the whole town – probably became an open-air stone quarry, the field began a long phase of agricultural use, as evidenced in the historical cartography (Zemignani forthcoming). Even at the time of the Brusin excavation, as mentioned, the area was a farm and a vineyard. This discontinuity of structures has allowed us to freely investigate the terrain, gathering many clues about its life over time.

## 13.4. Conclusion

In summary, it seems that the 5th century AD in Aquileia was a period of profound transformations in the natural and urban landscapes. On the one hand, one could say that the town in this period continued to play an important commercial role in the context of the Northern Adriatic, as demonstrated by the articulated mercantile structure we investigated – which appears to be without equal in the Empire for its dimensions and the structure of its diversified commercial areas – and probably also by a new system of docks along the Natissa, a substitute for the old river port then in disuse (Maselli Scotti & Rubinich 2009, 103–106; Tiussi 2009, 81; Groh 2011, 172).

Besides this urban sector, other important public monuments continued to be vital in this period, such as the so-called 'Great Baths', where archaeologists from the University of Udine found evidence from the 5th century AD of the restoration of floors and the construction of new rooms in the northeast sector (Rubinich & Braidotti 2021). Based on the written sources, even the *circus* and the hypothetical (but not yet located) imperial residence were still in use at least until the beginning of the 5th century AD, given that the former hosted the execution of John the Usurper in AD 423, and that Galla Placidia and her son Valentinian III, the last emperor who we know to have resided in the town, lodged in the palace until the autumn of AD 425 (Tiussi 2009, 80; Tiussi & Villa 2019, 124–129).

As in many other urban centers in the Empire, in the 5th century AD Aquilea witnessed the monumentalisation of places of worship, which by these years had become the community's new gathering places, marking a decisive change in the town's topography: one may consider the new religious buildings that extended outside the walls sometime between the 4th and 5th centuries AD, like Saint John in the Forum, the basilica of Saint Felix and Fortunatus and other two basilicas in the southern locality 'Beligna' (named 'del Fondo Tullio') and in the northern locality 'Monastero' (Cuscito 2004; 2009, 143–151; Lusuardi Siena & Baratto 2013, 194–198); within the walls there was also the construction, in the time of Chromatius, of the southern post-Theodoran basilica and of the baptistery (Cuscito 2009, 139–142; Lusuardi Siena & Baratto 2013, 193).

However, in contrast with this monumental continuity, other archaeological data seem to suggest a completely different urban landscape, with signs of discontinuity and radical and irreversible transformations. Consider the amphitheatre, in the area of today's Palazzo Brunner (via Roma), where the excavations conducted by the University of Verona under my direction between 2015 and 2017 have shown the defunctionalisation of the building by the second half of the 4th century AD and, from the middle of the 5th century AD, the reuse of its radial walls for housing (Soriano 2018, 103–106). These were perhaps modular houses, trapezoidal in plan, of perishable materials, which unloaded their domestic garbage in the ancient arena, as proved by the microstratigraphic analysis of organic levels (almost one meter thick) from the arena (Nicosia 2018, 172–176). If this public building was reappropriated for private purposes and underwent a decisive transformation of its monumental structure, profound alterations of the management of public space, albeit in different, more productive forms, also emerged in the theatre area. In fact, archaeological research suggests that, between the 4th and 5th centuries AD, facilities for the forging and beating of iron, as well as other metals, were created between the theatre buildings (Borsato 2021). Other similar productive structures have also been highlighted by excavations within the urban centre, such as the house of Titus Macro and the warehouses at the port, yet again clearly attesting to ongoing construction in a town that was still very much alive.

For the moment, however, with our incomplete data, the image of Aquileia in the 5th century AD remains blurry. We have long since overcome the idea that, after Attila's conquest in AD 452, Aquileia began a long decline that would lead to its definitive disappearance at the dawn of the early Middle Ages (Bratoz 2003; Sotinel 2003; Villa 2004; Marano 2009; 2012; Barca 2022). Nonetheless, this phase of the town's history still requires more multidisciplinary and integrated archaeological research to understand the environmental change, not to mention the transformation of politics, society, architecture, and material culture, it witnessed, and which may be fruitfully compared with other urban contexts. Like the phase of urban foundation, for which this volume offers wide-ranging discussions and case studies, Aquileia's history in the 5th century AD represents an extremely complex and therefore also extremely interesting period for the study of urban landscapes – one of radical changes and shifts, the collapse of old realities and the beginnings of other, completely new ones – which archaeology, with the refinement of its technique and analytical approaches, is ever more capable of grasping.

## Acknowledgements

I take this opportunity to thank the *Fondazione Aquileia* for generously supporting our work; the *Soprintendenza Archeologia, Belle Arti e Paesaggio per il Friuli Venezia Giulia* for their fieldwork support; the excavation team (Diana Dobreva, who directs it with me; the excavation supervisors Maria Bosco, Giacomo Fadelli, Marina Scalzeri, Fiammetta Soriano and Andrea Zemignani; the record supervisor Vittoria Canciani and Sabrina Zago; the graphic and photographic documentation supervisor Valeria Grazioli; the public archaeology activities supervisors Lisa Monaco, Angelica Gabrielli and Nicola Delbarba, and all university students, participating with commitment and enthusiasm both in the field and in the laboratory). I also wish to thank Alberto Manicardi (*SAP Società Archeologica*) for taking care of site logistics with grate competence; Marta Novello, director of the National Archeological Museum of Aquileia, and the archives supervisor Adriana Comar for kindly allowing us to study the documentation and for their help in finding it; Cristiano Nicosia for reading and interpreting the corings; Andrea Stella for studying the numismatic material; Barbara Bramanti and Jessica Mongillo (University of Ferrara) for the anthropological analysis of the human remains in the course of two undergraduate theses.

### Notes

1. On the theme of the 5th and 6th centuries in Aquileia with comparisons to other cities, see Buora *et al.* 2021.
2. The excavations were conducted with ministerial concession and in close scientific collaboration with the *Fondazione Aquileia*, which also funded our investigations.
3. To date, only initial excavation results have been published (Basso & Dobreva 2020a; 2020b; Basso 2021; Basso *et al.* 2021a; 2021b; 2022; forthcoming) and an initial volume on the research conducted in the archives of National Archaeological Museum of Aquileia (Basso & Dobreva forthcoming).
4. The bibliography on Aquileia's marked commercial character is extensive: e.g. Cuscito & Zaccaria 2007; Zaccaria & Pesavento Mattioli 2009; Ungaro *et al.* 2017, 147–228 together with the preceding bibliography. For an extensive summary of Aquileia market spaces, Tiussi 2004; Basso 2021.
5. Despite its important historical status, few environmental studies have been undertaken at Aquileia. The bibliography on the subject has recently expanded: e.g. Arnaud-Fassetta *et al.* 2003; Sichè *et al.* 2004; Cottica *et al.* 2018; Cottica & Ventura 2019; Kaniewsky *et al.* 2022.

6. The coin has not yet been published. Now on display in the National Archeological Museum of Aquileia.

## Bibliography

Alföldy, G. (1984) *Römische Statuen in Venetia et Histria. Epigraphische Quellen.* Heidelberg, Winter.

Arnaud-Fassetta, G., Carre, M.B., Marocco, R., Maselli Scotti, F., Pugliese, N., Zaccaria, C., Bandelli, A., Bresson, V., Manzoni, G., Montenegro, M., Morhange, C., Pipan, M., Prizzon, A. & Siché I. (2003) The site of Aquileia (northeastern Italy): example of fluvial geoarchaeology in a Mediterranean deltaic plain. *Géomorphologie: Relief, Processus, Environment* 9, 227–245.

Bandelli, G. (1988) *Ricerche sulla colonizzazione romana della Gallia Cisalpina. Le fasi iniziali e il caso aquileiese.* Rome, Quasar.

Bandelli, G. (1990) Gli scavi di Aquileia tra scienza e politica (1866–1918). In *Gli scavi di Aquileia, Uomini e Opere*, 163–188. Trieste, Editreg.

Bandera, S. (forthcoming) Gli scavi di Paola Lopreato. Le analisi dei resti faunistici. In P. Basso & D. Dobreva, *Aquileia, l'area delle mura e del mercato tardoantichi: gli scavi negli archivi.* Rome, Quasar.

Barca, N. (2022) *Roman Aquileia: The Impenetrable City-Fortress, a Sentry of the Alps.* Oxford, Oxbow Books.

Basso, P. (2018) *L'anfiteatro di Aquileia. Ricerche d'archivio e nuove indagini di scavo.* Quingentole, SAP.

Basso, P. (2021) *Aquileia's market spaces.* In F. Vermeulen, A. Zuiderhoek (eds) *Space, Movement and the Economy in Roman Cities in Italy and Beyond*, 180–200. London, Routledge.

Basso, P. (forthcoming) Gli scavi di Giovani Battista Brusin. I quaderni manoscritti. In P. Basso & D. Dobreva, *Aquileia, l'area delle mura e del mercato tardoantichi: gli scavi negli archivi.* Rome, Quasar.

Basso, P. & Dobreva, D. (2020a) Aquileia: first results from the market excavation and the Late Antiquity town walls (part one). *Fasti On Line Document & Research* 482, 1–20.

Basso, P. & Dobreva, D. (2020b) Aquileia: first results from the market excavation and the Late Antiquity town walls (part two). *Fasti On Line Document & Research* 483, 1–32.

Basso, P. & Dobreva, D. (forthcoming) *Aquileia, l'area delle mura e del mercato tardoantichi: gli scavi negli archivi.* Rome, Quasar.

Basso, P., Dobreva, D., Bosco, M., Soriano, F. & Zemignani, A. (2021a) Gli scavi nell'ex Fondo Pasqualis. I risultati delle indagini 2018. *Quaderni Friulani di Archeologia* 31, 91–117.

Basso, P., Dobreva, D., Bosco, M., Soriano, F. & Zemignani, A. (2021b) Trasformazioni e rinnovamenti urbanistici ad Aquileia nel V sec. d.C. In M. Buora, S. Magnani & L. Villa (eds) *Italia settentrionale e regioni dell'arco alpino fra V e VI secolo d.C.*, 253–275. Trieste, EUT Edizioni.

Basso, P., Dobreva, D. & Laserra, S. (2022) Aquileia: le mura tardoantiche nel settore meridionale della città fra indagini d'archivio e dati di scavo. *Atlante Tematico di Topografia Antica* 32, 87–112.

Basso, P., Dobreva, D. & Martinelli, N. (forthcoming) Fondazioni in legno e anfore: il caso delle mura tardoantiche di Aquileia. In C. Previato & J. Bonetto (eds) *Terra, legno e materiali deperibili nell'architettura antica.* Rome, Quasar.

Bertacchi, L. (2003) *Nuova pianta archeologica di Aquileia.* Udine, Edizioni del Confine.

Bonetto, J. (1998) *Mura e città nella transpadana romana.* Concordia Sagittaria, Fondazione A. Colluto.

Bonetto, J. (2009) Le mura. In F. Ghedini, M. Bueno & M. Novello (eds) *Moenibus et portu celeberrima, Aquileia, storia di una città*, 83–90. Rome, Istituto Poligrafico e Zecca dello Stato.

Bonetto, J. (2013) Le difese di Aquileia nel IV secolo. In C. Tiussi, L. Villa & M. Novello (eds) *Costantino e Teodoro. Aquileia nel IV secolo*, 72–74. Milano, Mondadori Electa.

Bonetto, J., Ghiotto, A.R. & Previato, C. (2019–2020) Le mura repubblicane di Aquileia: nuove indagini archeologiche lungo il lato occidentale della cinta urbica. *Aquileia Nostra* 90/91, 35–47.

Borsato, A. (2021) Il riuso artigianale dei vani sostruttivi del teatro romano di Aquileia. In M. Buora, S. Magnani & L. Villa (eds) *Italia settentrionale e regioni dell'arco alpino tra V e VI secolo d.C.*, 393–410. Trieste, EUT Edizioni.

Bratoz, R. (2003) Aquileia fra Teodosio e i Longobardi (379–568). In G. Cuscito (ed.) *Aquileia dalle origini alla costituzione del ducato longobardo. Storia - Amministrazione - Società*, 477–527. Trieste, Editreg.

Brusin, G. (1957) Gli scavi archeologici di Aquileia nell'anno 1954. *Aquileia Nostra* 38, 5–18.

Buonopane, A. (forthcoming) Gli scavi di Giovani Battista Brusin. Le iscrizioni. In P. Basso & D. Dobreva, *Aquileia, l'area delle mura e del mercato tardoantichi: gli scavi negli archivi*. Rome, Quasar.

Buora, M. (2016) Nuovi dati sulle mura urbiche (repubblicane, dell'età di Massimino e tetrarchiche) di Aquileia dalla documentazione relativa agli scavi per le nuove fognature. *Quaderni Friulani di Archeologia* 26.1, 9–19.

Buora, M., Magnani, S. & Villa, L. (eds) (2021) *Italia settentrionale e regioni dell'arco alpino tra V e VI secolo d.C.* Trieste, EUT Edizioni.

Carre, M.B. (2008) Les fouilles du port fluvial d'Aquilée. *Revue Archéologique* 1, 193–198.

Carre, M.B. & Maselli Scotti, F. (2001) Il porto di Aquileia: dati antichi e ritrovamenti recenti. In C. Zaccaria (ed.) *Strutture portuali e rotte marittime nell'Adriatico di età romana*, 211–243. Trieste, Editreg.

Chiabà, M. (2009) Dalla fondazione all'età tetrarchica. In F. Ghedini, M. Bueno & M. Novello (eds) *Moenibus et portu celeberrima, Aquileia, storia di una città*, 7–22. Rome, Istituto Poligrafico e Zecca dello Stato.

Cigaina, L. (2018) Giovanni Battista Brusin und die Archäologie in Aquileia und in den 'terre redente' (1919-1945). In D. Steuernagel (ed.) *Altertumswissenschaften in Deutschland und Italien. Zeit des Umbruchs (1870-1940)*, 143–166. Regensburg, Schnell & Steiner.

Cottica, D. & Ventura, P. (2019) Spunti per uno studio dell'interazione uomo e fiume in antico: il caso della sponda orientale del Natiso cum Turro ad Aquileia. In M. Auer (ed.) *Roman Settlements along the Drava River*, 11–34. Wiesbaden, Harrassowitz Verlag.

Cottica, D., Marchesini, M., Marvelli, S., Novello, M. & Ventura, P. (2018) Per uno studio integrato di uomo e ambiente ad Aquileia: alcune riflessioni a partire da recenti indagini archeologiche. *Rivista di Archeologia* 91, 99–123.

Cuscito, G. (2004) Lo spazio cristiano nell'urbanistica tardoantica di Aquileia. In *Aquileia dalle origini alla costituzione del ducato longobardo. Topografia - Urbanistica - Edilizia pubblica*, 511–559. Trieste, EUT Edizioni.

Cuscito, G. (2009) Lo spazio cristiano. In F. Ghedini, M. Bueno & M. Novello (eds) *Moenibus et portu celeberrima, Aquileia, storia di una città*, 133–151. Rome, Istituto Poligrafico e Zecca dello Stato.

Cuscito, G. & Lehmann, T. (eds) (2010) *La basilica di Aquileia: storia, archeologia e arte*. Trieste, Editreg.

Cuscito, G. & Zaccaria, C. (eds) (2007) *Aquileia dalle origini alla costituzione del ducato longobardo. Territorio - economia - società*. Trieste, Editreg.

Delbarba, N. (2021–22) Le mura tardoantiche di Aquileia: l'area dei fondi Pasqualis. Dallo studio alla ricostruzione (MA Dissertation; tutor P. Basso). Universities of Ferrara, Verona, Trento, Modena.

Dobreva, D. & Zago, S. (2021) *Aquileia e l'alto Adriatico nell'età della transizione. Aspetti di continuità e cambiamento commerciale alla luce dei contesti ceramici tardoantichi e altomedievali*. In M. Buora, S. Magnani & L. Villa (eds) *Italia settentrionale e regioni dell'arco alpino tra V e VI secolo d.C.*, 307-368. Trieste, EUT Edizioni.

Ghedini, F., Bueno, M., Novello, M. & Rinaldi, F. (eds) (2017) *I pavimenti romani di Aquileia. Contesti, tecniche, repertorio decorativo*. Padova, Padova University Press.

Ghiotto, A.R. (2018) Considerazioni sul teatro e sul 'quartiere degli spettacoli'. In P. Basso *L'anfiteatro di Aquileia. Ricerche d'archivio e nuove indagini di scavo*, 253-260. Quingentole, SAP.

Ghiotto, A.R., Berto, S., Fioratto, G. & Zanus Fortes, V. (2020) Lo scavo del teatro romano di Aquileia: ricerche in corso. *Quaderni Friulani di Archeologia* 30, 27–46.

Ghiotto, A.R., Fioratto, G. & Furlan, G. (2021) Il teatro romano di Aquileia: lo scavo dell'aditus maximus settentrionale e dell'edificio scenico. *Fasti On Line Document & Research* 495, 1-24.

Grazioli, V. (forthcoming) Gli scavi di Giovani Battista Brusin. Gli elementi architettonici. In P. Basso & D. Dobreva, *Aquileia, l'area delle mura e del mercato tardoantichi: gli scavi negli archivi*. Rome, Quasar.

Groh, S. (2011) Ricerche sull'urbanistica e le fortificazioni tardoantiche e bizantine di Aquileia. Relazione sulle prospezioni geofisiche condotte nel 2011. *Aquileia Nostra* 82, 153-204.

Kaniewski, D., Marriner, N., Sarti, G., Bertoni, D., Marchesini, M., Rossi, V., Lena, A., Bivolaru, A., Pourkeman, M., Vacchi, M., Cheddadi, R., Otto, T., Luce, F., Cottica, D. & Morhange, C. (2022) Northern Adriatic environmental changes since 500 AD reconstructed at Aquileia (Italy). *Quaternary Science Reviews* 287, 107565.

Lusuardi Siena, S. & Baratto, C. (2013) *Sguardo sull'edilizia religiosa e civile nella Venetia et Histria in età tardoantica*. In P. Basso & G. Cavalieri Manasse (eds) *Storia dell'architettura del Veneto. L'età romana e tardoantica*, 166-217. Venezia, Marsilio.

Maggi, P., Maselli Scotti, F., Pesavento Mattioli, S. & Zullini, E. (eds) (2017) *Materiali per Aquileia. Lo scavo del canale Anfora (2004-2005)*. Trieste, Editreg.

Mandruzzato, L. (1996) Notiziario archeologico. Aquileia. Immobile Pasqualis. *Aquileia Nostra* 67, 264-267.

Mandruzzato, L. & Maselli Scotti, F. (1994) Notiziario archeologico. Aquileia. Horrea. *Aquileia Nostra* 65, 354-358.

Marano, Y. (2009) La città tardoantica. In F. Ghedini, M. Bueno & M. Novello (eds) *Moenibus et portu celeberrima, Aquileia, storia di una città*, 23-33. Rome, Istituto Poligrafico e Zecca dello Stato.

Marano, Y. (2012) Urbanesimo e storia ad Aquileia fra V e VI secolo d.C. In J. Bonetto & M. Salvadori (eds) *L'architettura privata ad Aquileia in età romana*, 571-590. Rome, Quasar.

Maselli Scotti, F. (2009) Le fasi preromane. In F. Ghedini, M. Bueno & M. Novello (eds) *Moenibus et portu celeberrima, Aquileia, storia di una città*, 3-6. Rome, Istituto Poligrafico e Zecca dello Stato.

Maselli Scotti, F. & Rubinich, M. (2009) I monumenti pubblici. In F. Ghedini, M. Bueno & M. Novello (eds) *Moenibus et portu celeberrima, Aquileia, storia di una città*, 93-110. Rome, Istituto Poligrafico e Zecca dello Stato.

Maselli Scotti, F., Mandruzzato, L. & Tiussi, C. (2007) Primo impianto coloniario di Aquileia: l'area fra foro e macellum. In L. Brecciaroli Taborelli (ed.) *Forme e tempi dell'urbanizzazione nella Cisalpina (II secolo a.C.-I secolo d.C.)*, 35-40. Sesto Fiorentino, All'Insegna del Giglio.

Maselli Scotti, F., Mandruzzato, L. & Tiussi, C. (2009) La prima fase dell'impianto coloniario di Aquileia. La situazione attuale degli studi e delle ricerche. In *Aspetti e problemi della romanizzazione. Venetia, Histria e Arco Alpino Orientale*, 253-277. Trieste, EUT Edizioni.

Nicosia, C. (2018) Le analisi microstratigrafiche. In P. Basso, *L'anfiteatro di Aquileia. Ricerche d'archivio e nuove indagini di scavo*, 171-176. Quingentole, SAP.

Novello, M., Salvadori, M., Tiussi, C. & Villa, L. (2013) Il primo nucleo episcopale di Aquileia: struttura e decorazione. In C. Tiussi, L. Villa & M. Novello (eds) *Costantino e Teodoro. Aquileia nel IV secolo*, 143-153. Milano, Mondadori Electa.

Rubinich, M. (2020) Le Grandi Terme di Aquileia: passato, presente e futuro di un edificio pubblico tardoantico. *Quaderni Friulani di Archeologia* 30, 71-90.

Rubinich, M. (2022) Alcune considerazioni sulle 'Grandi Terme' e l'urbanistica di Aquileia. In M. Lavarone, S. Magnani & F. Prenc (eds) *MB. Maurizio Buora. La sua storia. Il suo Friuli*, 379-401. Trieste, Editreg.

Rubinich, M. & Braidotti, E. (2021) Le Grandi Terme costantiniane di Aquileia tra V e VI secolo: la fine di un edificio pubblico e l'inizio di nuovi modi di abitare. In M. Buora, S. Magnani & L. Villa (eds) *Italia settentrionale e regioni dell'arco alpino fra V e VI secolo d.C.*, 277-305. Trieste, EUT Edizioni.

Siché, I., Forte, E., Prizzon, A., Arnaud-Fassetta, G. & Fort, M. (2004) Cartographie hydrogéomorphologique et paléochenaux fluviatiles en milieux profondément modifiés par les sociétés. L'exemple du port fluvial antique d'Aquilée dans la plaine du Frioul (Italie septentrionale, Adriatique). *Mosella* 29, 247-259.

Soriano, F. (2018) Dopo l'anfiteatro: i dati di scavo. In P. Basso *L'anfiteatro di Aquileia. Ricerche d'archivio e nuove indagini di scavo*, 101–113. Quingentole, SAP.

Sotinel, C. (2003) Aquilée de Dioclétian à Théodose. In G. Cuscito (ed.) *Aquileia dalle origini alla costituzione del ducato longobardo. Storia - Amministrazione - Società*, 375–392. Trieste, Editreg.

Sotinel, C. (2005) *Identité civique et christianisme. Aquilée du IIIe au VIe siècle*. Rome, École française de Rome.

Tiussi, C. (2004) Il sistema di distribuzione di Aquileia: mercati e magazzini. In *Aquileia dalle origini alla costituzione del ducato longobardo. Topografia - Urbanistica - Edilizia pubblica*, 257–316. Trieste, EUT Edizioni.

Tiussi, C. (2009) *L'impianto urbano*. In F. Ghedini, M. Bueno & M. Novello (eds) *Moenibus et portu celeberrima, Aquileia, storia di una città*, 61–81. Rome, Istituto Poligrafico e Zecca dello Stato.

Tiussi, C. & Villa, L. (2018) Il circo. Dati archeologici e tentativo di ricostruzione. In P. Basso *L'anfiteatro di Aquileia. Ricerche d'archivio e nuove indagini di scavo*, 261–272. Quingentole, SAP.

Tiussi, C. & Villa, L. (2019) Aquileia in età tetrarchica e costantiniana. Trasformazioni urbanistiche e monumentali nel settore occidentale. *Aquileia Nostra* 26, 91–147.

Ungaro, L., Parisi Presicce, C., Pastor, S., Milella, M. & Giovannini, A. (eds) (2017) *Made in Roma and Aquileia*. Rome, Gangemi Editore.

Ventura, P. (2013) Mercati – horrea. In C. Tiussi, L. Villa & M. Novello (eds) *Costantino e Teodoro. Aquileia nel IV secolo*, 94–96. Milano, Mondadori Electa.

Verdonck, L., De Neef, W., Hoffelinck, A. & Vermeulen, F. (2020) The geophysical survey carried out by a team of the Department of Archaeology of Ghent University (Belgium). In P. Basso & Dobreva (eds) Aquileia: first results from the market excavation and the Late Antiquity town walls (part one). *Fasti On Line Document & Research* 482, 17–19.

Villa, L. (2004) Aquileia tra Goti, Bizantini e Longobardi: spunti per un'analisi delle trasformazioni urbane nella transizione fra Tarda Antichità e Alto Medioevo. In G. Cuscito & C. Zaccaria (eds) *Aquileia dalle origini alla costituzione del ducato longobardo. Territorio - economia - società*, 561–632. Trieste, Editreg.

Villa, L. (2012–13) Il complesso teodoriano. Una rilettura delle testimonianze archeologiche. *Aquileia Nostra* 83/84, 119–154.

Zaccaria, C. & Pesavento Mattioli, S. (2009) Uomini e merci. In Ghedini, F., Bueno & M., Novello, M. (eds) *Moenibus at portu celeberrima Aquileia: Storia di una città*, 257–287. Rome, Istituto Poligrafico e Zecca dello Stato.

Zemignani, A. (forthcoming) L'area nella cartografia storica. In P. Basso & D. Dobreva, *Aquileia, l'area delle mura e del mercato tardoantichi: gli scavi negli archivi*. Rome, Quasar.

## Website references

https://www.dizionariobiograficodeifriulani.it/brusin-giovanni-battista
https://www.fondazioneaquileia.it/it/cosa-vedere/fondo-pasqualis-mercati

# Chapter 14

## Bridging the gap: new data on the settlement continuity in Parma from the stone bridge

*Alessia Morigi*

### 14.1. Introduction

To explore the evidence of antiquity in the long-term context of the city of Parma, we could start from Italo Calvino's observation on the ideas underpinning this research:

> The city however does not tell its past, but contains it like the lines of a hand, written in the corners of the streets, the gratings of the windows, the banisters of the steps, the antennae of the lightning rods, the poles of the flags, every segment marked in turn with scratches, indentations, scrolls. (Calvino 1972, III).

In this view, the city mutates and changes over time, and bears, engraved on its surface, the signs of the different landscapes that have characterized it over time. The archaeological features of a centre with a long and continuous history can be traced in the material signs of these changes: stratigraphic studies, renovated remains of ancient buildings, topography, and those signs present that today have become part of the identity of the place and thus act as doors through which to glimpse a submerged history. In the collective imagination, the symbols of Parma are the Romanesque cathedral, the Baptistery, the Teatro Regio and its great artists: Correggio, Parmigianino, Verdi, Toscanini, and Bertolucci. But rather than these eminent aspects, this study focuses on the history of undiscovered Parma using data from new research promoted by *Programma S.F.E.R.A. Spazi e Forme dell'Emilia Romagna Antica dell'Università di Parma* (Morigi 2016a; 2018; 2021b; Morigi *et al.* 2019). This study in fact looks at what is called the Roman bridge, the only monument in Parma which makes the invisible visible to us today (Plate 14.1). The research project is in a preliminary phase, and what follows is an initial presentation of some early results and an outline of challenges faced by the research.

## 14.2. Unearthing the bridge

Parma today is located in a heavily industrialised area and, as in many Italian cities, the urban plan of ancient times has been erased by two thousand years of life and construction. Roman Parma today is confined to the renowned archaeological museum, the *Complesso Monumentale della Pilotta*, which displays the magnificent art of which the town was the centre. Otherwise, as noted by Andrew Wallace Hadrill (2022) at the 'Symposium Parma 2200' (Morigi & Quintelli 2018), the ancient plan survives in Parma indirectly in the imprint it left on the urban grid (Fig. 14.1A). Such traces are evident in the ancient and modern cities of Emilia Romagna, which share as their centre of gravity the Roman *via Aemilia* (today 'via Emilia'). The *via Aemilia* was the *decumanus maximus* of the entire Roman centuriation still visible in Emilia Romagna (Chevallier 1961; Bermond Montanari 1983; Calzolari 1995; Dall'Aglio 1996; Brighi 1997; Giorgetti 2000; Quilici 2000; Di Cocco & Viaggi 2003; Maraldi 2006; Franceschelli & Marabini 2007; Lenzi 2009; Marchesini & Marvelli 2009; Cantoni & Capurso 2017). It is as though the whole region were a gigantic chessboard, coherent in that the main road is also the main axis of its agrarian division.

This centuriation is well preserved and is the most important identifying landscape feature in the region of Emilia Romagna. The close interconnection between town and countryside means that a town cannot be studied without its territory, and there have been urban cartography projects carried out using excavations, surveys, and GIS models (Morigi *et al.* 2016; 2020a; 2020b; 2021a; 2021b; 2021c; Fontana & Garbasi 2018; Morigi & Bergamini 2019; Morigi & Villicich 2019a; 2019b; 2021a; 2021b; 2022). In this context, the Parma bridge, positioned along the consular road leading out of the town, is to all intents and purposes a link between the town and the territory. This is how it is framed in our description.

However, the bridge as a monument has not been able to 'speak'. Until recently there was very little information. Next to nothing was known about its shape, its chronology, its exact location, or its significance in relation to the town and the territory. Until a few years ago, it was also quite difficult to see. It was only in 2018 that a joint project between the University, the Municipality, and Ministry of Culture restored the part of the town where the bridge had been almost hidden underground. Today the area has been reopened for public use as an underpass and is also home to a new Information Centre of the University of Parma (Morigi 2015a; 2016b; 2019; Quintelli 2015; Morigi & Tedeschi 2018). The bridge is thus not only an ancient passage but also a bridge between the city and its university, metaphorically and physically.

The project is important; beforehand the surroundings and remains of the bridge were in very poor condition. But since the renovation, the bridge can be clearly viewed in spite of the modern buildings that have sprung up around it. Two new ramps have been put in to cross the bridge from one side to the other and an access ramp, at different heights, allows people to view the bridge from various perspectives. The site of the ancient riverbed has also been restored. And importantly, a permanent

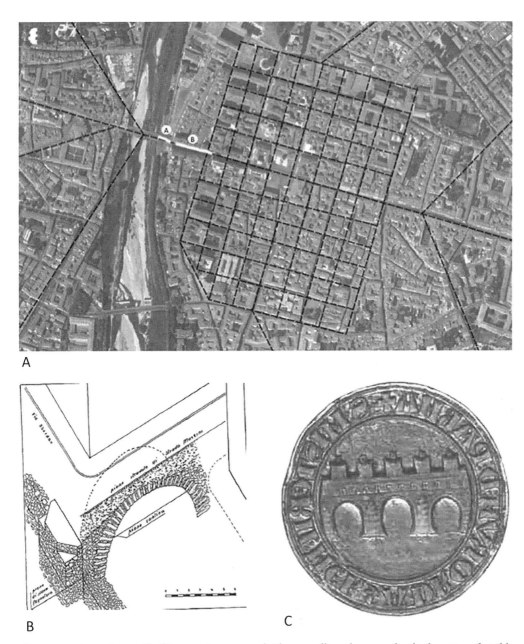

A

B

C

*Figure 14.1. A. ancient grid of Roman Parma overlaid on satellite photography (A: location of visible arches; B: buried arches); B. survey of the buried arch discovered in 1948; C. seal of Parma merchant guild (14th century AD) showing the bridge arches.*

open-air museum displaying archaeological discoveries from excavations on the site has already been opened in advance of further study or specific publication. Emergency measures were adopted by the municipality to restore the bridge, and the restoration has radically changed what we know about the history of settlement in Parma. Previously, neither the shape, location nor history of the bridge was known.

Focusing first on the shape, the new restoration has made visible only two of the bridge's arches, along the ancient *via Aemilia*, which runs through the city centre. Geoarchaeological investigations on the site show the location of the palaeo-riverbed. They confirm that the riverbed was very wide in ancient times, as it is in fact today. Stratigraphy of the area also shows that in the earliest times the riverbed included an islet and was therefore very large (Cremaschi &Trombino 2012; Malnati *et al.* 2013). It is impossible to find and count the remaining arches 'in the field' since today the bridge is enclosed between the present-day riverbed and modern buildings built after the Second World War bombing. We thus carried out an archaeological 'excavation' in the most important historical archives of Parma (*Archivio Storico Comunale*), where dozens of city maps are conserved. The maps are currently being digitized in GIS in order to reconstruct the evolution of the settlement (Fig. 14.1A).

Documents from the archive of the National Archaeological Museum show that in 1858, the Municipal Inspector Martelli discovered the extremity of a bridge along the *via Aemilia* after the demolition of the building above it. Almost 100 years later, in 1948, an arch was found in the same area and recognised by the Inspector of Antiquities, Corradi Cervi, as part of the ancient bridge (Fig. 14.1B). The distance between the newly discovered arch and the two which are visible today indicates that the bridge was very long. The discovery was very important because it indicates the connection between the bridge and city. But in spite of this *coup de théâtre*, no further explorations were made until another stroke of luck in 1951. The main road through the town, the modern via Emilia, at the point called today 'via Mazzini', began to subside under the pressure of motor traffic. The owners of the buildings with cellars situated under the road wrote to the Parma Municipality, which commissioned a series of technical surveys. Dozens of documents in the Parma City Archives reveal the cellar owners' alarm and describe the measures taken by the Municipality between the 1950s–60s. These included a number of maps and surveys, which reveal the extent of the bridge. They show the relationship between the ancient arches of the bridge and the small arches of the cellars built inside them clearly. The first series of maps from the 1950s shows seven arches above the cellars of the buildings along the modern 'via Mazzini'. The second series, from the 1960s, shows the same arches, plus two more on the left, which correspond to those now visible in the underpass today (Corradi Cervi 1963; Catarsi 1993). Cross-checking data from the two-map series shows that the bridge had ten arches. Only two can be seen today and eight cannot; seven were buried under 'via Mazzini', and one was destroyed by a bomb in the Second World War (Fig. 14.2A).

The second series of surveys is, not surprisingly, more detailed. In fact, at that time new building sites were opening along the via Emilia, and there was consolidation of

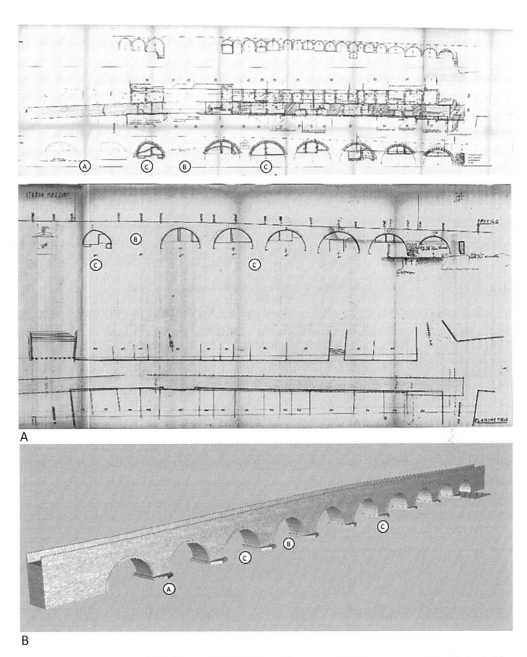

Figure 14.2. A. surveys of the 'Roman' bridge from the 1960s; B. 3D reconstruction of the bridge (A: two arches visible today; B: the arch destroyed by bombing; C: seven buried arches).

the areas which had become unstable due to heavy traffic. The building sites inevitably became archaeological sites, and an important sequence of urban archaeological excavations began in Parma. The images, again from the archives, are spectacular. Under the via Emilia, the buried arches, which had been repeatedly reported since the end of the 19th century, came to light. They remained, however, embedded in the foundations of the buildings, and were only partially visible (Fig. 14.3A). Only the arches nearest to the river could be seen in all their splendour under the modern road (Fig. 14.3B).

At this point in the story of the bridge, the human factor entered the sequence of events. The excavations provoked heated debate between those who wanted to create an open-air museum encompassing the whole bridge, and those for whom the requirements of modern life were the priority. The issue was significant in that the construction site and the excavations interrupted the city's main traffic route. The impact of the old town on the modern city was considered a threat. There was a clash involving the Municipality and the Ministry of Culture, as it is called today, and neither side was prepared to give way (Morigi 2016b; 2019; 2022). In the end, the cause of the rebirth of the bridge was also the cause of its premature death. The road became dangerously unstable and the Municipality hastily covered all the arches of the bridge with the asphalt of the modern via Emilia. Only the two arches next to the river, which lay under the road but not under buildings, were saved. In 1967 they were enclosed inside the underpass of the modern via Emilia, from which they were only freed in 2018.

## 14.3. The architecture of the bridge

So, in shape the bridge comprised ten, or rather, *at least* ten, arches. To give a definitive shape to the bridge, we need to explore precisely where it stands. The bridge was narrow and ran between the colony and the suburban road hub (Bottazzi 2000; Quilici 2000; Dall'Aglio & Di Cocco 2006; Morigi 2011; 2012; 2015b; 2015c; Bottazzi *et al.* 2017; Fontana & Garbasi 2018; Fontana 2020). On the town side, the bridge was bordered by the perimeter of the Roman colony of 183 BC. The urban grid of the colony on the river side is missing a corner and changes shape in line with the course of the palaeo-river (Dall'Aglio 1990; 2009; Catarsi 2009; Morigi 2009; 2015b).

The bridge borders the junction of the Roman roads leading both to the plain and to the mountains. Towards the plain the roads led to the River Po, the most important Italian waterway, with its important inland ports. Towards the mountains a road led to the most famous Roman town in the area, Lunae. The starting point of these Roman roads is easily recognised because the roads themselves are preserved beneath the modern ones and because they are archaeologically documented (Dall'Aglio 1990; 2009; Catarsi & Malavasi 2006; Morigi 2009; Bottazzi *et al.* 2017). The position of the junction confirms that the bridge was longer than the surviving one: the arches do not, in fact, fully span the palaeo-river. That the bridge was longer than today is also

A

B

*Figure 14.3. The 1960s excavations of the 'Roman' bridge: A. arches now buried under the via Emilia; B. arches visible today.*

confirmed by the arches themselves: they in fact rise in the direction of the river so must have descended equally on the opposite side. The bridge is humpbacked with a gradual raising of the road surface from east to west.

However, the question is complex, because the length of the bridge must have depended on the position of the palaeo-river, which moved over the years (Balista 1997; Cremaschi 1997; Cremaschi & Trombino 2012; Catarsi *et al.* 2013b, 26). New data on this are provided by the stratigraphic excavation made next to the bridge in what is today 'Piazza Ghiaia' (Malnati *et al.* 2013; Capelli 2017) (Fig. 14.4A). 'Piazza Ghiaia', the name of which derives from *glarea*, corresponds in position to the ancient riverbed over which the bridge once stood. The excavation revealed banks of alluvial gravel, confirming the presence of an active riverbed. We know that the riverbed dried up during the disastrous flood of AD 1180 described in medieval chronicles. However, the excavation revealed the history of the riverbed in Roman times, confirming that it had changed course several times (Fig. 14.4B). Defensive structures have in fact been found on its banks, and these structures altered over time according to the changes in the riverbed (Malnati *et al.* 2013).

There are three examples of the defence of the riverbanks. The oldest consists of a series of wooden posts and can be dated to the Republican period thanks to the finding of a coin dated to around 211 BC. The second, a wooden palisade from the Imperial period, has large blocks of travertine and spolia (Catarsi 2009) reinforcing the posts, and was possibly put in place in response to a sudden shift in the course of the river. The third defence involved wooden structures, perhaps pertaining to a basin or dock (Malnati *et al.* 2013).

The stratigraphic data, along with these three defences, show that the riverbed shifted over the years in different parts of the site. Geological data confirm this and, given that the river is a 'torrente' whose level fluctuates hugely, it is not surprising. The mapping of findings, on the other hand, is surprising, as it shows that the riverbed is not where it was expected to be, but further away from the town. This revised location for the riverbed is also confirmed by geoarchaeological analysis, which also shows that the alluvial deposits brought by flooding tend to be associated with post-antique landscaping and construction (Catarsi 2009; Marchi & Serchia 2022).

Geoarchaeological analysis changes our perspective: it is now certain that in the 2nd century AD, the river ran further away from the colony than had been thought, and the bridge would have needed more arches to cross it. Once the results of the geoarchaeological study are published, the picture will be clearer. What appears certain today, however, is that the bridge consisted of a series of arches supported by piers carrying a road over the river. This type of bridge, or viaduct, is well suited to the type of river, subject to heavy flooding and having a very wide and unstable bed, as it still does today. The grandeur of the bridge corresponded to its importance along the *via Aemilia*. It in fact served as link between two worlds: on one side the Roman colony and on the other the area outside town with roads leading into the province,

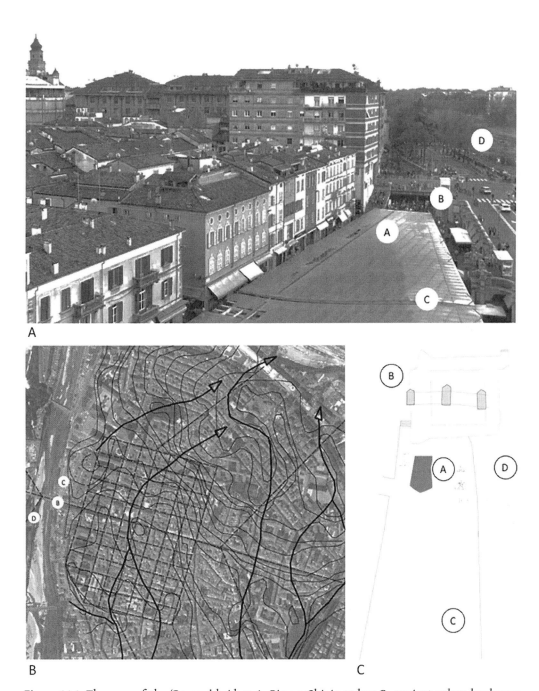

*Figure 14.4. The area of the 'Roman' bridge: A. Piazza Ghiaia today; B. ancient urban landscape and soil morphology (A: brick bridge; B: stone bridge; C: ancient riverbed; D: modern riverbed); C. contemporary excavations.*

burial grounds, and well-documented artisan centres (Catarsi & Malavasi 2006, 37; Catarsi 2009; Santoro 2009). There was a network of medium-distance centurial roads and long-distance trans-Apennine roads, and about ten miles from Parma runs the powerful waterway of the River Po. Parma thus lay at the centre of a strong system of roads and waterways. Their importance and durability are shown by the most famous of these, the Roman road between Parma, in Emilia, and Luni (Lunae), in Lunigiana, which, since the Middle Ages has been known by its medieval name, the 'Via Francigena' (Dall'Aglio 1998; Bottazzi *et al.* 2017; Medas 2017).

## 14.4. The chronology of the bridge

As regards the chronology of the bridge, a question mark hangs over the date it was built. Traditionally it was thought to have been built in Roman times and restored in Late Antiquity by King Theodoric (AD 493–526) (Affò 1792, 91; Catarsi 1993). It was thought that the appearance of the bridge in modern times was similar to that at the time of Theodoric, who also built the walls in Parma. Let us examine this question.

Theodoric, the Gothic king, was particularly important in the region of Emilia Romagna because of the presence of Ravenna. In Ravenna and across the region, particularly the Romagna part, his name is attached to palaces, monumental tombs, elegant *domus*, and his great villa at Galeata (Forlì-Cesena), currently under excavation by archaeologists from the University of Parma (Morigi & Villicich 2017; 2019a; 2019b; 2021a; 2021b; 2022; Morigi 2021b). Parma enjoyed a certain prosperity under the reign of Theodoric and the presence of the Goths is documented archaeologically in the city and in the local area (Fava 2006; Catarsi 2009; Catarsi *et al.* 2013a). There is, however, only one extant text which mentions Theodoric: Cassiodorus (*Var.* 8.29.1) reports on a letter from Atalaric, which says that Theodoric, in the manner of the Roman emperors, had brought large quantities of water to the town by restoring a watercourse towards Parma (*civitatem... saluberrima unda rigavit*). Archaeologically, however, no 6th-century AD aqueduct has been traced, and we therefore surmise that Theodoric intervened by restructuring the ancient aqueduct and the urban canals. In fact, as Cassiodorus notes, Atalaric recalls that Parma *curiales quia civis animum non habet, qui urbis suae gratia non tenetur.*

In Late Antiquity, the town grew on the foundations of its ancient palimpsest, conserving its ancient monuments and its civic identity. As observed by Wallace-Hadrill, the cities of Cassiodorus show 'the resilience of urban values' (Wallace-Hadrill 2022, 28). The resilience of Parma is fully confirmed by archaeological studies. Sewers and aqueducts had been defunct since the 4th century AD and Roman masonry pipelines were cut off from the town during the wars that led to the fall of the Western Roman Empire (Catarsi *et al.* 2013a). Canals, however, existed during Roman times. The *Canale Maggiore* ran along the walls, on the high ground on which the Roman colony was founded (Dall'Aglio 1990, 87). Recent research findings under the *S.F.E.R.A.* programme reveal that the *Canale Comune* ran along the ancient riverbed during the Bronze Age, and that the river itself reached the *forum*. At the time of the foundation of the colony, the *cardo maximus* ran along the canal for its entire length. The *Canale Comune* is therefore very important as the axis of the grid of the Roman colony and because it was used in medieval as well as modern times (Lucchetti 1965). Theodoric's intention to restore the town's internal water network was sound, as it was this network which generated the landscape of open canals and the Farnese aqueduct in post-antique Parma.

This data offers several insights in terms of the archaeology of waters systems. If the Goths intervened in the water infrastructure, it is in fact strange that Cassiodorus did not mention the bridge when describing water routes. We now focus on the second part of the traditional belief and ask whether Theodoric actually intervened on the walls. Over the last 200 years, archaeology has uncovered various sections of wall, but the documentation is patchy, both spatially and methodologically. Recent stratigraphic excavations show that the sections of wall made of concrete with stone facing date from the end of the 3rd century AD. The late walls are thought to have been built over previous Republican brick walls, which were preserved until the Imperial period. The epigraph of Quintus Munatius Apsirtos mentions a town gate in the 1st century AD (Arrigoni Bertini 2008). However, there is no reference to Theodoric regarding the walls, just as there is no reference to him regarding the bridge (Catarsi & Bianchi 2004, 45; Fava 2006; Marchi & Serchia 2022).

To answer our questions, we therefore return to the bridge. After the renovation, it was possible to conduct a new survey and technical analysis of the two accessible arches. The arches are between 9 and 11 m wide, all rounded (except for the eighth arch which has been reworked), and made of stone blocks (about 50 × 90 cm) and smaller stones mixed with cobblestones.

With regard to the piers, the documentation covers only the two easternmost ones, now buried, and the westernmost one, still visible. They were built with a concrete core lined with large pebbles and square stone blocks. All three have a breakwater rostrum facing upstream. At the eastern end of the bridge, an 8-m-long breakwater protected the town from flooding. The width of the road starts at 4.6 m and then narrows to 3.8 m. Regarding the building technique, both buried and visible structures show apparent differences, but the documentation offered by earlier photographs is often unclear.

The structures which are visible appear to be slightly misaligned and more reworked, and the buried structures appear to be straighter and more regular. Comparison of the less reworked part of both suggests, however, that the differences are not significant. And the direction of the bridge is certain as it can only lead towards the *via Aemilia* on the other side of the river.

It can be helpful to compare the characteristics of the Parma bridge with others in the area. Today only two bridges in the Parma area retain their arches: Parma and Fidenza. The Roman bridge at Fidenza runs along the via Emilia, like the bridge in Parma, and is dated to the 1st–2nd centuries AD. Discovered in 1847, it was surveyed by Astolfi and Pigorini and is still partly visible today. It would be therefore useful for comparison, but it uses the traditional Roman technique of square blocks and bears no resemblance to Parma bridge (Catarsi & Dall'Aglio 1993).

The only other Roman bridge known of nearby is at Bettola near Piacenza. This bridge, built of roughly shaped stones, was located near a Roman kiln and dated between the second and third century BC. It is not, however, visible today and there is no certainty about its origins (Catarsi & Dall'Aglio 1993). In the western part of Emilia, the bridges of Pontenure, Castellarquato, and Pieve di Campi were all built using regular building techniques with square blocks and have a double rostrum upstream and downstream (Catarsi & Dall'Aglio 1993). They have little or nothing in common with the Parma bridge.

Broadening the perspective to the whole Emilia Romagna region, the beginning of the *via Aemilia* in Rimini is marked by the famous 'Ponte di Tiberio'. This is a more usual isodomic bridge and very different from the one in Parma (Bondini *et al.* 2016). Looking at the widths of the road on the Parma bridge, as noted above, these range from 4.6 m to 3.8 m and are consistent with the sections of Roman roads found in Parma. These were usually 4 m wide; only the *cardo* and *decumanus* were paved, while the minor roads were gravel. Since, however, urban roads often keep the same dimensions over time, this is not diagnostic.

So the question arises: is this really a Roman bridge? And if not, where is the Roman bridge on the *via Aemilia* that connected the Roman colony with the outside world? The question can be answered using stratigraphy and laboratory analysis. The stratigraphic excavation in Piazza Ghiaia (Malnati *et al.* 2013) brought to light a bridge pier from the Roman period made of concrete and with a brick face (Fig. 14.4C). It dated from the early Imperial period and had collapsed after a serious flood at the end of the 2nd century AD (Capelli 2017). The stratigraphy shows that this was a bridge predating the one which we see today. It was built by Augustus, who also built the new *Capitolium,* theatre, and amphitheatre in Parma (Catarsi 2009). An epigraph from the 1st century AD recalls the work of Quinto Munazio Apsirto, who, at his own expense, had a stretch of the *via Aemilia*, that is the road running over the bridge, paved (*stravit*) (Arrigoni Bertini 2008). This must therefore be the Roman bridge which, until the 2nd century AD, was part of the *via Aemilia*. If this is in fact the case, there was more than one bridge in Parma: there would have been two bridges side by side.

The excavation in Piazza Ghiaia provided further information about the urban landscape within which the Roman bridge stood. The finding of a *sacellum* and a votive shrine show that there was also a ford. The shrine had coins and metal objects from between the 3rd and 2nd centuries BC, in all probability forfeited to the river deity for a safe crossing. A second votive shrine was used in the early Imperial period (Locatelli *et al.* 2013). Therefore, the ford existed before the Roman colony, perhaps making use of an islet. It is proof that there was a settlement of some type in Parma before the Romans came to build a colony there (Locatelli *et al.* 2013). The ford existed for a very long time, as did the main trade routes. The excavation in fact revealed traces of the wool trade, consisting of inscribed lead seals for semi-processed hanks of wool dated between the 1st century BC and the 2nd century AD (Cavalieri 2003). Along the many canals that crisscrossed the town, wool processing and dyeing were carried out for centuries until the Middle Ages. Piazza Ghiaia itself was always a centre of trade and commerce in the area around the bridge: in medieval times there were many shops, and from Farnese times onwards it became a marketplace (Conti *et al.* 2002).

But the Roman bridge was destroyed by flooding in the 2nd century AD. The two bridges, the brick and the stone bridge, were close to each other, and were probably not used at the same time, given the state of collapse of the brick bridge, which was buried in a sandbank. So we are left with the question of whether the bridge we see today is the one which replaced the Imperial bridge. There is no information about it until about AD 1180, when the three rivers around Parma were severely flooded. The floods are recounted in the *Chronicon Parmense* (Bonazzi 1902–04), kept in the *Biblioteca Palatina* in Parma. Even today Emilia is vulnerable to flooding, and Parma was severely flooded as recently as 2014. But in AD 1180 the floods diverted the course of the river and badly damaged the bridge, without completely destroying it. A medieval merchant guild seal (Fig. 14.1C) shows its arches supporting shops and dwellings, as it was the case with other more famous bridges, such as 'Ponte Vecchio' in Florence. The bridge functioned as a marketplace until AD 1547, when the first Duke of Parma, Pier Luigi Farnese, had the shops demolished and the bridge restored. In AD 1287 the *via Aemilia* had been diverted further upstream to the temporary *pons Solariorum,* but after almost 400 years it was brought back to life under the Farnese (Conti *et al.* 2002).

So, the bridge in question was built after the 2nd century AD and was not actually used to cross the river after the 12th century AD floods. Laboratory analyses provide some indications on what happened within that period. The analysis of a sample of mortar from the exposed part of the bridge suggests that it dates to between AD 332–433 (Lindroos *et al.* 2018). The sample comes from a reconstructed part of the bridge and the date implies that this bridge replaced the one that collapsed in AD 160 and that was restored in the 4th–5th centuries AD. As it happens, in the 4th century AD there was not only a flood but also an earthquake in Parma (Dall'Aglio 2000; Marini Calvani 2000; Catarsi & Bianchi 2004, 61). Stratigraphic confirmation of this come from the 'Domus degli Augustales', the 'Domus degli Stucchi' and the walls themselves. The *domus* were abandoned, but the walls, on a brick foundation, underwent restorations that can be dated on a stratigraphic basis to the 3rd–4th centuries AD. This is similar to what appears to have happened to the bridge.

This would mean that there was a Roman bridge which collapsed in the 2nd century AD, another one which collapsed in the 4th century AD, and a third one, which is the one which can be seen in the underpass today, which was taken out of use in the 12th century AD. The hasty rebuilding of the bridge after the earthquake would explain the uneven technique that characterises it.

Looking at the shape of the bridge in light of this new information, the recent renovation makes it possible to examine variations in the fabric of the wall (Fig. 14.5).

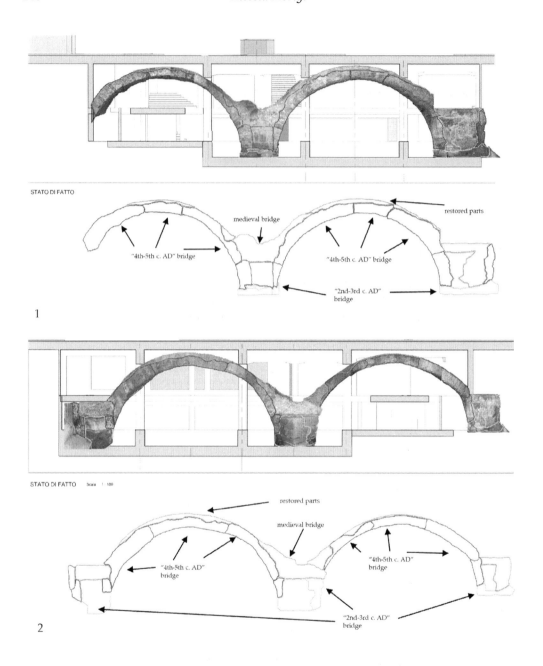

1 - North side
2 - South side

Figure 14.5. *Survey of the extant remains of the 'Roman' bridge of Parma (courtesy of F. Fontana): north sides (A) and south side (B).*

The bridge of the end of the 2nd to 3rd centuries may in fact survive in the bases of the piers. Although they were completely rebuilt, they make systematic use of isodomic blocks and support 9–10-m-wide arches like those of the 'Ponte di Tiberio' in Rimini, which measure 8–10 m, in keeping with the measurements usually used in Roman construction. This suggests that the project of the bridge may well date to this period. On the other hand, the portion of the bridge dated on the base of the mortar samples appears to date from around the 4th century AD or shortly afterwards. The most recent masonry work clearly corresponds to the medieval phase documented by the merchant guild seal. The remaining masonry corresponds to restoration of the bald arches for the construction of buildings above, which are often added when a bridge loses its function.

Certain aspects of the history of the bridge are clear and others less so. Not only the two mortar samples came from the same arch, but, since results were not technically obtainable for deep samples from Parma, they were taken from the surface: therefore, they may not be completely reliable and they cannot exclude the possibility that the bridge may be later than Roman. Under the Lombards, Parma underwent a great deal of reconstruction, and between the 6th–7th centuries AD the great Roman amphitheatre became the residence of the Lombard dukes (Gelichi 2011). In the 12th century AD, before the flood, Emperor Frederick I Barbarossa established a palace in the area, referred to in archival sources as *palacium de arena* (Guzzon 1995). At this time the bridge was in use and will certainly have undergone alterations to keep the town's main road in use.

## 14.5. Conclusions

If we look at the bridge without preconceptions, it clearly resembles bridges of the early Middle Ages. This broader perspective in fact simplifies the interpretation of the construction, the contextualisation of the chrono-typological characteristics and the dating of the walls and architectural characteristics. Until recently, these characteristics did not lead to a precise interpretation of the bridge and did not help to identify its history correctly. The bridge is in fact anomalous compared to other bridges identified as Roman, and also compared to bridges from the 13th–14th centuries AD built in the Age of Communes. A good example in a neighbouring area is the medieval bridge over the River Secchia near Rubiera, which used completely different building techniques. The structure in Rubiera includes a hexagonal pier equipped with two breakwaters in the manner of 1st–3rd centuries AD bridges. It also includes closely fitting pseudo-isodomic blocks and large square blocks at the top. The similarity with Roman bridges probably reflects that the skills typical of that period had reappeared in Medieval construction. The Rubiera bridge was for a long time thought to be Roman, but mensiochronological analysis from the rows of bricks interspersed with the stone blocks revealed that it is in fact medieval (Degani 1970). This clearly shows that it is impossible to date works of this type in western Emilia on a purely technical-stylistic basis.

Featuring medieval as well as ancient architectural elements, the bridge in Parma follows archetypal Roman measurements, and this is also true of the submerged isodomic piers. Analysis of the mortar from the arch shows that it could have been used between the 4th and 5th centuries AD (Lindroos *et al.* 2018) and was therefore presumably used from that point onwards. The arches appear to have been built by inexpert workers, and the building materials appear to have been chosen and used in haste. The lintels of the arches make use of rough-hewn materials and small pebbles, whereas fragments and scraps were used as padding to stabilise a vault rendered somewhat fragile by its size (which is what suggests a later date). They were probably also damaged by a 6th-century AD flood upstream of the bridge near the town walls in 'Via del Conservatorio' (Marchi & Serchia 2022). Looking further into the area, comparison can be made with the technique of the arches of the bridge at Vetto (13th century AD). Other bridges in the Upper Valley of the Parma River ('Alta Val Parma'), such as that over the River Prolo, used the same technique around the 14th century AD. In short, the Parma bridge was built over a lengthy period. And in this it is like one of the most famous bridges in western Emilia, the bridge of San Colombano Abbey in Bobbio (the one perhaps depicted by Leonardo da Vinci in the Mona Lisa portrait): this is a 7th-century AD bridge, coeval to the Abbey, built on a Roman structure, and it was, as we know, rebuilt countless times.

## Acknowledgements

I would like to thank Alessandro Launaro and Martin Millett, organizers of the Laurence Seminar, for the invitation, and the opportunity to present new research under the S.F.E.R.A. project on Roman cities in the Po Valley, especially Parma. I also thank Lorenzo Quilici for sharing useful information about the bridge in Parma and Filippo Fontana for sharing research on medieval bridges in Parma and for digitizing the land survey of the Parma bridge area.

## Bibliography

Affò, I. (1792) *Storia della Città di Parma*, Parma, Stamperia Carmignani.

Arrigoni Bertini, M. G. (2008) Le acque a Parma: donazioni pubbliche e fondazioni private. In P. Basso (ed.) Est enim ille flos Italiae... *vita economica e sociale nella Cisalpina romana*, 35–48. Verona, QuiEdit.

Balista, C. (1997) Fossati, canali e paleoalvei: connessioni nevralgiche per l'impianto e la sopravvivenza dei grandi siti terramaricoli di bassa pianura. In M. Bernabò Brea, A. Cardarelli & M. Cremaschi (eds) *Le Terramare. La più antica civiltà padana*, 126–136. Milan, Electa.

Bermond Montanari, G. (1983) La centuriazione in Emilia-Romagna. Problemi di tutela. In S. Settis (ed.) *Misurare la terra: centuriazione e coloni nel mondo romano*, 66–69. Modena, Panini.

Bonazzi, G. (1902–04) Chronicon Parmense ab anno 1038 usque ad annum 1338. In *Rerum Italicarum scriptores: raccolta degli storici italiani dal Cinquecento al Millecinquecento*, vol. 9. Città di Castello, S. Lapi.

Bondini, A., Cartoceti, M. & Curina, R. (2016) *Il ponte e le sue pietre: un contributo al patrimonio culturale della città di Rimini attraverso la salvaguardia di uno dei suoi simboli più importanti: il Ponte di Augusto e Tiberio*. Rimini, SGR.

Bottazzi, G. (2000) La rete itineraria. In M. Marini Calvani (ed.) *Aemilia. La cultura romana in Emilia-Romagna dal III sec. a.C. all'età costantiniana*. 79–85. Venezia, Marsilio.

Bottazzi, G., Ghiretti, A. & Magri, F. (eds) (2017) *Alla scoperta della Cisa romana. La Sella del Valoria*. Parma, Grafiche Step.

Brighi, G. (1997) *Le acque devono correre: le centuriazioni fra Rimini, Cervia e Cesena*. Cesena, Il Ponte Vecchio.

Calvino, I. (1972) *Le città invisibili*, Turin, Einaudi.

Calzolari, M. (1995) Interventi di bonifica nella Padania Centrale in età romana. *Atlante Tematico di Topografia Antica* 4, 7–16.

Cantoni, G. & Capurso A. (eds) (2017) *On the Road. Via Emilia 187 a.C.-2017*. Parma, Grafiche Step.

Capelli, G. (2017) Un attraversamento sul torrente Parma presso la via Emilia. In G. Cantoni, A & Capurso (eds) *On the Road. Via Emilia 187 a.C.-2017*, 107–108. Parma, Grafiche Step.

Catarsi, M. (1993) Il ponte romano di Parma. *Archivio Storico per le Province Parmensi* 45, 431–445.

Catarsi, M. (2009) Storia di Parma. Il contributo dell'archeologia. In D. Vera (ed.) *Storia di Parma, vol. 2. Parma romana*, 367–499. Parma, Monte Università Parma.

Catarsi, M. & Bianchi, A. (eds) (2004) *Il Museo Diocesano di Parma*. Parma, Soprintendenza per i beni archeologici dell'Emilia-Romagna.

Catarsi, M. & Dall'Aglio, P.L (1993) I ponti romani dell'Emilia Occidentale. *Atlante Tematico di Topografia Antica* 2, 209–221.

Catarsi, M. & Malavasi, I. (2006) *L'Oltretorrente di Parma romana. Nuovi dati dallo scavo archeologico di borgo Fornovo*. Firenze, All'Insegna del Giglio.

Catarsi, M., Anghinetti, C. & Bedini, E. (2013a) L'insediamento di Marore (Comune di Parma) tra Longobardi e Franchi. In *Atti IV Convegno Federarcheo*. Cosenza. http://www.archeobologna. beniculturali.it/pubblicazioni/2013_Catarsi_marore.pdf [accessed 10 January 2023].

Catarsi, M., Anghinetti, C., Raggio, P. & Usai, L. (2013b) Presenze longobarde nell'alta pianura parmense tra il torrente Parma e il fiume Enza. In *Atti IV Convegno Federarcheo*. Cosenza. http:// www.federarcheo.it/wp-content/uploads/Presenze-longobarde-nell-alta-pianura-parmense-tra-il-torrente-Parma-e-il-fiume-Enza1.pdf [accessed 10 January 2023]

Cavalieri, M. (2003) La produzione artigianale romana a Parma e nel suo territorio: un primo bilancio dei dati. *Aurea Parma* 1, 53–88.

Chevallier, R. (1961) La centuriazione e la colonizzazione romana dell'ottava regione augustea Emilia-Romagna. *L'universo* 40, 1077–1104.

Conti, G., Spocci, R., Sassi, F. & Zannoni, C. (2002) *Piazza Ghiaia. Teatro di un mercato*. Parma, Monte Università Parma.

Corradi Cervi, M. (1963) Il ponte dei salari sul torrente Parma. *Aurea Parma* 47, 146–150.

Cremaschi, M. (1997) Terramare e paesaggio padano. In M. Bernabò Brea, A. Cardaralli & M. Cremaschi (eds) *Le Terramare. La più antica civiltà padana*, 107–125. Milan, Electa.

Cremaschi, M. & Trombino, L. (2012) Osservazioni geoarcheologiche sulle serie stratigrafica portata alla luce dagli scavi. In M. Marini Calvani (ed.) *Ventidue secoli a Parma. Lo scavo sotto la sede centrale della Cassa di Risparmio in piazza Garibaldi*, 13–19. Oxford, Archaeopress.

Dall'Aglio, M. (2000) Il monastero di San Paolo a Parma. *Felix Ravenna* 4, 195–219.

Dall'Aglio, P.L. (1990) *Parma ed il suo territorio in età romana*. Parma, Editoria Tipolitotecnica.

Dall'Aglio, P.L. (1996) Modificazioni nell'assetto urbano e territoriale in Emilia tra età romana e altomedioevo. In N. Criniti (ed.) *Castrum Sermionense. Società e cultura della 'Cisalpina' nel primo medio evo*, 81–102. Brescia, Grafo.

Dall'Aglio, P.L. (1998) *Dalla Parma-Luni alla via Francigena*. Parma, Editoria Tipolitotecnica.

Dall'Aglio, P.L. (2009) Il territorio di Parma in età romana. In D. Vera (ed.) *Storia di Parma, vol. 2. Parma romana*, 555–602. Parma, Monte Università Parma.

Dall'Aglio, P.L. & Di Cocco, I. (2006) *La linea e la rete. Formazione storica del sistema stradale in Emilia-Romagna*, 98–104. Milano, Touring Club Italiano.

Degani, M. (1970) Gli antichi ponti di Rubiera sul fiume Secchia. *Atti e Memorie* 5, 105–113.

Di Cocco, I. & Viaggi, D. (2003) *Dalla scacchiera alla macchia.* Bologna, Ante Quem.

Fava, M. (2006) Il complesso episcopale parmense tra tarda antichità e Medioevo: dalla basilica paleocristiana alla cattedrale romanica. In *Vivere il Medioevo. Parma al tempo della cattedrale,* 71–88. Milano, Silvana.

Fontana, F. (2020) La *strata de Linario*: ricerca archeologica e valorizzazione di un itinerario storico. In A. Greci (ed.) *Cammini storici dell'Appennino parmense: la via di Linari,* 4–18. Parma, Club Alpino Italiano.

Fontana, F. & Garbasi, F. (2018) Luceria lungo la strada Parma-Lucca: ricerche e progetti di valorizzazione. In N. Cassone, C. Dazzi, F. Fontana & F. Garbasi, *Roma in Appennino: storia e civiltà lungo la via romana Parma-Lucca,* 103–135. Reggio Emilia, Compagnia Editoriale Aliberti.

Franceschelli, C. & Marabini, S. (2007) *Lettura di un territorio sepolto. La pianura lughese in età romana.* Bologna, Ante Quem.

Gelichi, S. (2011) Parma, il Medioevo e l'Archeologia. In D. Vera (ed.) *Storia di Parma, vol. 3. Parma medievale,* 89–115. Parma, Monte Università Parma.

Giorgetti, D. (2000) La centuriazione nell'Emilia occidentale. In M. Marini Calvani (ed.) *Aemilia. La cultura romana in Emilia Romagna dal III secolo a. C. all'età costantiniana,* 64–72. Venezia, Marsilio.

Guzzon, C. (1995) Il palazzo dell'Arena: uno dei più significativi edifici di Parma attraverso ricostruzioni e rifacimenti durati quasi duemila anni. *Archivio Storico per le Province Parmensi* 47, 247–261.

Lenzi F. (2009) (ed.) *Antichi paesaggi. Una proposta di valorizzazione della centuriazione romana in Emilia Romagna,* Bologna, Istituto per i Beni Artistici Culturali e naturali della regione Emilia Romagna.

Lindroos, A. Ringbom, Å., Heinemeie, J., Hodgins, G., Sonck-Koota, P., Sjöberg, P., Lancaster, L., Kaisti, R., Brock, F., Ranta, H., Caroselli, M. & Lugli, S. (2018) Radiocarbon dating historical mortars: lime lumps and/or binder carbonate? *Radiocarbon* 60, 875–899.

Locatelli, D., Malnati, L. & Maras, D.F. (eds) (2013) *Storie della prima Parma. Etruschi, Galli, Romani: le origini della città alla luce delle nuove scoperte archeologiche.* Rome, L'Erma di Bretschneider.

Lucchetti, G. (1965) Note e appunti sull'acquedotto farnesiano e sull'acquedotto di Marano. *Archivio Storico per le Province Parmensi* 49, 197–208.

Malnati, L., Catarsi, M. & Pedrelli, C. (2013) Il santuario al guado del fiume: prime risultanze dello scavo archeologico in Piazza Ghiaia. In D. Locatelli, L. Malnati & D.F. Maras (eds) *Storie della prima Parma. Etruschi, Galli, Romani: le origini della città alla luce delle nuove scoperte archeologiche,* 71–72. Rome, L'Erma di Bretschneider.

Maraldi, L. (2006) *Il popolamento di età romana nel territorio della centuriazione cesenate.* Cesena, Società di Studi Romagnoli.

Marchesini, M. & Marvelli S. (2009) Ricostruzione del paesaggio vegetale e antropico nelle aree centuriate dell'Emilia Romagna attraverso le indagini archeobotaniche. *Agri Centuriati* 6, 313–324.

Marchi, A. & Serchia, I. (2022) L'impatto delle alluvioni sullo sviluppo urbano ed economico della città di Parma, alla luce dei recenti rinvenimenti dallo scavo di via del Conservatorio. In E. Kefalidou (ed.) *Riverlands of Aegean Thrace: Production, Consumption and Exploitation of the Natural and Cultural Landscapes / River Valleys and Regional Economies, Panel 2.4 / 2.7, Archaeology and Economy in the Ancient World* 6, 87–99, Heidelberg, Propylaeum. https://doi.org/10.11588/propylaeum.871.c11428 [accessed 10 January 2023].

Marini Calvani, M. (2000) Parma. In Mariella Marini Calvani (ed.) *Aemilia. La cultura romana in Emilia-Romagna dal III sec. a.C. all'età costantiniana,* 394–403. Venezia, Marsilio.

Medas, S. (2017) La navigazione lungo le idrovie padane in epoca romana. In G. Cantoni & A. Capurso (eds) *On the Road. Via Emilia 187 a.C.-2017,* 146–161. Parma.

Morigi, A. (2009) La città dentro la città. Le trasformazioni di Parma antica. In D. Vera (ed.) *Storia di Parma: Parma romana,* 659–693, Parma, Grafiche Step.

Morigi, A. (2011) «... andone per la strata de pelegrino acosta in valdemozula et al borgo valdetaro a pontremuli ...». Calcaiola e la viabilità appenninica parmense tra Val di Taro e Val di Mozzola. In M. Catarsi (ed.) *Sei Oratori per Calcaiola*, 36–43. Parma, Guidotti.

Morigi, A. (2012) «...in un gomitolo di strade...». La formazione storica del paesaggio itinerario dell'alto appennino parmense. In G. Iacoli (ed.) *Discipline del paesaggio. Un laboratorio per le scienze umane*, 101–122, Milano-Udine, Mimesis.

Morigi, A. (2015a) Nuove carte d'identità. Topografia antica & progettazione urbana moderna per il restyling consapevole della forma di Parma. *Paideia* 70, 277–28.

Morigi, A. (2015b) Atlante stradale della terra di mezzo: tracciabilità delle rotte e dei flussi itinerari via Fornovo in età romana. In M. Catarsi (ed.) *Da Forum Novum a Fornovo Taro. Archeologia, arte e storia di un territorio*, 44–53. Fornovo Taro, Studio Guidotti.

Morigi, A. (2015c) Atlante stradale della terra di mezzo: tracciabilità delle rotte e dei flussi itinerari via Fornovo in età medievale. In M. Catarsi (ed.) *Da Forum Novum a Fornovo Taro. Archeologia, arte e storia di un territorio*, 162–171. Fornovo Taro, Studio Guidotti.

Morigi, A. (2016a) Progetto S.F.E.R.A. Ricerca scientifica, formazione universitaria, progettazione urbana e politiche occupazionali per l'archeologia dell'Emilia-Romagna. *Studi romagnoli* 66, 809–822.

Morigi, A. (2016b) *Pons lapidis*. Nuovi documenti per la morfologia, la storia edilizia e la continuità insediativa postantica del ponte romano nell'Archivio Storico Comunale di Parma. *Paideia* 71, 81–114.

Morigi, A. (2018) Archeologia in UniPr. Il Programma S.F.E.R.A. Spazi e Forme dell'Emilia Romagna Antica. In A. Morigi & C. Quintelli (eds) *Fondare e ri-fondare: origine e sviluppo della città di Parma. Costruzione di un'identità policentrica lungo la via Emilia tra Parma, Reggio e Modena*, 113–134. Padova, Il Poligrafo.

Morigi, A. (2019) Il linguaggio urbano. Segno, sopravvivenza e semantica dell'antico nel ponte di Parma e nelle città romane lungo la via Emilia. In S. Voce (ed.) *La città e le sue metamorfosi. Dal mondo antico all'età moderna*, 77–103. Bologna, Patron.

Morigi, A. (2021a) Archeologia al plurale. Galeata nel Programma S.F.E.R.A. dell'Università di Parma. In A. Morigi, (ed.) *Studi su Galeata e Santa Sofia*, 35–75, Cesena, Società di Studi Romagnoli.

Morigi, A. (ed.) (2021b) *Studi su Galeata e Santa Sofia*. Cesena, Società di Studi Romagnoli.

Morigi, A. (2022) Urban settlement in Emilia Romagna: between spontaneous development, grid-planning and post-antique adaptation. In S. Greaves & A. Wallace-Hadrill (eds) *Rome and the Colonial City: Rethinking the Grid*, 167–186. Oxford, Oxbow Books.

Morigi, A. & Bergamini, S. (2019) Vie urbane regolari e oblique: nuovi dati per la topografia e l'urbanistica di *Regium Lepidi*. In M. Podini & A. Losi (eds) *La città che si rinnova. Gli scavi di Palazzo Busetti e Piazza della Vittoria a Reggio Emilia*, 60–64. Parma, Grafiche Step.

Morigi, A. & Quintelli, C. (2018) (eds) *Fondare e ri-fondare: origine e sviluppo della città di Parma. Costruzione di un'identità policentrica lungo la via Emilia tra Parma, Reggio e Modena*. Padova, Il Poligrafo.

Morigi, A. & Tedeschi, A. M. (2018) Luoghi archeologici ritrovati: l'hub universitario del ponte romano di Parma. In A. Morigi & C. Quintelli (eds) *Fondare e ri-fondare: origine e sviluppo della città di Parma. Costruzione di un'identità policentrica lungo la via Emilia tra Parma, Reggio e Modena*, 355–374. Padova, Il Poligrafo.

Morigi, A. & Villicich, R. (2017) *Scavi nell''area della villa di Teoderico a Galeata. Le fasi di età romana*. Bologna, Bononia University Press.

Morigi, A. & Villicich, R. (eds) (2019a) *Di villa in villa: il 'Palazzo' di Teoderico nel nuovo allestimento museale*. Santa Sofia-Galeata, Stabilimento tipografico dei Comuni.

Morigi, A. & Villicich, R. (2019b) La campagna di scavo 2018 presso la villa di Teoderico a Galeata: il grande mosaico. *Studi romagnoli* 69, 169–192.

Morigi, A. & Villicich, R. (2021a) Mosaici in villa: nuovi dati sull'edilizia residenziale tardoantica dagli scavi della villa di Teoderico a Galeata. In I. Baldini & C. Sfameni (eds) *Abitare nel Mediterraneo tardoantico*, 243–252. Bari, Edipuglia.

Morigi, A. & Villicich, R. (2021b) Ieri oggi domani. La missione archeologica dell'Università di Parma presso la Villa di Teoderico a Galeata. In A. Morigi (ed.) *Studi su Galeata e Santa Sofia*, 9–128. Cesena, Società di Studi Romagnoli.

Morigi, A. & Villicich, R. (2022) Vivere in Appennino. Nuovi dati dallo scavo della villa di Teoderico a Galeata sull'insediamento repubblicano nella Romagna appenninica. In R. Perna, Riccardo C. & M. Giuliodori (eds) *Roma e il mondo adriatico. Dalla ricerca archeologica alla pianificazione del territorio*, 269–289. Rome, Quasar.

Morigi, A., Macellari, R. & Bergamini, S. (2016) La città invisibile. Per la carta archeologica e la forma urbana di *Regium Lepidi*. In M. Forte (ed.) *Regium@Lepidi Project 2200*, 77–95. Bologna, Ante Quem.

Morigi, A., Fontana, F. & Garbasi, F. (2019) Appennini in rete: archeologie e tecnologie dal Progetto *Inter Amnes* per la conoscenza e lo sviluppo dell'Appennino emiliano e romagnolo. *Studi romagnoli* 69, 997–1039.

Morigi, A., Fontana, F. & Garbasi, F. (2020a) *GIS Inter Amnes. Itinerari storici. Data base dei tracciati e degli itinerari storici nelle fonti documentali e archeologiche nelle valli di Enza, Parma e Baganza.*

Morigi, A., Fontana, F. & Garbasi, F. (2020b) *GIS Inter Amnes. Database delle emergenze archeologiche nelle valli di Parma, Enza e Baganza (PR).*

Morigi, A., Fontana, F. & Garbasi, F. (2021a) *GIS ParmAumentata: cartografia e rilievo digitali diacronici per l'elaborazione di app con riproduzione in realtà aumentata dei monumenti antichi.*

Morigi, A., Fontana, F. & Garbasi, F. (2021b) Ricerca archeologica, augmented reality e user experience nella ricostruzione del paesaggio urbano di Parma. *Archeologia e Calcolatori* 32, 269–290.

Morigi, A., Fontana, F., Garbasi, F. & Lommi, M. (2021c) Inter Amnes. Archeologia di superficie nel comprensorio delle valli di Enza, Parma e Baganza (PR). Dati preliminari dal settore parmense della Val d'Enza. *Fasti On Line Document & Research* 16, 1–30.

Quilici, L. (2000) Le strade dell'Emilia romana. *Orizzonti* 1, 115–138.

Quintelli, C. (2015) L'imprescindibile archeologia del progetto architettonico. *Paideia* 70, 331–339.

Santoro, S. (2009) Gusto, cultura artistica e produzione artigianale in Parma romana. In D. Vera (ed.) *Storia di Parma, vol. 2. Parma romana*, 501–554. Parma, Monte Università Parma.

Wallace-Hadrill, A. (2022) The cities of Cassiodorus: the resilience of urban values. In J. Martínez Jiménez & S. Ottewill Soulsby (eds) *Remembering and Forgetting the Ancient Cities*, 23–44. Oxford, Oxbow Books.

# Chapter 15

# Conclusion: recent discoveries and new directions

## John R. Patterson

The history of Italy under the Romans is to a significant extent the history of its cities. Not only did these act as a stage where the ruling elites could display their wealth and influence, but they also served to control the resources produced by the cities' own territories, and collectively formed a structure which enabled the whole peninsula to be administered and controlled under the oversight of Rome. This volume provides a rich and welcome overview of recent and current research on a selection of these cities, and many of the papers also serve as appetisers for important (and imminent) new publications of work carried out over many years. These include reports on major projects at Falerii Novi (Millett), and Interamna Lirenas (Launaro), and on excavations at Fregellae of a series of *domus*, notable for their early date and their degree of preservation, until their destruction by a Roman army in 125 BC (Diosono). Along with the more specifically archaeological acquisitions, the body of fieldwork outlined here has also identified new elements in the epigraphic record. In particular a calendar and consular *Fasti* painted on wall-plaster, the surviving portion covering the period from the 40s BC to the 30s AD, have been discovered during the excavation of a portico close to the *forum* at Alba Fucens. It is already clear that this document will cast new light on the political history and the prosopography of the triumviral period, and of the early Principate (Letta 2012–13; Tansey 2018). Collectively, then, the work being presented here is of great significance for the history of Roman Italy.

As Millett highlights in his contribution, and is also made abundantly clear by the other essays in the volume, 'cities' do not constitute a unified category in Italy in this period. While they do share essentially similar institutional frameworks, their formal status may be that of colonies (of various kinds) or municipalities. Urban frameworks may already be more or less familiar in the surrounding area; cities' physical extent, as defined by the surface area of the territory within their walls, may be large or small, as may the density of occupation, and so the population occupying that area. They may have extensive and agriculturally rich territories, and access to external resources by means of political control, trade and commerce, and connectivity with the world beyond the city's boundary. Alternatively, they may occupy a small territory, hemmed in by neighbouring cities, controlling only marginal and unproductive lands, and far away from the networks to which roads, major rivers and the sea give access. Cities may of course combine these various features to a greater or lesser extent. The central challenge for the scholar in analysing patterns of urbanism in Roman Italy is how to balance general trends with local combinations of circumstances, across the centuries which we define as 'Roman history'.

The essays in the volume raise a wide variety of important issues, methodological and historical, only a few of which can be highlighted here.

One central theme is the way in which multiple remote sensing technologies are now being used, often in combination, and alongside more traditional approaches to landscape history, to explore the cities of Italy. Ground-penetrating radar and resistivity have been deployed alongside magnetometry (itself extensively used since the 1990s), allowing a greater sense of depth to emerge from the imaging of a site, although the outcome is still inevitably in the form of a palimpsest (Kay *et al.*; Millett; Vermeulen). This geophysical analysis can in turn be followed by more targeted excavation, as at Aeclanum (Russell & De Simone) and/or combined with surface survey within the urban centre, as for example at Interamna (Launaro). Various forms of aerial photography and photogrammetry, using drones as well as conventional aircraft, are being deployed alongside geophysical techniques to reconstruct the urban layout, as at Aquinum and Septempeda (Ceraudo; Vermeulen). While remote sensing techniques have produced their most spectacular results on 'greenfield' sites (where there is very little post-Roman settlement), the work carried out on the Caelian Hill at Rome demonstrates how they can also be deployed with success in densely occupied and deeply stratified urban contexts, alongside structural archaeology, and the use of boreholes (Haynes *et al.*). As a result, a dossier of information is being built up for the towns of Italy, combining both the high-resolution data provided by stratigraphic excavation, and the lower-resolution knowledge of cityscapes enabled by the extensive deployment of remote sensing techniques, and by surface survey, which can in turn be set alongside epigraphic and literary evidence.

It is also worth highlighting in particular the potential importance for the understanding of urban – and indeed rural – landscapes of the detailed study of commonware pottery, as the strikingly different reconstructions of settlement dynamics at Interamna between the late Republic and the 3rd century AD demonstrate. The field survey carried out there in the 2010s, characterised by particular attention to commonwares, suggests a general continuity of habitation on the site into the high Empire, by contrast to the striking pattern of decline suggested by the survey of Hayes and Wightman in the late 1970s and early 1980s, which predominantly focused on fineware pottery (Launaro; Hayes & Wightman 1984).

Much recent research on the Roman city has been concerned with the phenomenon of colonisation in the mid-Republic, and this is also true of many of the papers here. Fregellae, Interamna, Alba Fucens, Cosa, and Aquileia, all founded as Latin colonies, are represented (Diosono; Launaro; Evers; De Giorgi; Basso): the precise knowledge derived from literary texts about when, and in what circumstances, these settlements were founded, and sometimes reinforced, provides a fundamental – if sometimes elusive – starting point for understanding their urban frameworks. The circumstances of the destruction of Fregellae, following that colony's rebellion against Rome in 125 BC, and the absence of significant later settlement on the site, makes the city a 'closed context' of particular interest. Recent work on Latin colonies has tended to move away from Aulus Gellius' idea of these being standardised 'little images and copies' of Rome (Gell. *NA* 16.13.9, with *e.g.* the essays in Stek & Pelgrom, 2014); instead, scholars have stressed the different circumstances of their foundation, and the diversity of the sites themselves and of their populations of settlers, which may in some cases have included indigenous inhabitants. The papers presented here further contribute to this picture of complexity. De Giorgi for example relates the reinforcement of Cosa at the beginning of the 2nd century BC to the decline of the fortified settlement at Orbetello on the coast below. On the other hand, the module used for laying out rooms adjacent to the *forum* at Alba Fucens is the same as that used at Paestum, another Latin colony established some 25 years later (Evers), suggesting a certain standardisation in this respect at least. Lunae (founded 177 BC) was a Roman citizen colony, and here the archaeology has cast light on the earliest phases of the settlement, with a stockade containing huts built in clay and straw, and perhaps constituting the original habitation of the colonists. The burial of dogs in locations close to the city walls, as also attested at Ariminum and Paestum, seems to be related to foundational rites (Menchelli *et al.*). Colonial foundations thus continue to emerge as a striking combination of innovation and traditionalism.

Unsurprisingly, both broad historical trends and more specific circumstances can be seen to be contributing to the history of urban centres. The process of municipalisation after the grants of Roman citizenship to Italians in the years following the Social War is clearly fundamental, for example (Vermeulen), but individual episodes are important too. The reconstruction of Aeclanum following that town's sack in 89 BC is led by Sulla's associates, including C. Quinctus Valgus, who are attested building walls and other fortifications (Russell & De Simone). Similarly, it has been suggested that the impressive walls and towers at Septempeda should be related to the settlement at the site of Social War veterans who had served under Sulla (Vermeulen). A generation later, local elites again had to manoeuvre carefully, and make decisions of crucial importance for the fate of their community, as more conflict broke out, first between Julius Caesar and Pompey, and then between Caesar's heir Octavian and Mark Antony. Both Alba Fucens and Interamna – wisely, as it turned out – chose Caesar as patron of their community, and Alba Fucens subsequently chose to support his adoptive son in a stand-off with Antony at the town late in 44 BC (Evers; Launaro). Following the establishment of the Principate, the support of the emperor, or someone close to him, might similarly have affected the urban fabric. At Alba Fucens, the amphitheatre was constructed with funds bequeathed to what was probably his home town by Q. Naevius Cordus Sutorius Macro, Praetorian Prefect of the emperor Tiberius in succession to Sejanus; Macro we also know to have owned brickworks nearby (Evers). The 2nd century AD enhancement of the cityscape of Aeclanum may in part be linked to the grant of colonial status to the town by the emperor Hadrian (Russell & De Simone; Boatwright 1989, 238–240).

This wealth of recent work has also allowed the identification of a number of previously unknown public monuments in Italian cities: the location of the *forum* itself has been identified at Aeclanum (Russell & De Simone), theatres have been located at Interamna and Aeclanum (Launaro; Russell & De Simone), *macella* at Falerii and Interamna (Launaro; Millett), and important bath-buildings at Fregellae and Aquinum. The Fregellae baths are of particular interest because of their early date (in three phrases between the 3rd and 2nd centuries BC) and the ways in which they can be compared with Greek models (Tsiolis 2013; revised chronology suggested by Diosono); the Aquinum baths are remarkable for their scale, and because they preserve a mosaic inscription recording the name of the man who constructed them in the Augustan period, M. Veccius (Ceraudo, with Ceraudo *et al.* 2017–18; Ceraudo 2019). Monuments of these types are arguably the product not only of elite munificence and inter-city competitive emulation within Italy, but also influenced by examples of monumental building at Rome: the Theatre of Marcellus and the Macellum Magnum of Nero, to cite only a couple of examples. More specific influences can be seen in the Corinthian capitals recalling those of the Forum of Augustus found in the 'Columnar Hall' excavated at Alba Fucens (Evers) and the so-called 'Forum Adiectum' of Claudian date, adjacent to the main *forum* at Lunae (Menchelli *et al.*: this example should be added to the list of multiple *fora* in Italian towns discussed in Patterson 2022) which seems to have been influenced by the Fora of Caesar and Augustus adjacent to the Forum Romanum. Similarly, the Sessorian palace complex, a 'new city' on the eastern Caelian at Rome, containing as it does the Amphitheatrum Castrense and Varian Circus, which were subsequently incorporated into the Aurelianic Wall, can be compared with the later Tetrarchic palatial residences established in key locations around the Empire (Haynes *et al.*). This sector of Rome became more militarised in the late 2nd century AD, with the establishment of a new camp for the imperial horse-guards, and the provision of military supplies thus became particularly important, just as it did at Aquileia, where soldiers were often stationed, as the city served as a supply base for the Danubian frontier to the North (Haynes *et al.*; Basso).

The distinctive appearance of monuments such as theatres and *macella* makes them particularly easy to spot in the geophysical record. Equally, the ability to see the layout of an entire city also allows us to pay appropriate attention to structures and spaces which are less standardised but nevertheless played an important role in the urban landscape. These include the courtyard buildings identified as *horrea*, the finely decorated halls plausibly to be associated with sub-elite bodies like *collegia* and the *Augustales*, as at Alba, Lunae, and Interamna (Evers; Menchelli *et al.*; Launaro), and defined open areas, such as the *campus* outside the city walls at Septempeda

(Vermeulen), or the space interpreted as the *forum pecuarium*, an animal market, at Interamna (Launaro).

Similarly, a recurrent theme in the studies contained in this volume is an interest in those areas on the margins of the cities – both inside and outside the city walls – which have tended to be neglected in past fieldwork, mostly concerned with the monumental public buildings in the vicinity of a city's *forum*. At Falerii Novi and at Septempeda, geophysical survey was carried out in the area outside the walls, illustrating the way in which the approach to a city might be characterised both by the commemoration of the dead, and by activities excluded from the city by virtue of their hazardous or offensive character, such as quarrying or pottery production (Millett; Vermeulen; Hay *et al.* 2010). The bridge at Parma over the river of the same name served as a kind of monumental entrance to the city, from a location primarily characterised by tombs, workshops, and road-junctions, but separated from the urban centre proper by the river channel (Morigi), while the lofty position of the horse-guards' barracks at Rome served to intimidate anyone approaching the Severan city from the southeast (Haynes *et al.*), just as the Praetorian Camp had previously done for travellers approaching from the northeast. Once inside the city of Falerii, the series of temples located inside the wall-circuit highlighted to the visitor the particular importance of the sacred in the urban topography of that city (Millett).

The practicalities of community life were likewise a major focus of the peripheral areas of the city. The *forum pecuarium* at Interamna was located at the southeast end of the city, presumably in order to avoid flocks of animals having to be herded through the streets. Likewise storage and marketing facilities were often located on the periphery. This was the case in Rome under the Principate, where the Macellum of Republican date adjacent to the Forum Romanum was supplemented (under Augustus) by the Macellum of Livia on the Esquiline, and later replaced by the Macellum of Nero on the Caelian, both of which locations were more easily accessible from the city's southeastern hinterland (Coarelli 1986, 42–43). At Cosa and Aquileia, markets and storage buildings were located at the edge of the city, whether concerned with commercial activities or for the supply of the community itself; *horrea* might however also be found in more central locations (De Giorgi; Basso; Launaro; Russell & De Simone; for an important recent discussion of the phenomenon of storage, see van Oyen 2020). Similarly, the periphery of towns was often also characterised by infrastructure relating to water supply, especially where one part of the city was at a physically higher level, for example the Caelian hill at Rome, where there was a concentration of the aqueducts which supplied much of the city (Haynes *et al.*). Provision of water was a particular issue at Cosa, where there was no perennial water source on the hilltop, and both cisterns and what appears to be a mechanism for transporting water up the hill from a spring in the vicinity of the harbour have been identified (De Giorgi).

The advent of Christianity, too, can be seen to have had a particular impact on the periphery of the cities: at Rome, the Lateran basilica was constructed on the

site of the former barracks (Haynes *et al.*), well away from the traditional religious
and political spaces of the city; likewise the first, Constantinian, basilica at Aquileia
was located close to the Late Antique market and walls, shifting 'the urban centre of
gravity from the *forum*, the heart of Aquileia in the Republican and Imperial periods,
to this southwestern part of the town' (Basso).

It is worth stressing that peripheral areas of the city were not only indeterminate
and marginal in character, but also were liable to change over time. In particular, as
new defences were created in response to security threats, areas which had previously
been outside the city subsequently came to be included within it. This can be seen in
particular at Rome: in the late Republic and early Principate the city grew beyond the
so-called Servian Walls, and so the Lateran and Caelian hills came to be characterised
not only by tombs but by the *horti* of the wealthy; subsequently these were included
in the late 3rd-century AD Aurelianic wall. At Aquileia, too, we can see the wall-circuit
being extended more than once, the Republican walls being replaced by a new circuit
in the late 3rd/early 4th centuries AD, and in turn by another in the 5th century AD,
in response to a change in the course of the river (Basso).

As suggested at the outset, the history of a Roman city, and in particular the
extent of its civic superstructure, was closely linked to the resources available to
that city, whether from its own territory or beyond. Crucial here were the ways in
which roads, rivers, and the sea provided connectivity beyond the city's boundaries.
Under the Republic, Latin colonies were often established in close relation to road-
building schemes, although the foundation of the colony might either precede or
follow the laying out of the road in chronological terms (Bradley 2014, 66–69). While
Fregellae and Interamna were both located on the *via Latina*, the exact relationship
between the foundation of the colonies and the laying out of the road as a long-
distance route is unclear; the establishment of Alba Fucens was subsequent to the
construction of the *via Valeria*, which extended the route of the *via Tiburtina* eastwards
into the territory of the Marsi. Septempeda seems to have developed along the road
which connected the *via Flaminia* with the Adriatic at Ancona (Vermeulen), while
the relationship of the early phases of settlement at Aeclanum with the laying out
of the *via Appia* remains obscure (Russell & De Simone). Main roads typically, but not
always, ran through the centres of towns: the latter served as sources of provisions
for travellers, but the roads also provided a means of social networking with Rome,
the Roman elite in particular, and other communities in Italy (Wiseman 1971, 28–29).
Being bypassed by a major road, however, need not necessarily have been disastrous
for a community: the survey results suggest that Interamna continued to prosper
even though, from the late Republic onwards, long-distance travellers journeying
South along the *via Latina* headed direct from Aquinum to Casinum; likewise the
institution of the more direct *via Traiana* route between Beneventum and Brundisium
seems not to have been detrimental to the fortunes of Aeclanum (Launaro; Russell
& De Simone), where Hadrian intervened to enhance the road-network in the area,
presumably in relation to his grant of colonial status to the community (Boatwright

1989, 238–240; Ceraudo 2022). While urban centres were often laid out giving emphasis to the main road – the *via Amerina* at Falerii being a case in point (Millett) – this was not invariably the case: the public monuments of Aeclanum and Interamna seem to have been directed to the viewer in the territory as well, creating impressive vistas from afar (Launaro; Russell & De Simone).

Access to ports was similarly of major importance in terms of connectivity, in cases where a town had access to the sea or to a navigable river. At Interamna, a group of buildings outside the city walls, but close to the River Liri, has been identified as the river-port of the town (Launaro). At Lunae, investigations in the southeast quarter of the city, along the road that gave access to the port, have revealed a complex of wealthy houses: one of these, dating to the late Republic, was decorated with a mosaic depicting ships, perhaps reflecting the source of the owner's wealth. In both cities, the existence of the port facilities seems to have been important in determining the wealth available to the town, whether related to the export of marble (as at Lunae) or of agricultural produce (as at Interamna) (Menchelli *et al.*; Launaro). In general, much of a city's wealth was likely to be locally generated, the prosperity of Aeclanum largely relating to its extensive and fertile territory (Russell & De Simone). The case of Alba Fucens is a particularly interesting one in this context, given that we can explicitly see the extent of the agricultural land available to the community increasing in size, as the draining of the Fucine Lake seems finally to have taken place in the mid–2nd century AD, after various false starts. This does indeed seem to have been reflected in the changes in the urban superstructure of the town (Evers).

Needless to say, the papers contained in the volume also flag up topics and debates which seem to me to be worthy of further investigation. To take just three:

1. Survey at Lucus Feroniae has confirmed that the town centre there is one essentially characterised by public monuments, without significant areas of urban habitation, although a number of villas have been identified in the vicinity, notably that of the Volusii Saturnini (Kay *et al.*). The particular history of this site, and especially the presence of the sanctuary of Feronia, seems of special relevance, given also that the geophysics has identified what seems to be a sacred grove here. Equally, geophysical survey at Forum Novum, in Sabine territory on the opposite side of the Tiber, showed that this site too had little in the way of a population resident in its urban centre (Gaffney *et al.* 2001), and Kay *et al.* note that recent surveys at other small urban sites in the central Appennines, such as Amiternum, Iuvanum, and Peltuinum, have suggested similar patterns. Septempeda, however, does appear to have had a significant urban population (Vermeulen, who cautiously refers to 'the demographic bloom of the settlement from the 1st century BC onwards, when living quarters perhaps gradually filled the intra-mural space once the town wall was built'). Why do some small towns have substantial populations resident in the urban centre, and others not?

2. It is clear that extensive patterns of population movement, both as a result of state policy and individual initiative, formed a backdrop to the process of urban development in the periods under consideration here (Isayev 2017 provides a recent overview). Scheidel has argued that in the last two centuries BC, between two and two-and-a-half million people relocated permanently as a result of urban growth and colonial settlement in Italy (Scheidel 2004, 1); if a broader definition of mobility is used, to include seasonal and temporary migration, the number of people on the move may well have been significantly larger (Erdkamp 2008). Furthermore, those enslaved and brought to Italy would need to be added to these figures. In the 180s and early 170s BC, for example, we hear about migration of Latins to Rome, and of Samnites and Paelignians to Fregellae (Liv. 39.3.4–6; 41.8.6–8, with Diosono), as also the deportation of Ligurians to Samnium, in the lead-up to the establishment of the Roman colony at Lunae (Liv. 40. 38, 41. 3–4, with Menchelli *et al.*). To what extent can these processes be detected in the physical spaces of the cities of Italy? There are some hints in the case studies presented here: Diosono suggests that patterns of supply and consumption of foodstuffs at Fregellae may reflect the presence of Carthaginian hostages, whom we know from Nepos (*Hann.* 7.2) to have lived at the town: significant quantities of Punic amphorae have been found there. Similarly, the sacred topography at Falerii Novi may in some way reflect that of nearby Falerii Veteres, from where the inhabitants of the new town were transferred by the Romans (Millett; Millett 2007). We ought to be aware, however, that there may be a tension between the fixed images of habitation areas generated by geophysical survey, and the populations of the cities, which may well have fluctuated over time. Both under the Republic and under the Principate, a significant proportion of those moving to Rome in particular are likely to have been drawn from Italy (Tacoma 2016, 58–61).

3. We know that there were particularly substantial movements of populations in Italy in the 1st century BC, with land distribution to veterans being a factor of key importance in this period. Keppie estimates that between 47 and 13 BC 'at least 130,000 time-served veterans' received land grants in Italy (Keppie 1983, ix). It is clear from the centuriation grids laid out in this period, from the tombstones commemorating the veterans' military service, and from allusions to evictions in the poetry of Vergil (esp. Verg. *Ecl.* 1.1–12, 64–79; *Ecl.* 9.1–6, 26–29) and Propertius (Prop. 4.1.121–130), both of whom we know to have had personal experience of the confiscation and redistribution of land, that the impact of the settlement process on the Italian countryside was very significant (Keppie 1983; Osgood 2006, 108–151). Equally, the public spaces of those cities where veterans were settled were often enhanced as a result of the process of colonial settlement, as the cities received public buildings thanks to the generosity of the Emperor and of the colonies' newly promoted elites (Keppie 1983, 114–117). The baths of M. Veccius at Aquinum, dating as they do to the Augustan period, may be a product of this process, though Veccius' dedicatory inscription makes no explicit reference to his having been involved in military service (Ceraudo *et al.* 2017–18, 33).

How far did this process affect urban space more broadly, though? Keppie (1983, 102–104) suggests that urban centres may have been less affected by the process of colonization than the cities' territories, though he also notes Dio's reference to widespread street-fighting taking place between veterans and the dispossessed, within Italian towns as well as at Rome (Cass. Dio 48.9.4–5); wealthy individuals may have had urban as well as rural properties. Many of the cities targeted by the triumvirs Octavian, Antony, and Lepidus for the confiscation and redistribution of land remained substantial urban centres into the mediaeval period and beyond, so there are few opportunities to undertake the kind of greenfield remote-sensing survey that has been carried out with such success at a number of Latin colonies. Aquinum, if – as seems likely – it is correctly identified as a triumviral colony (Keppie 1983, 137–138; Ceraudo *et al.* 2017–18, 12), may potentially be an important case study here: the city stands out from the others discussed in this volume in terms of its surface area, the land enclosed within the walls being some 100 ha (by contrast with Cosa [13 ha]; Septempeda [15 ha]; Aeclanum [21 ha]; Alba Fucens [34 ha]; Interamna [23 ha]; Lunae [24 ha]; and Falerii [31 ha]). The only other sites on an analogous scale discussed here are Fregellae (about 90 ha, but destroyed in 125 BC), and Aquileia (80 ha), where the city's strategic and commercial position on the Adriatic, and its connections with the Danube frontier, clearly made it a regional centre of considerable importance. Ceraudo indeed highlights the large scale of Aquinum, especially after the arrival of the colonists, and tentatively suggests an urban population of 25,000 in the mid imperial period (Ceraudo 2019, 109–111), but rightly stresses the need for further investigations in the urban centre. Another site discussed here, Lucus Feroniae, also received a late Republican colonial settlement, an early 1st-century BC date for which has been proposed by Stanco; if so, the formal title of the community, Colonia Iulia Felix Lucus Feroniae, suggests that there may have been a further colonial intervention, later in the century (Keppie 1983, 168–169; Stanco 2016). Despite this, as we have seen, there were few residents in the urban centre of Lucus Feroniae. Just as mid-Republican Latin colonies displayed diversity in their urban form, perhaps late Republican veteran colonies did too, reflecting the fact that such settlements tended to be imposed on already existing centres of population.

There is still much more to be learnt about the cities of Roman Italy: alongside their own very substantial contributions, the papers in this volume are both suggesting new questions, and providing ways in which archaeologists and historians might attempt to answer them.

## Bibliography

Boatwright, M.T. (1989) Hadrian and Italian cities. *Chiron* 19, 235–271.
Bradley, G. (2014) The nature of Roman strategy in Mid-Republican colonization and road building. In T.D. Stek & J. Pelgrom (eds) *Roman Republican Colonization: New Perspectives from Archaeology and Ancient History*, 60–72. Rome, Palombi.
Ceraudo, G. (2019) Il *balneum* di Marcus Veccius ad Aquinum. Considerazioni sull'edificio termale e sulle sue potenzialità ricettive. *Atlante Tematico di Topografia Antica* 29, 89–113.

Ceraudo, G. (2022) Su un miliario dimenticato della Via Appia: il ripristino di Adriano del tratto Beneventum – Aeclanum. *Atlante Tematico di Topografia Antica* 32, 125–143.

Ceraudo, G., Molle, C. & Nonnis, D. (2017–18) L'iscrizione musiva di M. Veccius M. f. nelle terme centrali di Aquinum. *Atti della Pontificia Accademia di Archeologia - Rendiconti* 90, 3–53.

Coarelli, F. (1986) L'urbs e il suburbio. In A. Giardina (ed.) *Società romana e impero tardoantico* 2, 1–58. Rome and Bari, Laterza.

Erdkamp, P. (2008) Mobility and migration in Italy in the second century BC. In L. de Ligt & S. Northwood (eds) *People, Land and Politics. Demographic Developments and the Transformation of Roman Italy, 300 BC - AD 14*, 417–449. Leiden and Boston, Brill.

Gaffney, V., Patterson, H. & Roberts, P. (2001) Forum Novum – Vescovio: studying urbanism in the Tiber valley. *Journal of Roman Archaeology* 14, 59–79.

Hay, S., Johnson, P., Keay, S. & Millett, M. (2010) Falerii Novi: further survey of the northern extramural area. *Papers of the British School at Rome* 78, 1–38.

Hayes, J.W. & Wightman, E.M. (1984) Interamna Lirenas: risultati di ricerche in superficie 1979–1981. In S. Quilici-Gigli (ed.), *Archeologia Laziale VI*, 137–148. Rome, Consiglio Nazionale delle Ricerche.

Isayev, E. (2017) *Migration, Mobility and Place in Ancient Italy*. Cambridge, Cambridge University Press.

Keppie, L. (1983) *Colonisation and Veteran Settlement in Italy, 47-14 BC*. London, British School at Rome.

Letta, C. (2012–13) Prime osservazioni sui *Fasti Albenses*. *Atti della Pontificia Accademia di Archeologia - Rendiconti* 85, 315–335.

Millett, M. (2007) Urban topography and social identity in the Tiber valley. In R. Roth & J. Keller (eds) *Roman by Integration: Dimensions of Group Identity in Material Culture and Text*, 71–82. Portsmouth RI, Journal of Roman Archaeology.

Osgood, J. (2006) *Caesar's Legacy: Civil War and the Emergence of the Roman Empire*. Cambridge, Cambridge University Press.

Patterson, J.R. (2022) Transformations of public space in the cities of Italy under the Principate: the case of the Forum. In D. Filippi (ed.) *Rethinking the Roman city: the Spatial Turn and the Archaeology of Roman Italy*, 226–243. London, Routledge.

Scheidel, W. (2004) Human mobility in Roman Italy, 1: the free population. *Journal of Roman Studies* 94, 1–26.

Stanco, E.A. (2016) Dalla distruzione del santuario alla colonia romana. In A. Russo Tagliente, G. Ghini & L. Caretta (eds) *Lucus Feroniae: il santuario, la città, il territorio*, 91–100. Rome, Scienze e Lettere.

Stek, T.D. & Pelgrom, J. (2014) *Roman Republican Colonization: New Perspectives from Archaeology and Ancient History*. Rome, Palombi.

Tacoma, L.E. (2016) *Moving Romans: Migration to Rome in the Principate*. Oxford, Oxford University Press.

Tansey, P. (2018) *Notabilia varia* in the *fasti* of Alba Fucens. *Studi Classici e Orientali* 64, 199–269.

Tsiolis, V. (2013) The baths at Fregellae and the transition from Balaneion to Balneum. In S.K. Lucore & M. Trümper (eds) *Greek Baths and Bathing Culture: New Discoveries and Approaches*, 89–111. Leuven, Paris, Walpole MA: Peeters.

van Oyen, A. (2020) *The Socio-Economics of Roman Storage: Agriculture, Trade and Family*. Cambridge, Cambridge University Press.

Wiseman, T.P. (1971) *New Men in the Roman Senate 139 BC-AD 14*. Oxford, Oxford University Press.

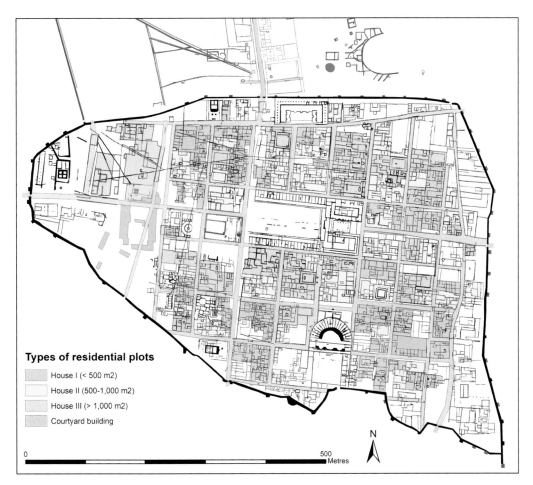

Plate 2.1. Plan of Falerii Novi based on gradiometry and GPR surveys showing the distribution of different types of residential plots (illustration by Alessandro Launaro, based on data from Keay et al. 2000 and collected by Lieven Verdonck for the AHRC-funded Beneath the surface of Roman Republican cities project).

Plate 3.1. Project visualisation ('provocation') showing the northwest corner of the early 4th century AD portico of the domus under the Ospedale di San Giovanni (Thea Ravasi, Ian Haynes, Paolo Liverani & Iwan Peverett).

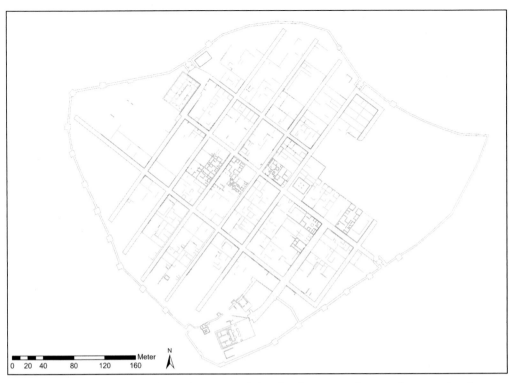

Plate 5.1. Cosa: the geophysical survey and the plan (courtesy of Maximilian Rönnberg).

Plate 7.1. Alba Fucens. Southern part of the forum (with the Belgian excavations on the right) and central part of the town (copyright ULB CreA-Patrimoine).

*Plate 9.1. Coverage of the site of Septempeda by different geophysical techniques. The proposed location of the Roman wall circuit is also indicated (D. Taelman).*

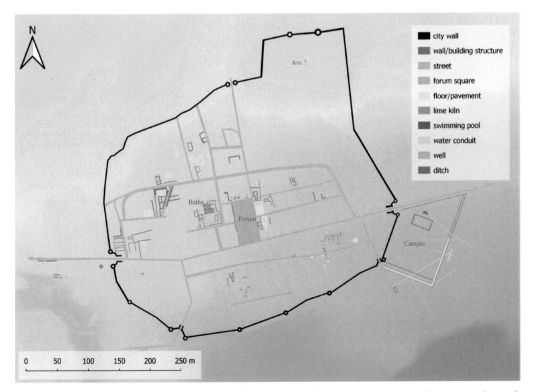

*Plate 9.2. Provisional mapping of all important features detected in the town area of Septempeda, with proposed functional identification (F. Vermeulen and D. Taelman).*

*Plate 10.1. A: Detail of the* navalia *mosaic (Domus B). B: aerial photo of the eastern part of Domus B; featuring alae (B1, B9a and B9b), tablinum (B7), peristyle (B12), triclinium (B5) and room B8 (aerial photo by Domingo Belcari).*

**Types of building**

- Public (baths)
- Public (religious)
- Public (other)
- Courtyard building
- Tabernae
- House I
- House II
- House III
- Other
- Undetermined
- Empty

FORUM

0    100    200    300    400    500
Metres

N

*Plate 11.1. The plan of Interamna Lirenas as revealed by the geophysical prospection (2010–17), showing the distribution of different types of building.*

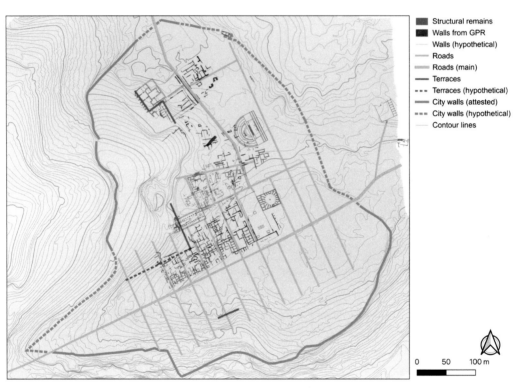

Plate 12.1. Plan of Aeclanum, showing the results of excavation and geophysical survey alongside reconstructed plans of the known public buildings and hypothesised street network (image: G.F. De Simone).

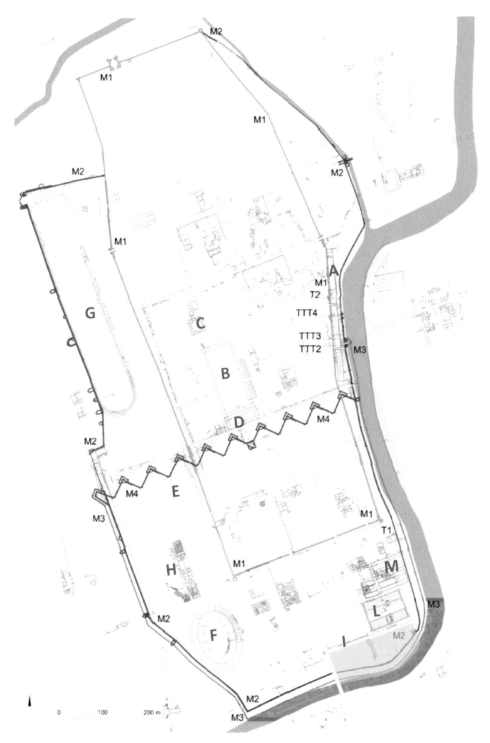

Plate 13.1. *The archaeological map of Aquileia: in yellow, our excavation area, named 'ex Fondo Pasqualis' after the old owner (reworked by V. Grazioli from Bonetto 2009, fig. 1).*

*Plate 14.1. The 'Roman' bridge as it is visible today.*